Twin Star Exorcists

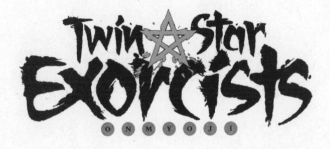

ONMYOJI

Twin ☆ Star Exorcists

ONMYOJI

14

STORY & ART
YOSHIAKI SUKENO

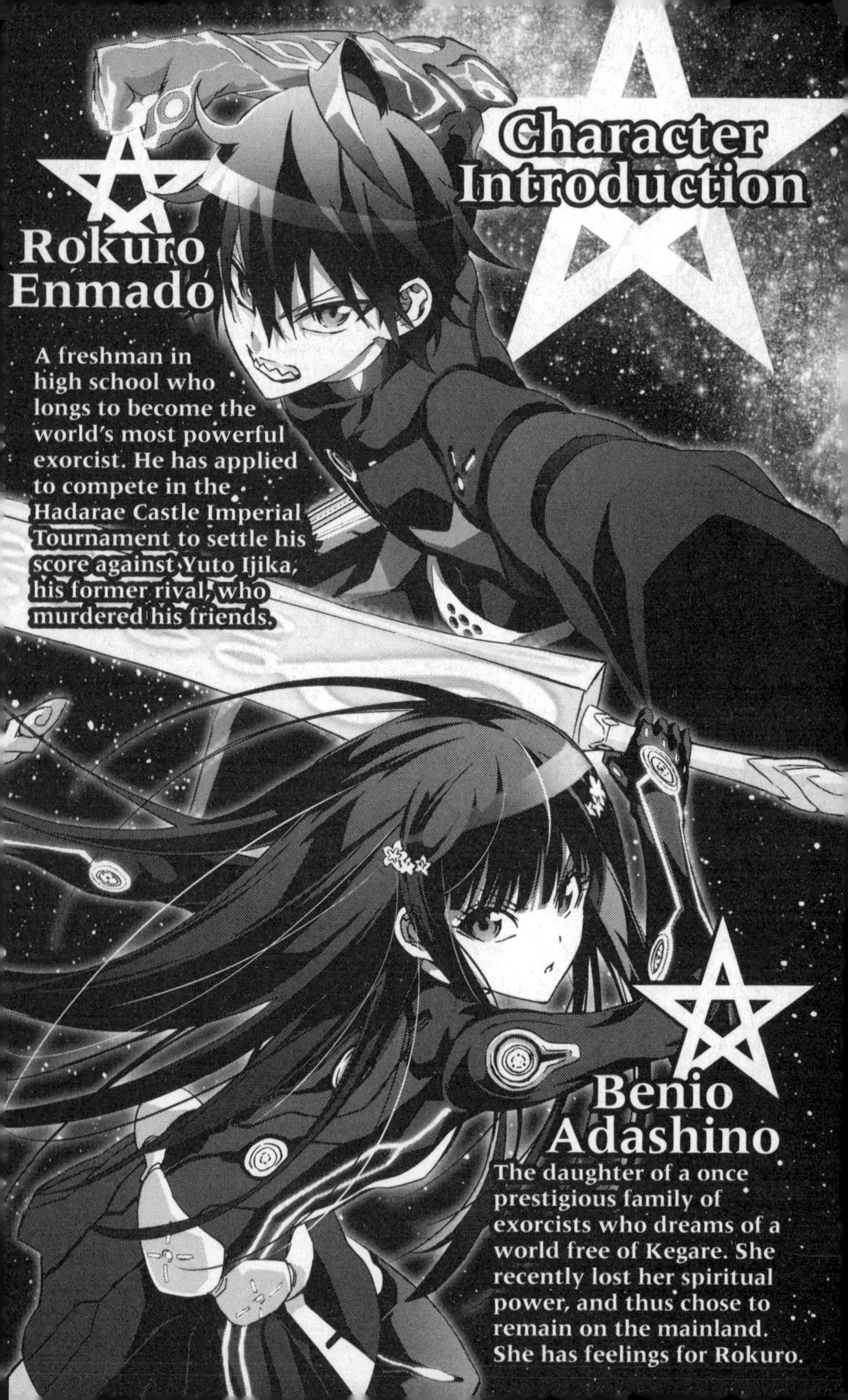
Character Introduction
Rokuro Enmado
A freshman in high school who longs to become the world's most powerful exorcist. He has applied to compete in the Hadarae Castle Imperial Tournament to settle his score against Yuto Ijika, his former rival, who murdered his friends.
Benio Adashino
The daughter of a once prestigious family of exorcists who dreams of a world free of Kegare. She recently lost her spiritual power, and thus chose to remain on the mainland. She has feelings for Rokuro.

Shimon Ikaruga

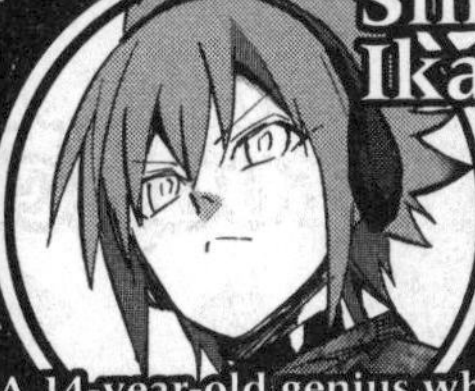

A 14-year-old genius who succeeded as Vermillion Bird of the Twelve Guardians. He has deep respect for his mentor, Seigen.

Tenma Unomiya

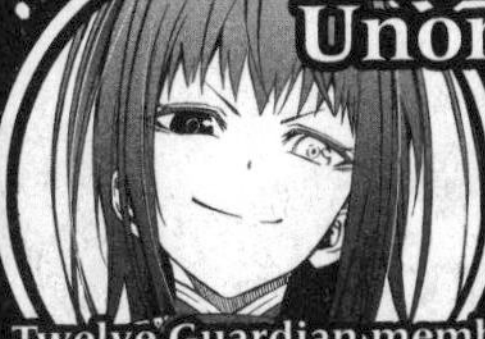

Twelve Guardian member God of the In-Between. Head of the Unomiya Family and said to be the most powerful exorcist. He habitually gives people weird nicknames.

Kamui

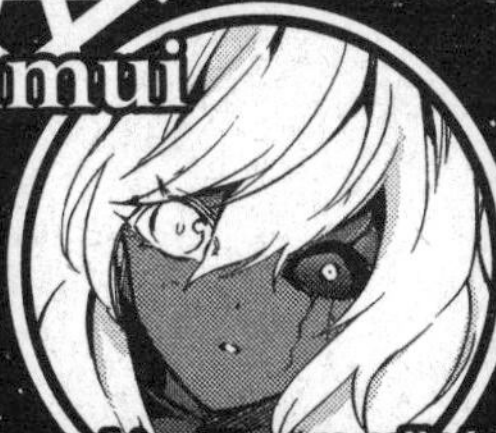

A high-ranking Kegare called a Basara who has the ability to communicate in the human tongue. Kamui killed Benio's parents.

Mayura Otomi

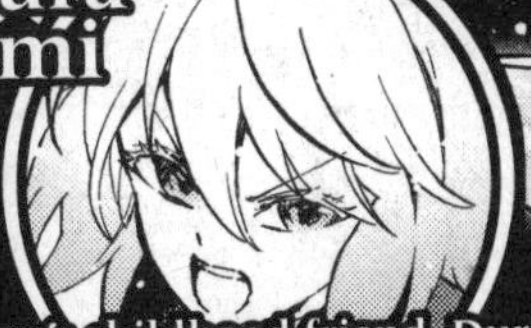

Rokuro's childhood friend. During a fierce battle in Magano, her commitment to protecting others earned her the spiritual protector White Tiger. She has become the new head of the Amawaka Family.

Kankuro Mitosaka

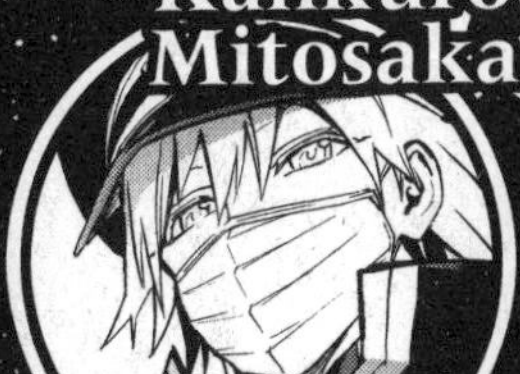

Twelve Guardian Azure Dragon, one of the most powerful guardians. Head of the Mitosaka Family and a doctor as well.

Arimori Tsuchimikado

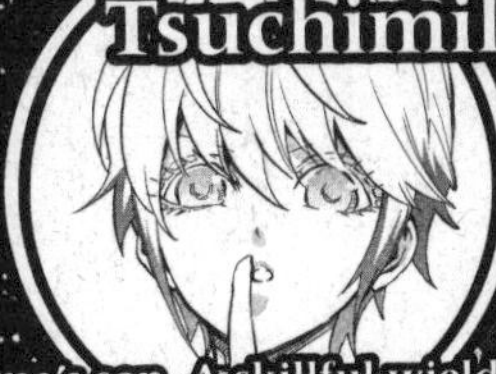

Arima's son. A skillful wielder of shikigami. He joined the Enmado Family to get his father's attention.

Story Thus Far...

Kegare are creatures from Magano, the underworld, and it is the duty of an exorcist to hunt, exorcise and purify them. Rokuro and Benio are the Twin Star Exorcists, fated to bear the Prophesied Child who will defeat the Kegare. Their goal is to go to Tsuchimikado Island to get revenge on Yuto, Benio's brother and the mastermind behind the Hinatsuki Tragedy.

After two years, Rokuro qualifies to go to the island, but Benio loses her spiritual power in battle. Leaving her behind, Rokuro instead moves to the island with his childhood friend and newbie exorcist Mayura. In order to compete in the Hadarae Castle Imperial Tournament to earn the right to join the hunt for Yuto Ijika, Rokuro founds a new clan in his name, the Enmado Family, and surprises everyone by defeating his opponent, Kankuro. Kankuro makes good on his promise to join the Enmado Family if he lost. And now, in the final match, Shimon is up against invincible and ruthless exorcist Tenma...

Twin Star Exorcists

ONMYOJI

EXORCISMS

ONMYOJI have worked for the Imperial Court since the Heian era.
In addition to exorcising evil spirits, as civil servants they performed a
variety of roles, including advising nobles by foretelling the future, creating
the calendar, observing the movements of the stars, measuring time…

#49: End of the Party

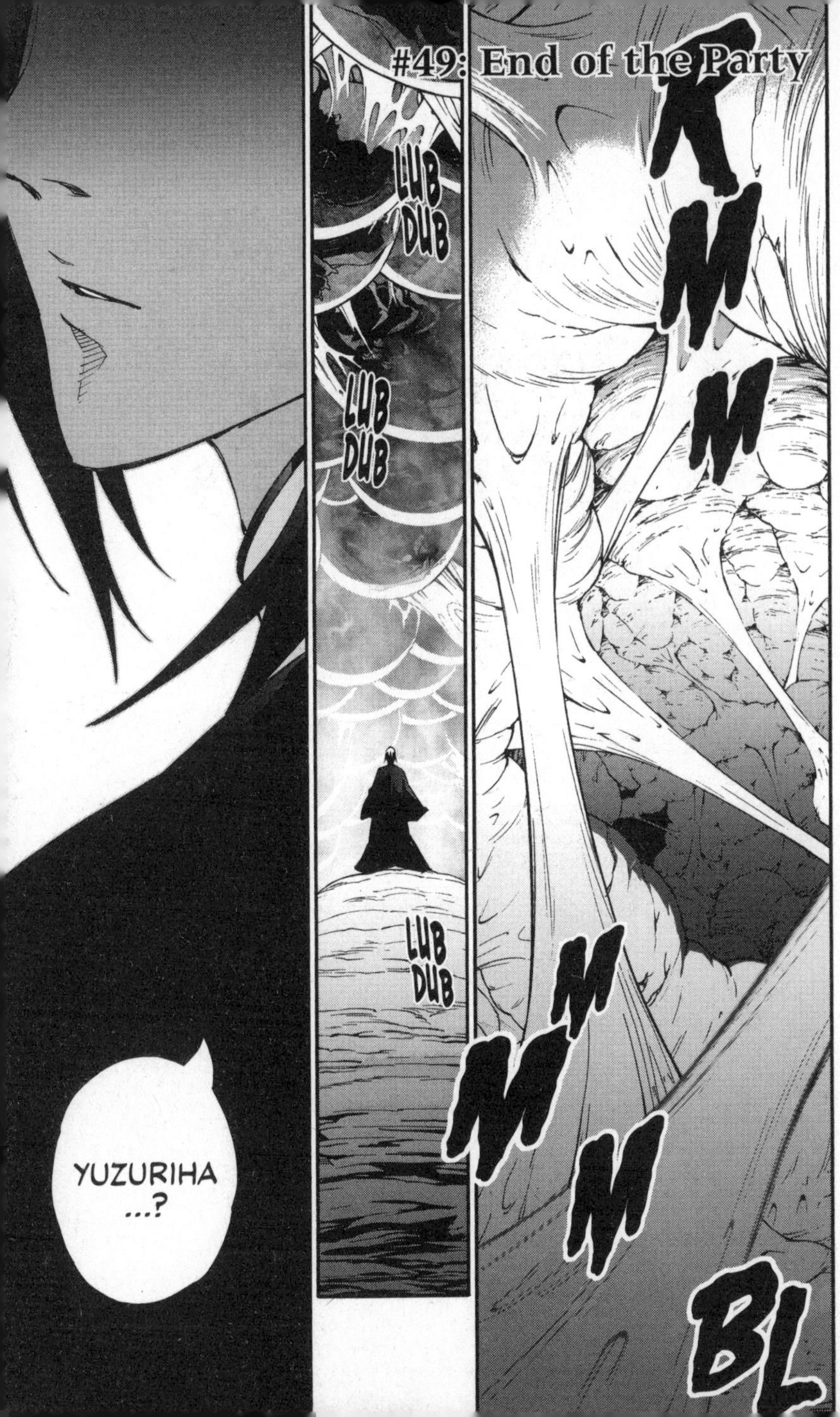
MM
MMMMBL
LUB DUB
LUB DUB
LUB DUB
YUZURIHA ...?

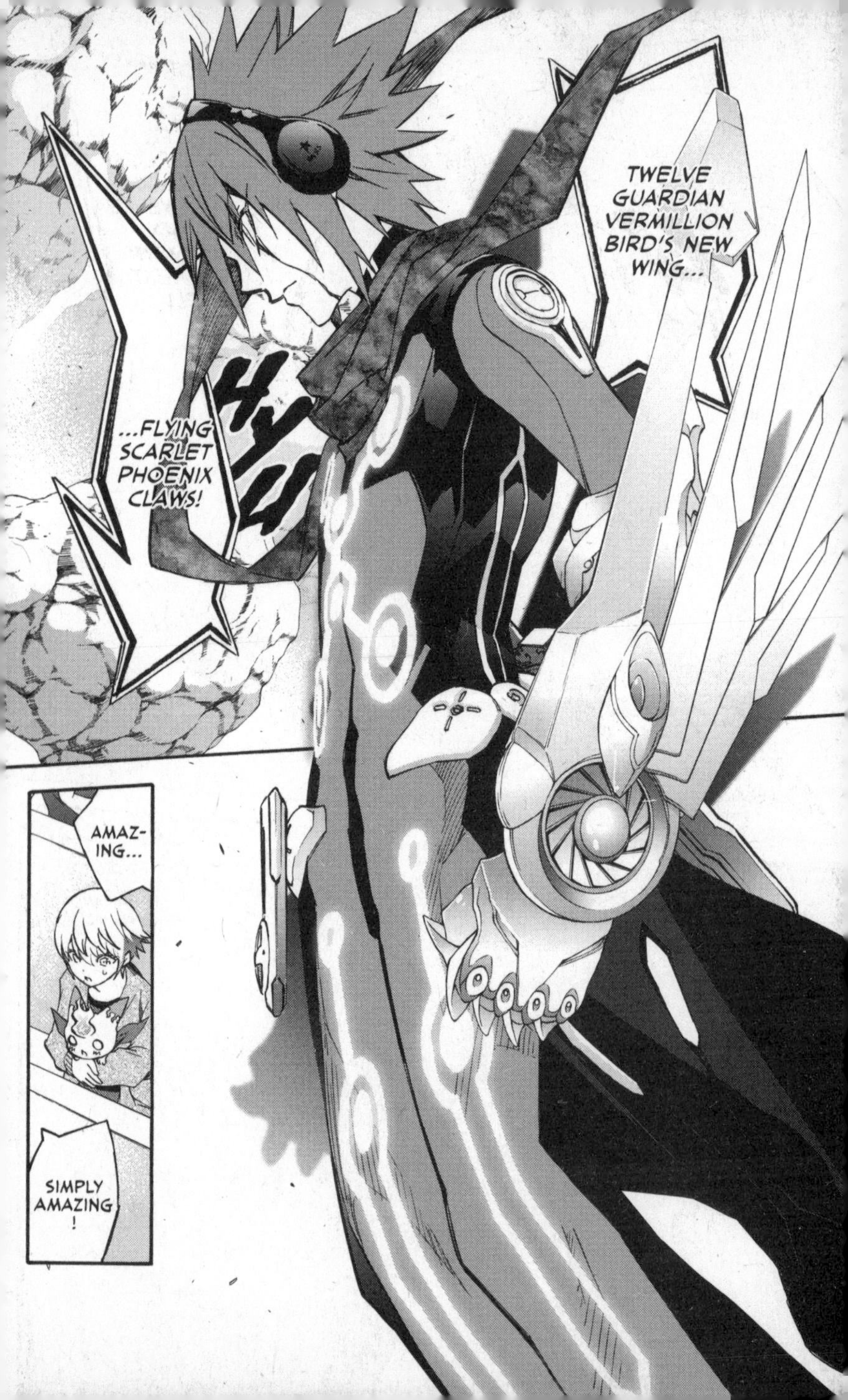
TWELVE GUARDIAN VERMILLION BIRD'S NEW WING...
...FLYING SCARLET PHOENIX CLAWS!
AMAZ-ING...
SIMPLY AMAZING!

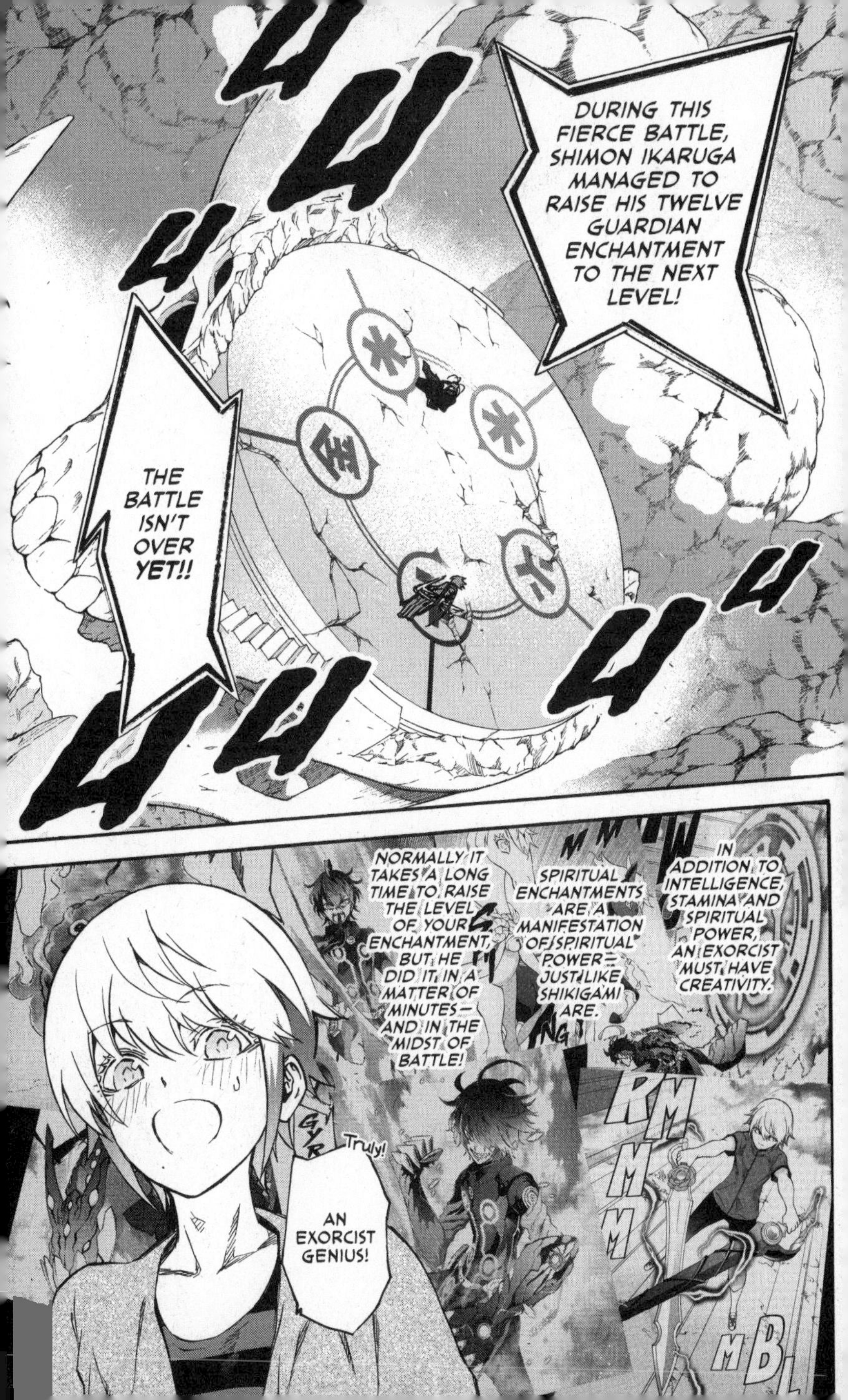
DURING THIS FIERCE BATTLE, SHIMON IKARUGA MANAGED TO RAISE HIS TWELVE GUARDIAN ENCHANTMENT TO THE NEXT LEVEL!
THE BATTLE ISN'T OVER YET!!
IN ADDITION TO INTELLIGENCE, STAMINA AND SPIRITUAL POWER, AN EXORCIST MUST HAVE CREATIVITY.
SPIRITUAL ENCHANTMENTS ARE A MANIFESTATION OF SPIRITUAL POWER—JUST LIKE SHIKIGAMI ARE.
NORMALLY IT TAKES A LONG TIME TO RAISE THE LEVEL OF YOUR ENCHANTMENT, BUT HE DID IT IN A MATTER OF MINUTES—AND IN THE MIDST OF BATTLE!
Truly!
AN EXORCIST GENIUS!

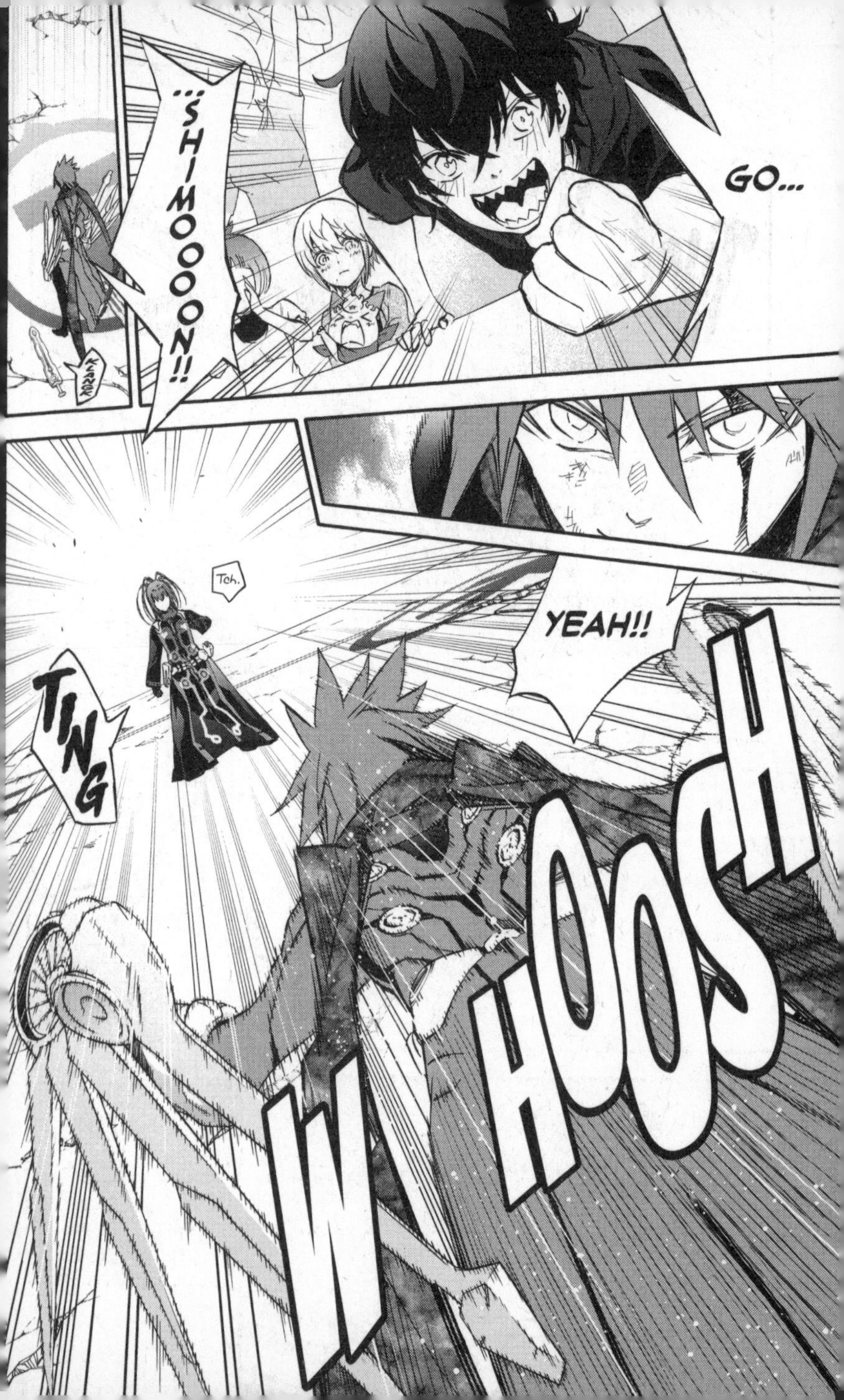
GO...
...SHIMOOOON!!
KLANCK
YEAH!!
Tch.
TING
WHOOSH

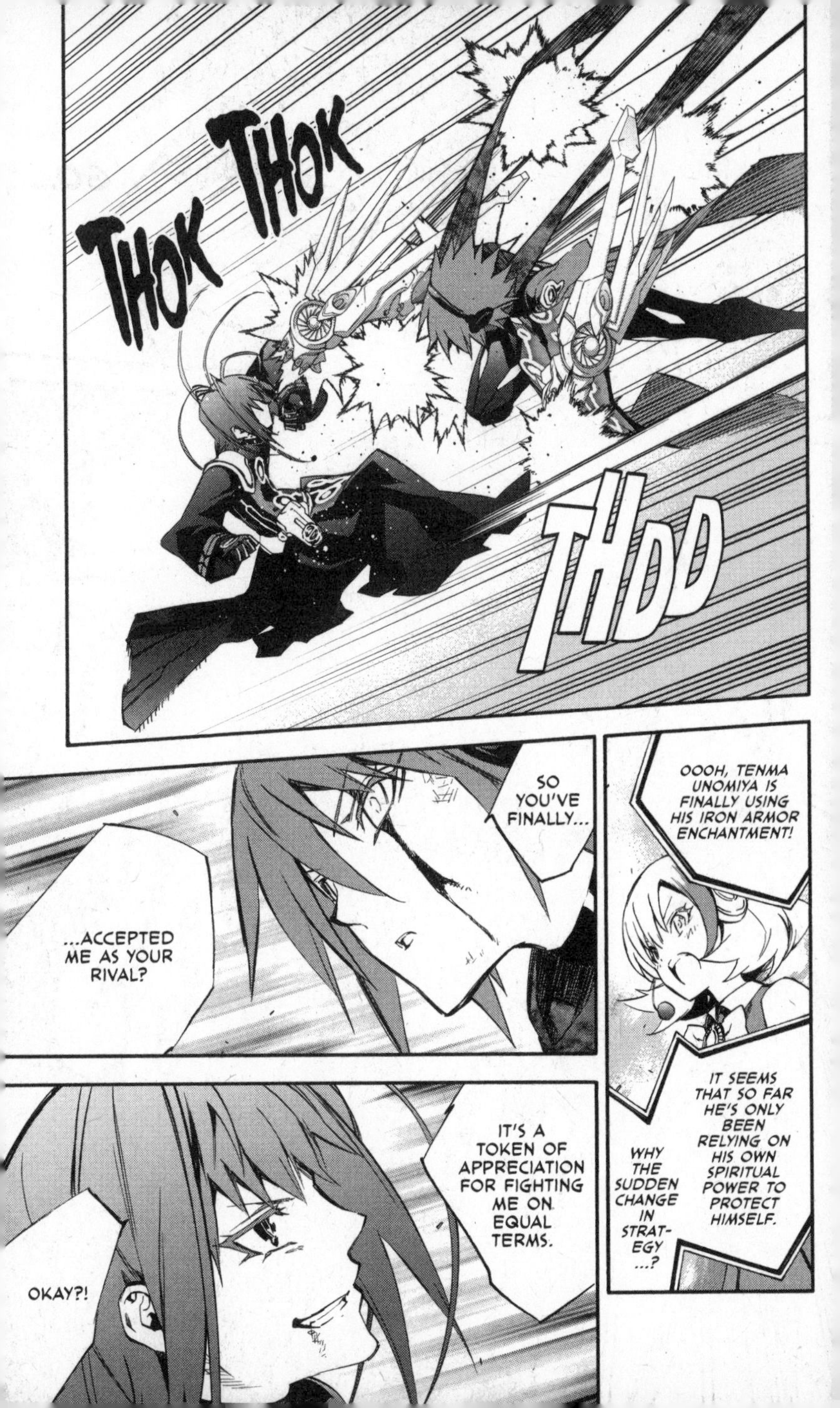
THOK THOK
THDD
OOOH, TENMA UNOMIYA IS FINALLY USING HIS IRON ARMOR ENCHANTMENT!
IT SEEMS THAT SO FAR HE'S ONLY BEEN RELYING ON HIS OWN SPIRITUAL POWER TO PROTECT HIMSELF.
WHY THE SUDDEN CHANGE IN STRAT-EGY ...?
SO YOU'VE FINALLY...
...ACCEPTED ME AS YOUR RIVAL?
IT'S A TOKEN OF APPRECIATION FOR FIGHTING ME ON EQUAL TERMS.
OKAY?!

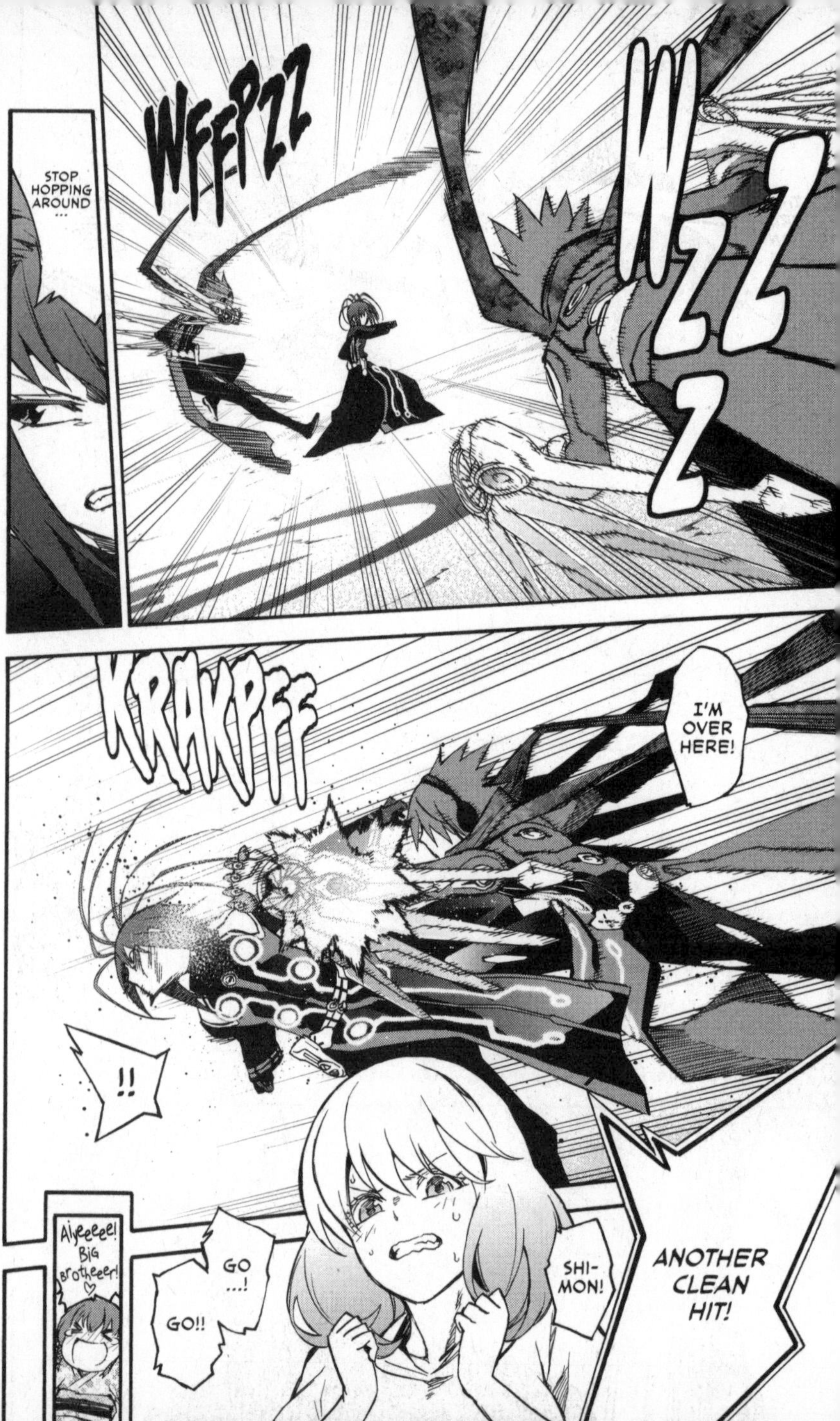
WZZZ
WFFPZZ
STOP HOPPING AROUND ...
KRAKPFF
I'M OVER HERE!
!!
ANOTHER CLEAN HIT!
SHI-MON!
GO ...!
GO!!
Aiyeeeee! Big brotheeer! ♡

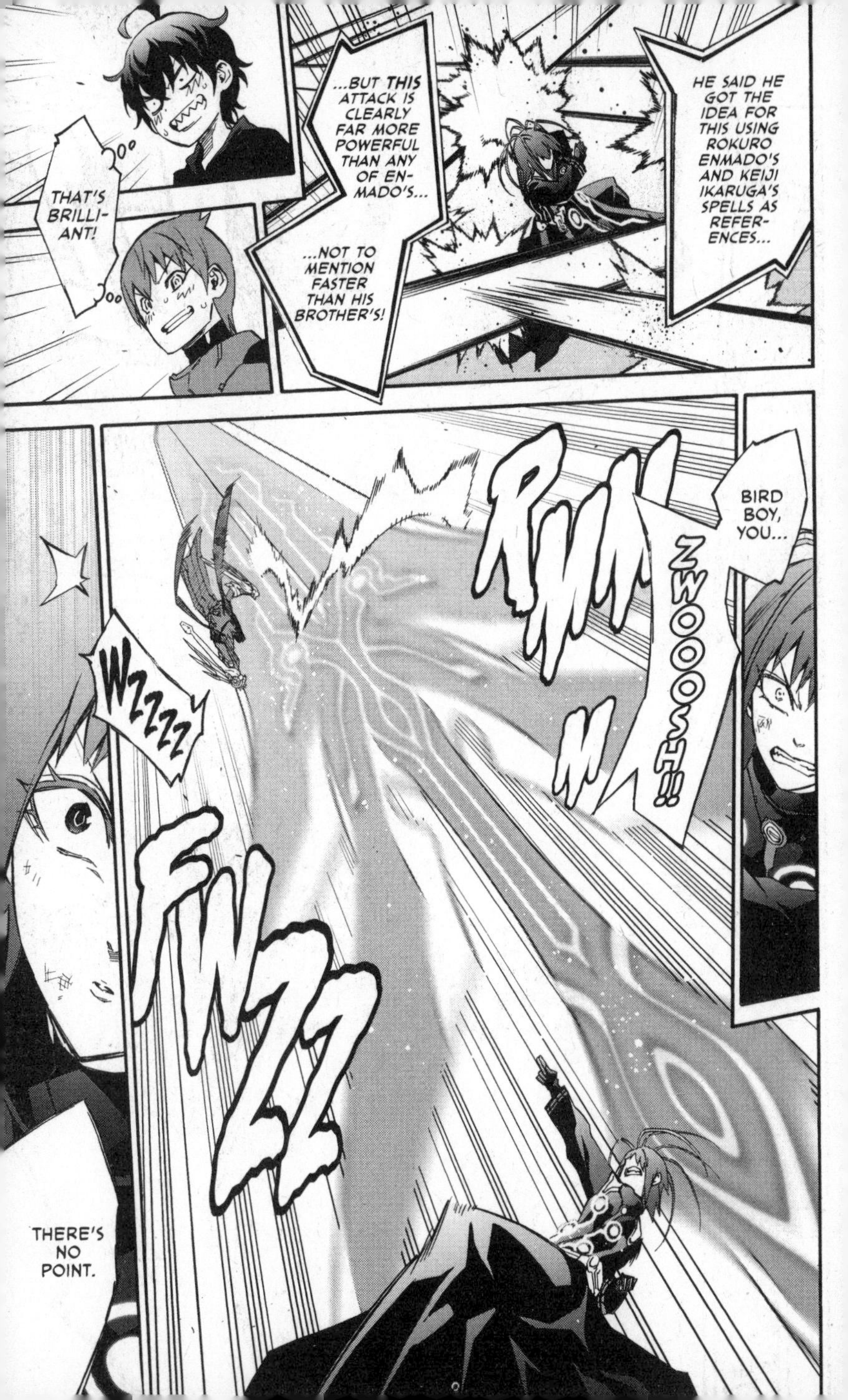

HE SAID HE GOT THE IDEA FOR THIS USING ROKURO ENMADO'S AND KEIJI IKARUGA'S SPELLS AS REFERENCES...
...BUT THIS ATTACK IS CLEARLY FAR MORE POWERFUL THAN ANY OF ENMADO'S...
...NOT TO MENTION FASTER THAN HIS BROTHER'S!
THAT'S BRILLIANT!
BIRD BOY, YOU...
RMMM
ZWOOOOSH!!
WZZZZ
FWZZ
THERE'S NO POINT.

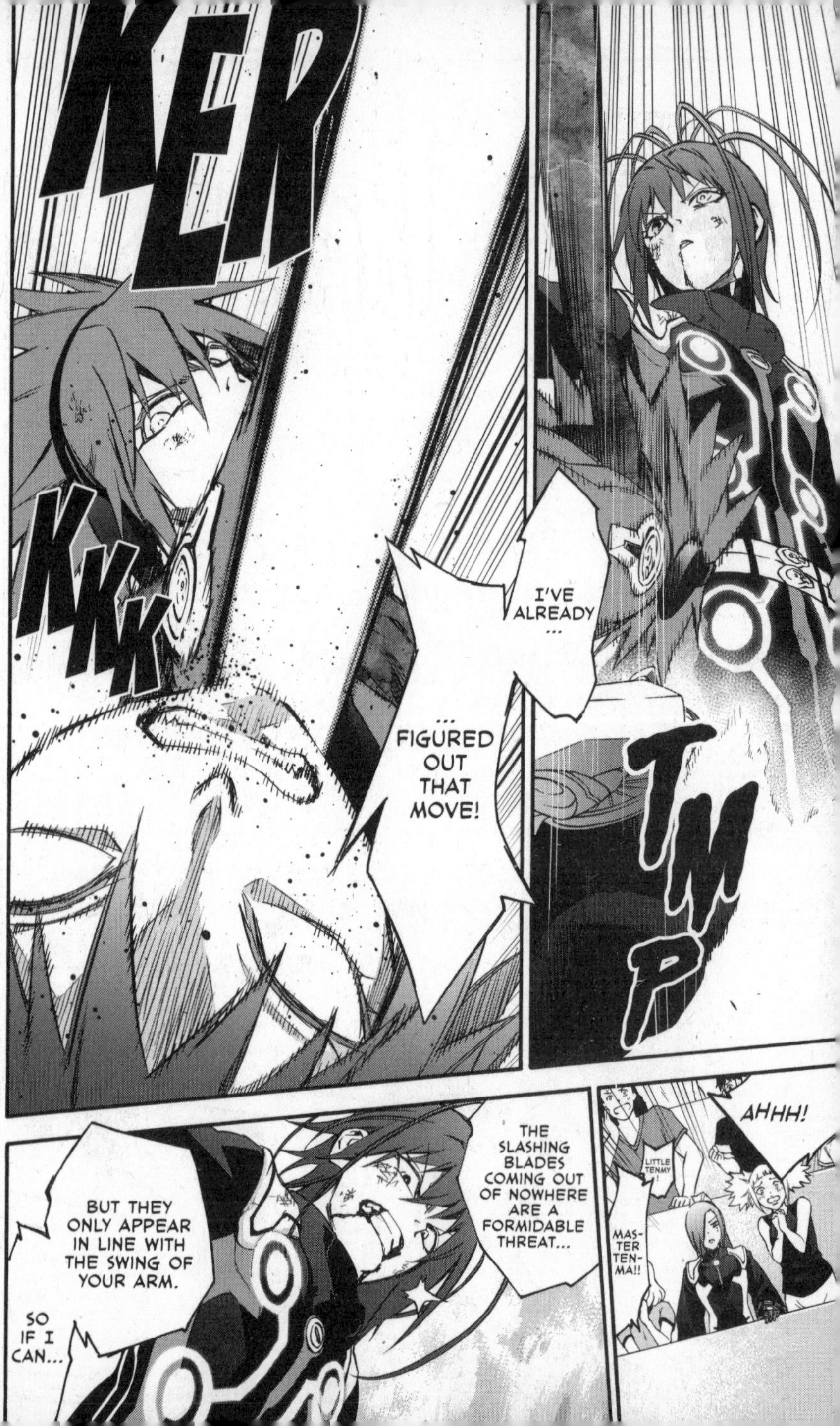
TMP
I'VE ALREADY...
KER
KKK
...FIGURED OUT THAT MOVE!
AHHH!
LITTLE TENMY!
MASTER TENMA!!
THE SLASHING BLADES COMING OUT OF NOWHERE ARE A FORMIDABLE THREAT...
BUT THEY ONLY APPEAR IN LINE WITH THE SWING OF YOUR ARM.
SO IF I CAN...

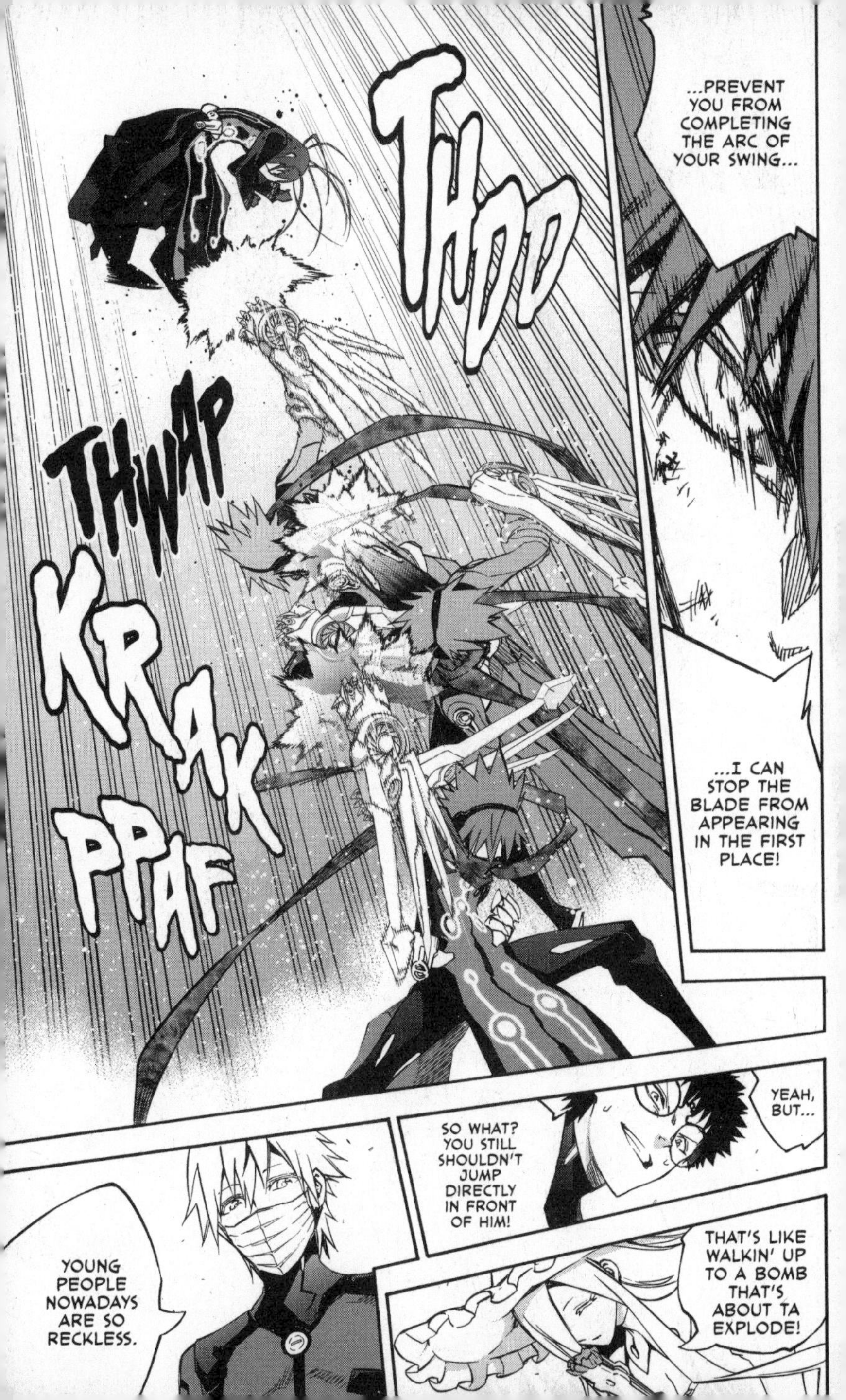
...PREVENT YOU FROM COMPLETING THE ARC OF YOUR SWING...
...I CAN STOP THE BLADE FROM APPEARING IN THE FIRST PLACE!
THDD
THWAP
KRAK
PPAF
YEAH, BUT...
SO WHAT? YOU STILL SHOULDN'T JUMP DIRECTLY IN FRONT OF HIM!
THAT'S LIKE WALKIN' UP TO A BOMB THAT'S ABOUT TA EXPLODE!
YOUNG PEOPLE NOWADAYS ARE SO RECKLESS.

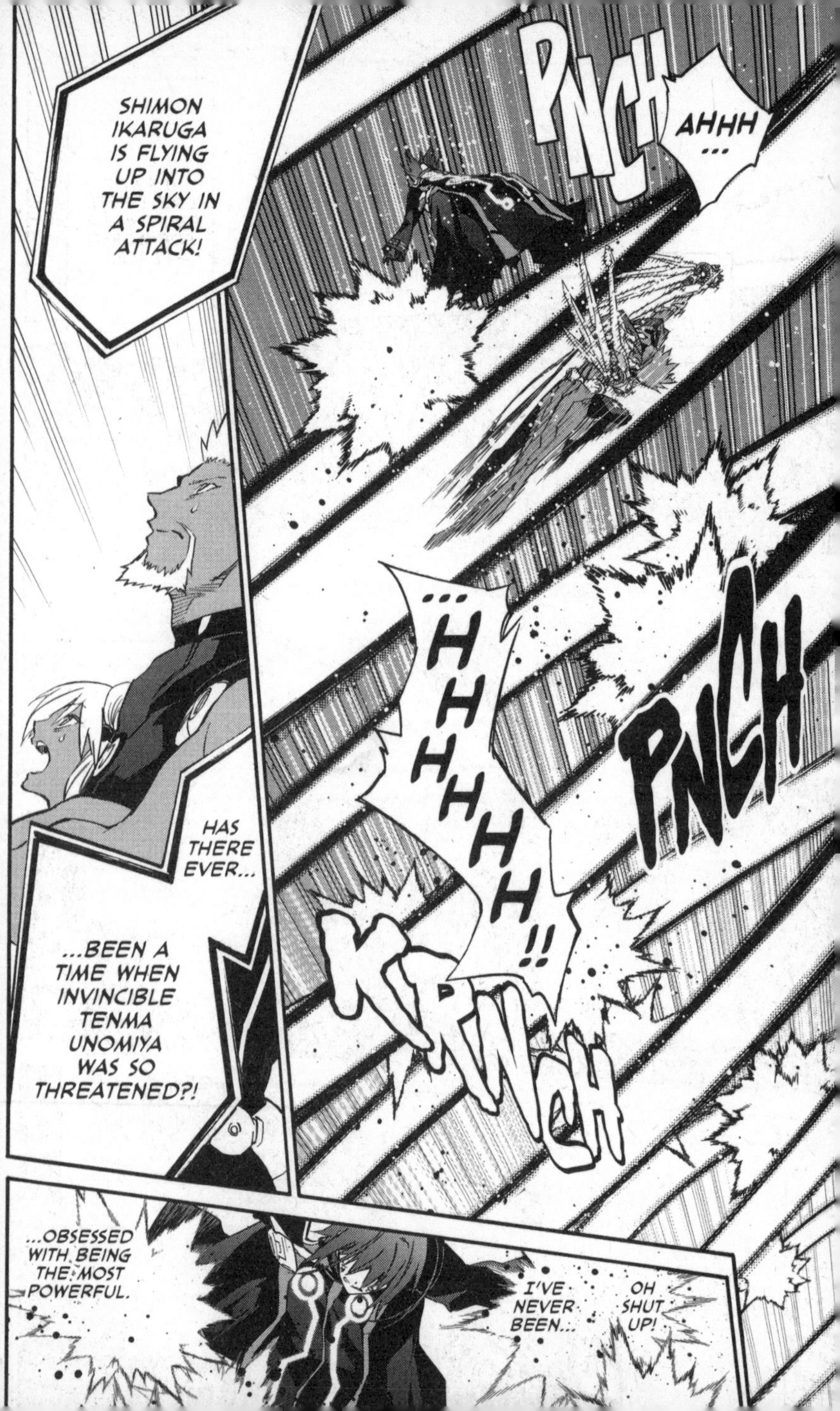

PNCH
AHHH...
...HHHHHHH!!
PNCH
KRNCH
SHIMON IKARUGA IS FLYING UP INTO THE SKY IN A SPIRAL ATTACK!
HAS THERE EVER...
...BEEN A TIME WHEN INVINCIBLE TENMA UNOMIYA WAS SO THREATENED?!
OH SHUT UP!
I'VE NEVER BEEN...
...OBSESSED WITH BEING THE MOST POWERFUL.

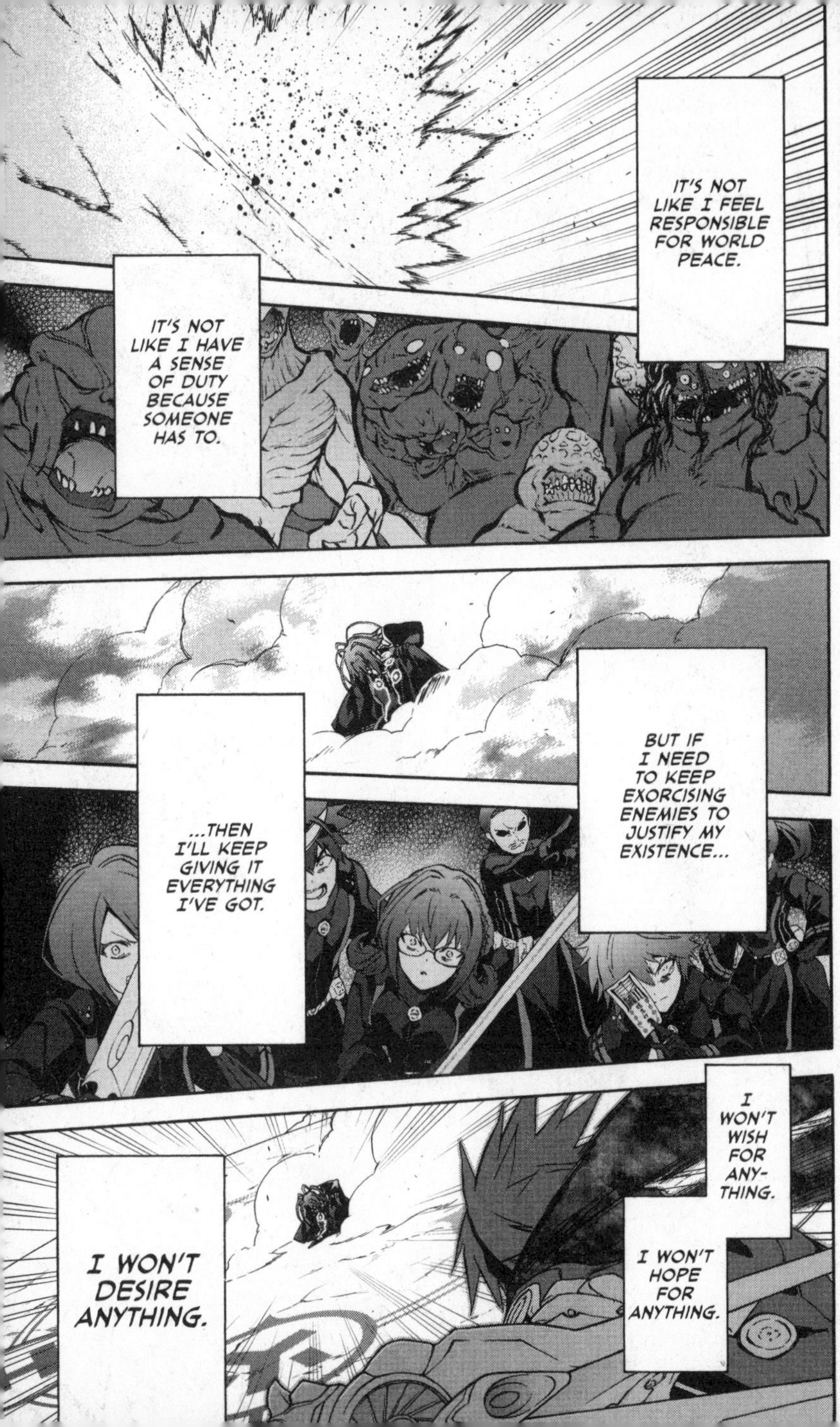
IT'S NOT LIKE I FEEL RESPONSIBLE FOR WORLD PEACE.
IT'S NOT LIKE I HAVE A SENSE OF DUTY BECAUSE SOMEONE HAS TO.
BUT IF I NEED TO KEEP EXORCISING ENEMIES TO JUSTIFY MY EXISTENCE...
...THEN I'LL KEEP GIVING IT EVERYTHING I'VE GOT.
I WON'T WISH FOR ANY-THING.
I WON'T HOPE FOR ANYTHING.
I WON'T DESIRE ANYTHING.

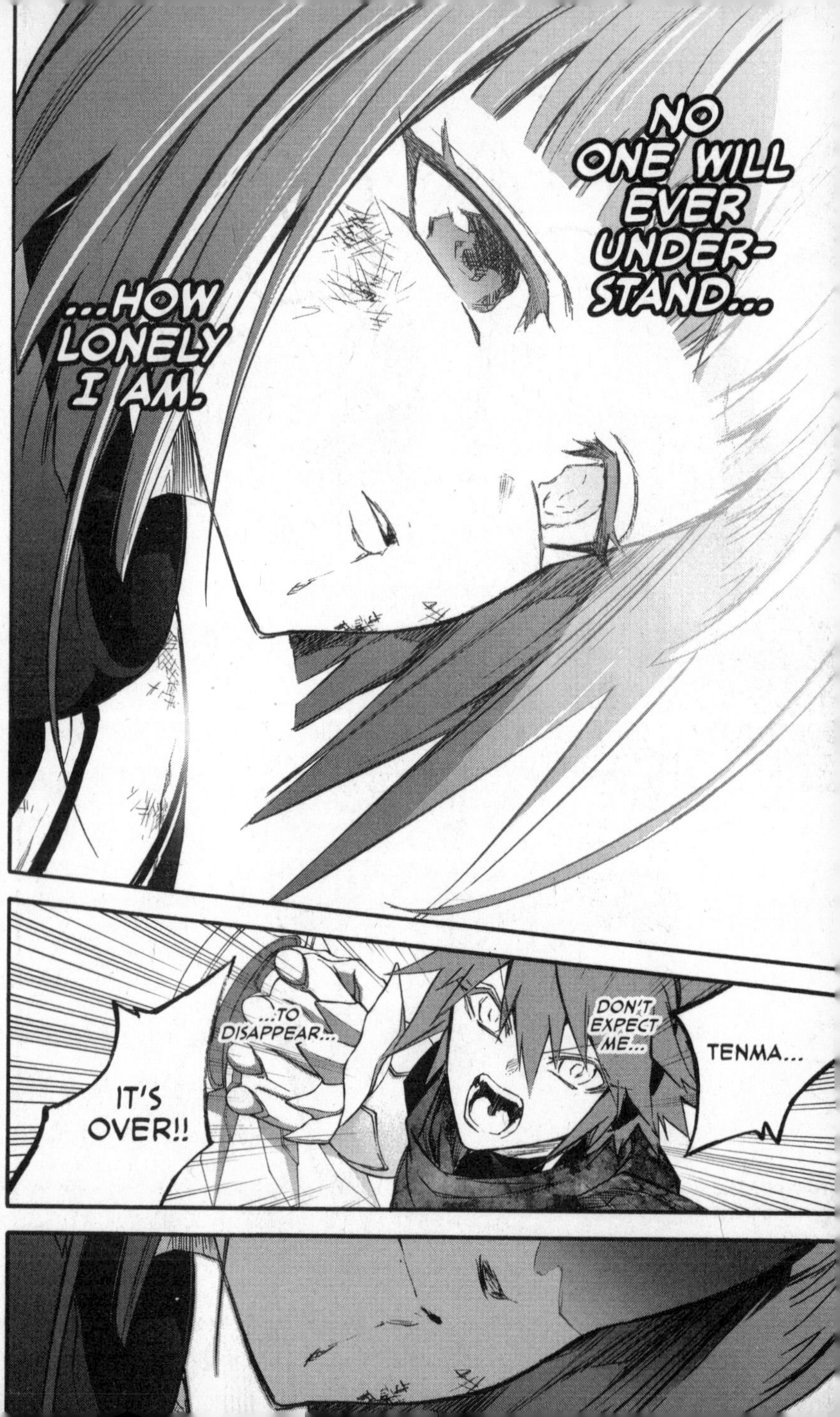
NO ONE WILL EVER UNDER-STAND...
...HOW LONELY I AM.
TENMA...
DON'T EXPECT ME...
...TO DISAPPEAR...
IT'S OVER!!

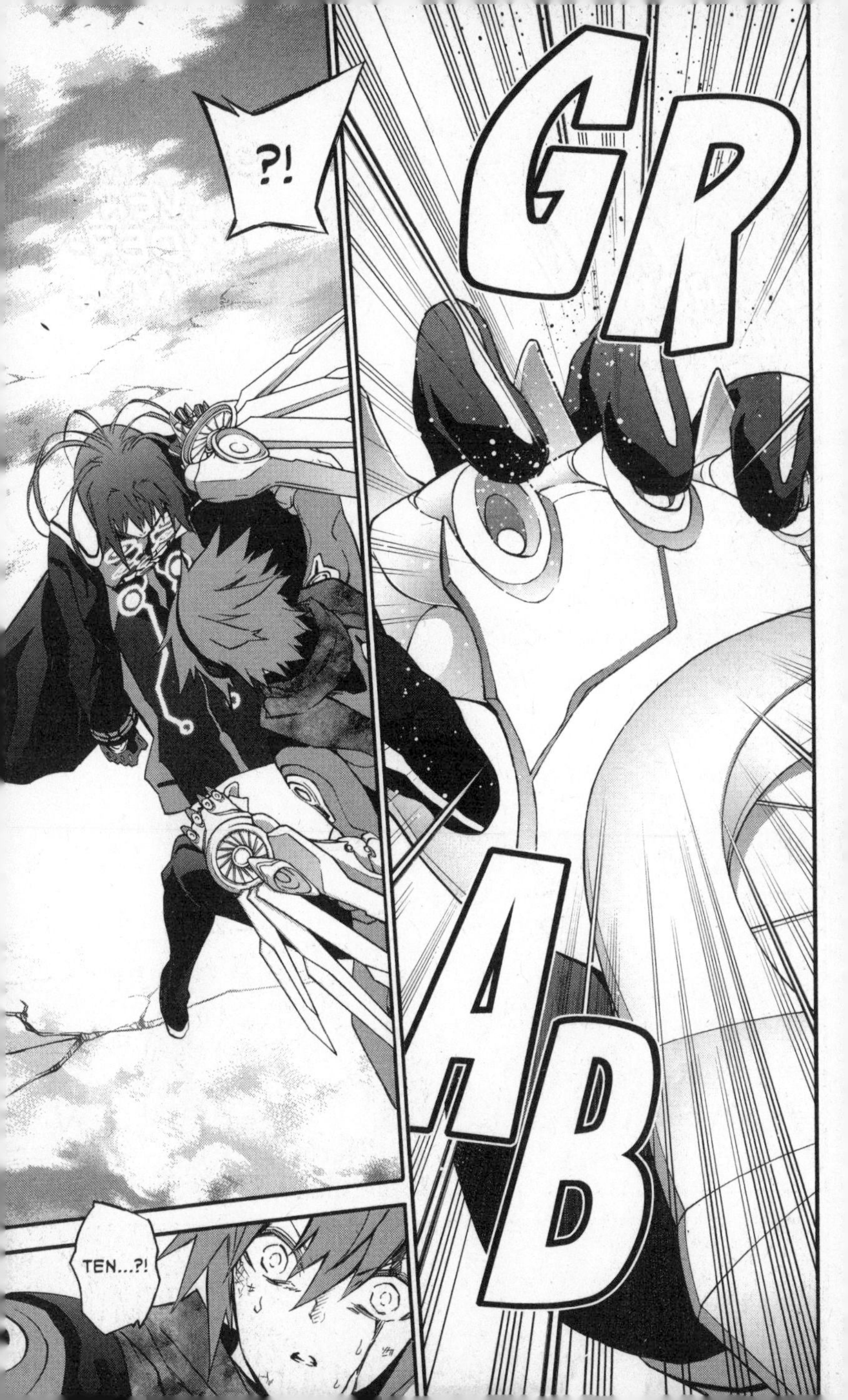
GRAB
?!
TEN...?!

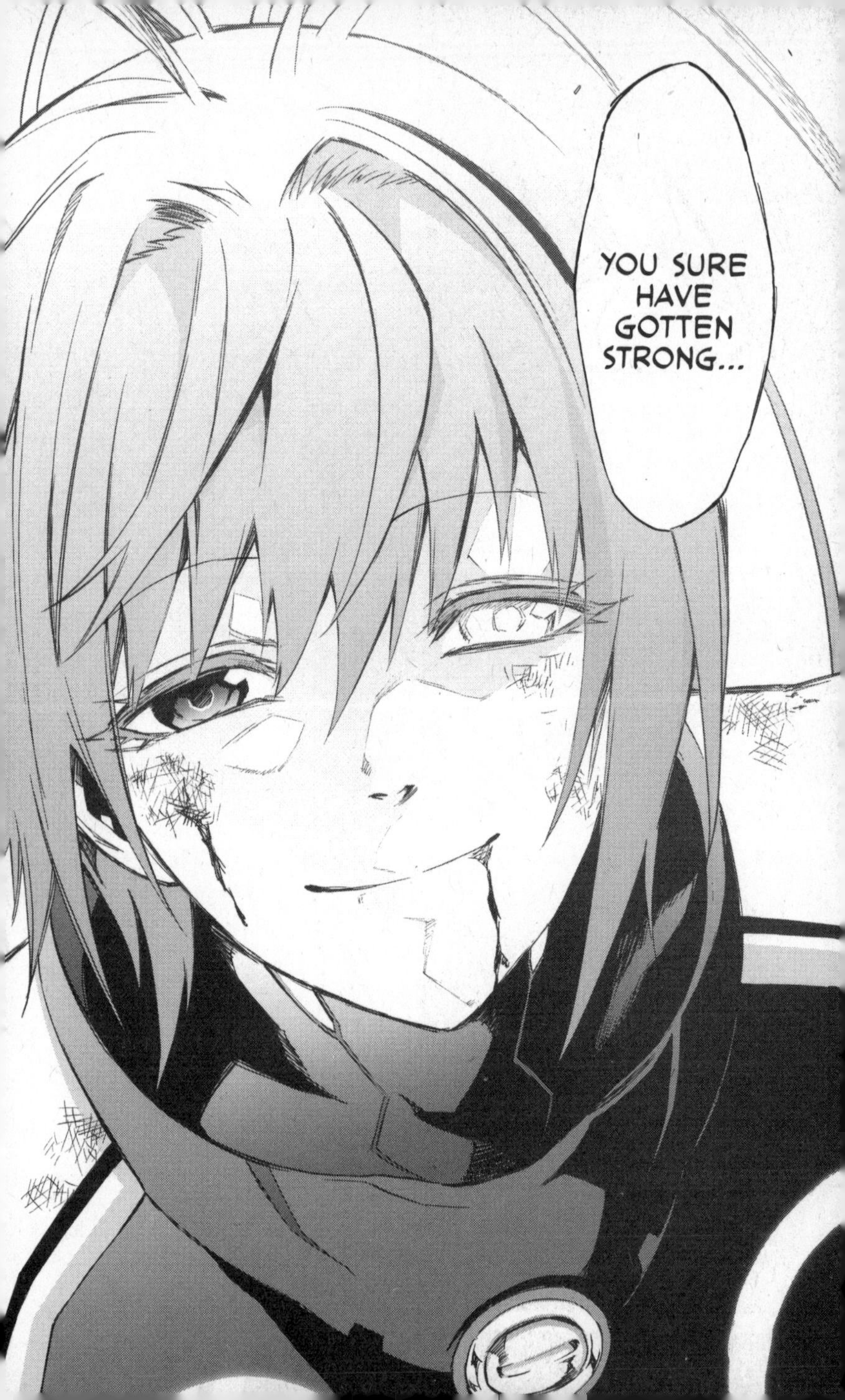
YOU SURE HAVE GOTTEN STRONG...

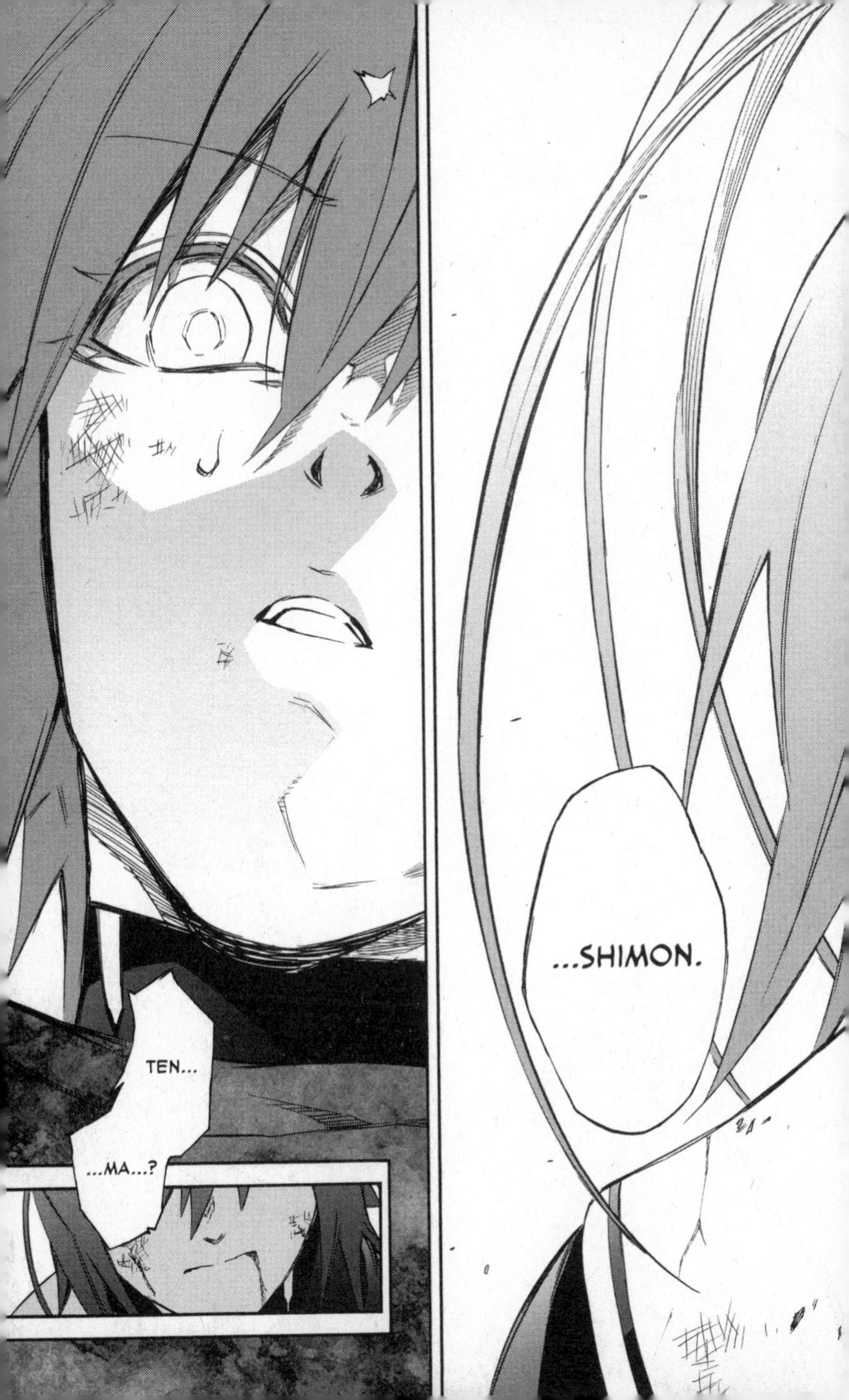
...SHIMON.
TEN...
...MA...?

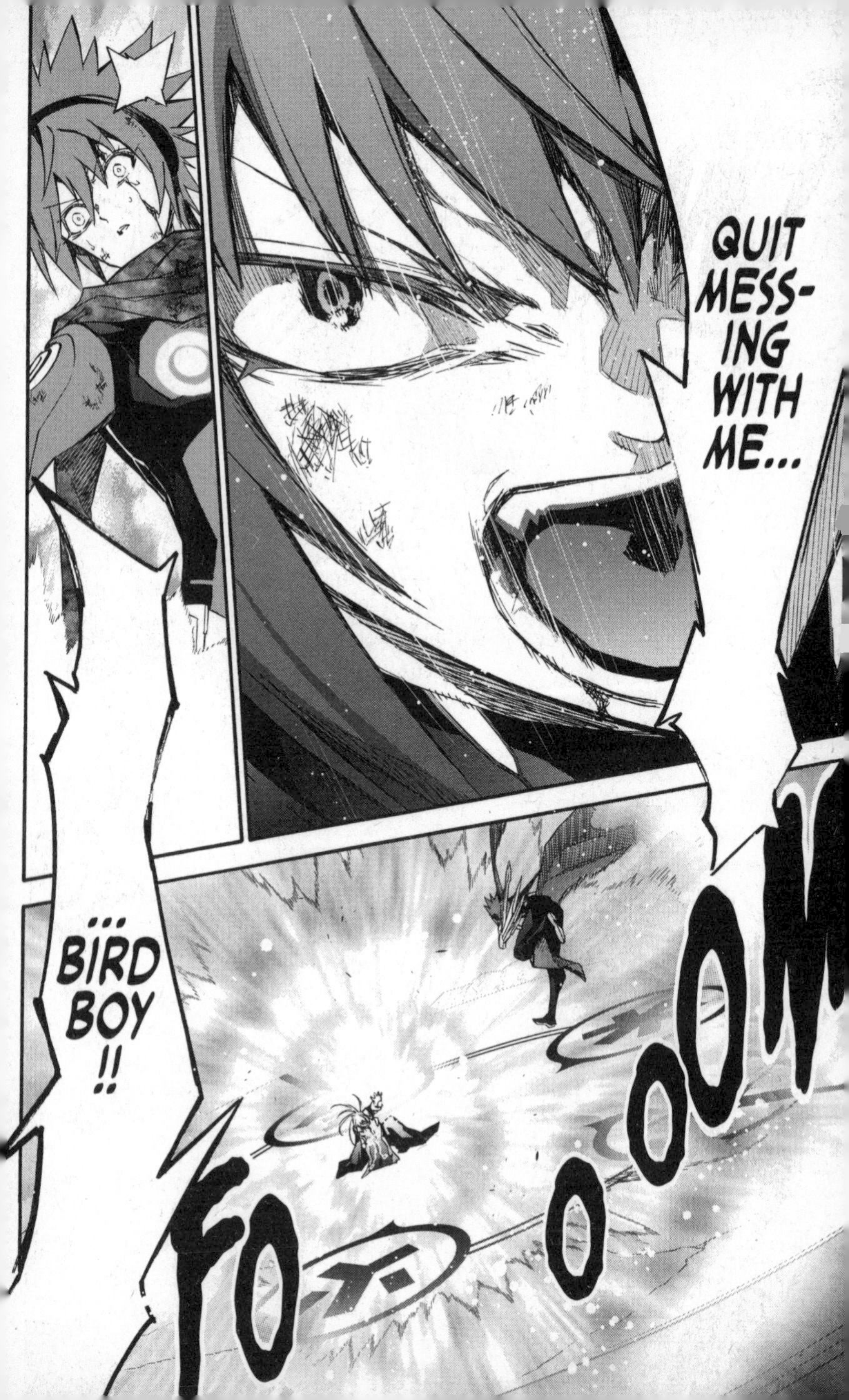
QUIT MESSING WITH ME...
...BIRD BOY!!
FOOOOOM

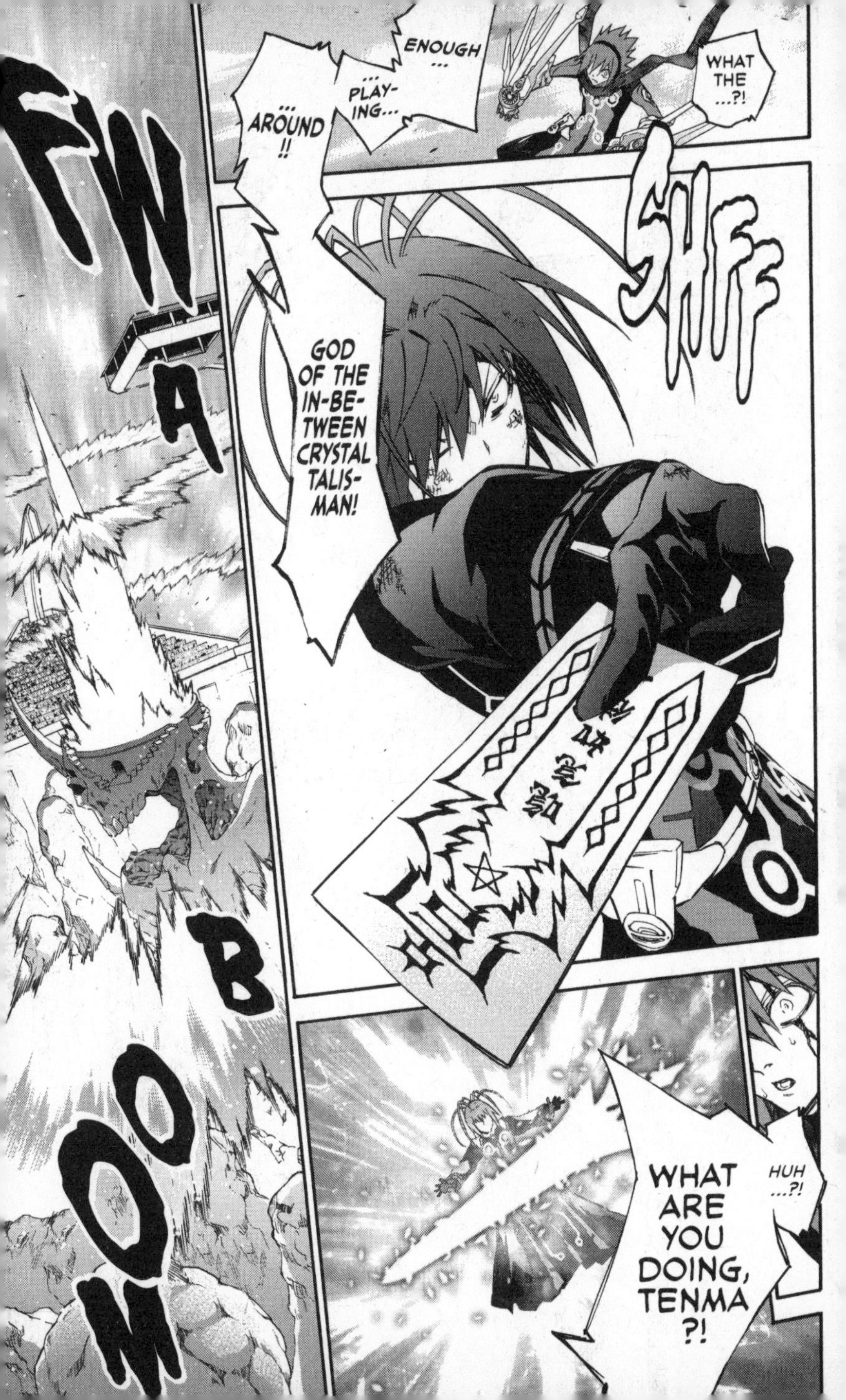
WHAT THE ...?!
ENOUGH ...
... PLAYING...
... AROUND !!
SHFF
GOD OF THE IN-BE-TWEEN CRYSTAL TALIS-MAN!
HUH ...?!
WHAT ARE YOU DOING, TENMA ?!
FWA
B
OOM

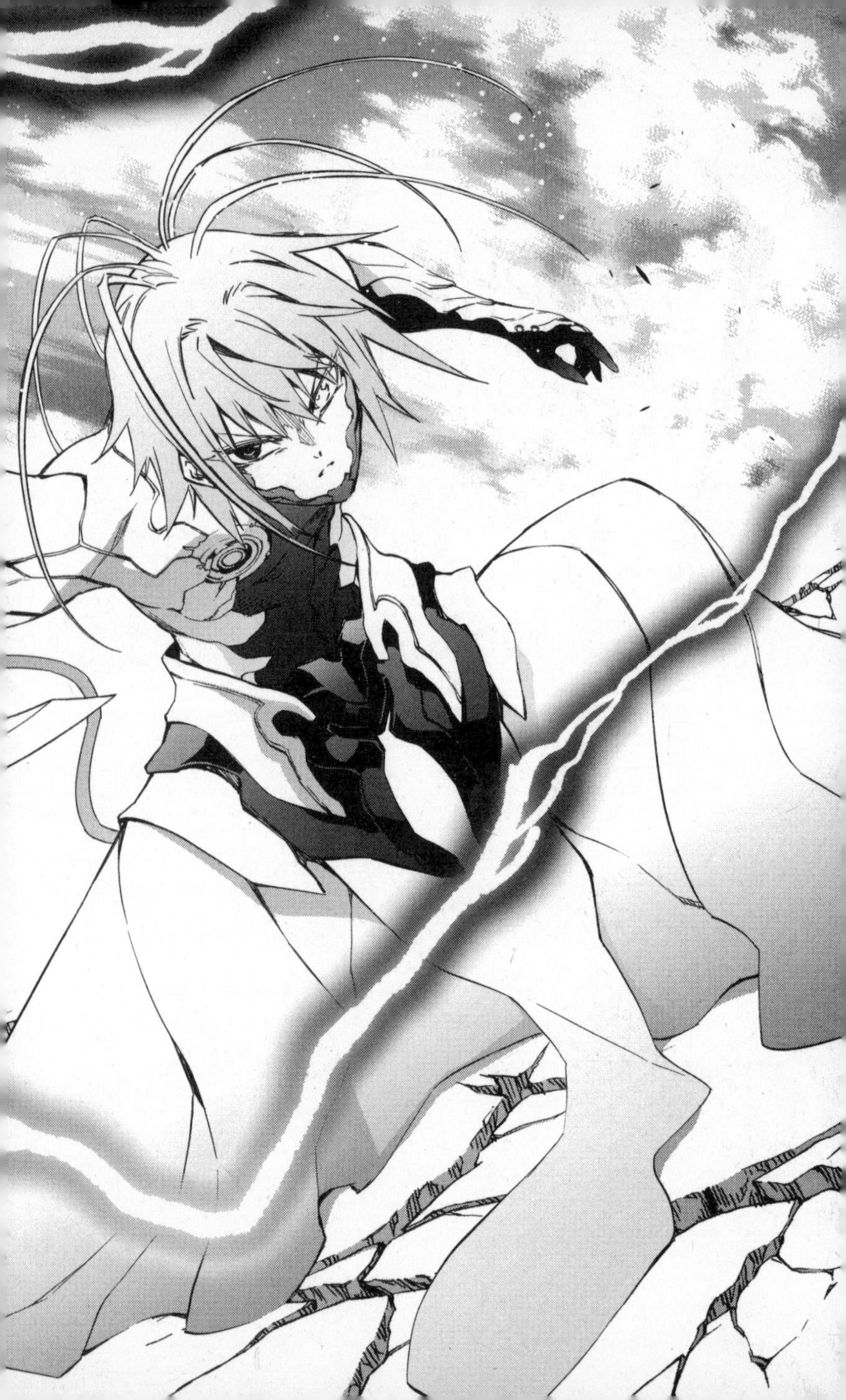

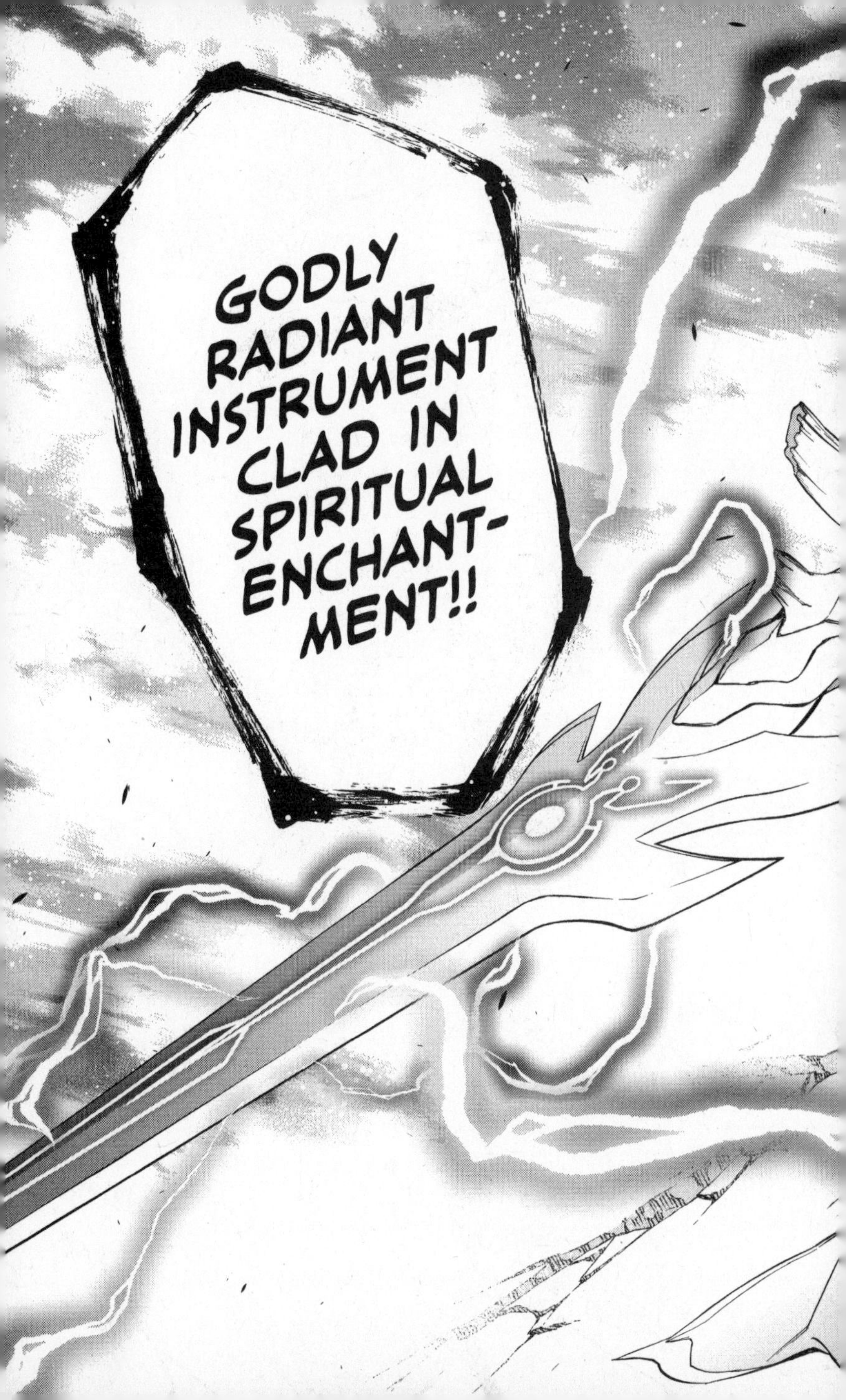
GODLY RADIANT INSTRUMENT CLAD IN SPIRITUAL ENCHANT-MENT!!

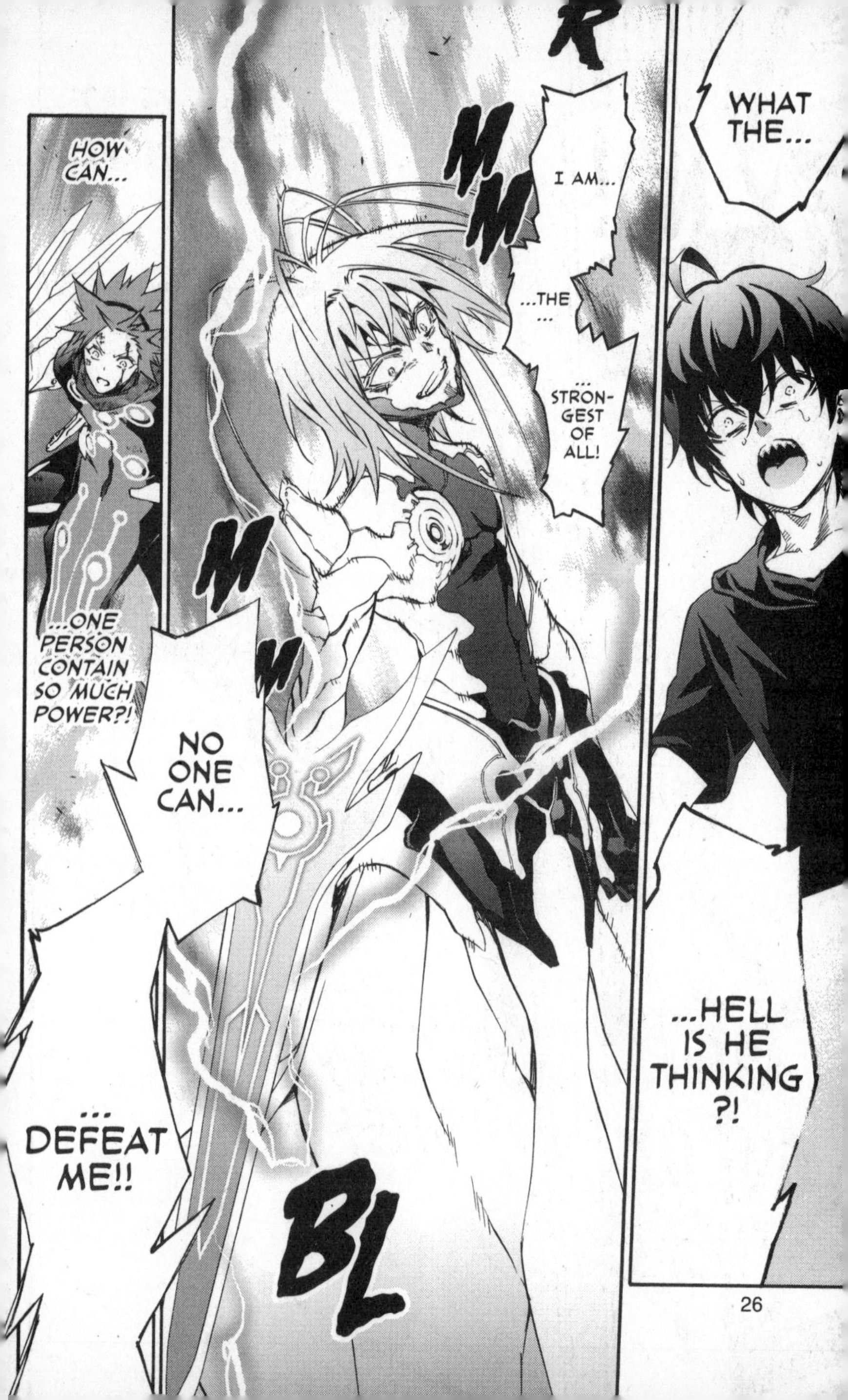
WHAT THE...
...HELL IS HE THINKING?!
R
MM
I AM...
...THE...
...STRONGEST OF ALL!
M
M
HOW CAN...
...ONE PERSON CONTAIN SO MUCH POWER?!
NO ONE CAN...
...DEFEAT ME!!
BL

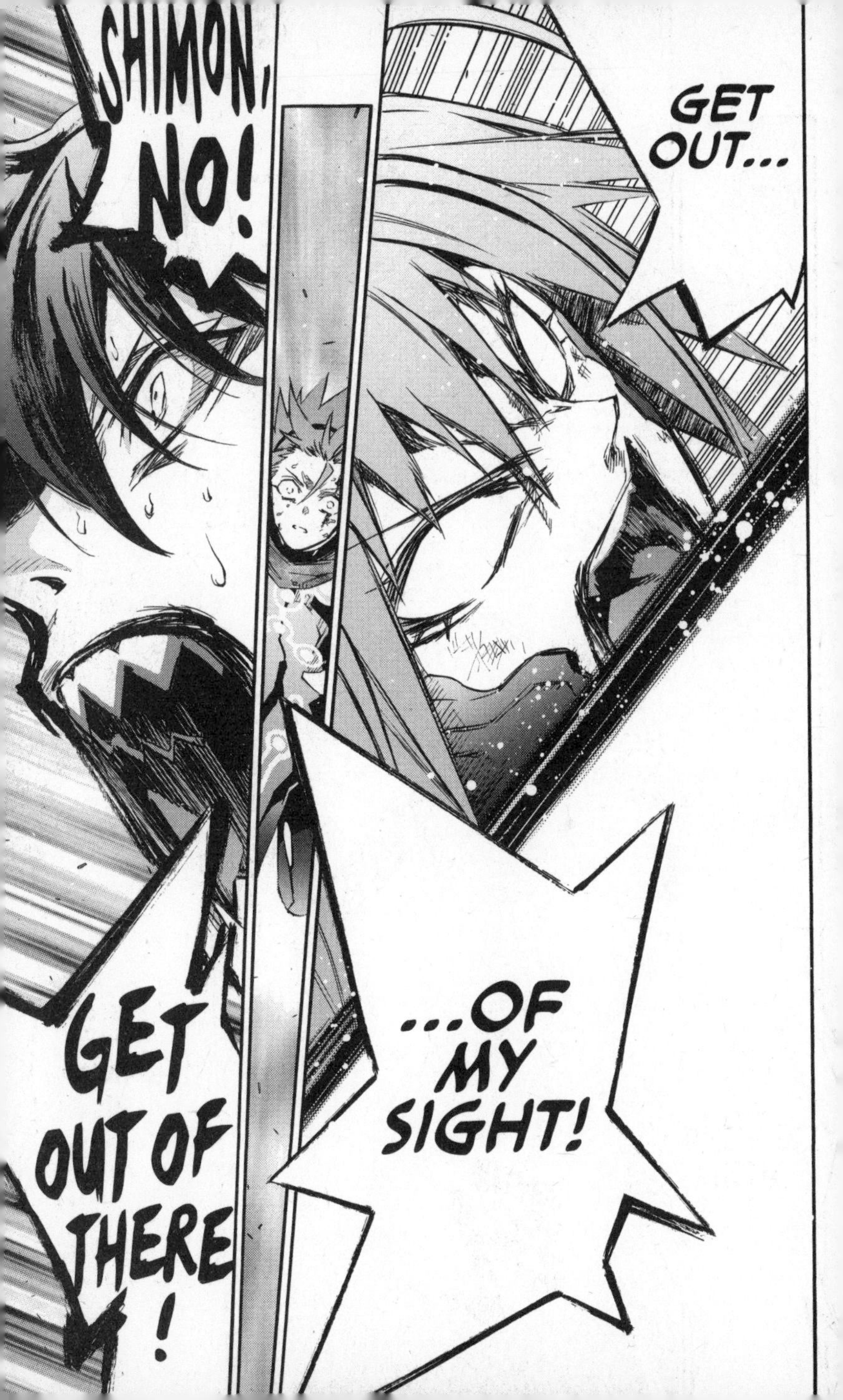
GET OUT...
...OF MY SIGHT!
SHIMON, NO!
GET OUT OF THERE!

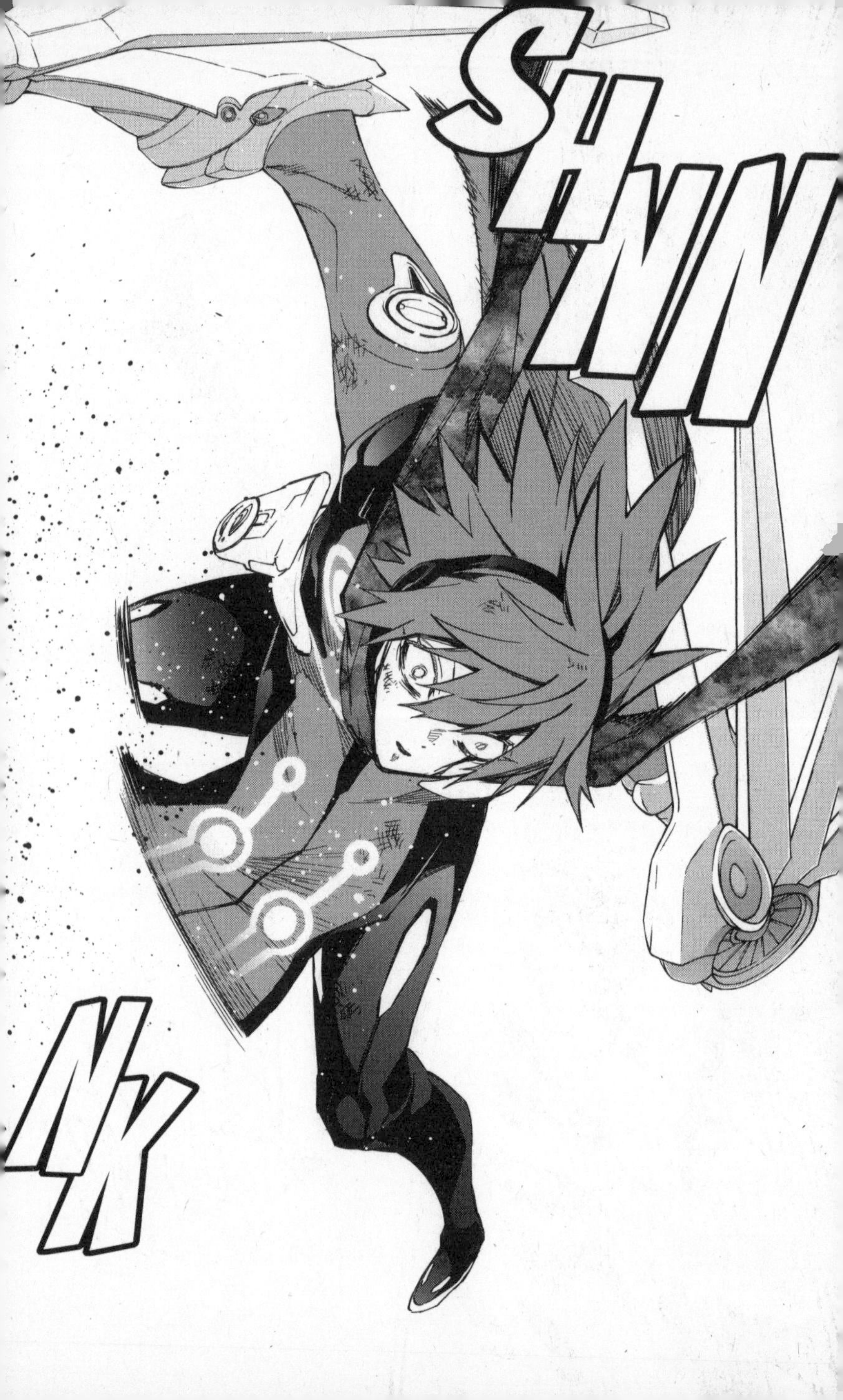
SHNN
NK

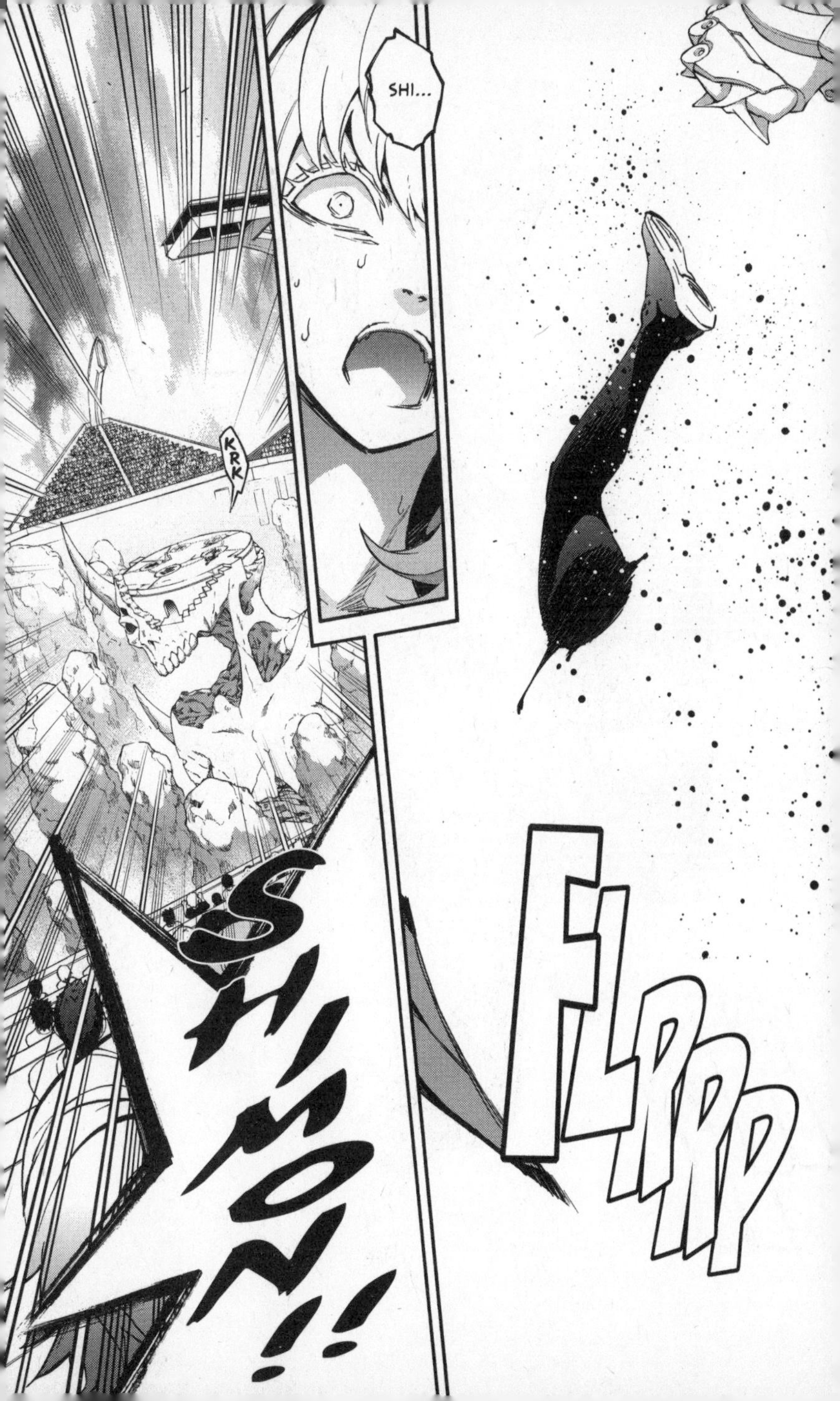

FLRRP
SHI...
KRK

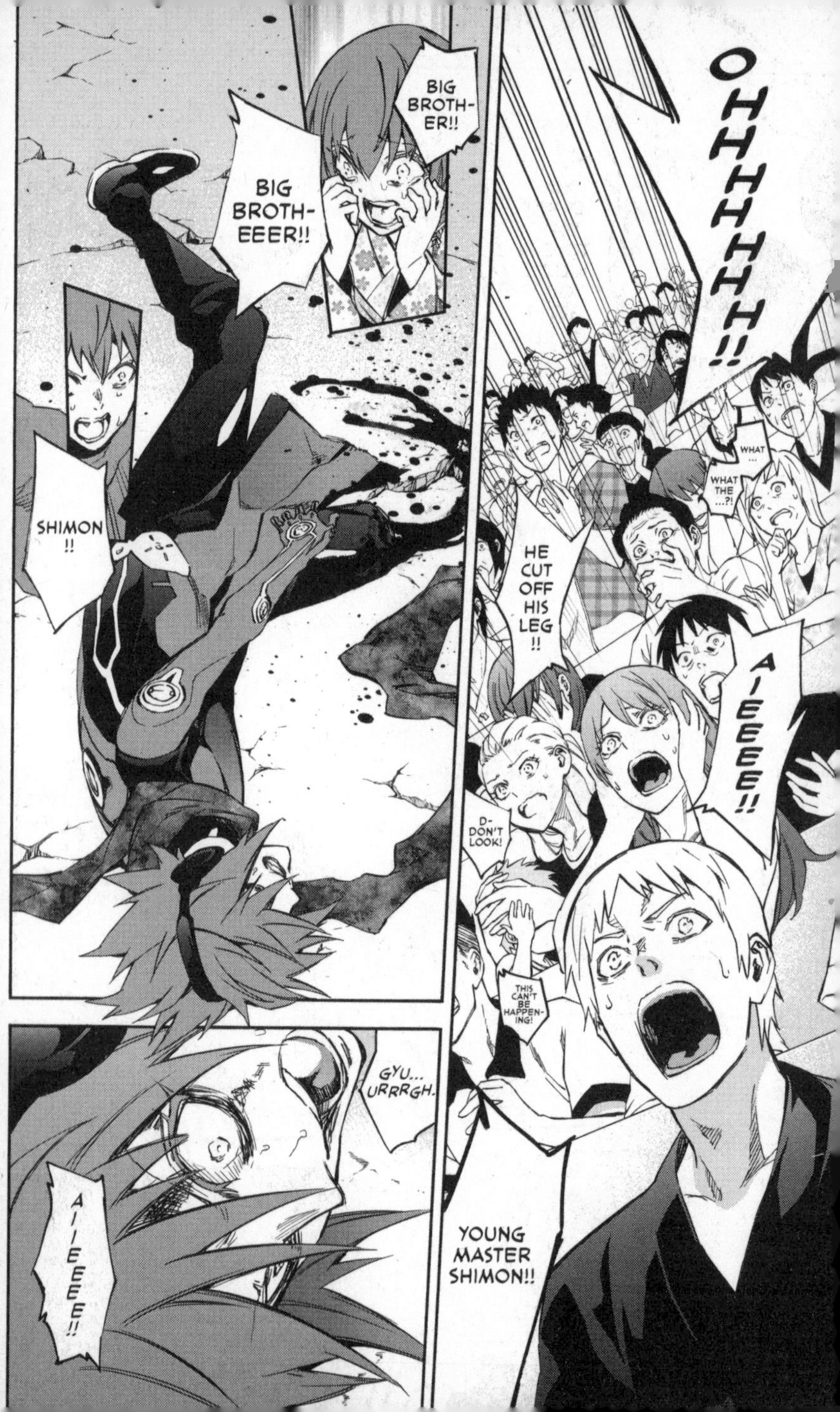
OHHHHHHH!!
WHAT... WHAT THE...?!
HE CUT OFF HIS LEG!!
AIEEEE!!
D-DON'T LOOK!
THIS CAN'T BE HAPPENING!
YOUNG MASTER SHIMON!!
BIG BROTHER!!
BIG BROTHEEER!!
SHIMON!!
GYU... URRRGH.
AIIEEEE!!

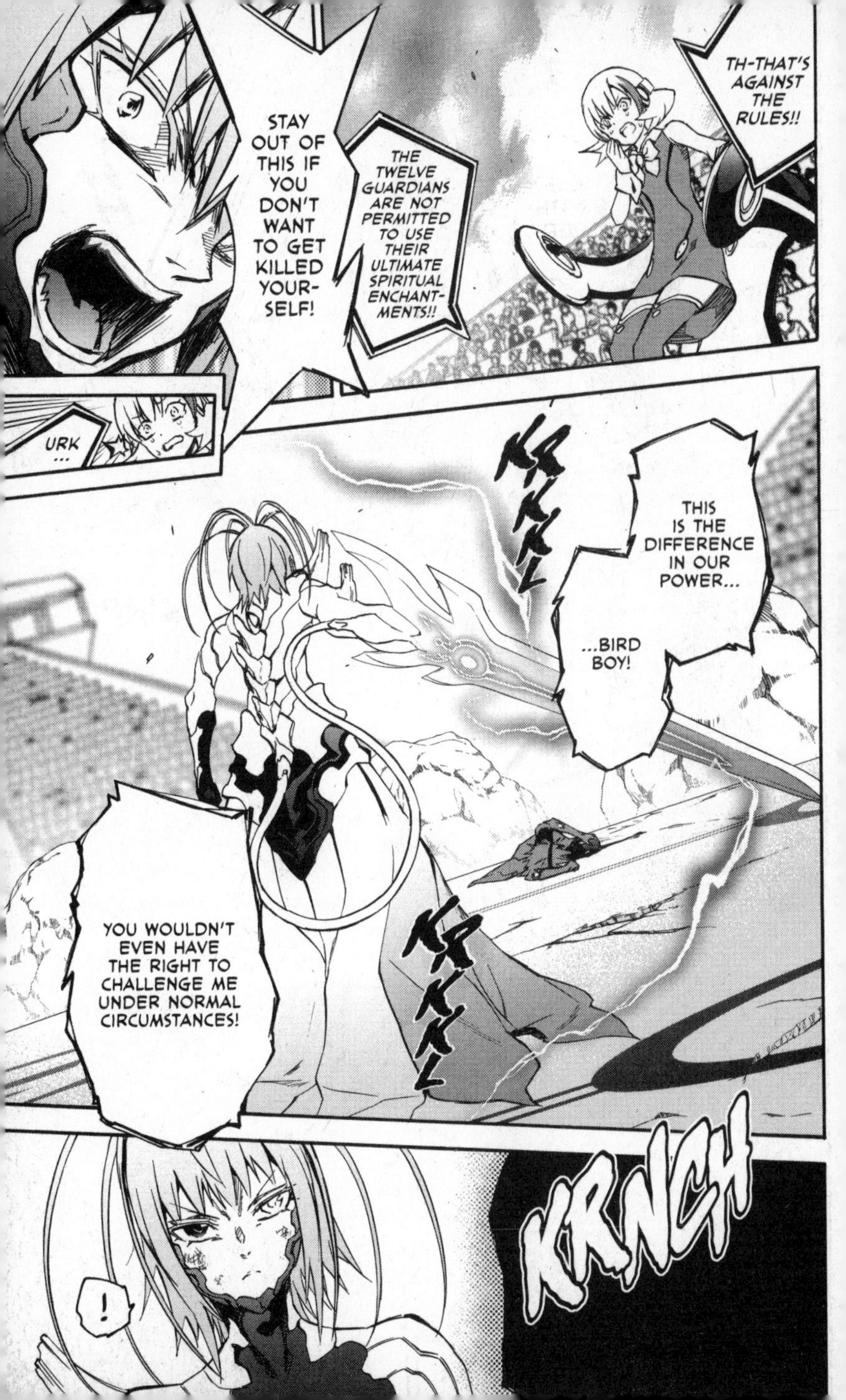

TH-THAT'S AGAINST THE RULES!!
THE TWELVE GUARDIANS ARE NOT PERMITTED TO USE THEIR ULTIMATE SPIRITUAL ENCHANT-MENTS!!
STAY OUT OF THIS IF YOU DON'T WANT TO GET KILLED YOUR-SELF!
URK ...
KRAKKL
THIS IS THE DIFFERENCE IN OUR POWER...
...BIRD BOY!
YOU WOULDN'T EVEN HAVE THE RIGHT TO CHALLENGE ME UNDER NORMAL CIRCUMSTANCES!
KRAKKL
KRNCH
!

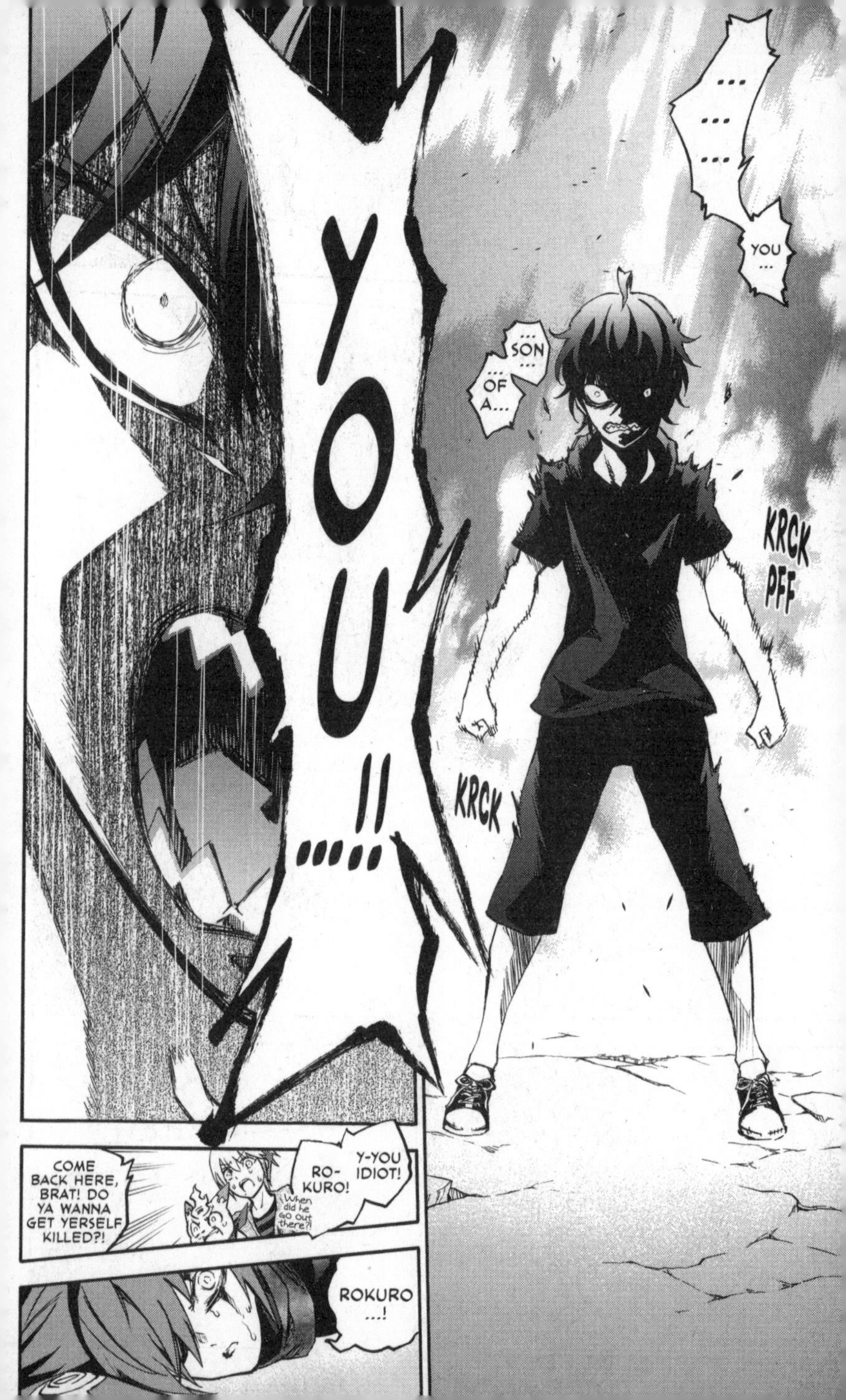
...
...
...
YOU...
...SON... ...OF A...
KRCK PFF
KRCK
YOU...!!
Y-YOU IDIOT!
RO-KURO!
When did he go out there?!
COME BACK HERE, BRAT! DO YA WANNA GET YERSELF KILLED?!
ROKURO...!

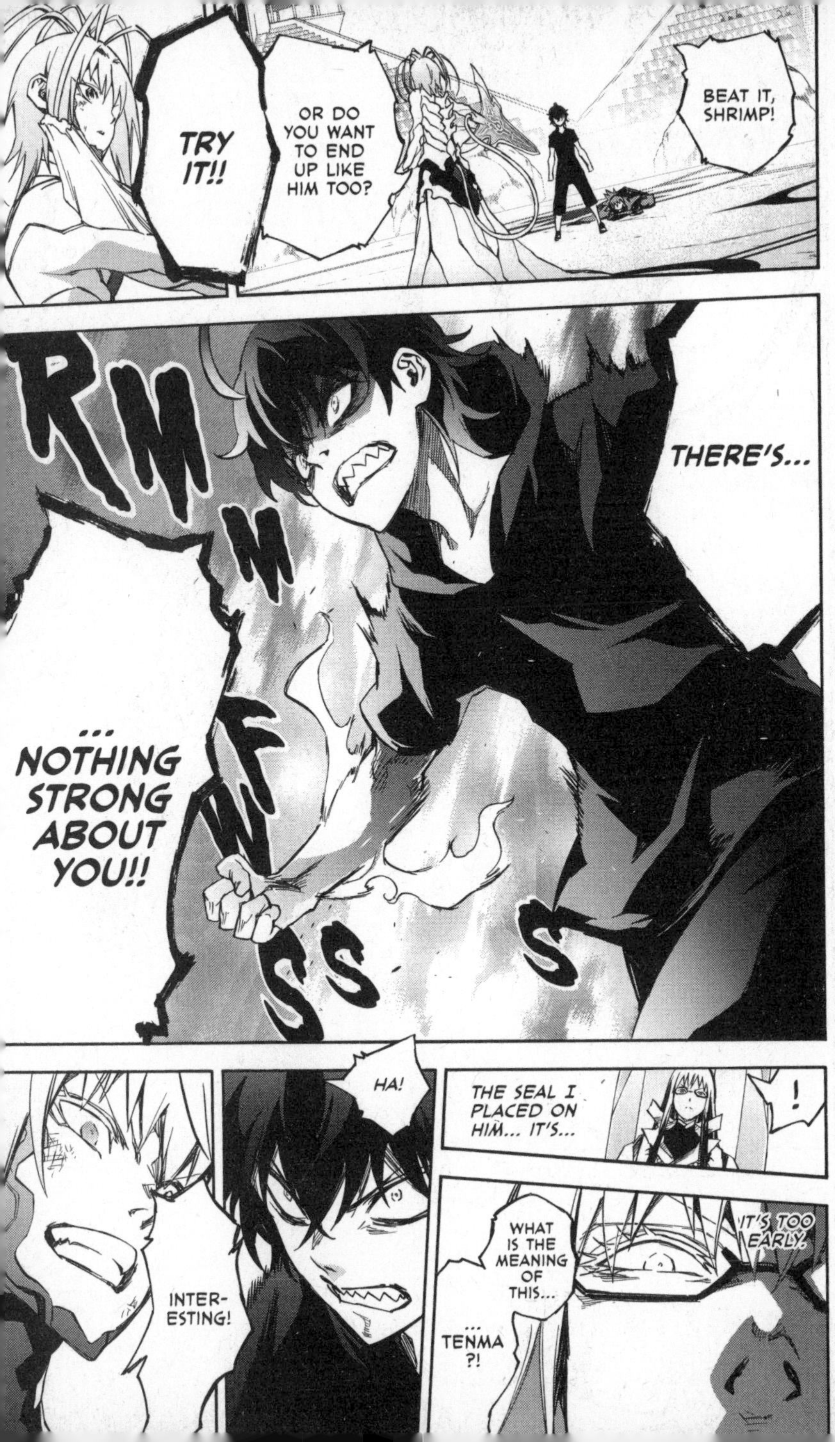
BEAT IT, SHRIMP!
OR DO YOU WANT TO END UP LIKE HIM TOO?
TRY IT!!
THERE'S...
RIMMWFSSS
...NOTHING STRONG ABOUT YOU!!
!
THE SEAL I PLACED ON HIM... IT'S...
IT'S TOO EARLY.
WHAT IS THE MEANING OF THIS...
...TENMA?!
HA!
INTER-ESTING!

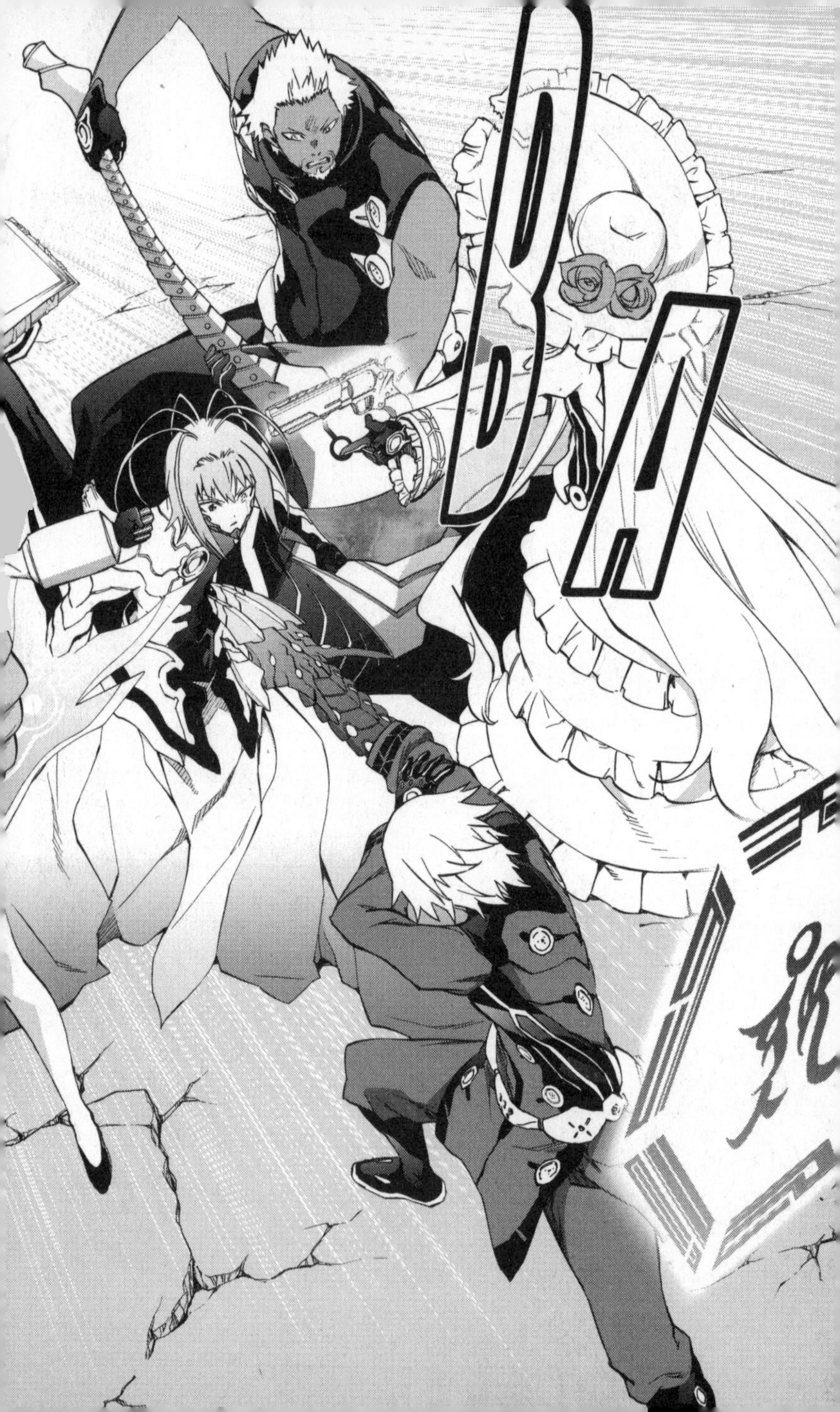

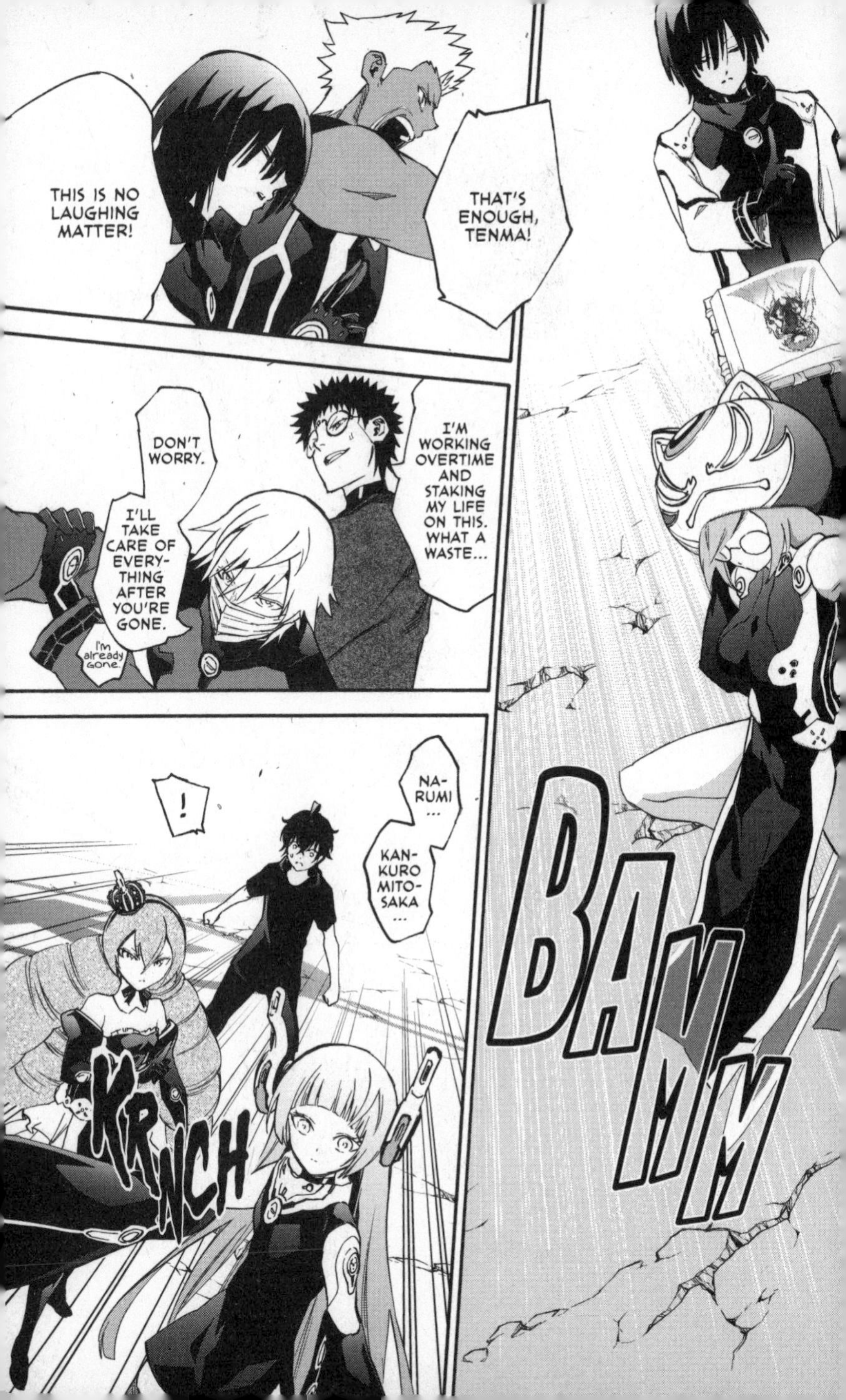
BAMMM
THAT'S ENOUGH, TENMA!
THIS IS NO LAUGHING MATTER!
I'M WORKING OVERTIME AND STAKING MY LIFE ON THIS. WHAT A WASTE...
DON'T WORRY.
I'LL TAKE CARE OF EVERY-THING AFTER YOU'RE GONE.
I'm already gone.
NA-RUMI...
KAN-KURO MITO-SAKA...
!
KRNCH

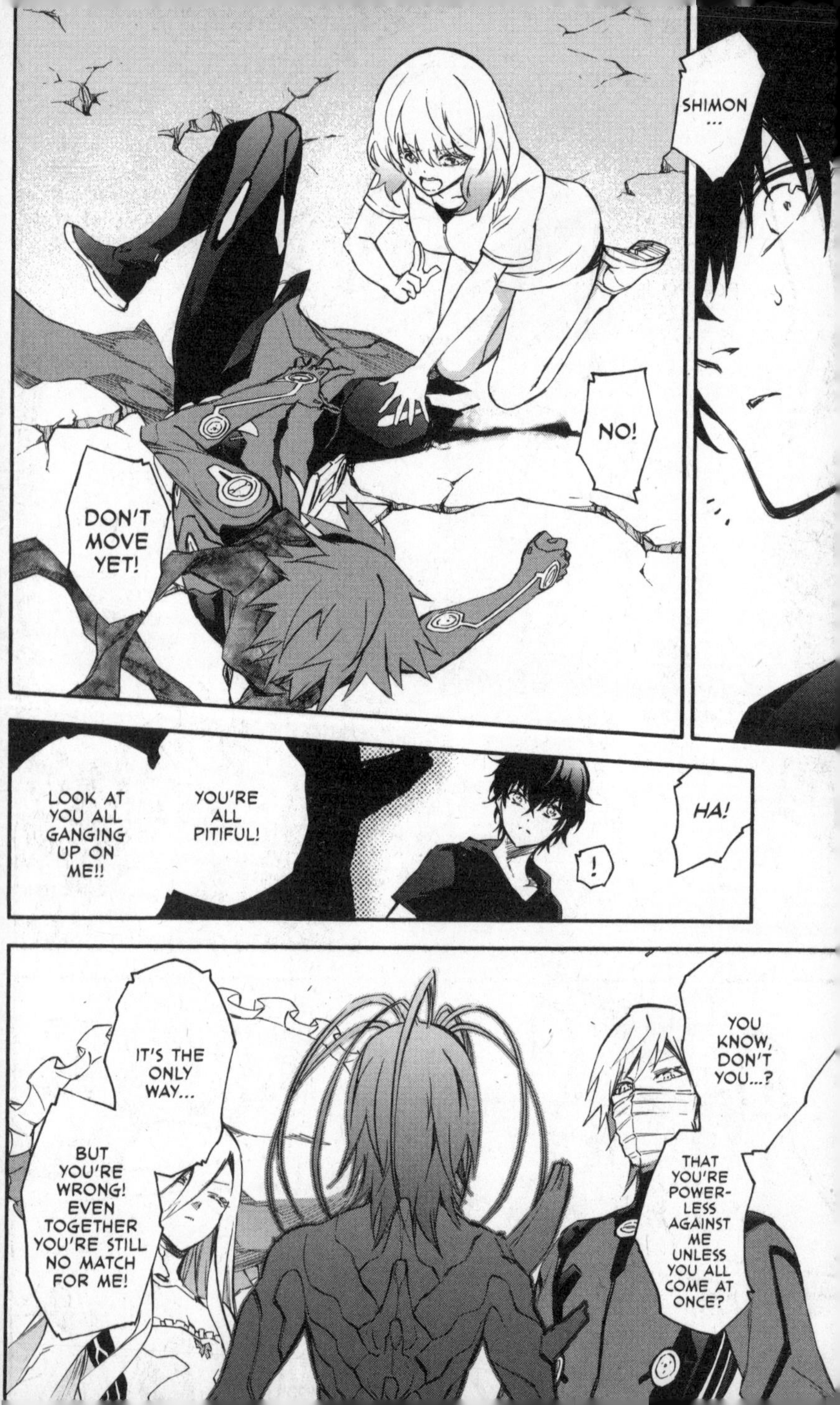
SHIMON ...
NO!
DON'T MOVE YET!
HA!
!
YOU'RE ALL PITIFUL!
LOOK AT YOU ALL GANGING UP ON ME!!
YOU KNOW, DON'T YOU...?
THAT YOU'RE POWERLESS AGAINST ME UNLESS YOU ALL COME AT ONCE?
IT'S THE ONLY WAY...
BUT YOU'RE WRONG! EVEN TOGETHER YOU'RE STILL NO MATCH FOR ME!

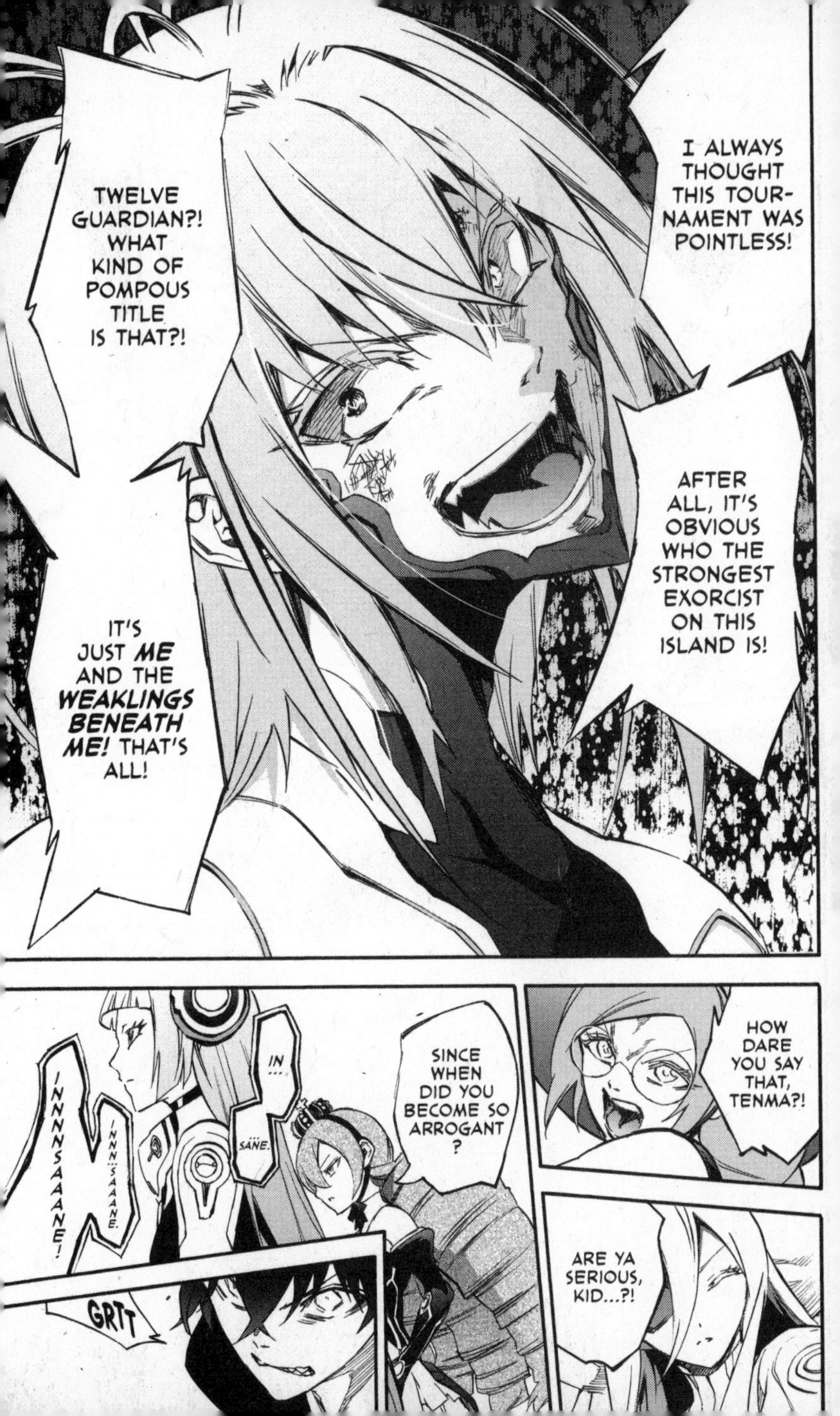
I ALWAYS THOUGHT THIS TOURNAMENT WAS POINTLESS!
TWELVE GUARDIAN?! WHAT KIND OF POMPOUS TITLE IS THAT?!
AFTER ALL, IT'S OBVIOUS WHO THE STRONGEST EXORCIST ON THIS ISLAND IS!
IT'S JUST *ME* AND THE *WEAKLINGS BENEATH ME!* THAT'S ALL!
HOW DARE YOU SAY THAT, TENMA?!
ARE YA SERIOUS, KID...?!
SINCE WHEN DID YOU BECOME SO ARROGANT?
IN... SÄNE.
INNN...SAAAANE.
INNNNSAAAANE!
GRTT

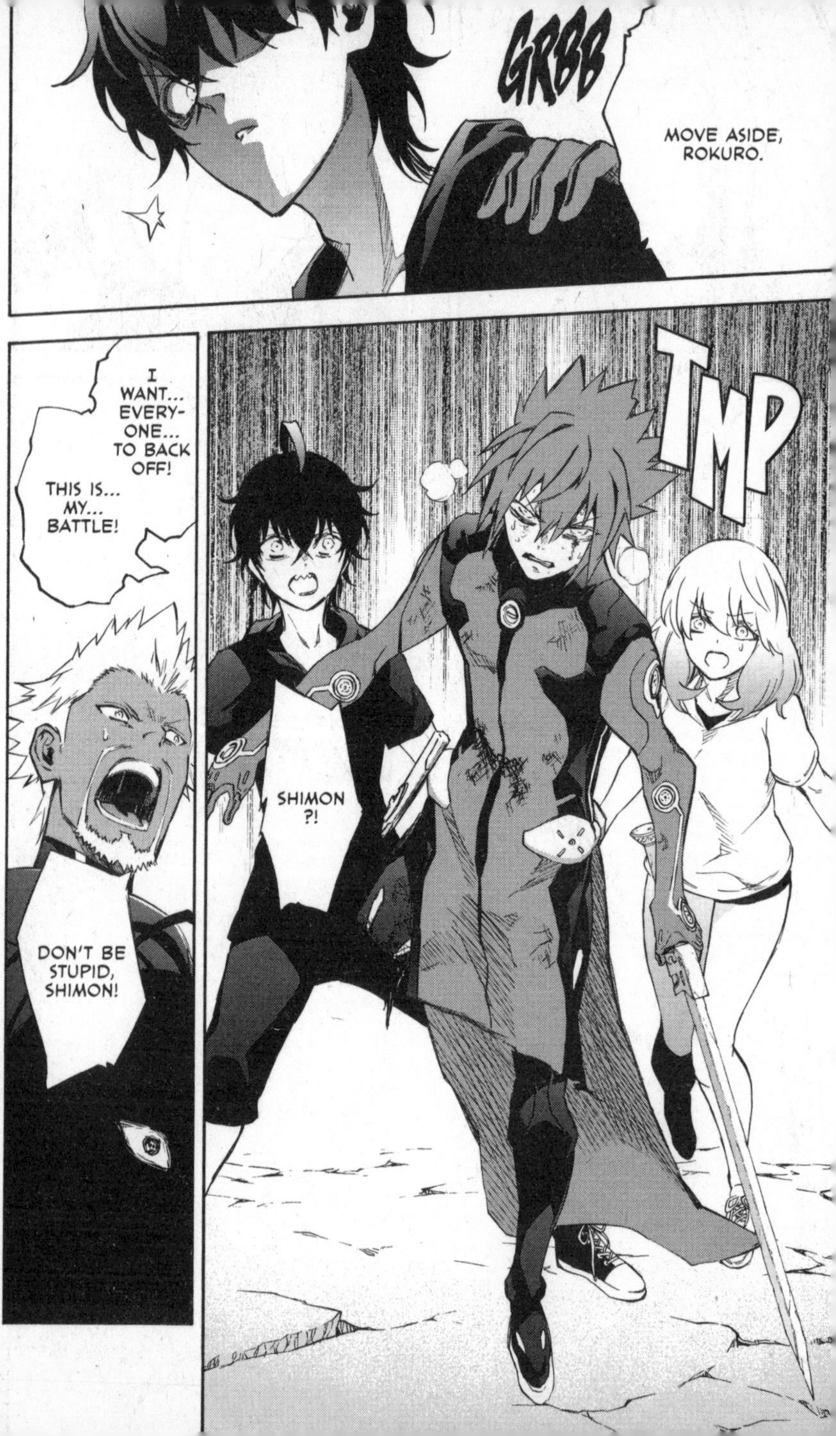
GRBB
MOVE ASIDE, ROKURO.
TMP
SHIMON ?!
I WANT... EVERYONE... TO BACK OFF! THIS IS... MY... BATTLE!
DON'T BE STUPID, SHIMON!

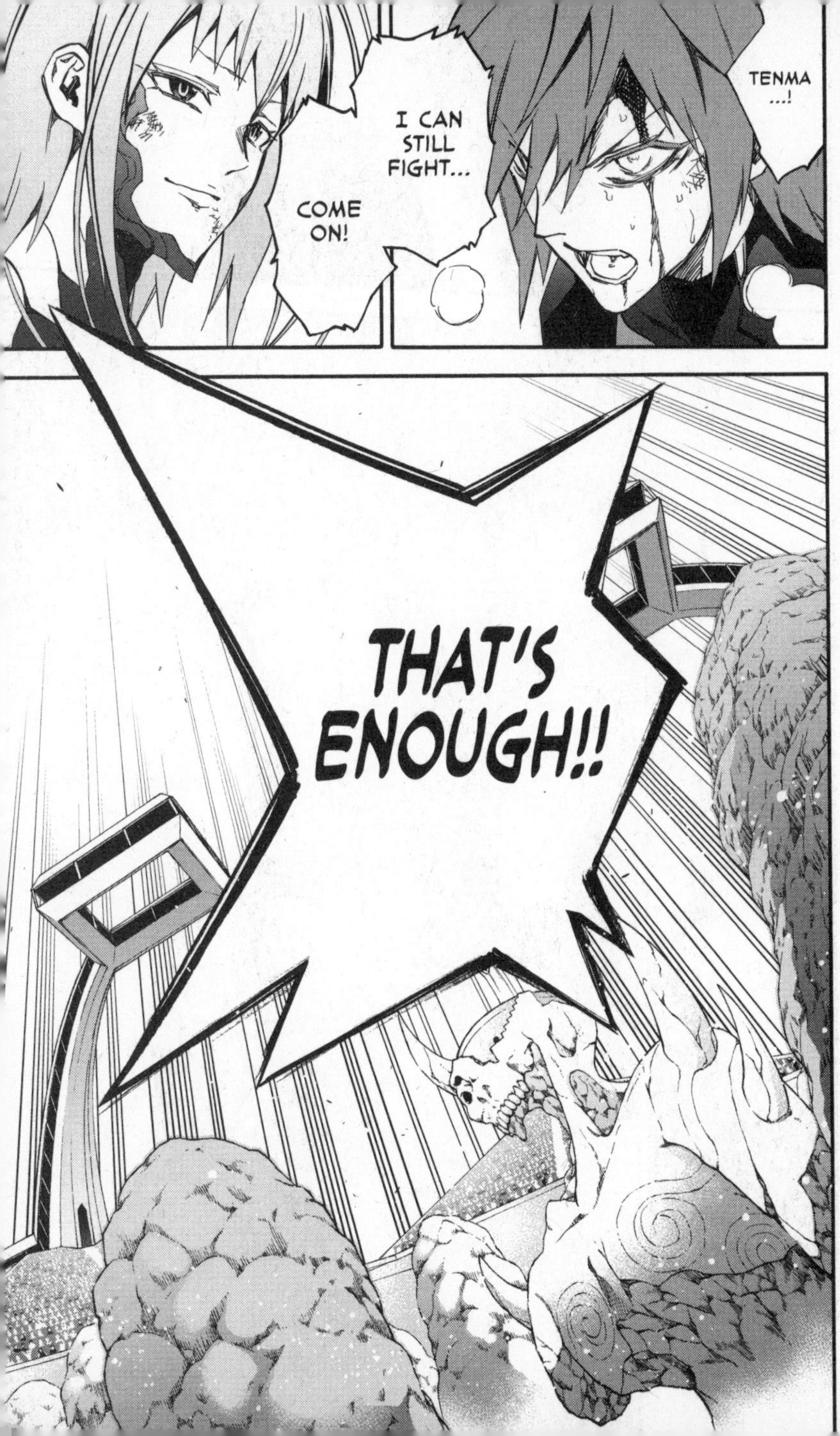
TENMA ...!
I CAN STILL FIGHT...
COME ON!
THAT'S ENOUGH!!

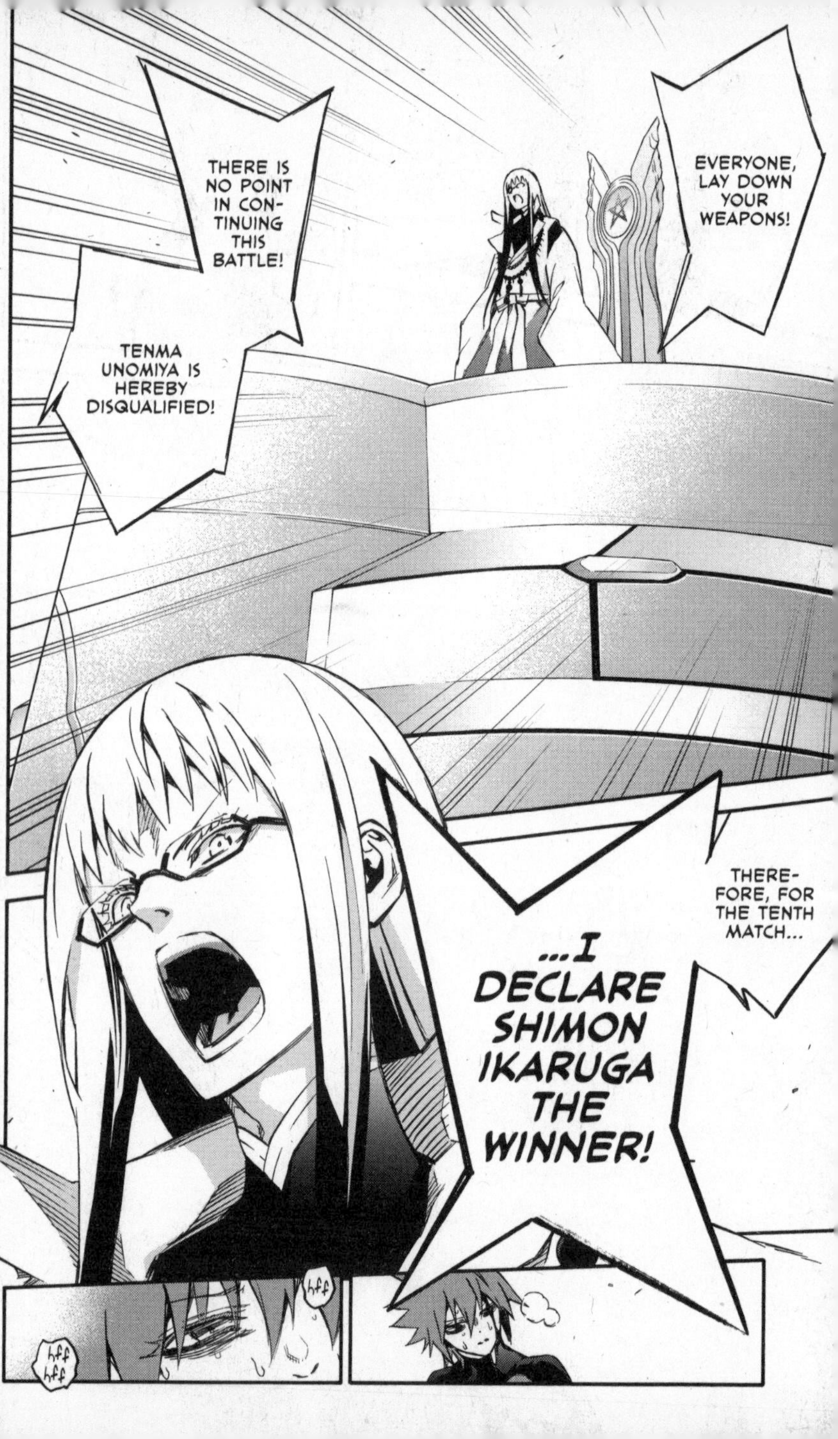
EVERYONE, LAY DOWN YOUR WEAPONS!
THERE IS NO POINT IN CONTINUING THIS BATTLE!
TENMA UNOMIYA IS HEREBY DISQUALIFIED!
THEREFORE, FOR THE TENTH MATCH...
...I DECLARE SHIMON IKARUGA THE WINNER!
hff
hff hff

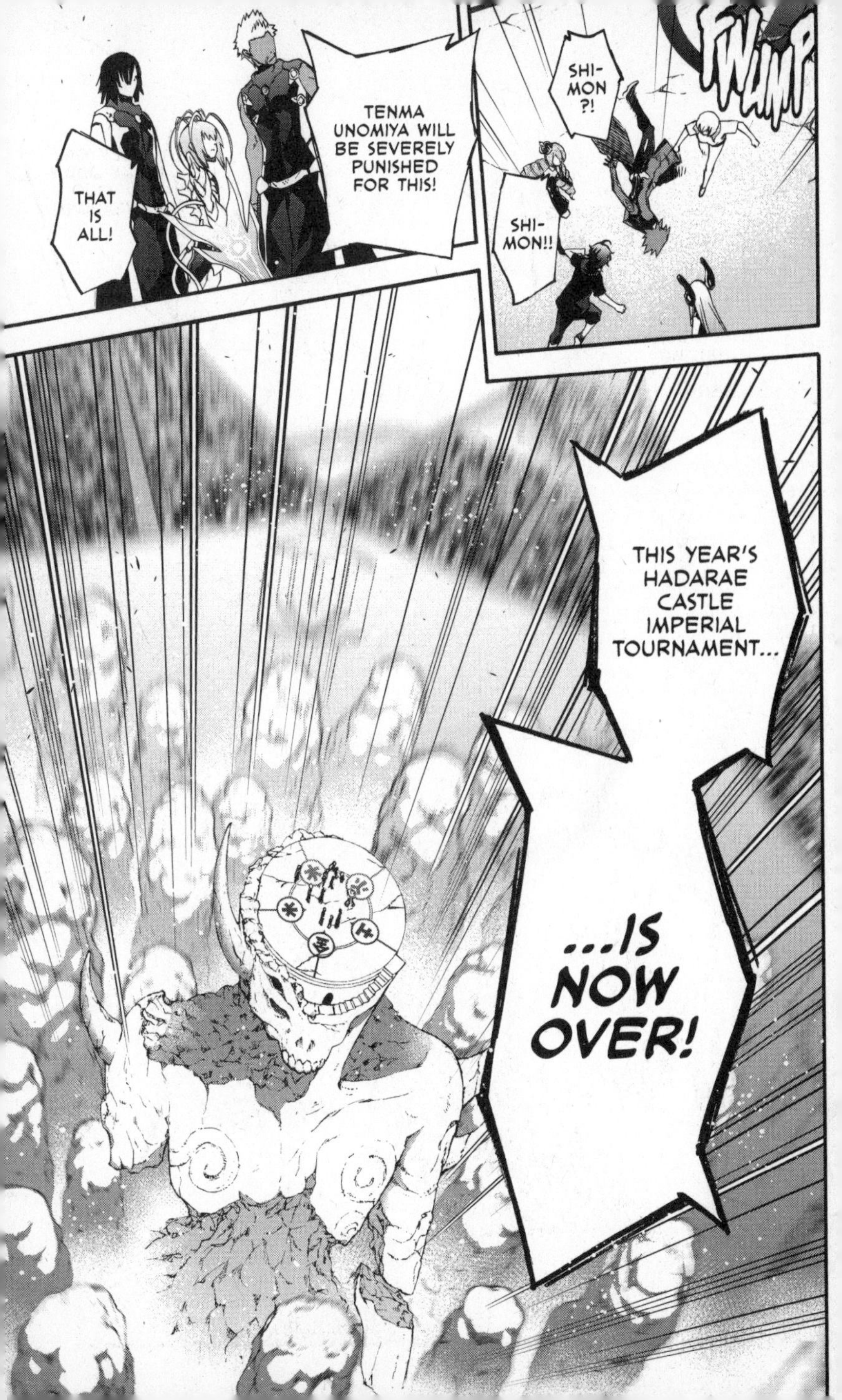
FWUMP
SHI-MON?!
SHI-MON!!
TENMA UNOMIYA WILL BE SEVERELY PUNISHED FOR THIS!
THAT IS ALL!
THIS YEAR'S HADARAE CASTLE IMPERIAL TOURNAMENT...
...IS NOW OVER!

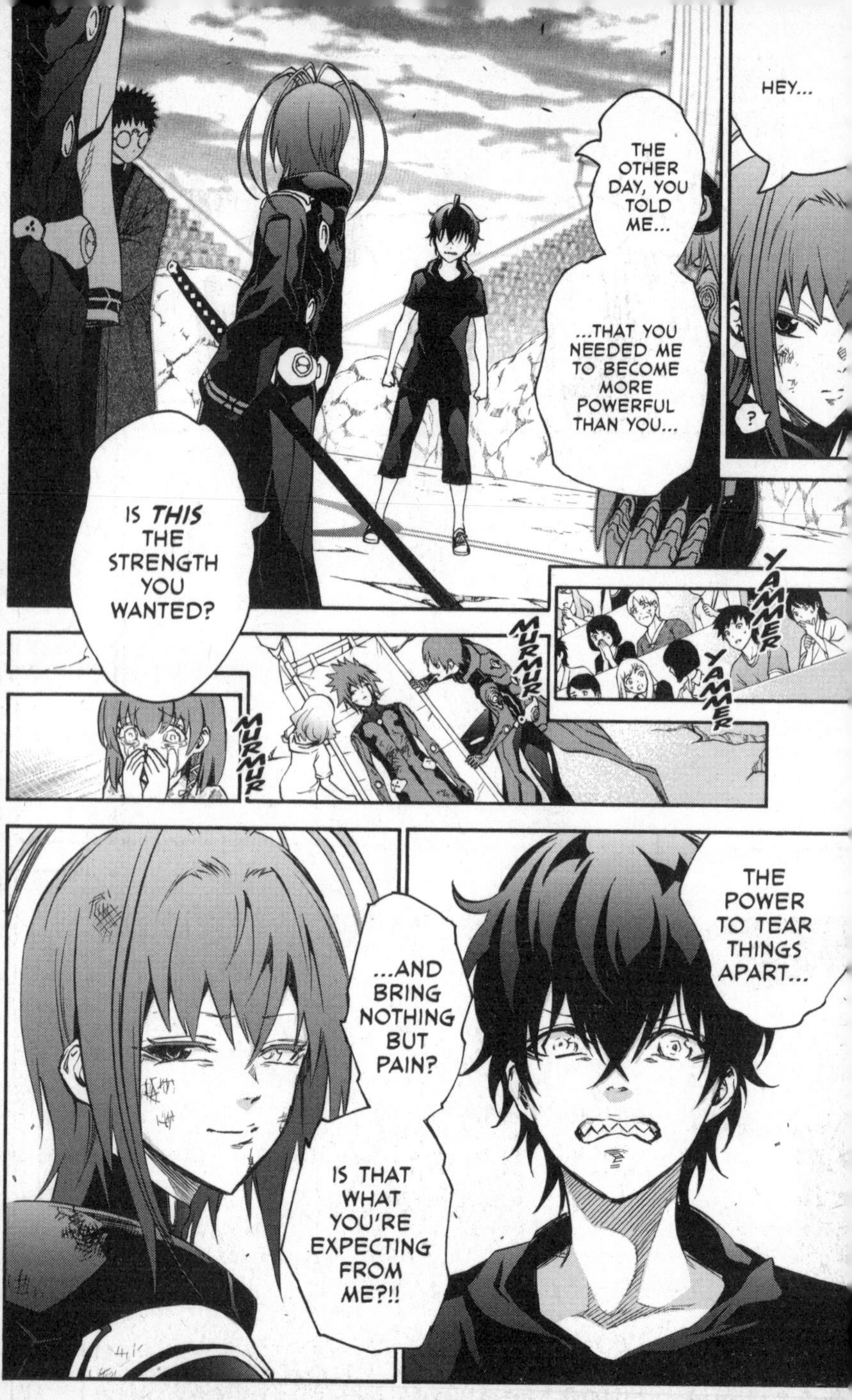
HEY...
?
THE OTHER DAY, YOU TOLD ME...
...THAT YOU NEEDED ME TO BECOME MORE POWERFUL THAN YOU...
IS *THIS* THE STRENGTH YOU WANTED?
YAMMER
YAMMER
MURMUR
MURMUR
THE POWER TO TEAR THINGS APART...
...AND BRING NOTHING BUT PAIN?
IS THAT WHAT YOU'RE EXPECTING FROM ME?!!

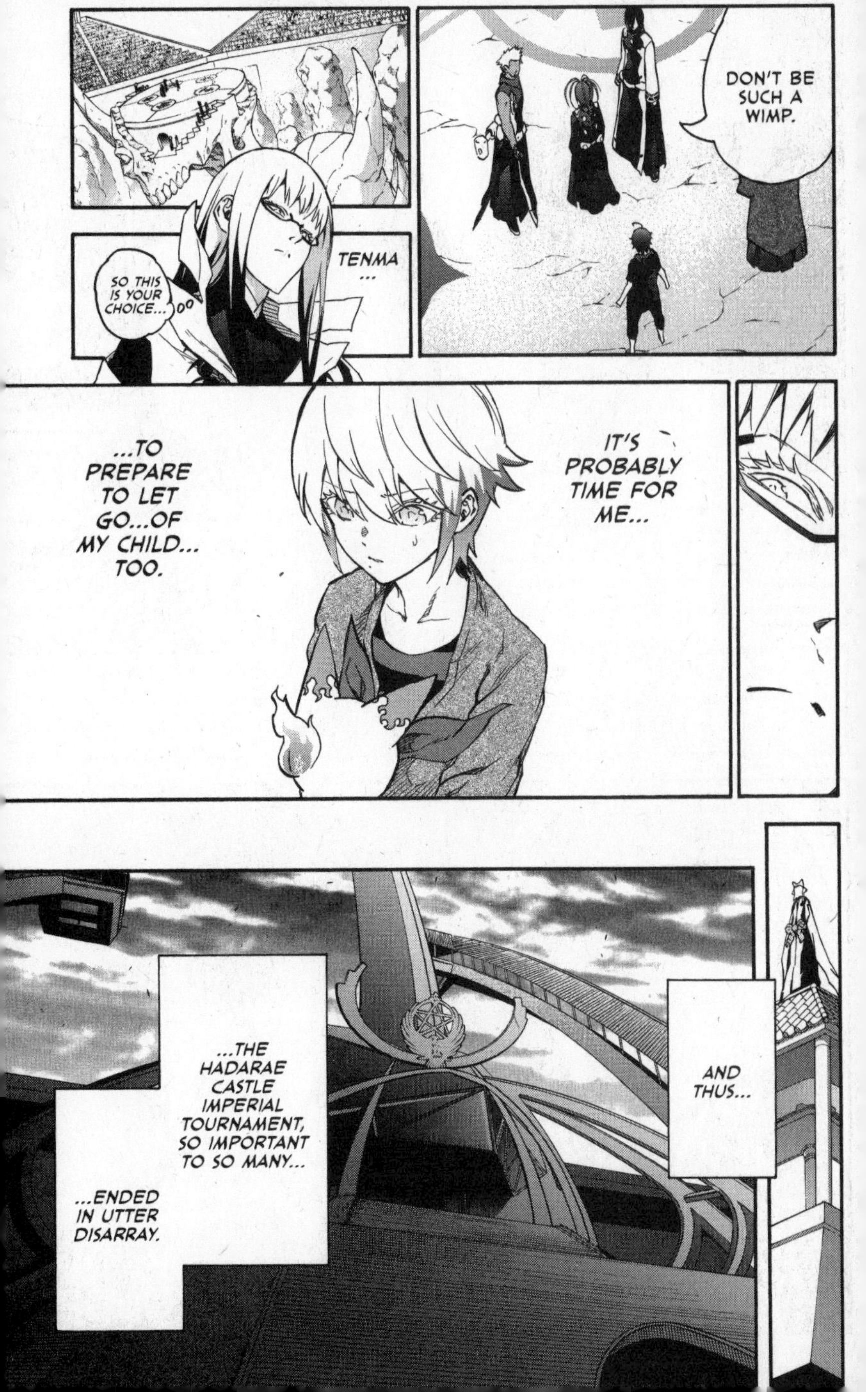
DON'T BE SUCH A WIMP.
TENMA ...
SO THIS IS YOUR CHOICE...
IT'S PROBABLY TIME FOR ME...
...TO PREPARE TO LET GO...OF MY CHILD... TOO.
AND THUS...
...THE HADARAE CASTLE IMPERIAL TOURNAMENT, SO IMPORTANT TO SO MANY...
...ENDED IN UTTER DISARRAY.

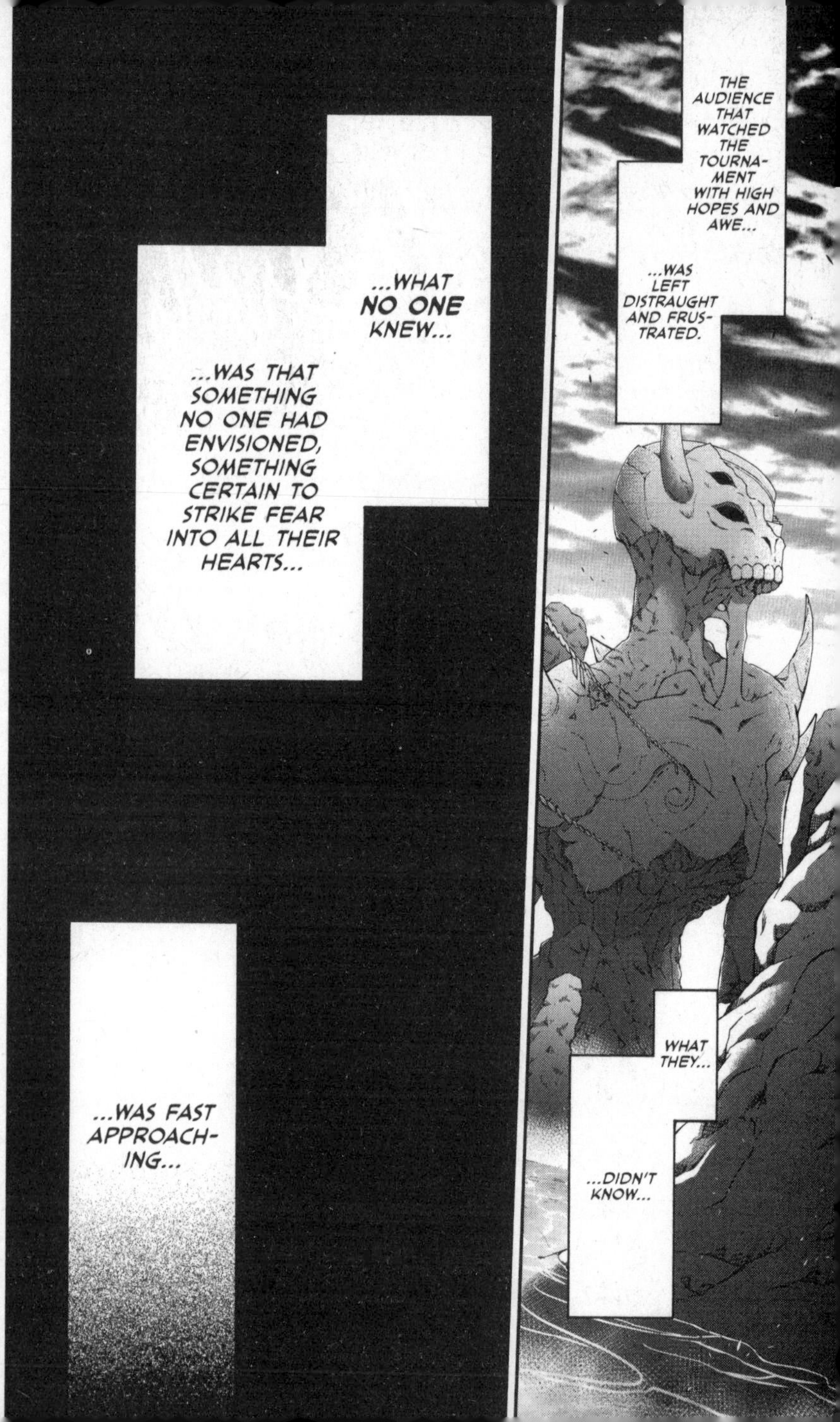
THE AUDIENCE THAT WATCHED THE TOURNAMENT WITH HIGH HOPES AND AWE...
...WAS LEFT DISTRAUGHT AND FRUSTRATED.
WHAT THEY...
...DIDN'T KNOW...
...WHAT NO ONE KNEW...
...WAS THAT SOMETHING NO ONE HAD ENVISIONED, SOMETHING CERTAIN TO STRIKE FEAR INTO ALL THEIR HEARTS...
...WAS FAST APPROACHING...

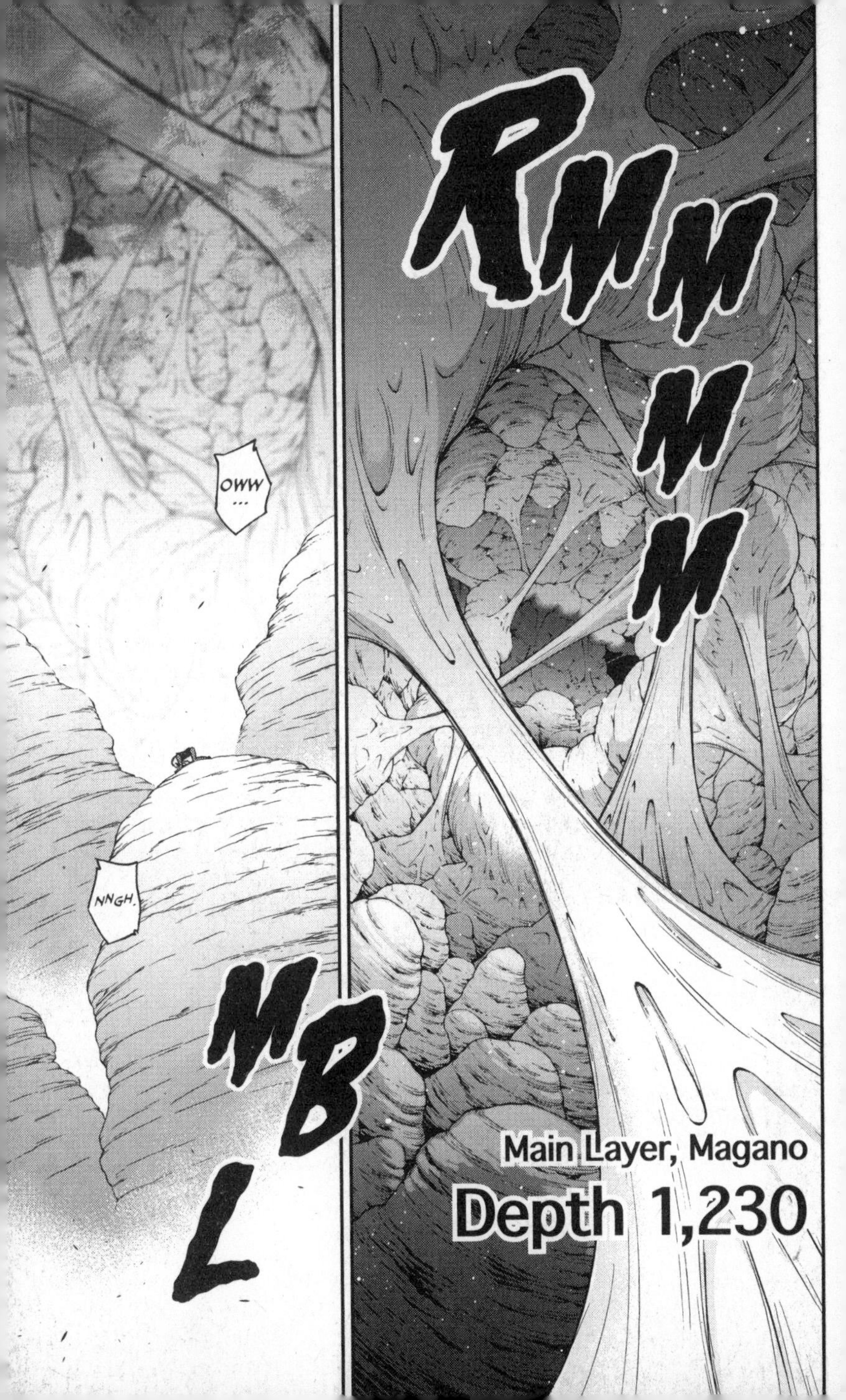
RMMMMM
Main Layer, Magano
Depth 1,230
OWW...
NNGH.
MBL

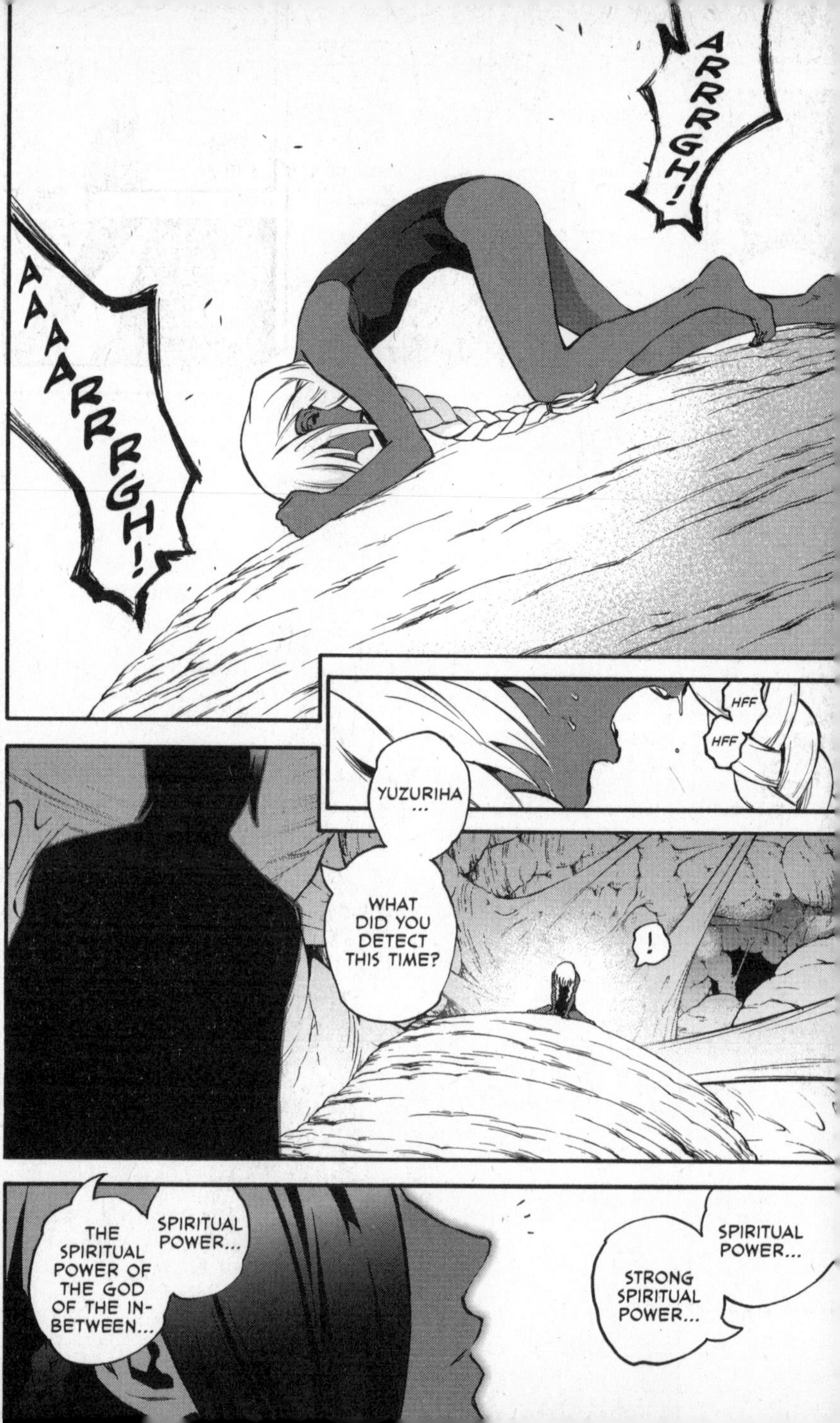
ARRRGH!
AAAARRRGH!
HFF
HFF
YUZURIHA ...
WHAT DID YOU DETECT THIS TIME?
!
SPIRITUAL POWER...
STRONG SPIRITUAL POWER...
SPIRITUAL POWER...
THE SPIRITUAL POWER OF THE GOD OF THE IN-BETWEEN...

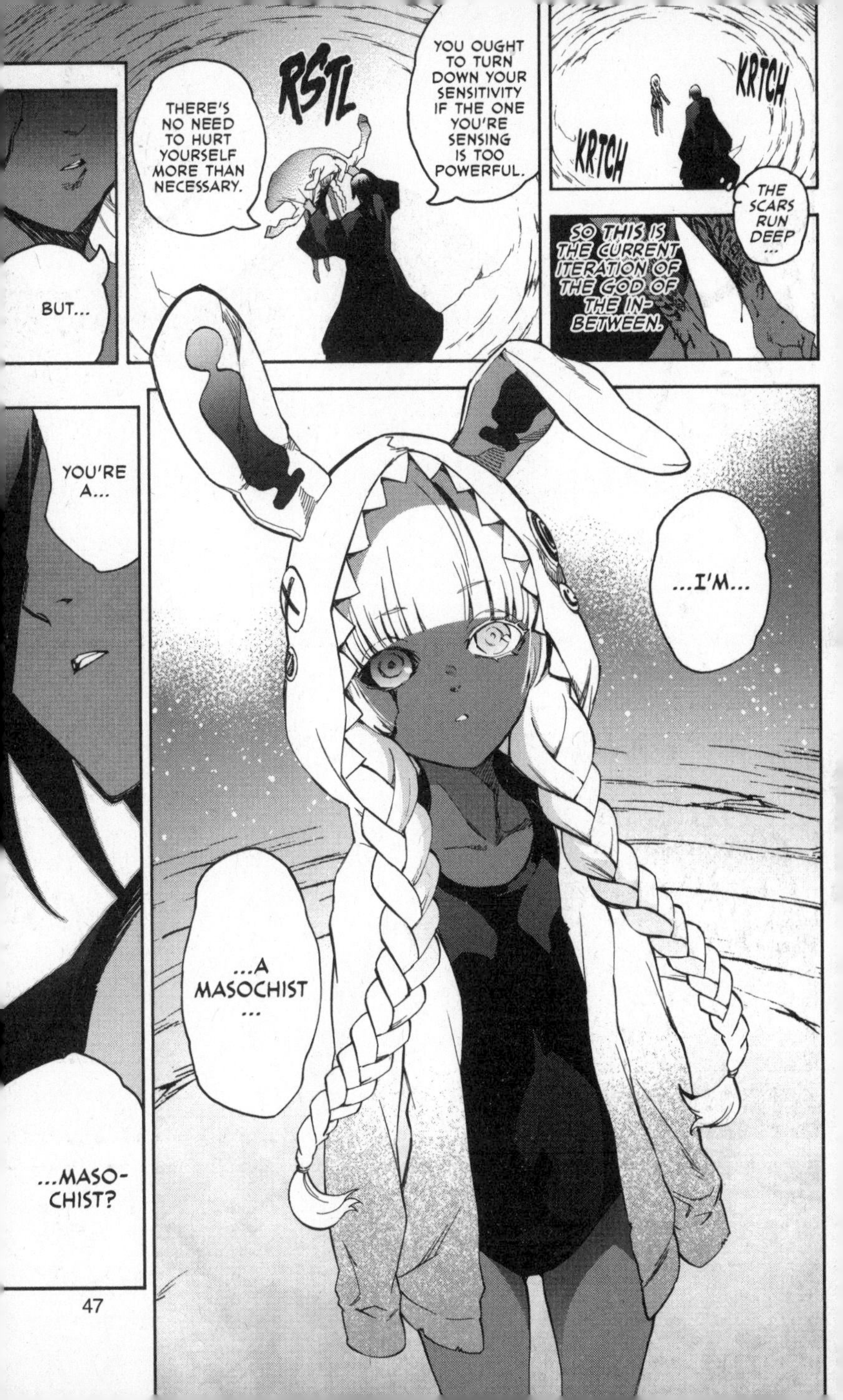
KRTCH
KRTCH
THE SCARS RUN DEEP...
SO THIS IS THE CURRENT ITERATION OF THE GOD OF THE IN-BETWEEN.
RSTL
YOU OUGHT TO TURN DOWN YOUR SENSITIVITY IF THE ONE YOU'RE SENSING IS TOO POWERFUL.
THERE'S NO NEED TO HURT YOURSELF MORE THAN NECESSARY.
BUT...
...I'M...
...A MASOCHIST...
YOU'RE A...
...MASO-CHIST?

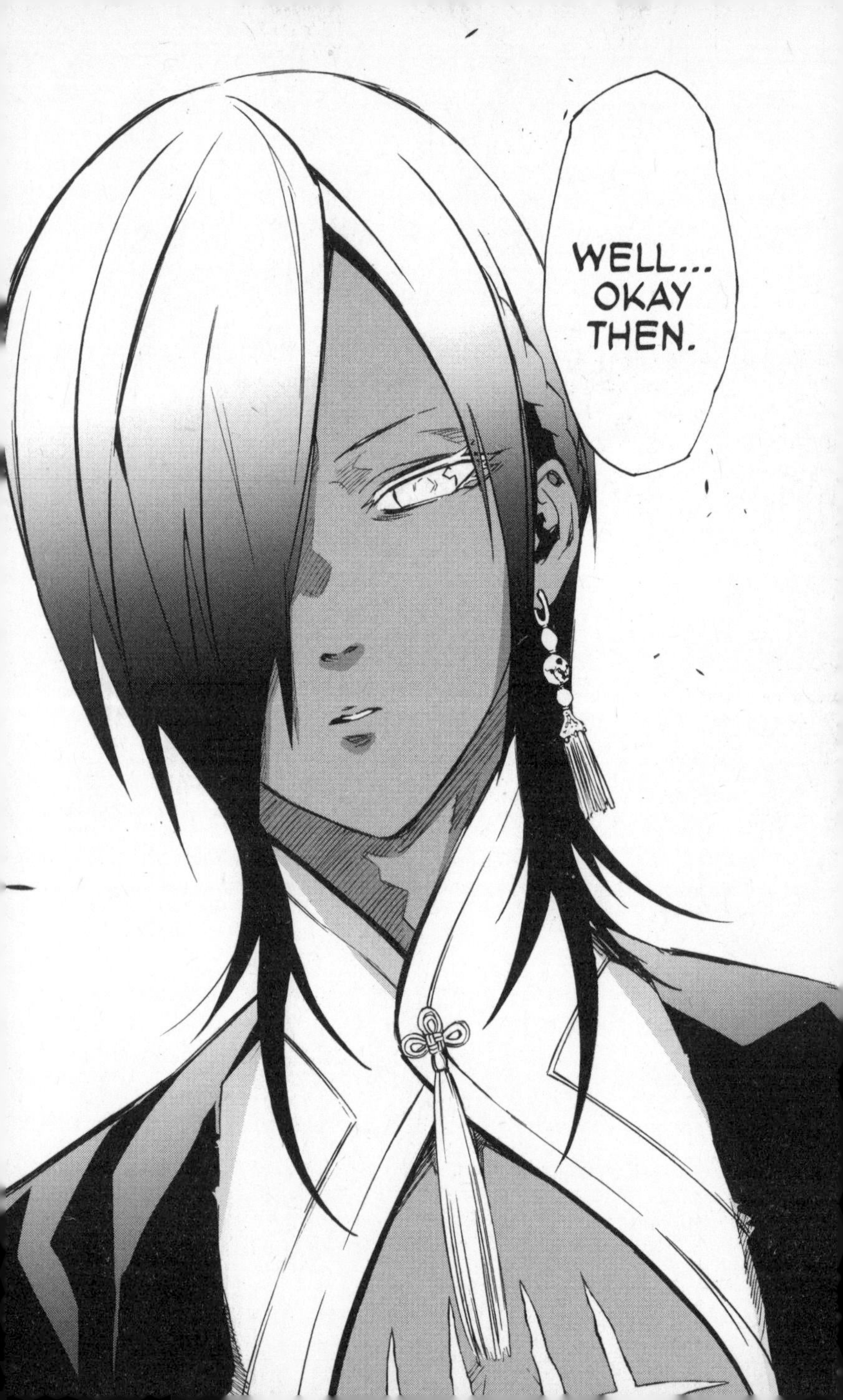
WELL... OKAY THEN.

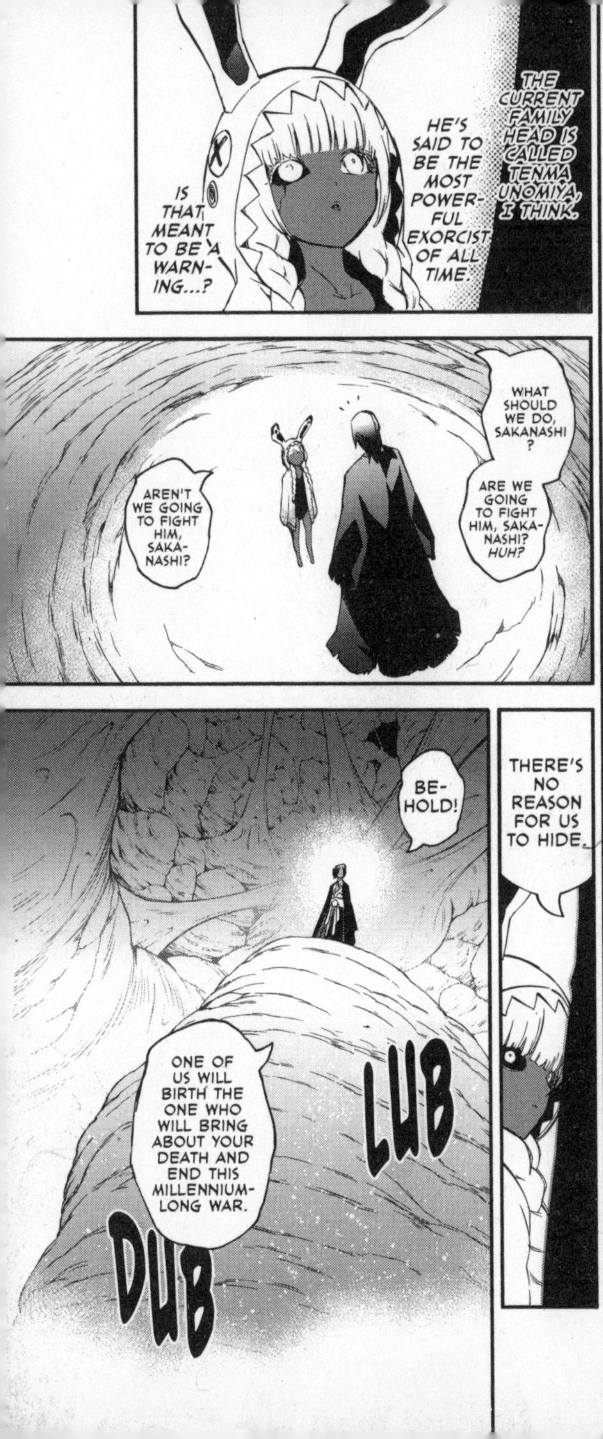
THE CURRENT FAMILY HEAD IS CALLED TENMA UNOMIYA, I THINK.
HE'S SAID TO BE THE MOST POWERFUL EXORCIST OF ALL TIME.
IS THAT MEANT TO BE A WARNING...?
WHAT SHOULD WE DO, SAKANASHI?
ARE WE GOING TO FIGHT HIM, SAKANASHI? HUH?
AREN'T WE GOING TO FIGHT HIM, SAKANASHI?
THERE'S NO REASON FOR US TO HIDE.
BEHOLD!
LUB
ONE OF US WILL BIRTH THE ONE WHO WILL BRING ABOUT YOUR DEATH AND END THIS MILLENNIUM-LONG WAR.
DUB

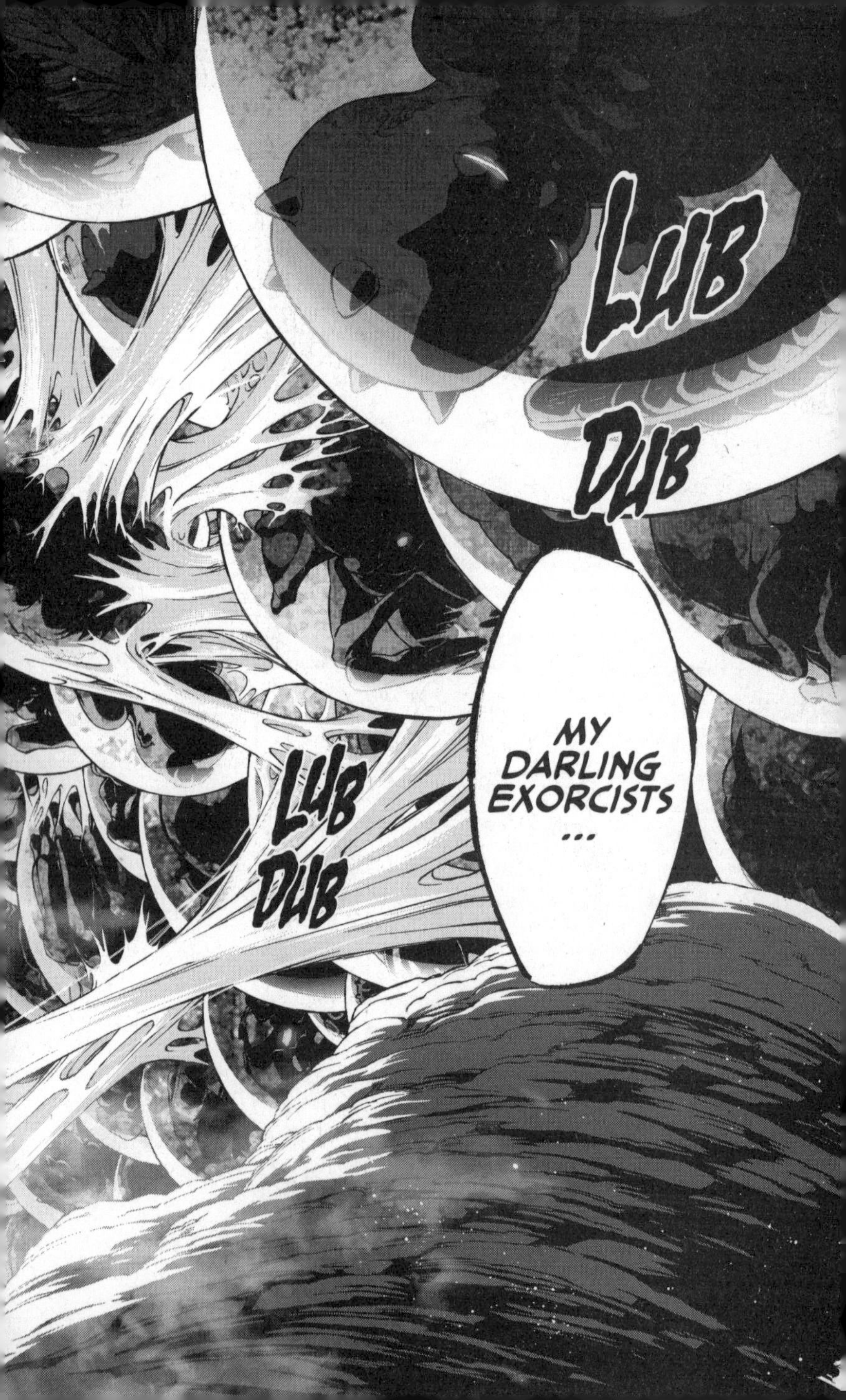
LUB
DUB
MY DARLING EXORCISTS ...
LUB
DUB

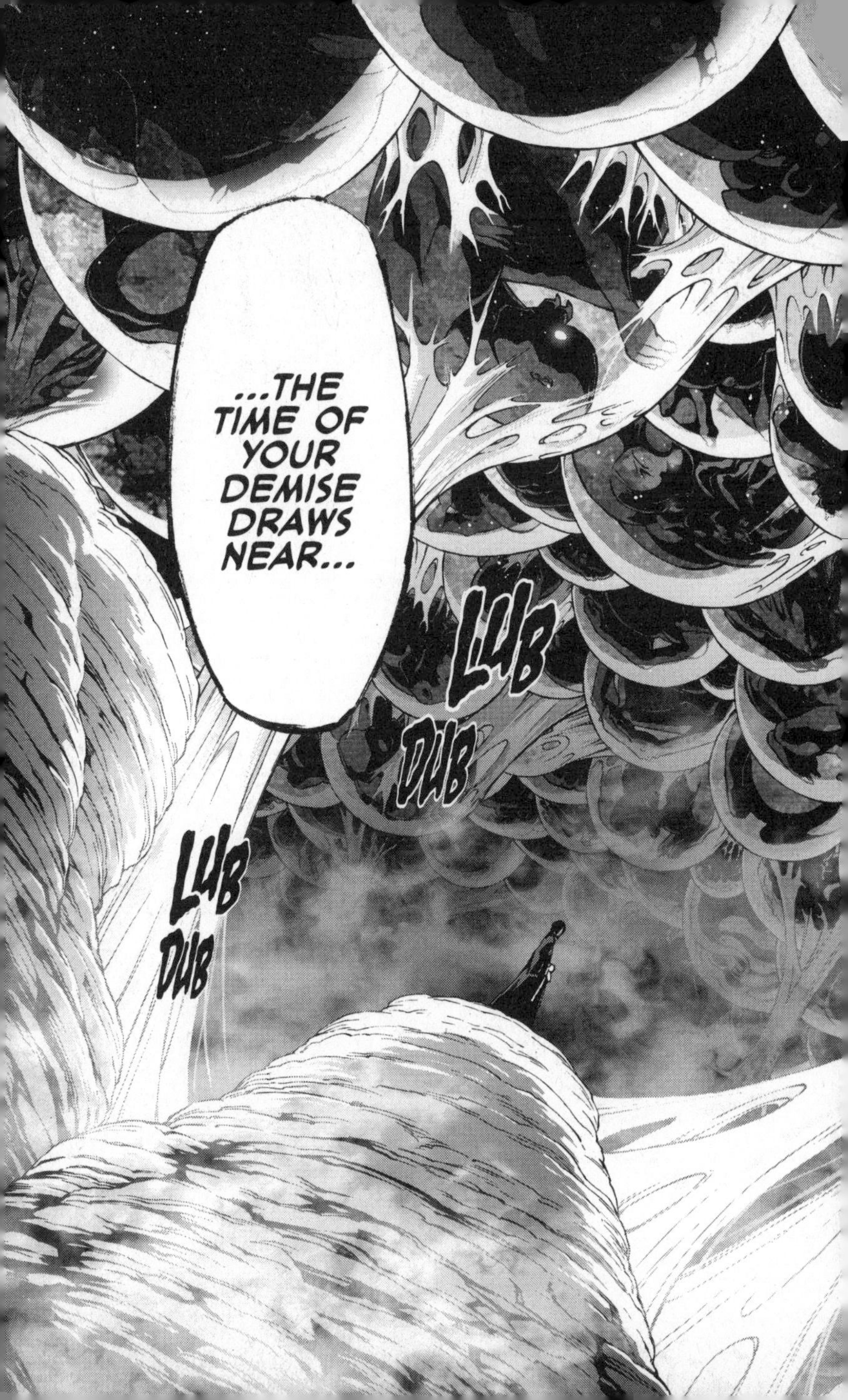
...THE TIME OF YOUR DEMISE DRAWS NEAR...
LUB DUB
LUB DUB

QQnyoritsuryo!

Question Corner

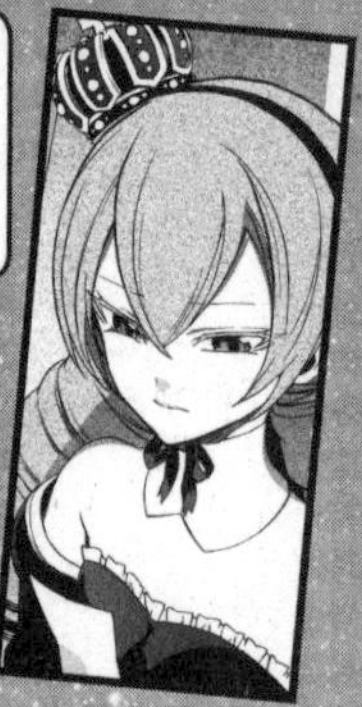

Q Please tell me the secret behind Miku's beauty! I want to be like her! Please! (Laugh)
(From Glen 15)

A She channels her dormant spiritual power to rejuvenate her cells and stay youthful. ♡

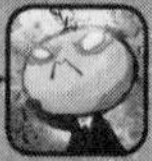

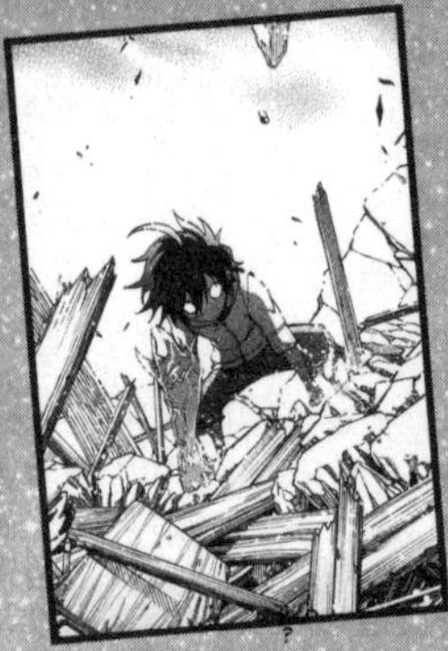

Q Rokuro was found alone inside Magano, so how did he get the name "Rokuro Enmado"?
(From Nekopon)

A Seigen named him. "Enmado" is the name of a man who took care of Seigen as a child. He died in Magano without any descendants, so his family line came to an end about 30 years ago. The first name "Rokuro" came about because Seigen found him on Roku-gatsu Roku-nichi.*

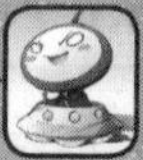

*June 6, plus a common ending for a male name

Q What do I need to do to get good at drawing? (Other than drawing a lot...)
(From Manga-Loving Grim Reaper)

A Copy the illustrations of good artists from top to bottom. Personally, I think the idea that you'll improve just by drawing a lot isn't true. You'll never improve no matter how much you draw if you don't study good drawing techniques.

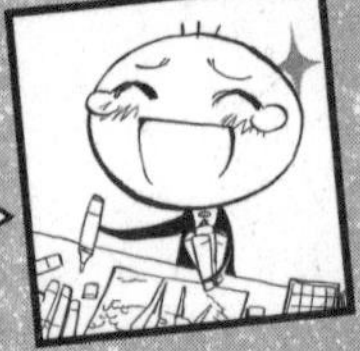

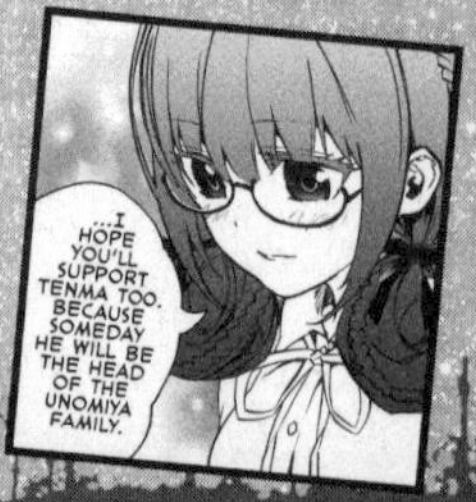
...I HOPE YOU'LL SUPPORT TENMA TOO. BECAUSE SOMEDAY HE WILL BE THE HEAD OF THE UNOMIYA FAMILY.

R (Request) I have a request for you, Sensei. Please make Senri's birthday August 24!
(From Singing Voice)

A Sure. Senri's birthday will be that day!

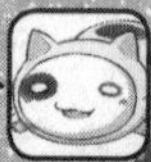

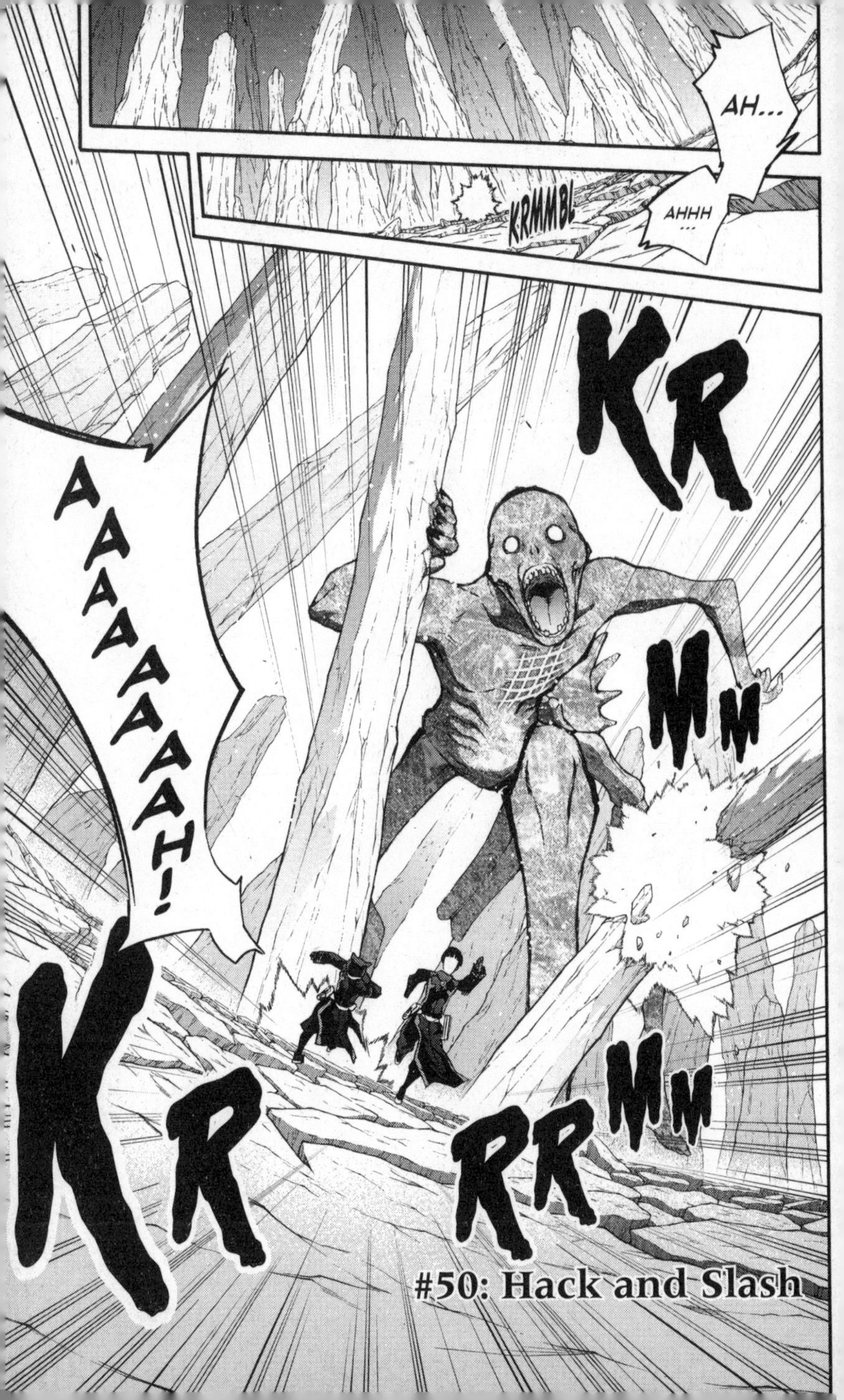
AH...
AHHH ...
KRMMBL
KR
MM
AAAAAAAAH!
KR
RRMM

#50: Hack and Slash

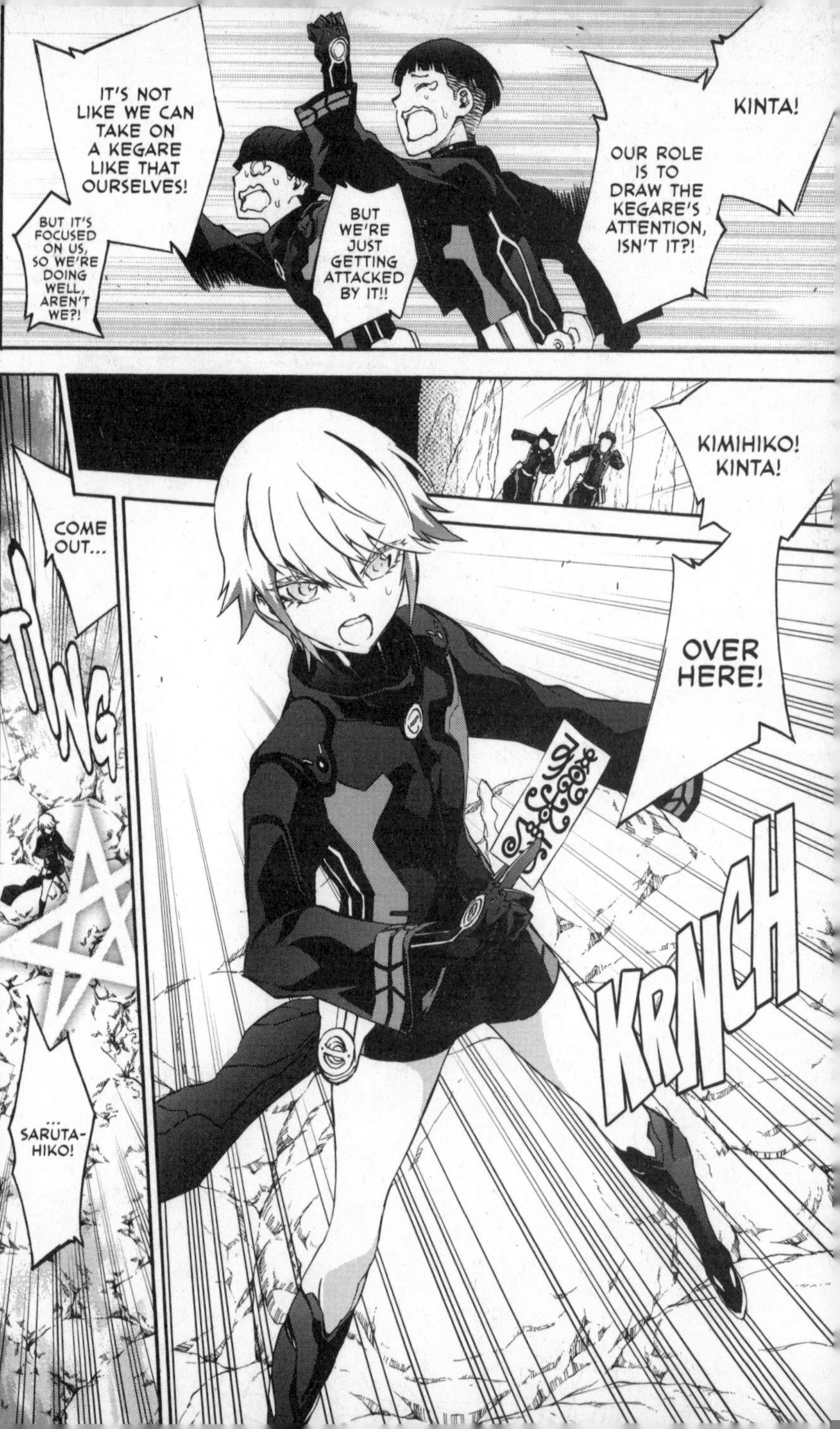
KINTA!
OUR ROLE IS TO DRAW THE KEGARE'S ATTENTION, ISN'T IT?!
BUT WE'RE JUST GETTING ATTACKED BY IT!!
IT'S NOT LIKE WE CAN TAKE ON A KEGARE LIKE THAT OURSELVES!
BUT IT'S FOCUSED ON US, SO WE'RE DOING WELL, AREN'T WE?!
KIMIHIKO! KINTA!
OVER HERE!
KRNCH
COME OUT...
TING
...SARUTA-HIKO!

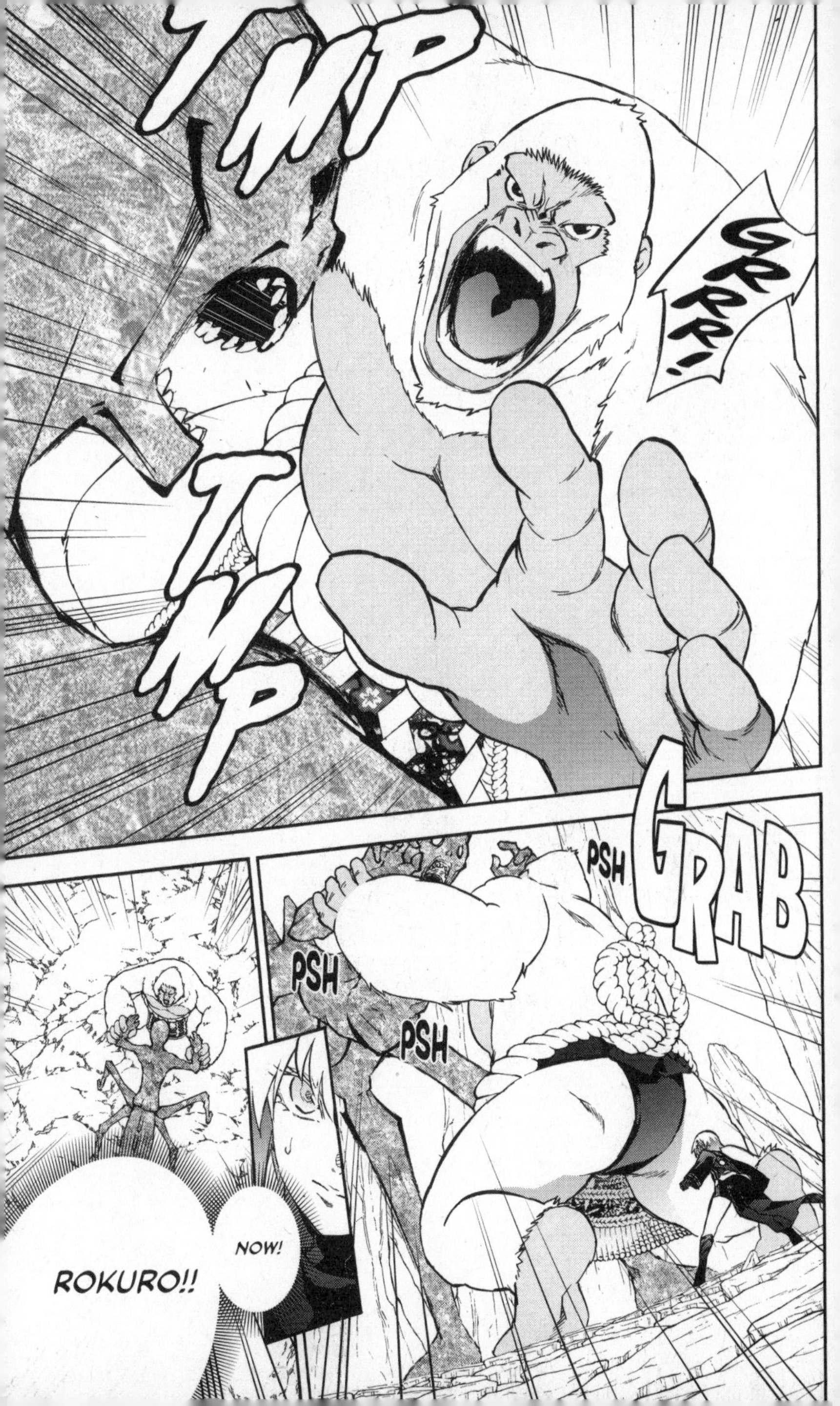

THMP
GRRR!
THMP
GRAB
PSH
PSH
PSH
NOW!
ROKURO!!

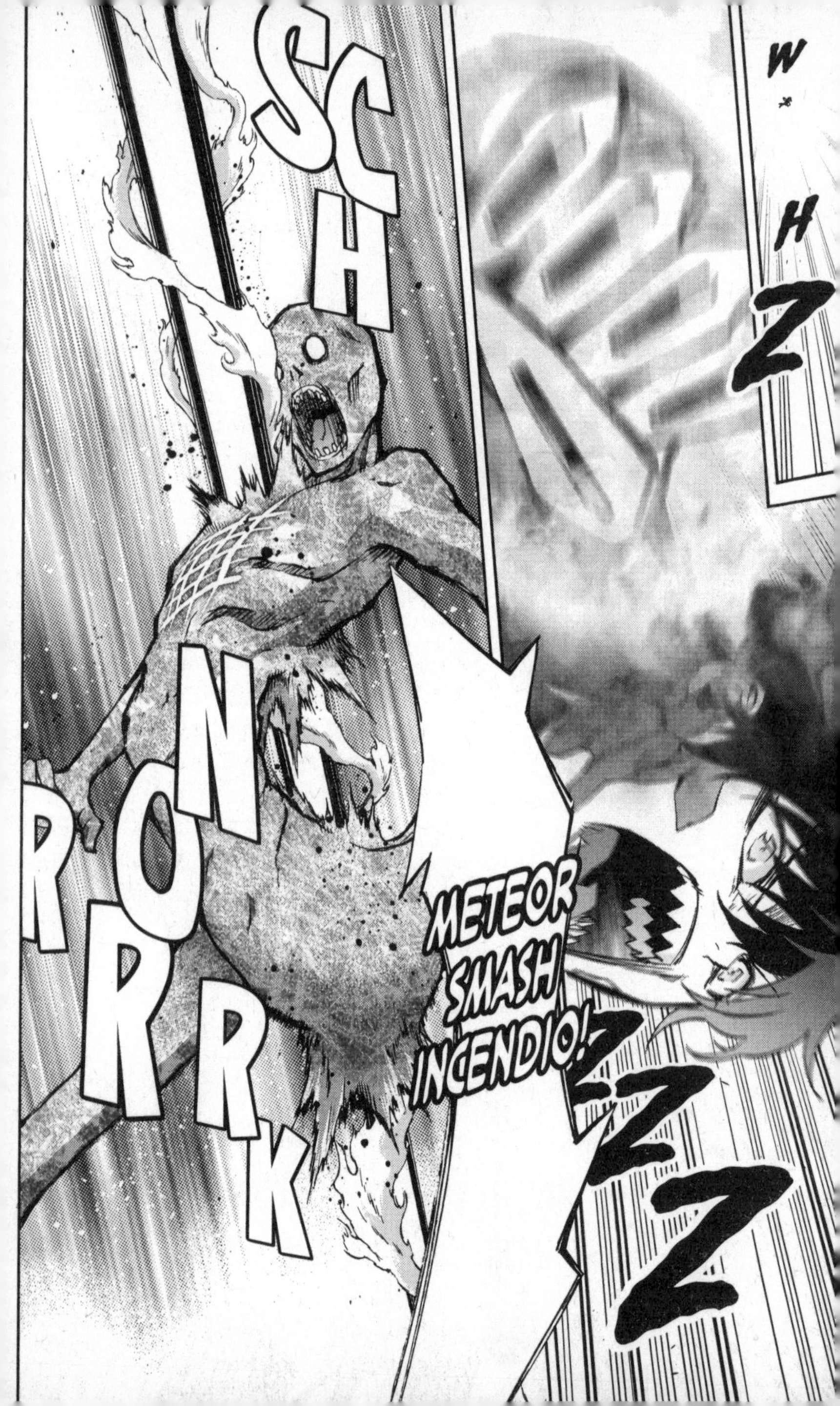
WHZ
METEOR SMASH INCENDIO!
ZZZ
SCHNORRRK

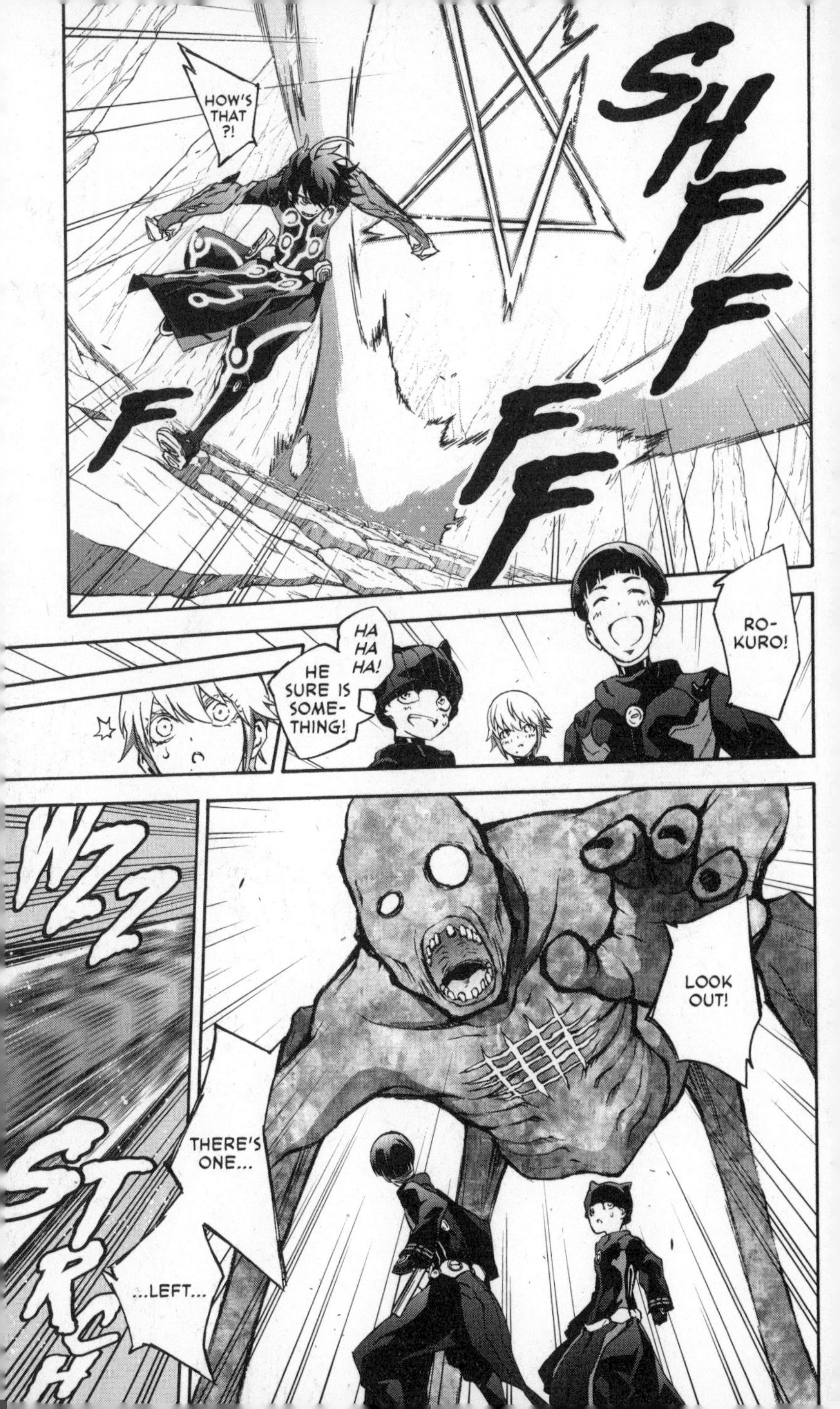
SHFFFFF
HOW'S THAT ?!
RO-KURO!
HA HA HA!
HE SURE IS SOME-THING!
LOOK OUT!
WZZ
THERE'S ONE...
...LEFT...

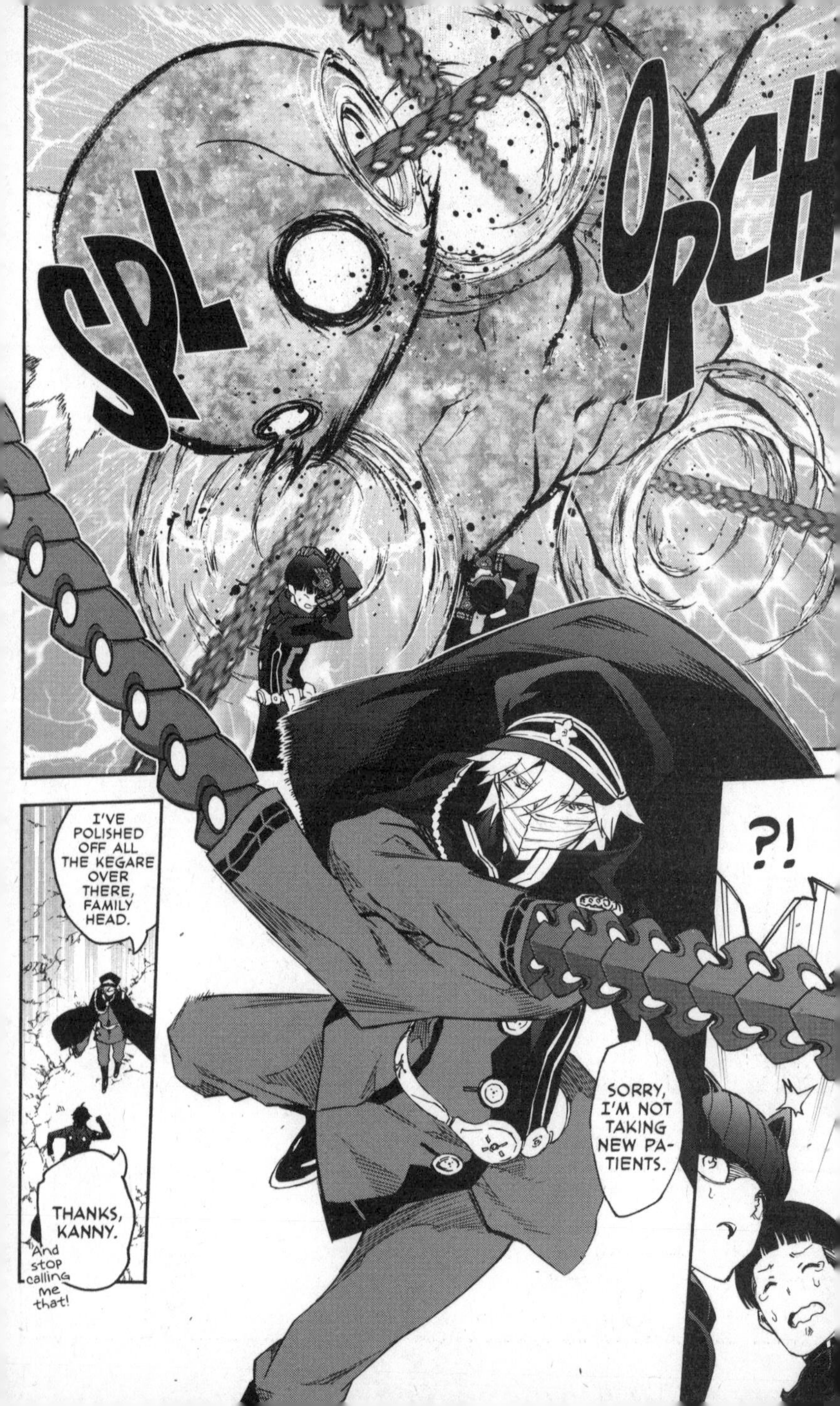
SPLORCH
?!
SORRY, I'M NOT TAKING NEW PATIENTS.
I'VE POLISHED OFF ALL THE KEGARE OVER THERE, FAMILY HEAD.
THANKS, KANNY.
And stop calling me that!

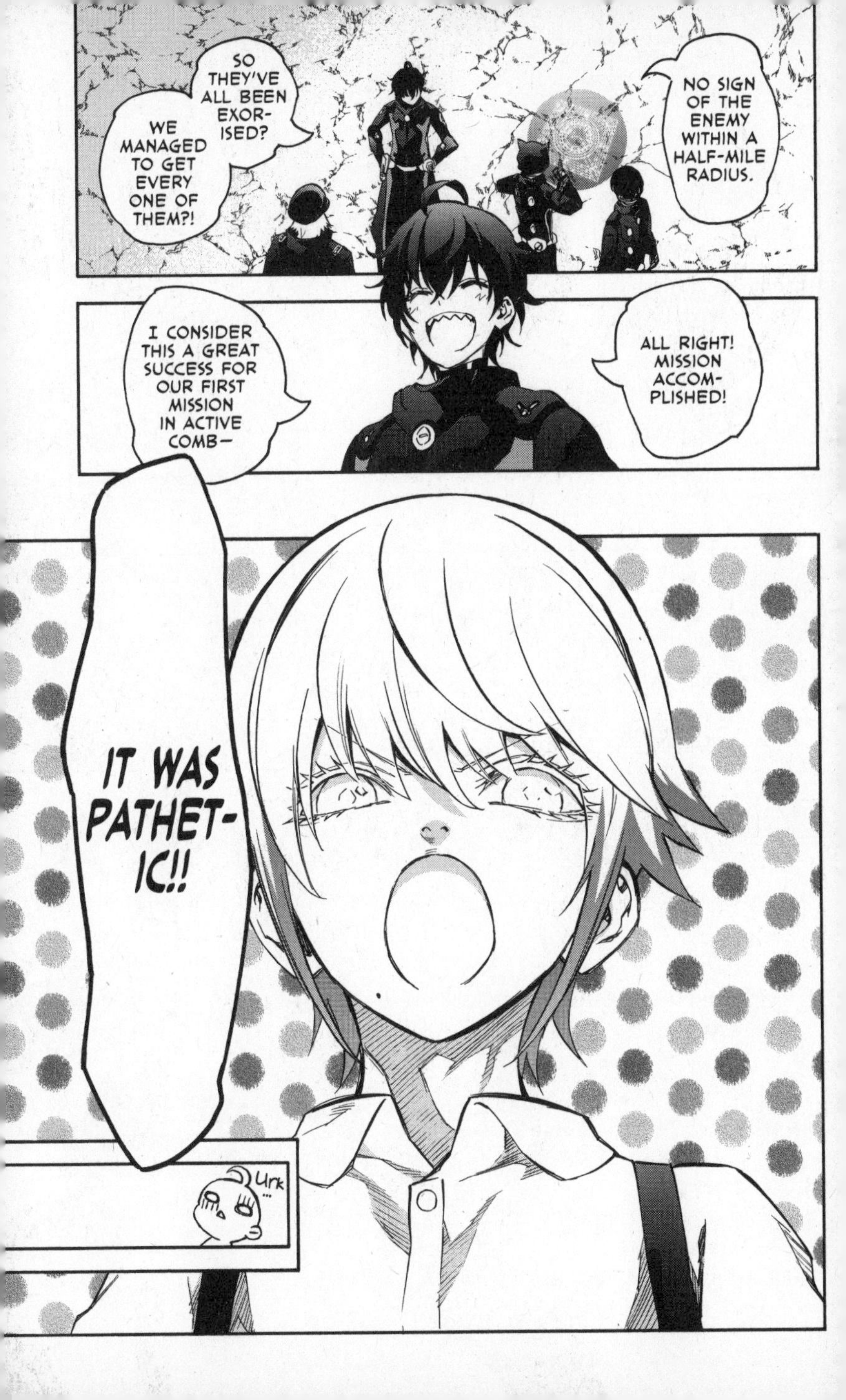
NO SIGN OF THE ENEMY WITHIN A HALF-MILE RADIUS.
SO THEY'VE ALL BEEN EXOR-ISED?
WE MANAGED TO GET EVERY ONE OF THEM?!
ALL RIGHT! MISSION ACCOM-PLISHED!
I CONSIDER THIS A GREAT SUCCESS FOR OUR FIRST MISSION IN ACTIVE COMB—
IT WAS PATHET-IC!!
Urk...

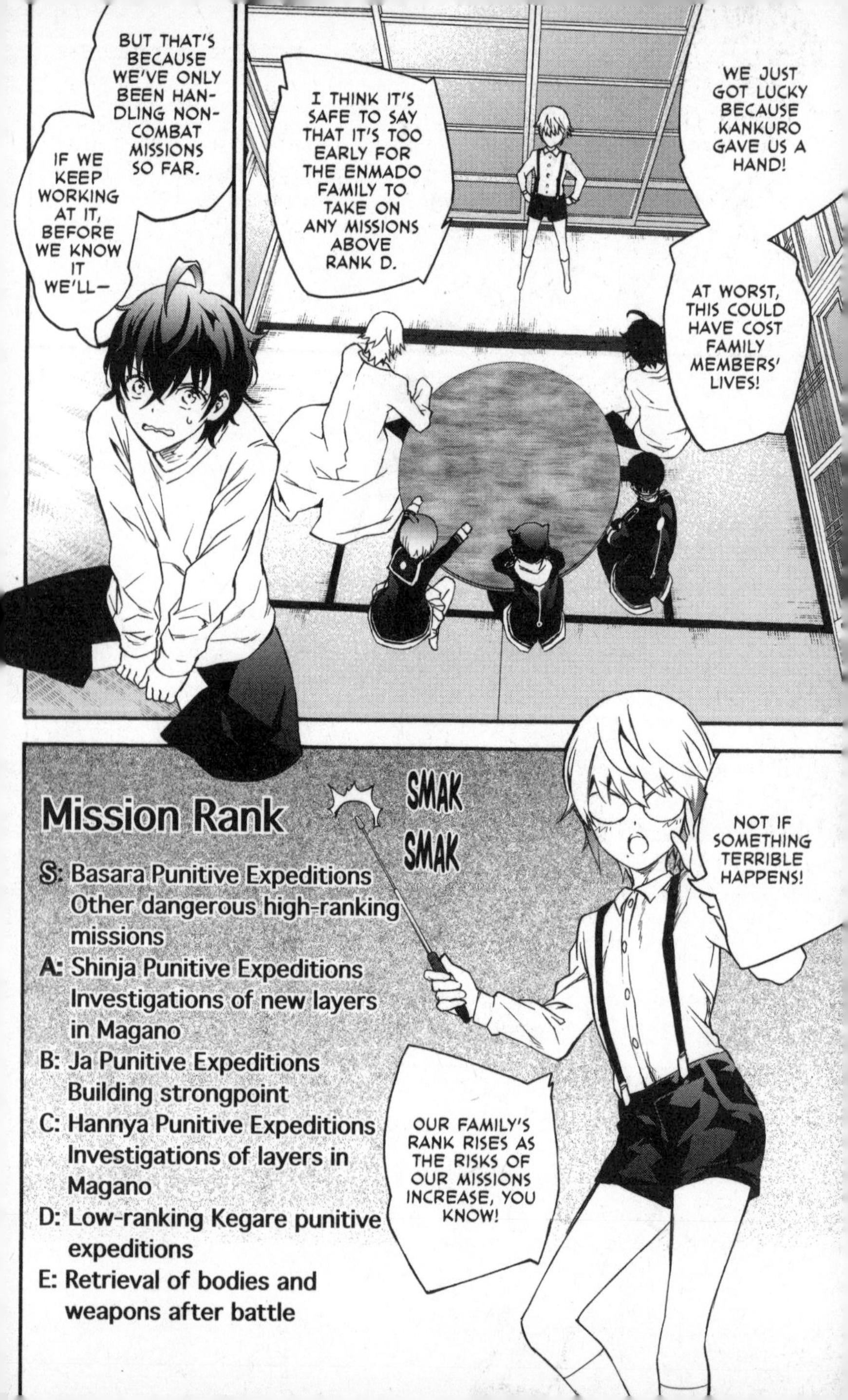
WE JUST GOT LUCKY BECAUSE KANKURO GAVE US A HAND!
AT WORST, THIS COULD HAVE COST FAMILY MEMBERS' LIVES!
I THINK IT'S SAFE TO SAY THAT IT'S TOO EARLY FOR THE ENMADO FAMILY TO TAKE ON ANY MISSIONS ABOVE RANK D.
BUT THAT'S BECAUSE WE'VE ONLY BEEN HAN-DLING NON-COMBAT MISSIONS SO FAR.
IF WE KEEP WORKING AT IT, BEFORE WE KNOW IT WE'LL—
NOT IF SOMETHING TERRIBLE HAPPENS!
SMAK
SMAK
OUR FAMILY'S RANK RISES AS THE RISKS OF OUR MISSIONS INCREASE, YOU KNOW!
Mission Rank
S: Basara Punitive Expeditions
Other dangerous high-ranking missions
A: Shinja Punitive Expeditions
Investigations of new layers in Magano
B: Ja Punitive Expeditions
Building strongpoint
C: Hannya Punitive Expeditions
Investigations of layers in Magano
D: Low-ranking Kegare punitive expeditions
E: Retrieval of bodies and weapons after battle

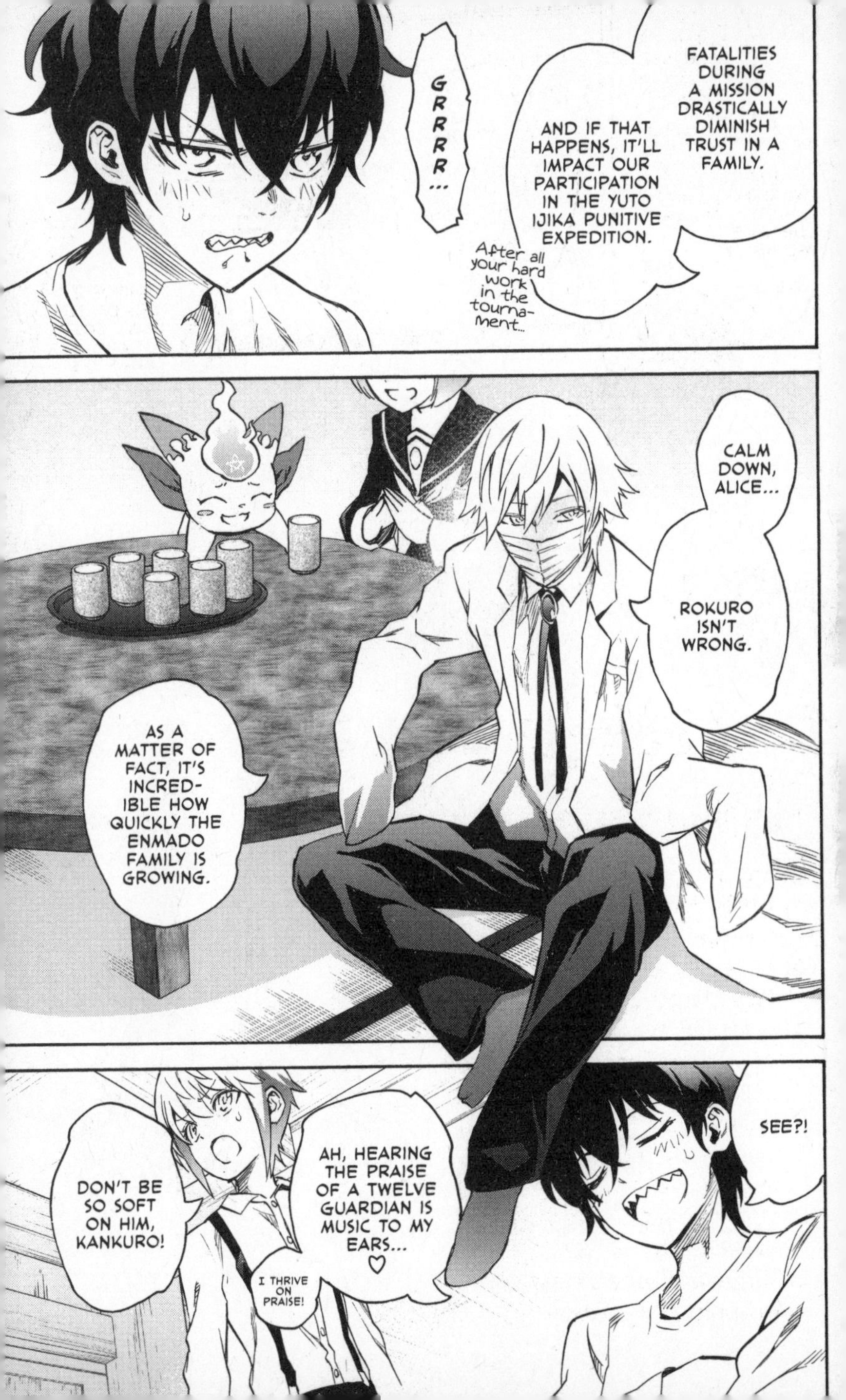
FATALITIES DURING A MISSION DRASTICALLY DIMINISH TRUST IN A FAMILY.
AND IF THAT HAPPENS, IT'LL IMPACT OUR PARTICIPATION IN THE YUTO IJIKA PUNITIVE EXPEDITION.
After all your hard work in the tourna-ment...
GRRRR...
CALM DOWN, ALICE...
ROKURO ISN'T WRONG.
AS A MATTER OF FACT, IT'S INCRED-IBLE HOW QUICKLY THE ENMADO FAMILY IS GROWING.
SEE?!
AH, HEARING THE PRAISE OF A TWELVE GUARDIAN IS MUSIC TO MY EARS... ♡
I THRIVE ON PRAISE!
DON'T BE SO SOFT ON HIM, KANKURO!

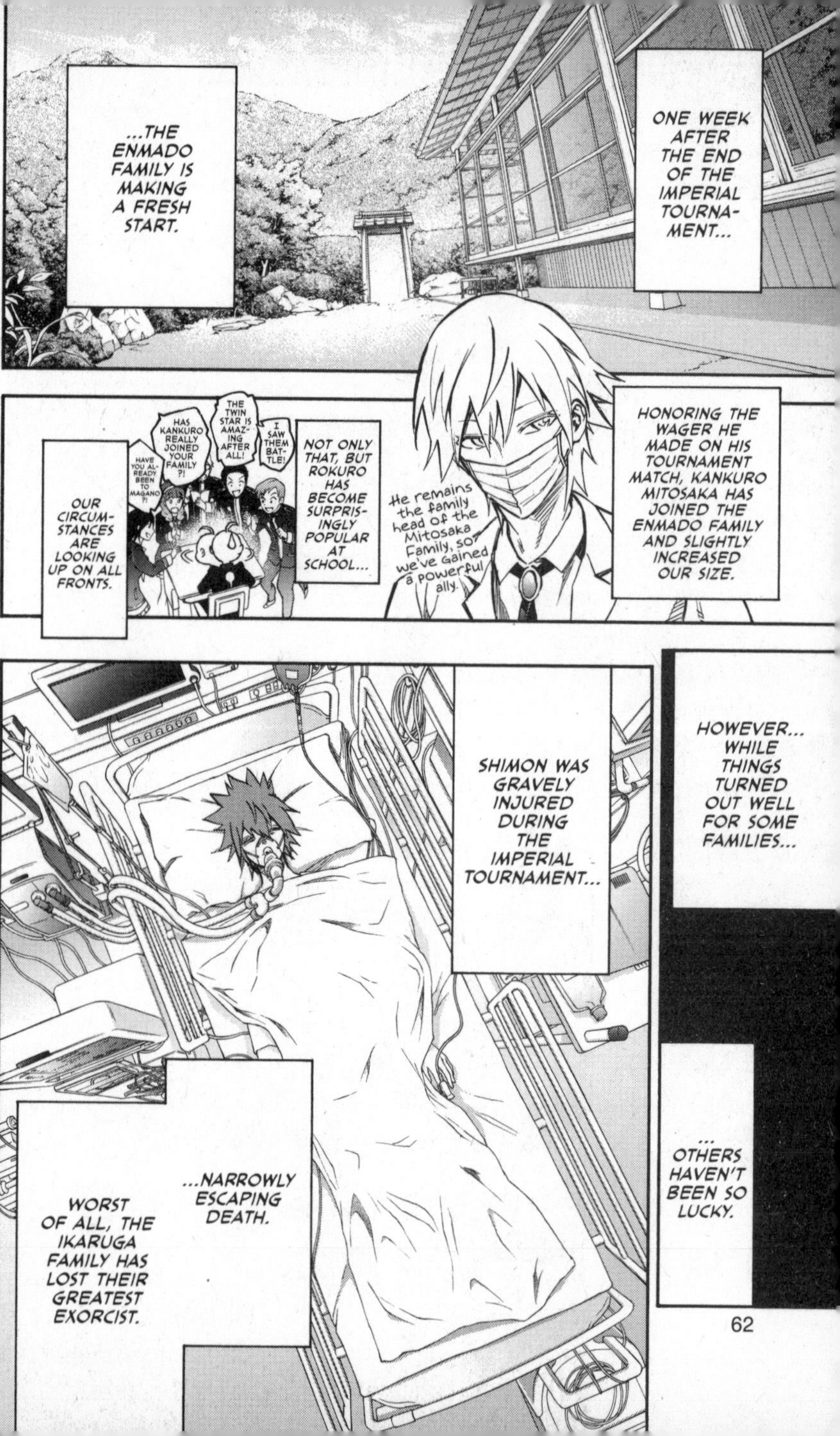
ONE WEEK AFTER THE END OF THE IMPERIAL TOURNAMENT...
...THE ENMADO FAMILY IS MAKING A FRESH START.
HONORING THE WAGER HE MADE ON HIS TOURNAMENT MATCH, KANKURO MITOSAKA HAS JOINED THE ENMADO FAMILY AND SLIGHTLY INCREASED OUR SIZE.
He remains the family head of the Mitosaka Family, so we've gained a powerful ally.
NOT ONLY THAT, BUT ROKURO HAS BECOME SURPRISINGLY POPULAR AT SCHOOL...
I SAW THEM BATTLE!
THE TWIN STAR IS AMAZING AFTER ALL!
HAS KANKURO REALLY JOINED YOUR FAMILY?!
HAVE YOU ALREADY BEEN TO MAGANO?!
OUR CIRCUMSTANCES ARE LOOKING UP ON ALL FRONTS.
HOWEVER... WHILE THINGS TURNED OUT WELL FOR SOME FAMILIES...
...OTHERS HAVEN'T BEEN SO LUCKY.
SHIMON WAS GRAVELY INJURED DURING THE IMPERIAL TOURNAMENT...
...NARROWLY ESCAPING DEATH.
WORST OF ALL, THE IKARUGA FAMILY HAS LOST THEIR GREATEST EXORCIST.

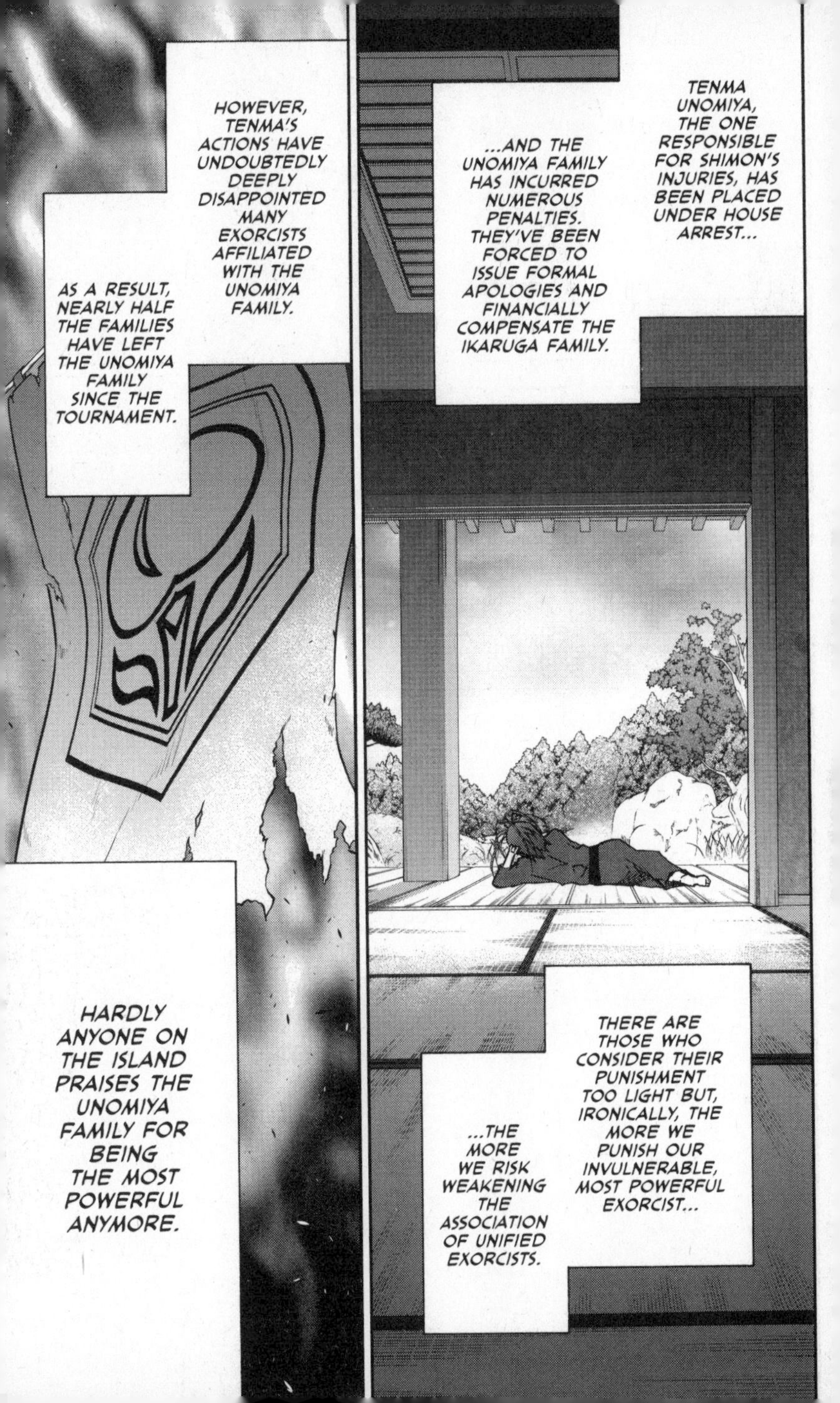
TENMA UNOMIYA, THE ONE RESPONSIBLE FOR SHIMON'S INJURIES, HAS BEEN PLACED UNDER HOUSE ARREST...
...AND THE UNOMIYA FAMILY HAS INCURRED NUMEROUS PENALTIES. THEY'VE BEEN FORCED TO ISSUE FORMAL APOLOGIES AND FINANCIALLY COMPENSATE THE IKARUGA FAMILY.
THERE ARE THOSE WHO CONSIDER THEIR PUNISHMENT TOO LIGHT BUT, IRONICALLY, THE MORE WE PUNISH OUR INVULNERABLE, MOST POWERFUL EXORCIST...
...THE MORE WE RISK WEAKENING THE ASSOCIATION OF UNIFIED EXORCISTS.
HOWEVER, TENMA'S ACTIONS HAVE UNDOUBTEDLY DEEPLY DISAPPOINTED MANY EXORCISTS AFFILIATED WITH THE UNOMIYA FAMILY.
AS A RESULT, NEARLY HALF THE FAMILIES HAVE LEFT THE UNOMIYA FAMILY SINCE THE TOURNAMENT.
HARDLY ANYONE ON THE ISLAND PRAISES THE UNOMIYA FAMILY FOR BEING THE MOST POWERFUL ANYMORE.

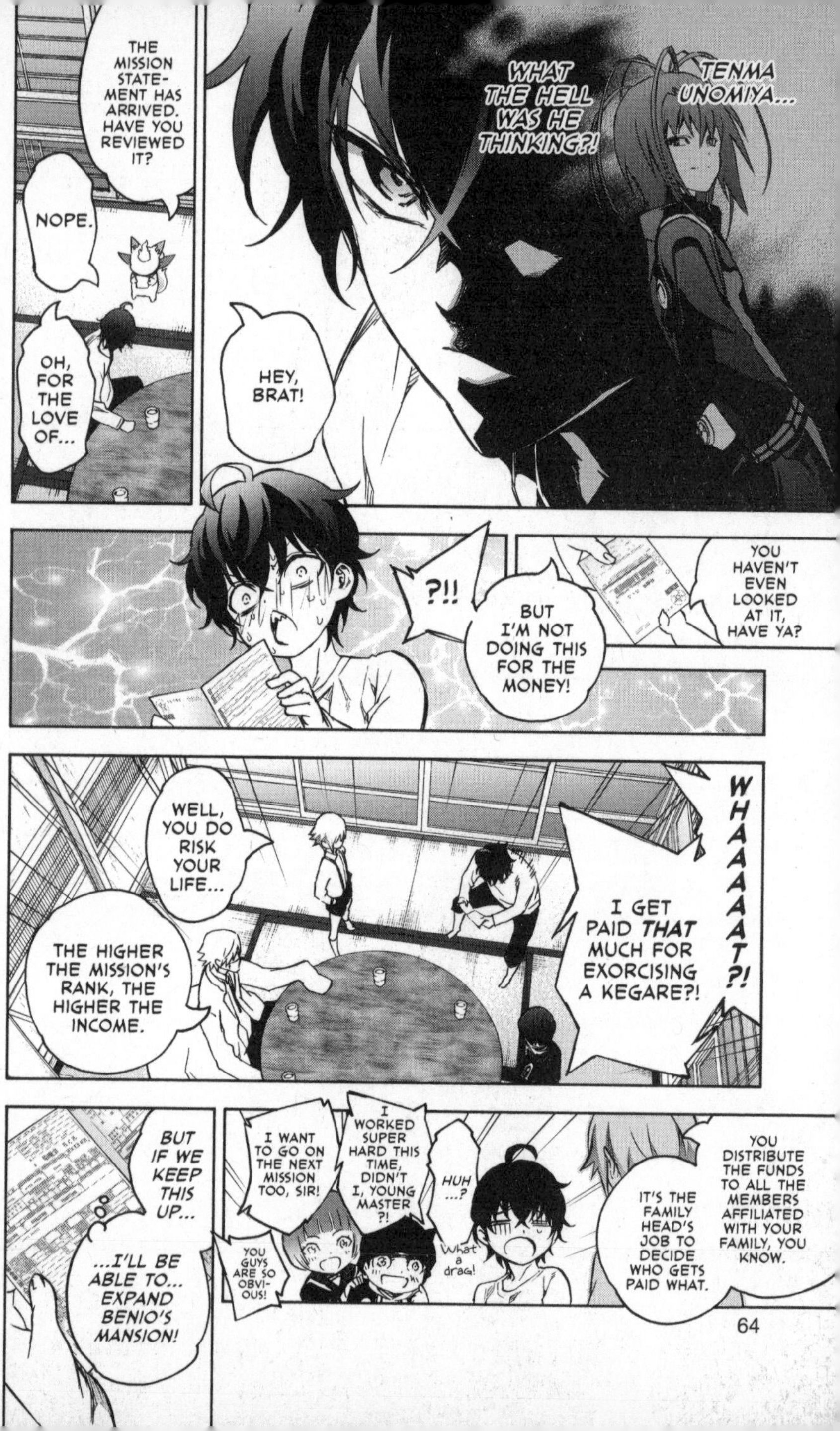
TENMA UNOMIYA...
WHAT THE HELL WAS HE THINKING?!
HEY, BRAT!
THE MISSION STATEMENT HAS ARRIVED. HAVE YOU REVIEWED IT?
NOPE.
OH, FOR THE LOVE OF...
YOU HAVEN'T EVEN LOOKED AT IT, HAVE YA?
BUT I'M NOT DOING THIS FOR THE MONEY!
?!!
WHAAAAAAT?!
I GET PAID *THAT* MUCH FOR EXORCISING A KEGARE?!
WELL, YOU DO RISK YOUR LIFE...
THE HIGHER THE MISSION'S RANK, THE HIGHER THE INCOME.
YOU DISTRIBUTE THE FUNDS TO ALL THE MEMBERS AFFILIATED WITH YOUR FAMILY, YOU KNOW.
IT'S THE FAMILY HEAD'S JOB TO DECIDE WHO GETS PAID WHAT.
HUH ...?
I WORKED SUPER HARD THIS TIME, DIDN'T I, YOUNG MASTER ?!
I WANT TO GO ON THE NEXT MISSION TOO, SIR!
What a drag!
YOU GUYS ARE SO OBVIOUS!
BUT IF WE KEEP THIS UP...
...I'LL BE ABLE TO... EXPAND BENIO'S MANSION!

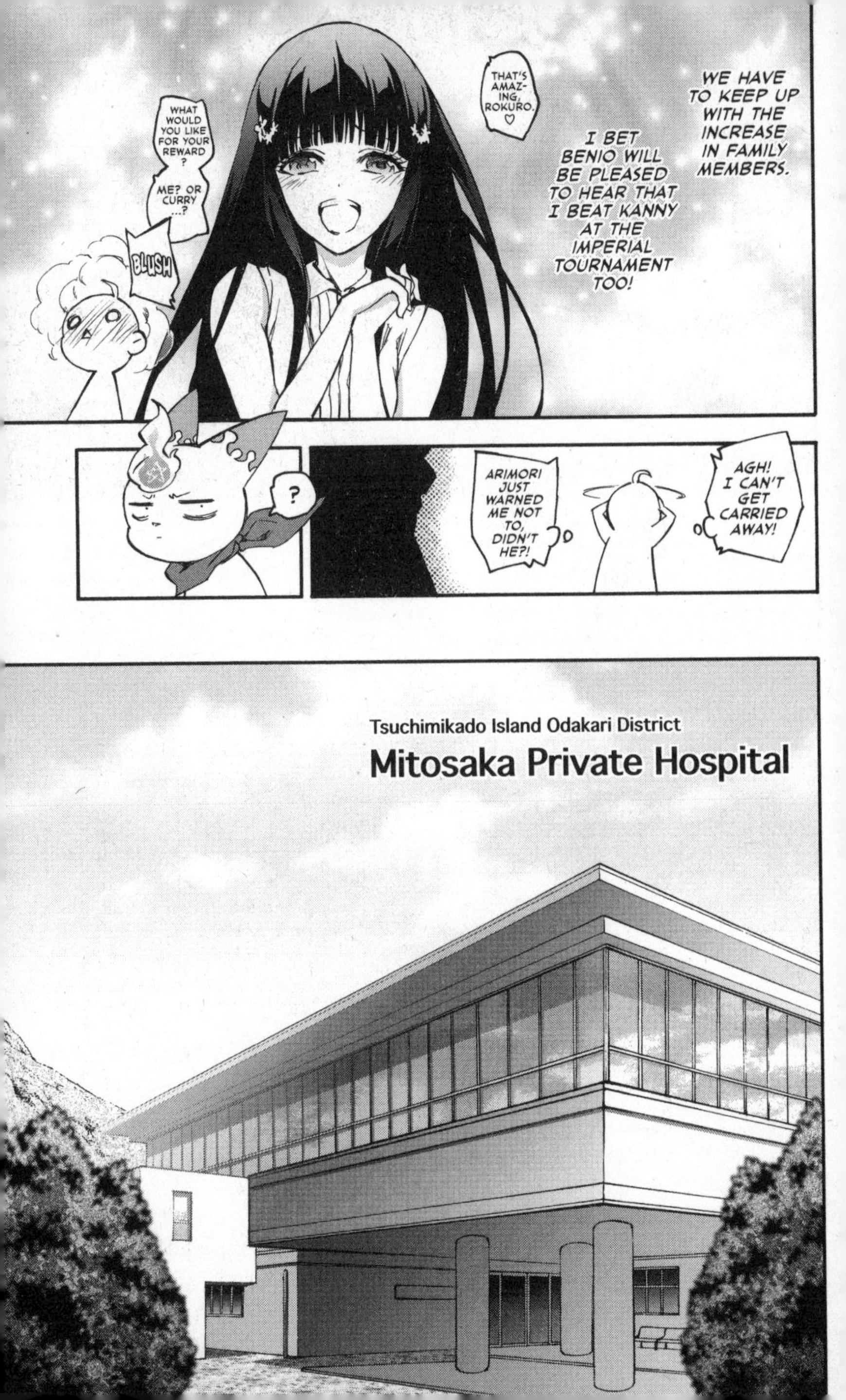
WE HAVE TO KEEP UP WITH THE INCREASE IN FAMILY MEMBERS.
I BET BENIO WILL BE PLEASED TO HEAR THAT I BEAT KANNY AT THE IMPERIAL TOURNAMENT TOO!
THAT'S AMAZING, ROKURO. ♡
WHAT WOULD YOU LIKE FOR YOUR REWARD?
ME? OR CURRY...?
BLUSH
AGH! I CAN'T GET CARRIED AWAY!
ARIMORI JUST WARNED ME NOT TO, DIDN'T HE?!
?
Tsuchimikado Island Odakari District
Mitosaka Private Hospital

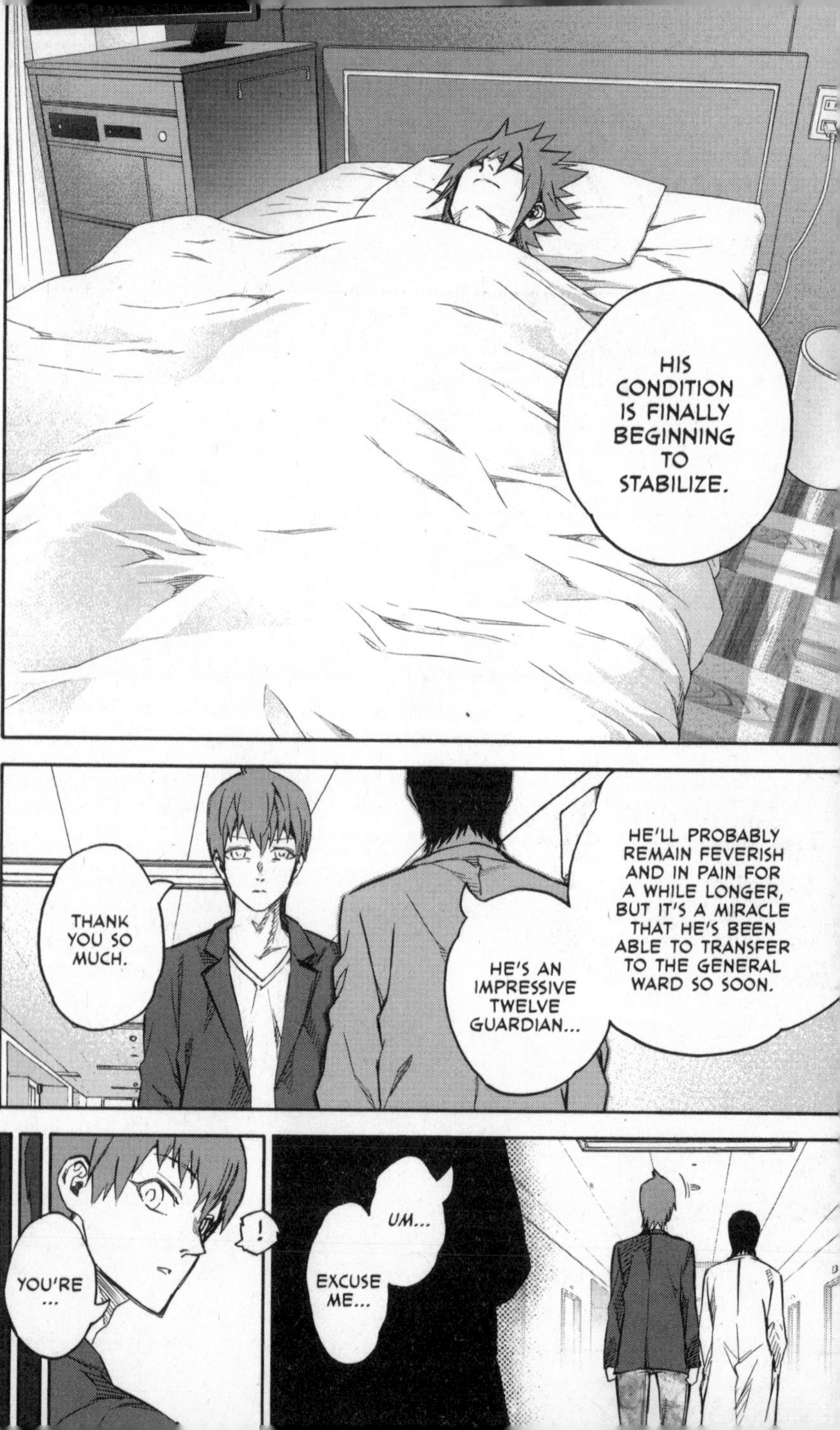
HIS CONDITION IS FINALLY BEGINNING TO STABILIZE.
HE'LL PROBABLY REMAIN FEVERISH AND IN PAIN FOR A WHILE LONGER, BUT IT'S A MIRACLE THAT HE'S BEEN ABLE TO TRANSFER TO THE GENERAL WARD SO SOON.
HE'S AN IMPRESSIVE TWELVE GUARDIAN...
THANK YOU SO MUCH.
UM...
EXCUSE ME...
!
YOU'RE ...

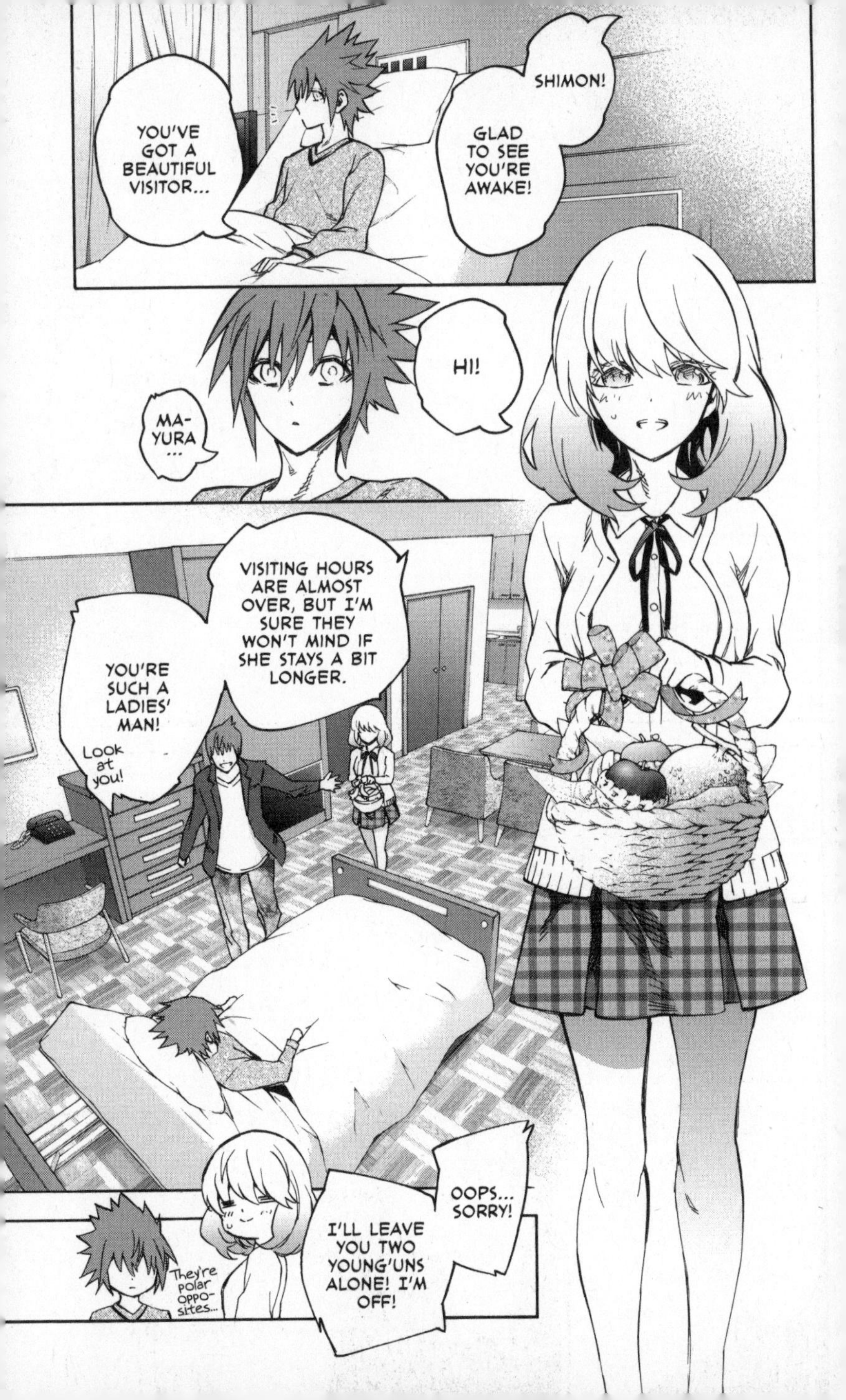
SHIMON!
GLAD TO SEE YOU'RE AWAKE!
YOU'VE GOT A BEAUTIFUL VISITOR...
HI!
MA-YURA...
VISITING HOURS ARE ALMOST OVER, BUT I'M SURE THEY WON'T MIND IF SHE STAYS A BIT LONGER.
YOU'RE SUCH A LADIES' MAN!
Look at you!
OOPS... SORRY!
I'LL LEAVE YOU TWO YOUNG'UNS ALONE! I'M OFF!
They're polar opposites...

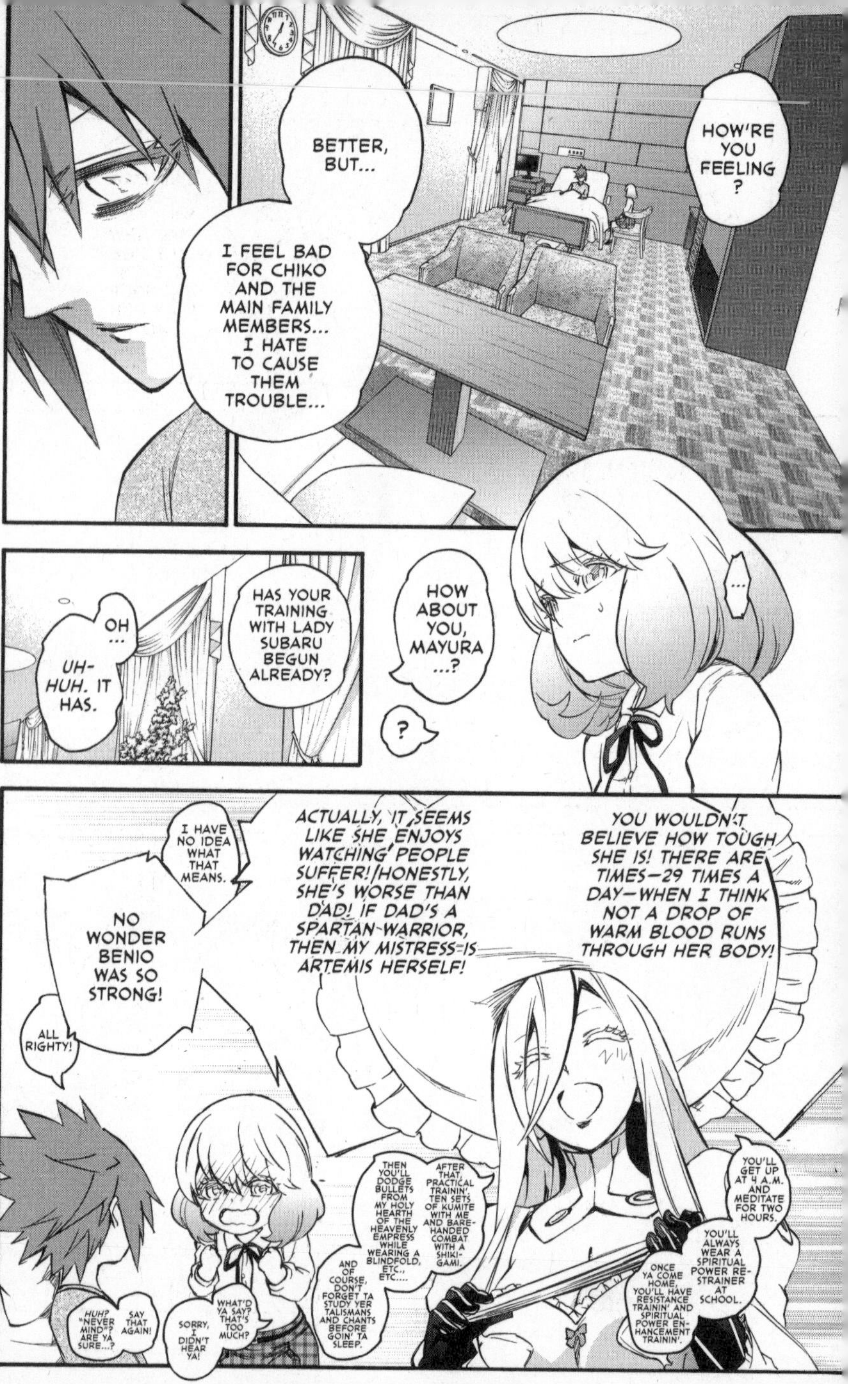

HOW'RE YOU FEELING?
BETTER, BUT...
I FEEL BAD FOR CHIKO AND THE MAIN FAMILY MEMBERS... I HATE TO CAUSE THEM TROUBLE...
...
HOW ABOUT YOU, MAYURA...?
?
HAS YOUR TRAINING WITH LADY SUBARU BEGUN ALREADY?
OH... UH-HUH. IT HAS.
YOU WOULDN'T BELIEVE HOW TOUGH SHE IS! THERE ARE TIMES—29 TIMES A DAY—WHEN I THINK NOT A DROP OF WARM BLOOD RUNS THROUGH HER BODY!
ACTUALLY, IT SEEMS LIKE SHE ENJOYS WATCHING PEOPLE SUFFER! HONESTLY, SHE'S WORSE THAN DAD! IF DAD'S A SPARTAN WARRIOR, THEN MY MISTRESS IS ARTEMIS HERSELF!
I HAVE NO IDEA WHAT THAT MEANS.
NO WONDER BENIO WAS SO STRONG!
ALL RIGHTY!
YOU'LL GET UP AT 4 A.M. AND MEDITATE FOR TWO HOURS.
YOU'LL ALWAYS WEAR A SPIRITUAL POWER RESTRAINER AT SCHOOL.
ONCE YA COME HOME, YOU'LL HAVE RESISTANCE TRAININ' AND SPIRITUAL POWER ENHANCEMENT TRAININ'.
AFTER THAT, PRACTICAL TRAININ', TEN SETS OF KUMITE WITH ME AND BARE-HANDED COMBAT WITH A SHIKIGAMI.
THEN YOU'LL DODGE BULLETS FROM MY HOLY HEARTH OF THE HEAVENLY EMPRESS WHILE WEARING A BLINDFOLD, ETC....
AND OF COURSE, DON'T FORGET TA STUDY YER TALISMANS AND CHANTS BEFORE GOIN' TA SLEEP.
WHAT'D YA SAY? THAT'S TOO MUCH?
SORRY, I DIDN'T HEAR YA!
SAY THAT AGAIN!
HUH? "NEVER MIND"? ARE YA SURE...?

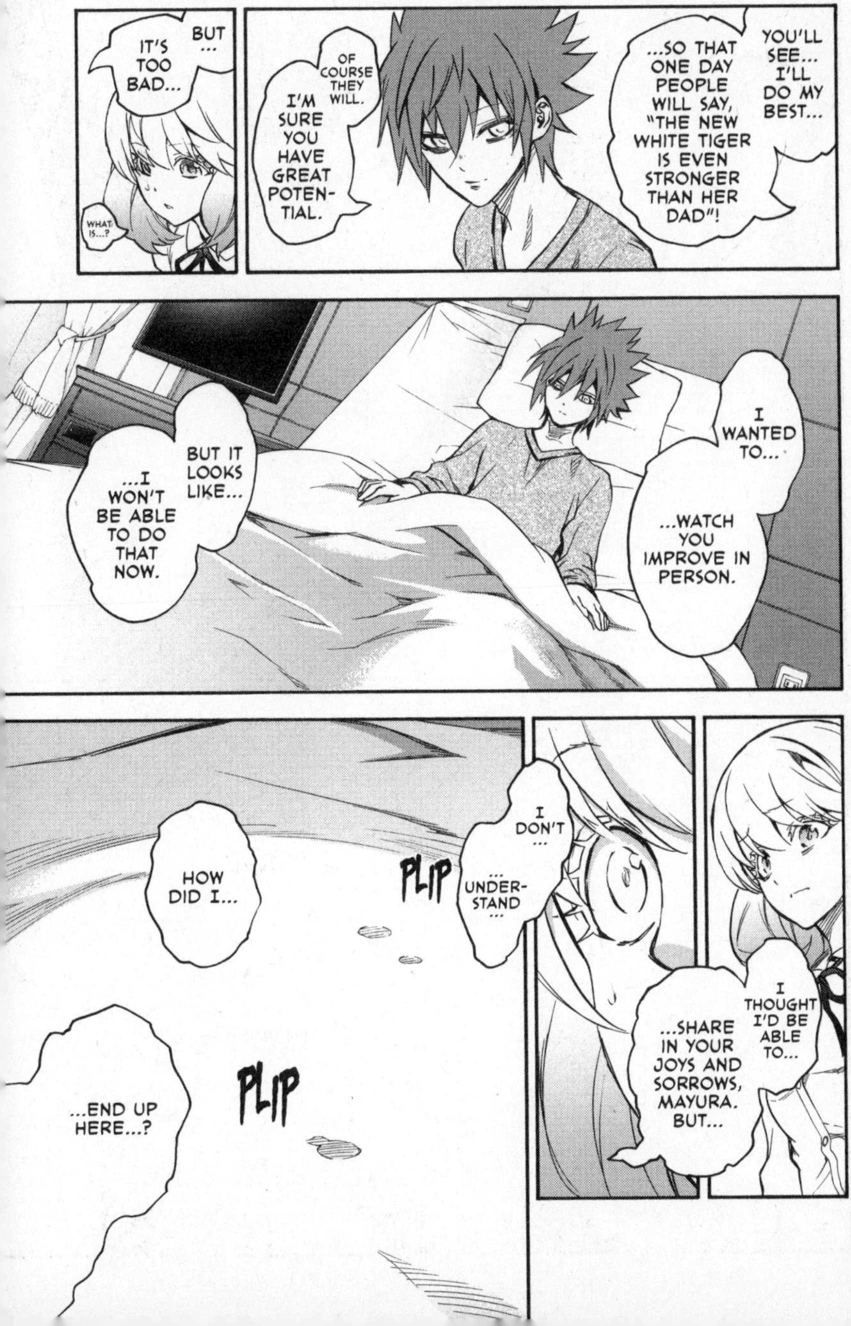
YOU'LL SEE... I'LL DO MY BEST...
...SO THAT ONE DAY PEOPLE WILL SAY, "THE NEW WHITE TIGER IS EVEN STRONGER THAN HER DAD"!
OF COURSE THEY WILL.
I'M SURE YOU HAVE GREAT POTENTIAL.
BUT...
IT'S TOO BAD...
WHAT IS...?
I WANTED TO...
...WATCH YOU IMPROVE IN PERSON.
BUT IT LOOKS LIKE...
...I WON'T BE ABLE TO DO THAT NOW.
I THOUGHT I'D BE ABLE TO...
...SHARE IN YOUR JOYS AND SORROWS, MAYURA. BUT...
I DON'T...
...UNDERSTAND...
PLIP
HOW DID I...
PLIP
...END UP HERE...?

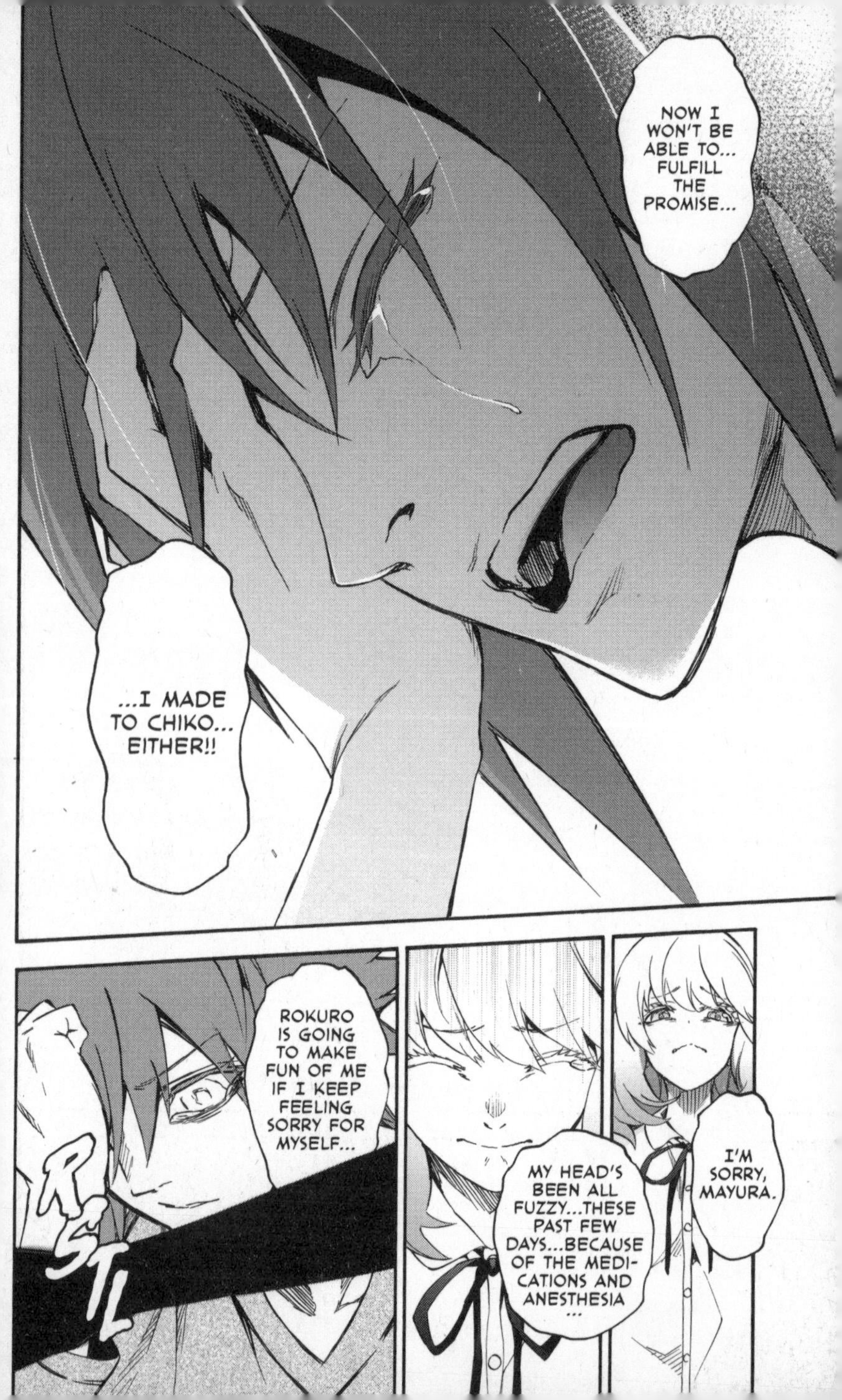
NOW I WON'T BE ABLE TO... FULFILL THE PROMISE...
...I MADE TO CHIKO... EITHER!!
I'M SORRY, MAYURA.
MY HEAD'S BEEN ALL FUZZY...THESE PAST FEW DAYS...BECAUSE OF THE MEDI-CATIONS AND ANESTHESIA...
ROKURO IS GOING TO MAKE FUN OF ME IF I KEEP FEELING SORRY FOR MYSELF...
RSTL

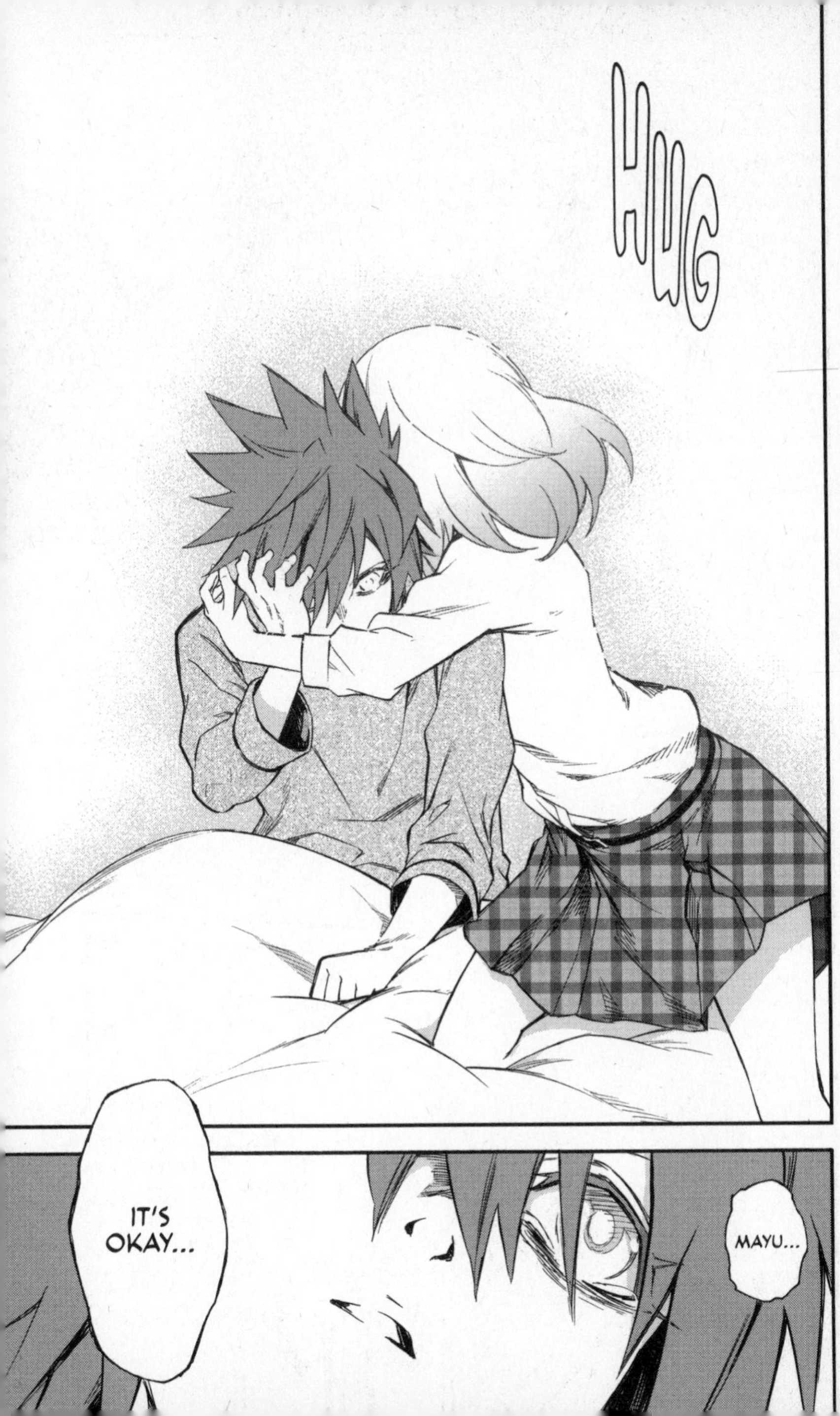
HUG
MAYU...
IT'S OKAY...

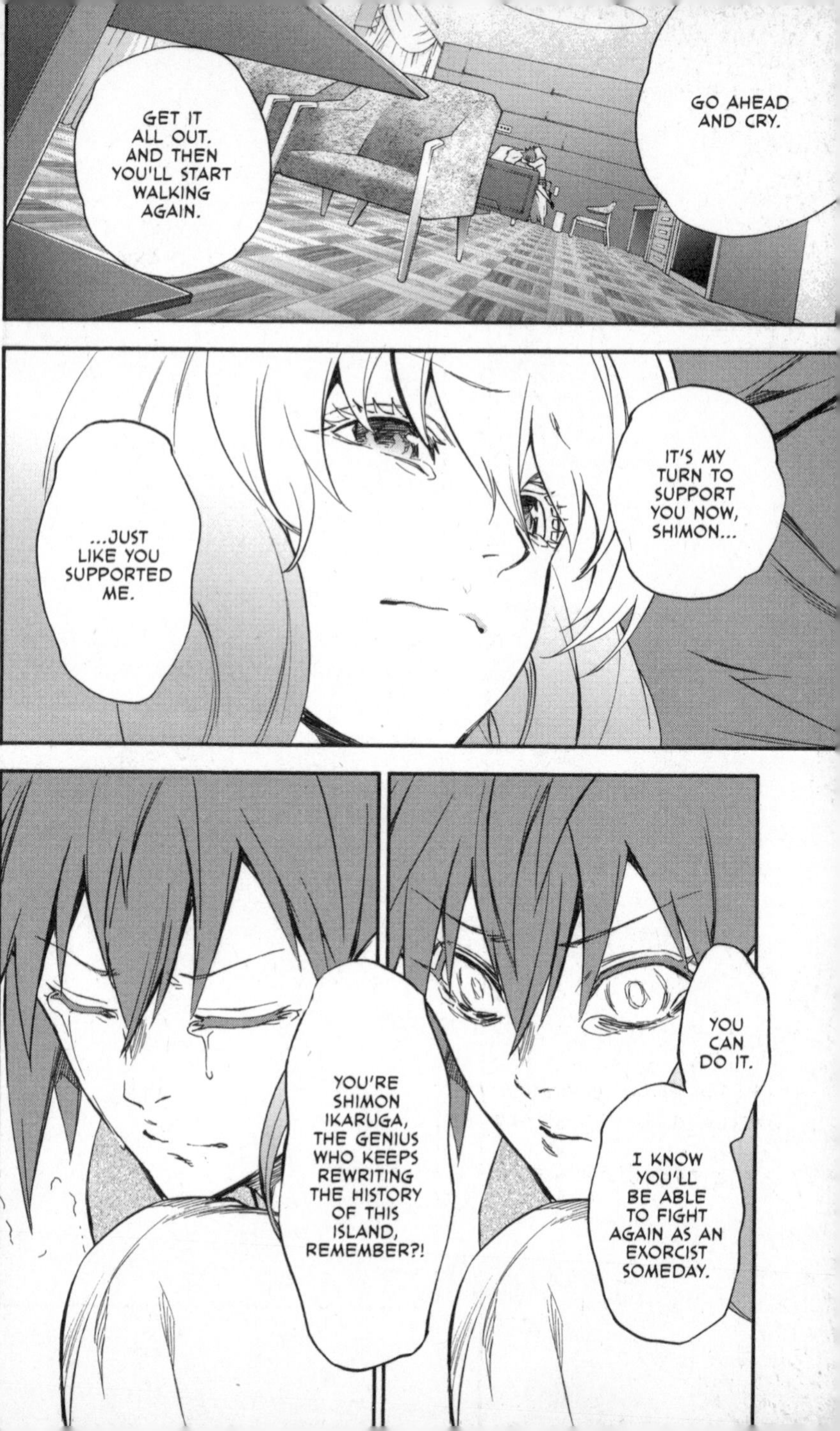
GO AHEAD AND CRY.
GET IT ALL OUT. AND THEN YOU'LL START WALKING AGAIN.
IT'S MY TURN TO SUPPORT YOU NOW, SHIMON...
...JUST LIKE YOU SUPPORTED ME.
YOU CAN DO IT.
YOU'RE SHIMON IKARUGA, THE GENIUS WHO KEEPS REWRITING THE HISTORY OF THIS ISLAND, REMEMBER?!
I KNOW YOU'LL BE ABLE TO FIGHT AGAIN AS AN EXORCIST SOMEDAY.

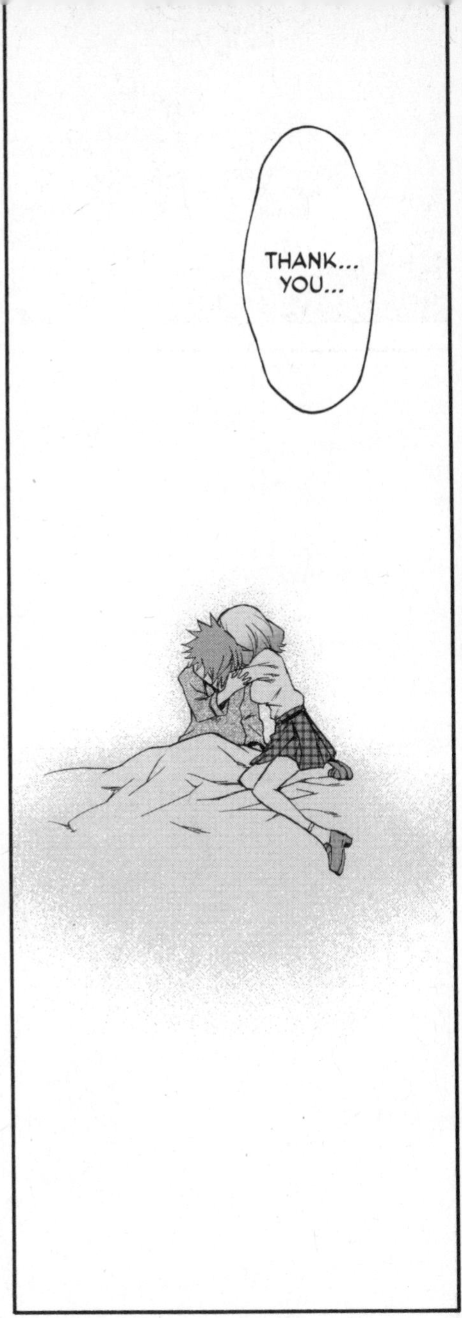
THANK... YOU...

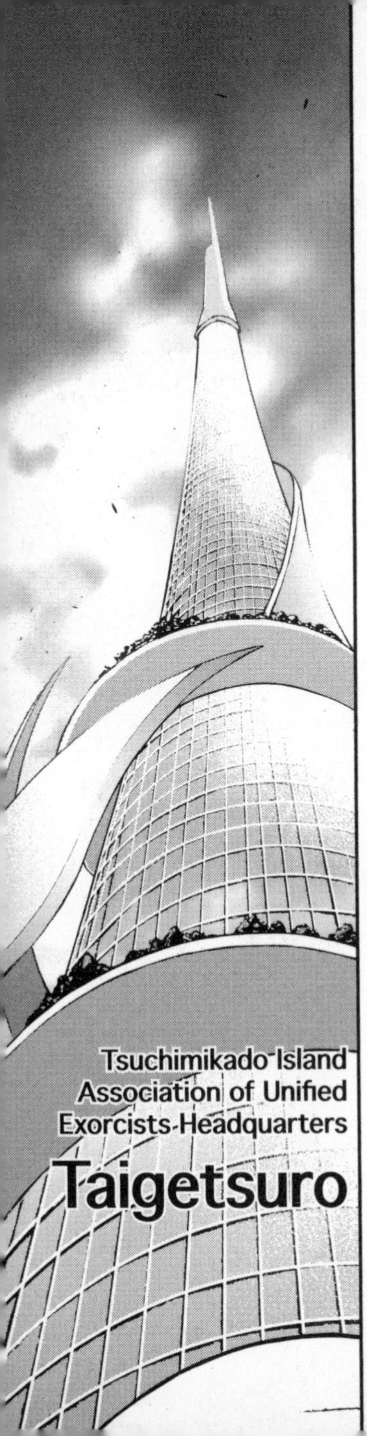
Tsuchimikado Island
Association of Unified
Exorcists-Headquarters
Taigetsuro

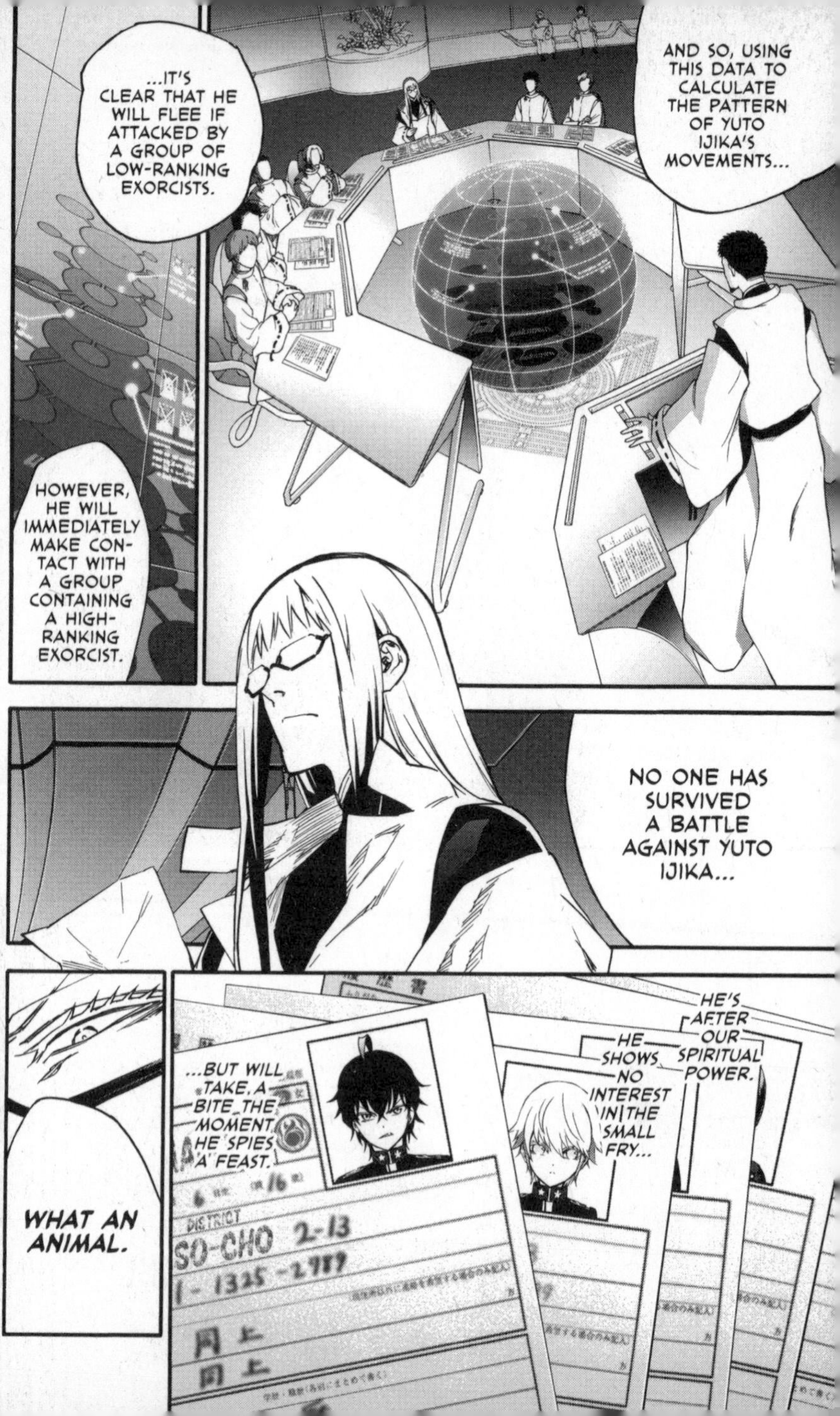
AND SO, USING THIS DATA TO CALCULATE THE PATTERN OF YUTO IJIKA'S MOVEMENTS...
...IT'S CLEAR THAT HE WILL FLEE IF ATTACKED BY A GROUP OF LOW-RANKING EXORCISTS.
HOWEVER, HE WILL IMMEDIATELY MAKE CON-TACT WITH A GROUP CONTAINING A HIGH-RANKING EXORCIST.
NO ONE HAS SURVIVED A BATTLE AGAINST YUTO IJIKA...
HE'S AFTER OUR SPIRITUAL POWER.
HE SHOWS NO INTEREST IN THE SMALL FRY...
...BUT WILL TAKE A BITE THE MOMENT HE SPIES A FEAST.
WHAT AN ANIMAL.

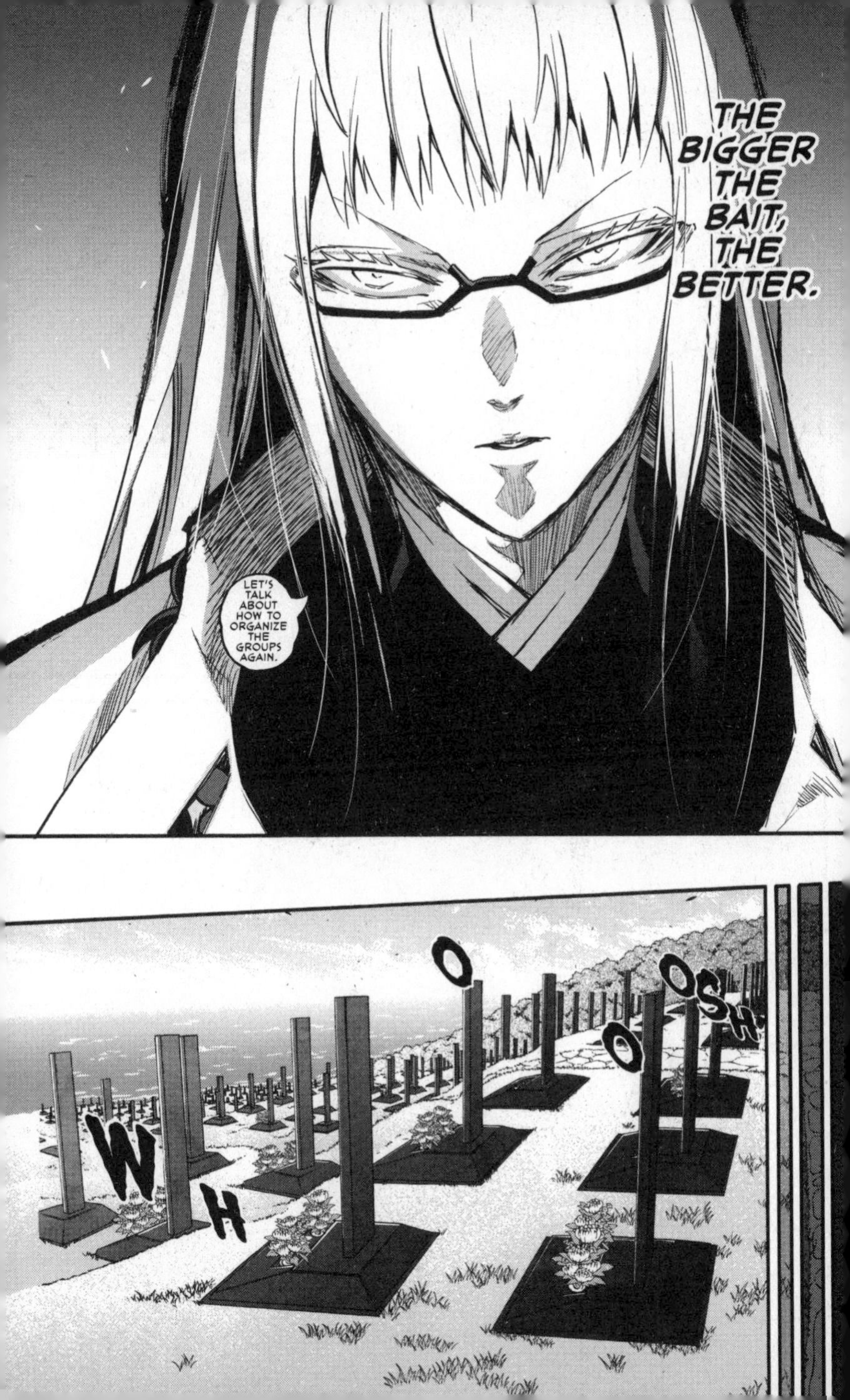
THE BIGGER THE BAIT, THE BETTER.
LET'S TALK ABOUT HOW TO ORGANIZE THE GROUPS AGAIN.
WHOOOSH

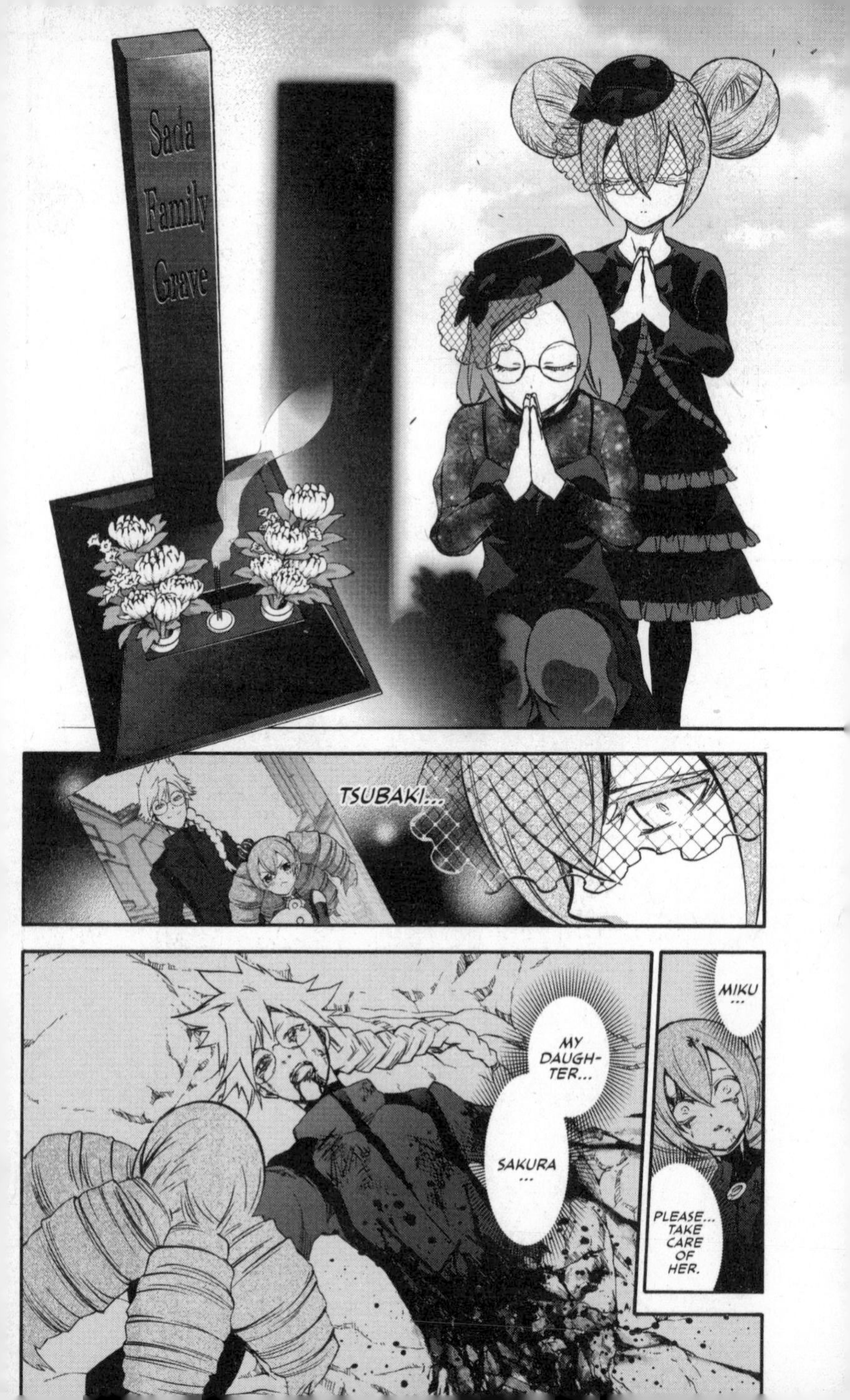
Sada Family Grave
TSUBAKI...
MIKU...
MY DAUGHTER...
SAKURA...
PLEASE... TAKE CARE OF HER.

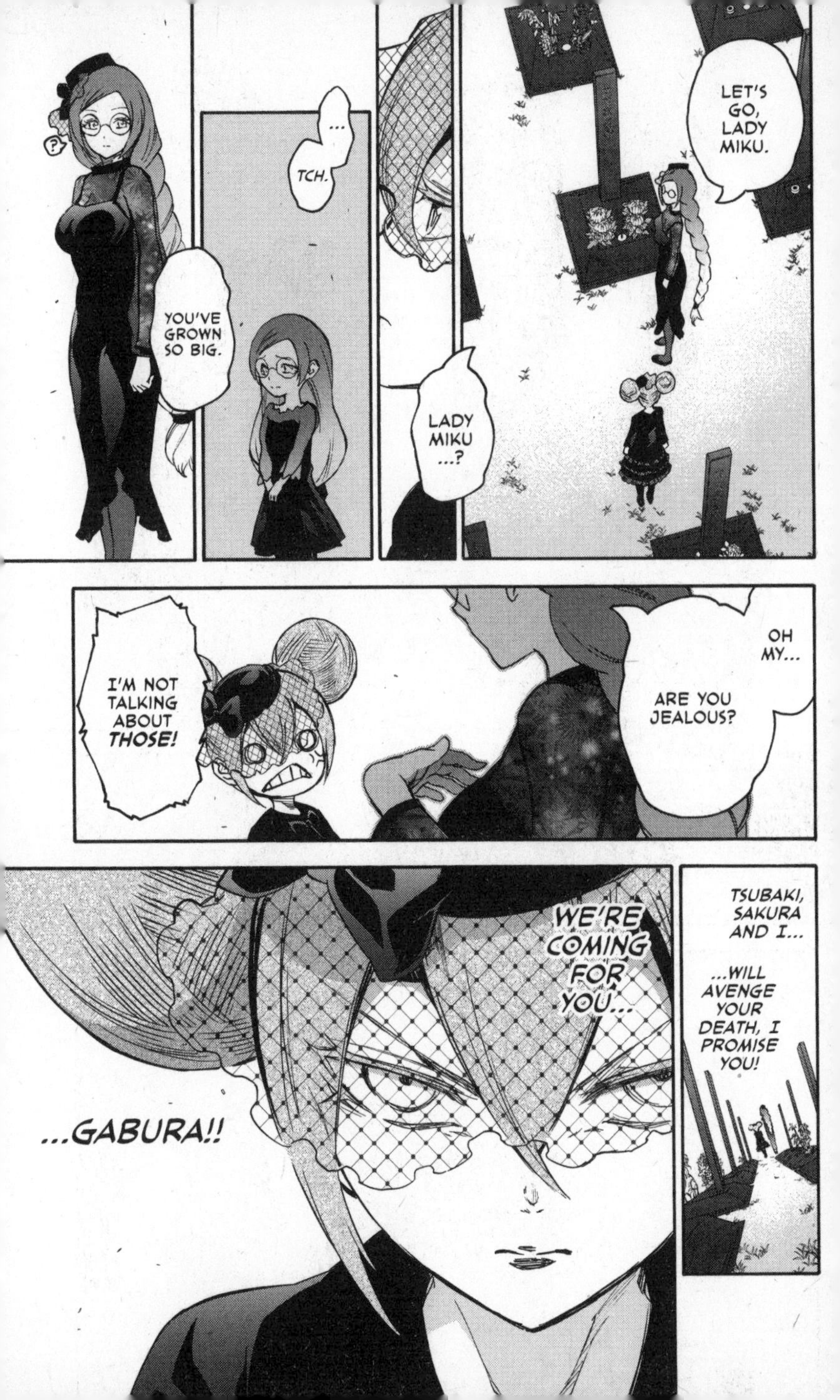
LET'S GO, LADY MIKU.
LADY MIKU ...?
...
TCH.
?
YOU'VE GROWN SO BIG.
OH MY...
ARE YOU JEALOUS?
I'M NOT TALKING ABOUT *THOSE!*
TSUBAKI, SAKURA AND I...
...WILL AVENGE YOUR DEATH, I PROMISE YOU!
WE'RE COMING FOR YOU...
...GABURA!!

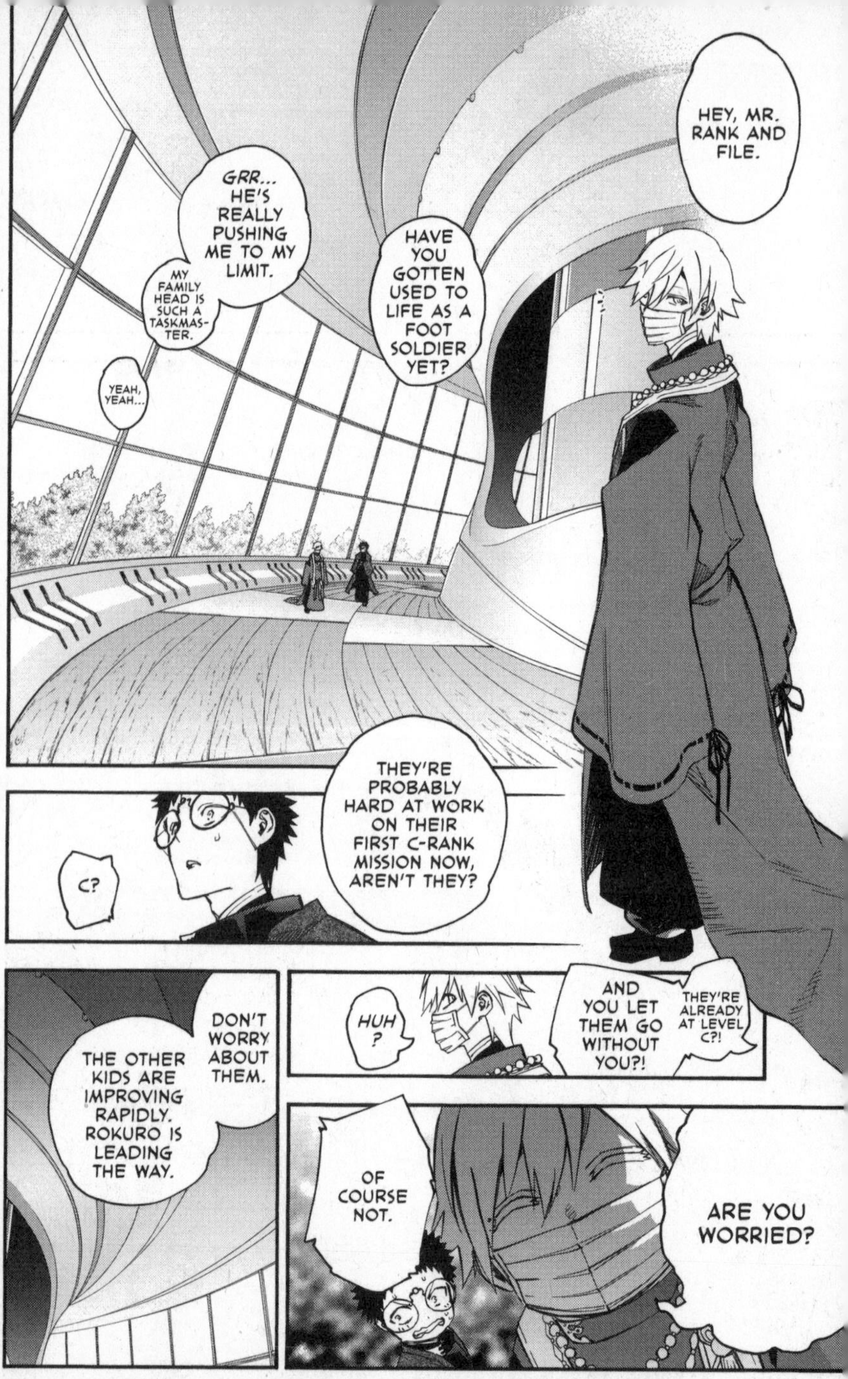
HEY, MR. RANK AND FILE.
HAVE YOU GOTTEN USED TO LIFE AS A FOOT SOLDIER YET?
GRR... HE'S REALLY PUSHING ME TO MY LIMIT.
MY FAMILY HEAD IS SUCH A TASKMASTER.
YEAH, YEAH...
THEY'RE PROBABLY HARD AT WORK ON THEIR FIRST C-RANK MISSION NOW, AREN'T THEY?
C?
THEY'RE ALREADY AT LEVEL C?!
AND YOU LET THEM GO WITHOUT YOU?!
HUH?
ARE YOU WORRIED?
OF COURSE NOT.
DON'T WORRY ABOUT THEM.
THE OTHER KIDS ARE IMPROVING RAPIDLY. ROKURO IS LEADING THE WAY.

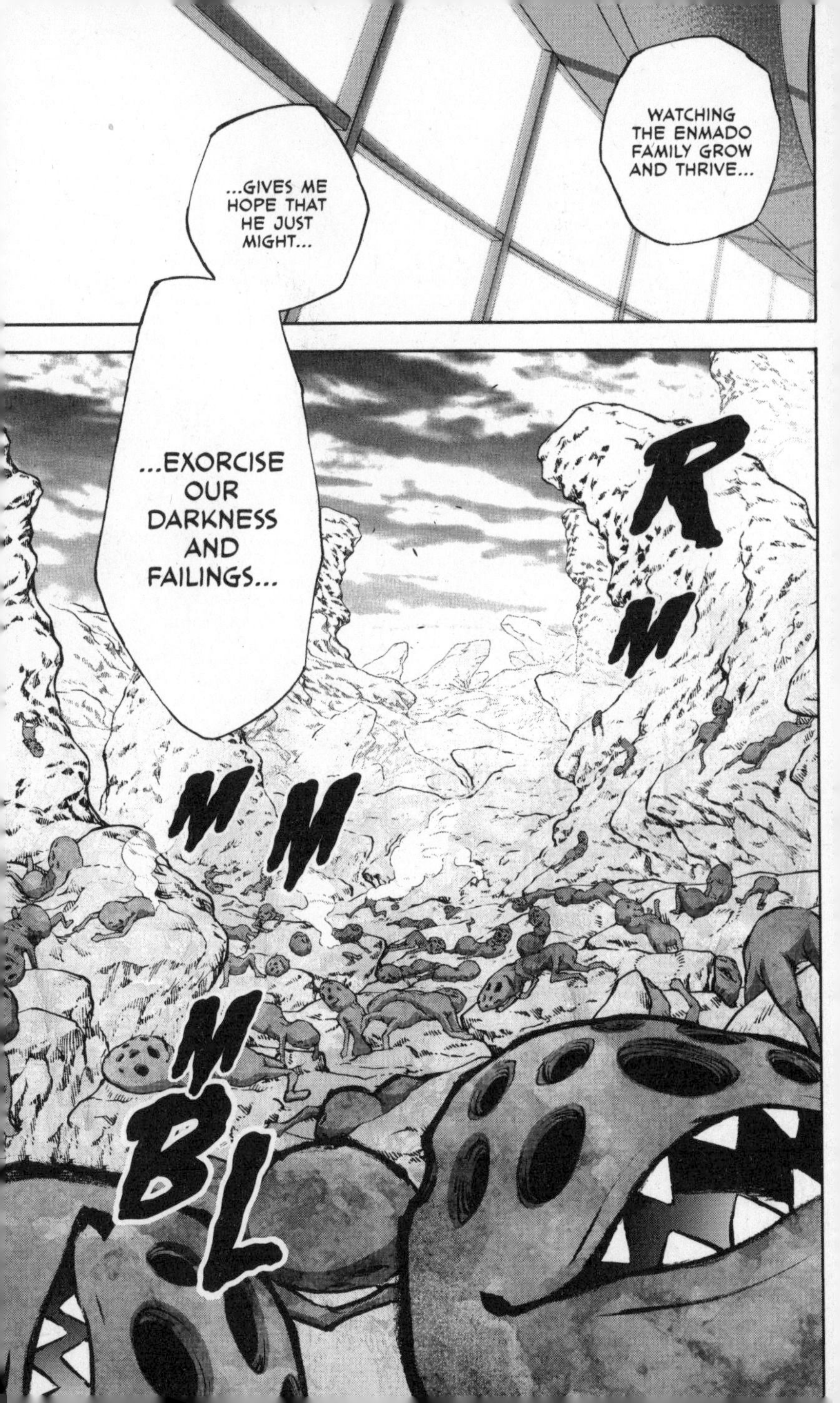
WATCHING THE ENMADO FAMILY GROW AND THRIVE...
...GIVES ME HOPE THAT HE JUST MIGHT...
...EXORCISE OUR DARKNESS AND FAILINGS...
RMMMMMMBL

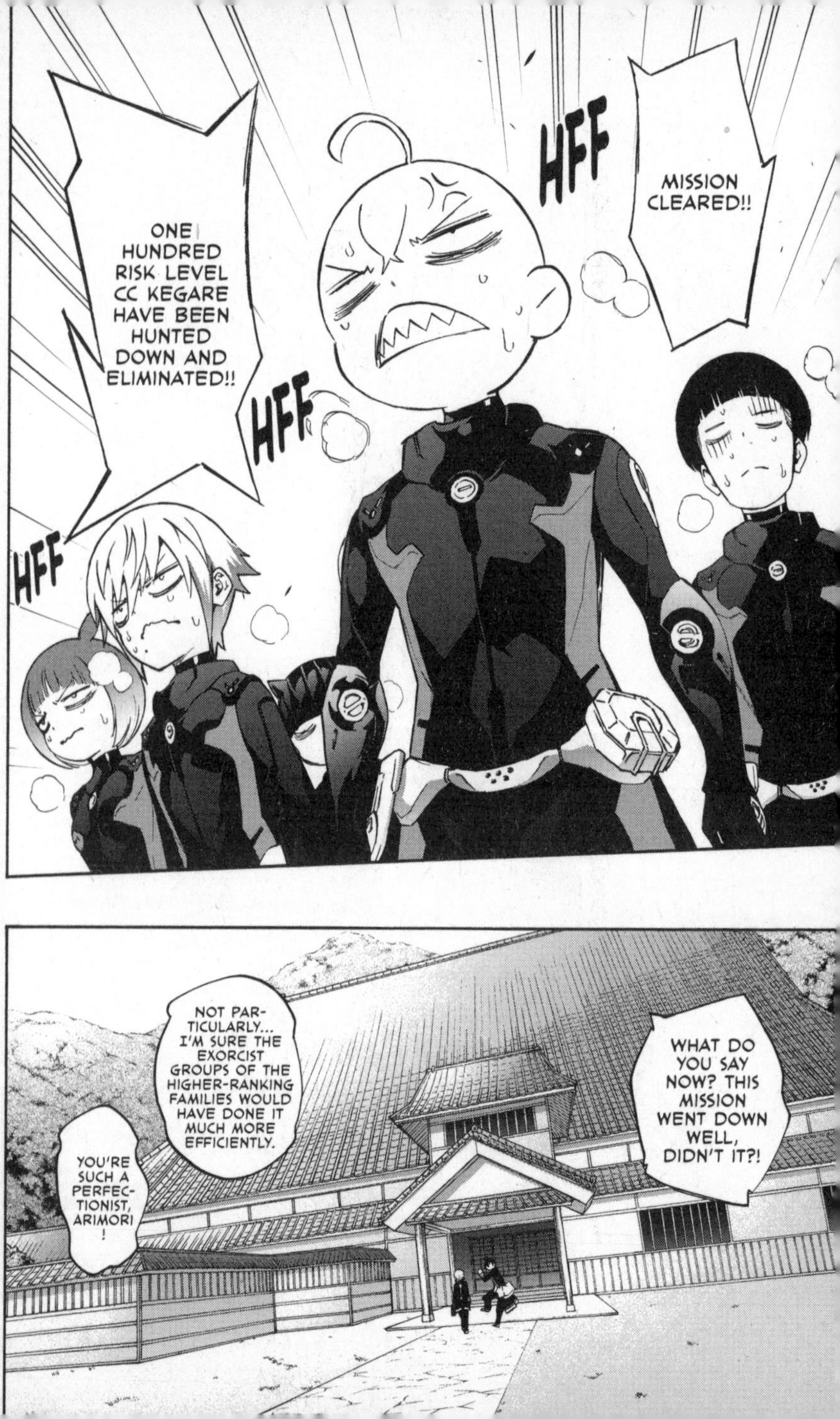
MISSION CLEARED!!
HFF
HFF
ONE HUNDRED RISK LEVEL CC KEGARE HAVE BEEN HUNTED DOWN AND ELIMINATED!!
HFF
WHAT DO YOU SAY NOW? THIS MISSION WENT DOWN WELL, DIDN'T IT?!
NOT PARTICULARLY... I'M SURE THE EXORCIST GROUPS OF THE HIGHER-RANKING FAMILIES WOULD HAVE DONE IT MUCH MORE EFFICIENTLY.
YOU'RE SUCH A PERFECTIONIST, ARIMORI!

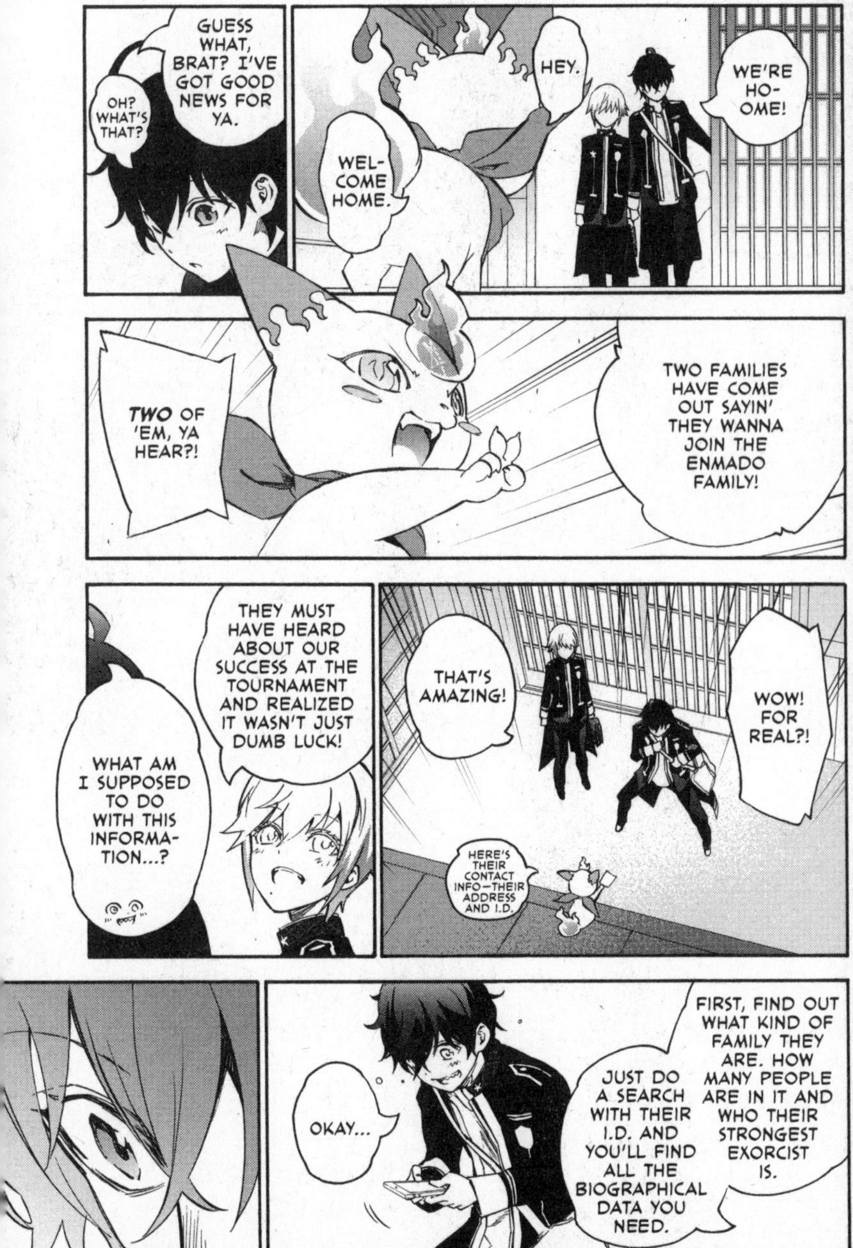
WE'RE HO-OME!
HEY.
WEL-COME HOME.
GUESS WHAT, BRAT? I'VE GOT GOOD NEWS FOR YA.
OH? WHAT'S THAT?
TWO FAMILIES HAVE COME OUT SAYIN' THEY WANNA JOIN THE ENMADO FAMILY!
TWO OF 'EM, YA HEAR?!
WOW! FOR REAL?!
THAT'S AMAZING!
HERE'S THEIR CONTACT INFO—THEIR ADDRESS AND I.D.
THEY MUST HAVE HEARD ABOUT OUR SUCCESS AT THE TOURNAMENT AND REALIZED IT WASN'T JUST DUMB LUCK!
WHAT AM I SUPPOSED TO DO WITH THIS INFORMA-TION...?
FIRST, FIND OUT WHAT KIND OF FAMILY THEY ARE. HOW MANY PEOPLE ARE IN IT AND WHO THEIR STRONGEST EXORCIST IS.
JUST DO A SEARCH WITH THEIR I.D. AND YOU'LL FIND ALL THE BIOGRAPHICAL DATA YOU NEED.
OKAY...

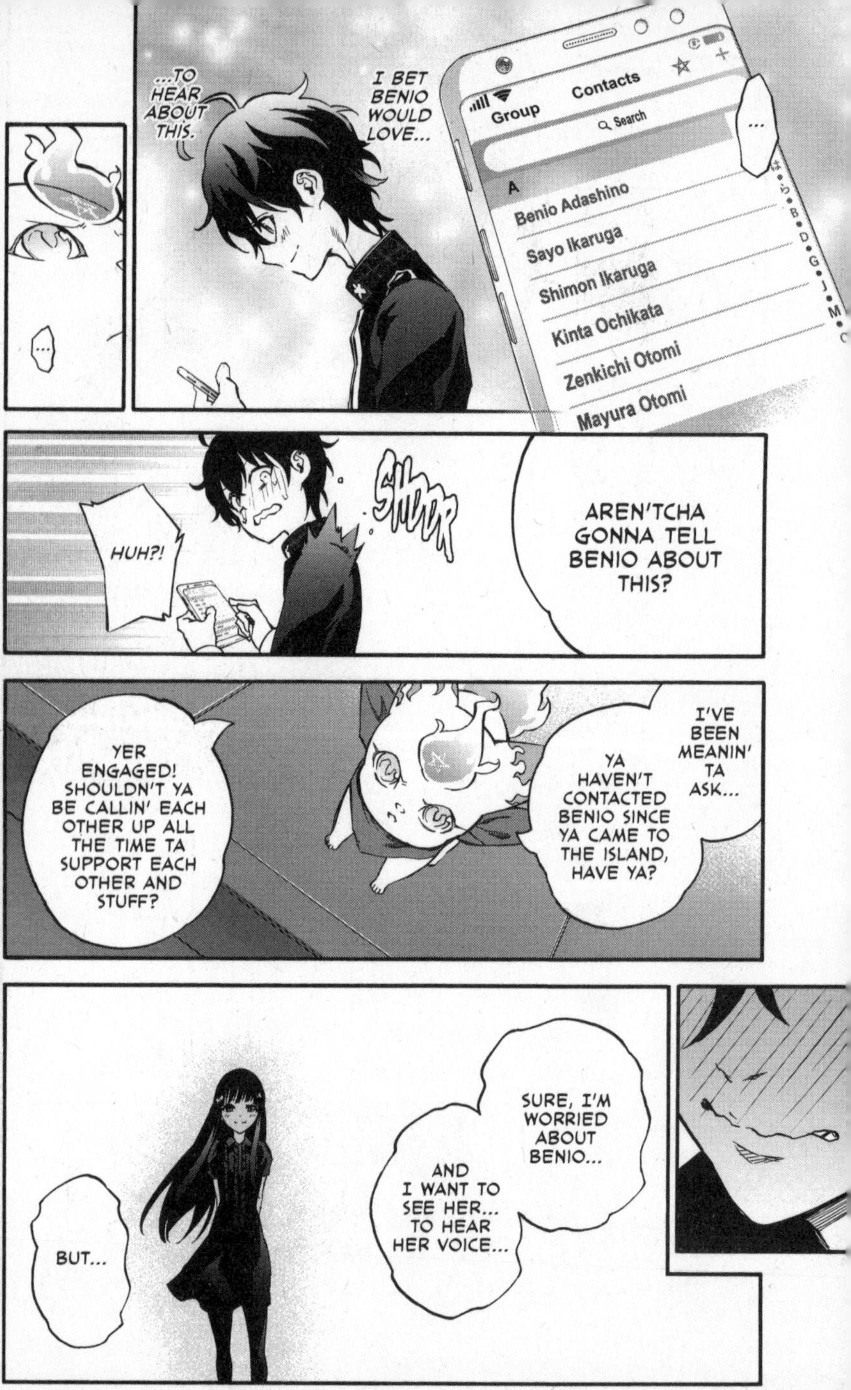
Group
Contacts
Search
A
Benio Adashino
Sayo Ikaruga
Shimon Ikaruga
Kinta Ochikata
Zenkichi Otomi
Mayura Otomi
...
I BET BENIO WOULD LOVE...
...TO HEAR ABOUT THIS.
...
AREN'TCHA GONNA TELL BENIO ABOUT THIS?
SHUDDR
HUH?!
I'VE BEEN MEANIN' TA ASK...
YA HAVEN'T CONTACTED BENIO SINCE YA CAME TO THE ISLAND, HAVE YA?
YER ENGAGED! SHOULDN'T YA BE CALLIN' EACH OTHER UP ALL THE TIME TA SUPPORT EACH OTHER AND STUFF?
SURE, I'M WORRIED ABOUT BENIO...
AND I WANT TO SEE HER... TO HEAR HER VOICE...
BUT...

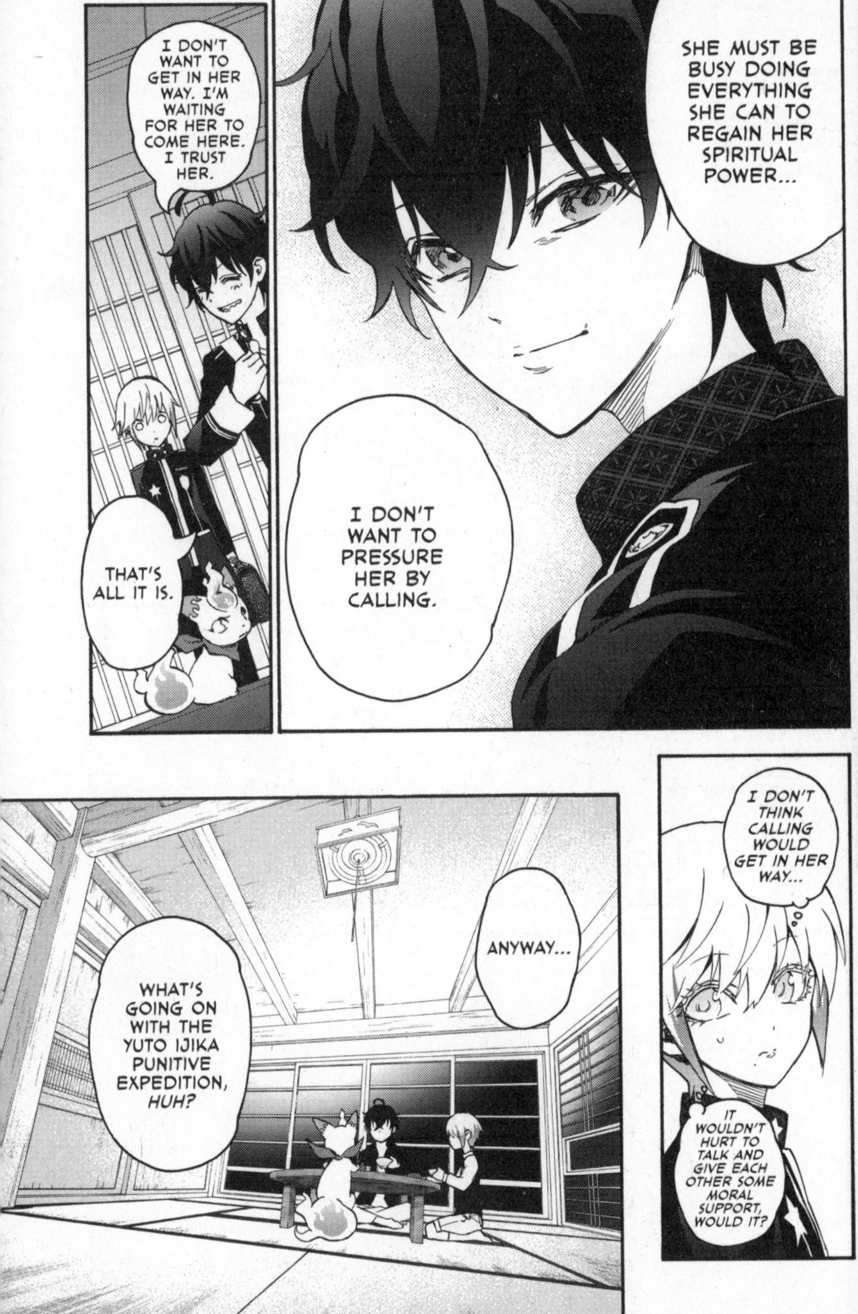
SHE MUST BE BUSY DOING EVERYTHING SHE CAN TO REGAIN HER SPIRITUAL POWER...
I DON'T WANT TO PRESSURE HER BY CALLING.
I DON'T WANT TO GET IN HER WAY. I'M WAITING FOR HER TO COME HERE. I TRUST HER.
THAT'S ALL IT IS.
I DON'T THINK CALLING WOULD GET IN HER WAY...
IT WOULDN'T HURT TO TALK AND GIVE EACH OTHER SOME MORAL SUPPORT, WOULD IT?
ANYWAY...
WHAT'S GOING ON WITH THE YUTO IJIKA PUNITIVE EXPEDITION, *HUH?*

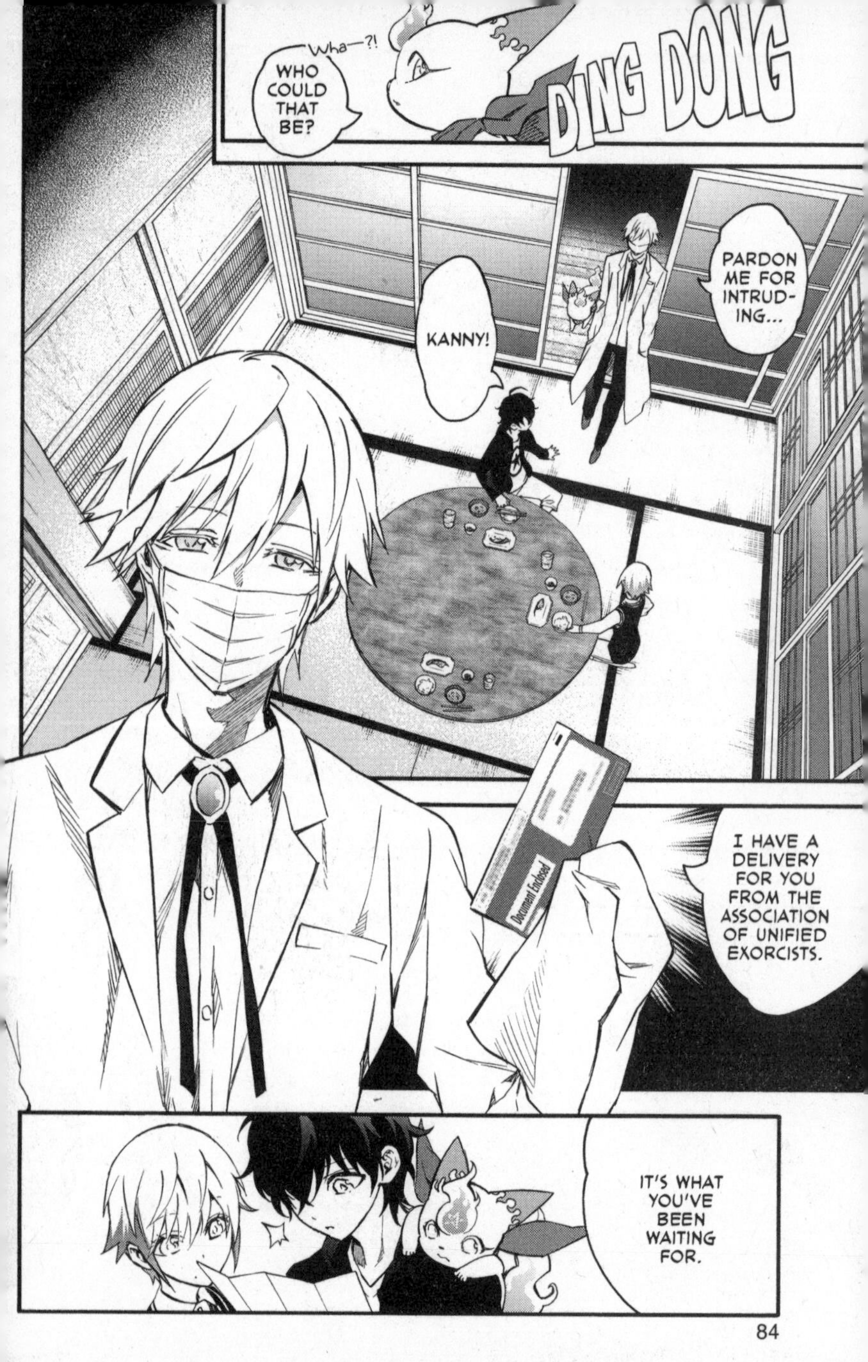
DING DONG
Wha—?!
WHO COULD THAT BE?
PARDON ME FOR INTRUD-ING...
KANNY!
I HAVE A DELIVERY FOR YOU FROM THE ASSOCIATION OF UNIFIED EXORCISTS.
Document Enclosed
IT'S WHAT YOU'VE BEEN WAITING FOR.

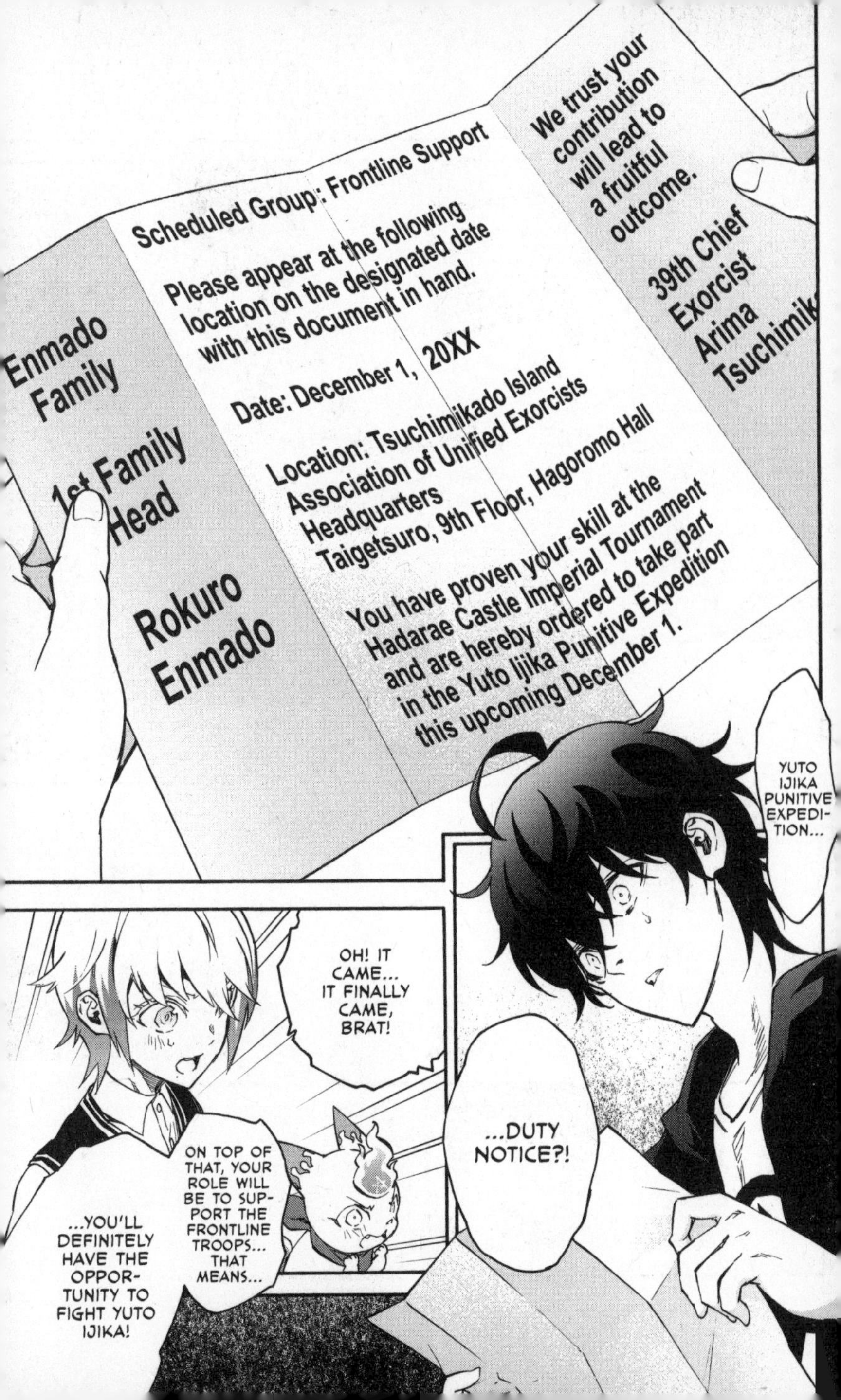
Enmado Family
1st Family Head
Rokuro Enmado
Scheduled Group: Frontline Support
Please appear at the following location on the designated date with this document in hand.
Date: December 1, 20XX
Location: Tsuchimikado Island Association of Unified Exorcists Headquarters Taigetsuro, 9th Floor, Hagoromo Hall
You have proven your skill at the Hadarae Castle Imperial Tournament and are hereby ordered to take part in the Yuto Ijika Punitive Expedition this upcoming December 1.
We trust your contribution will lead to a fruitful outcome.
39th Chief Exorcist Arima Tsuchimik
YUTO IJIKA PUNITIVE EXPEDITION...
...DUTY NOTICE?!
OH! IT CAME... IT FINALLY CAME, BRAT!
ON TOP OF THAT, YOUR ROLE WILL BE TO SUPPORT THE FRONTLINE TROOPS... THAT MEANS...
...YOU'LL DEFINITELY HAVE THE OPPORTUNITY TO FIGHT YUTO IJIKA!

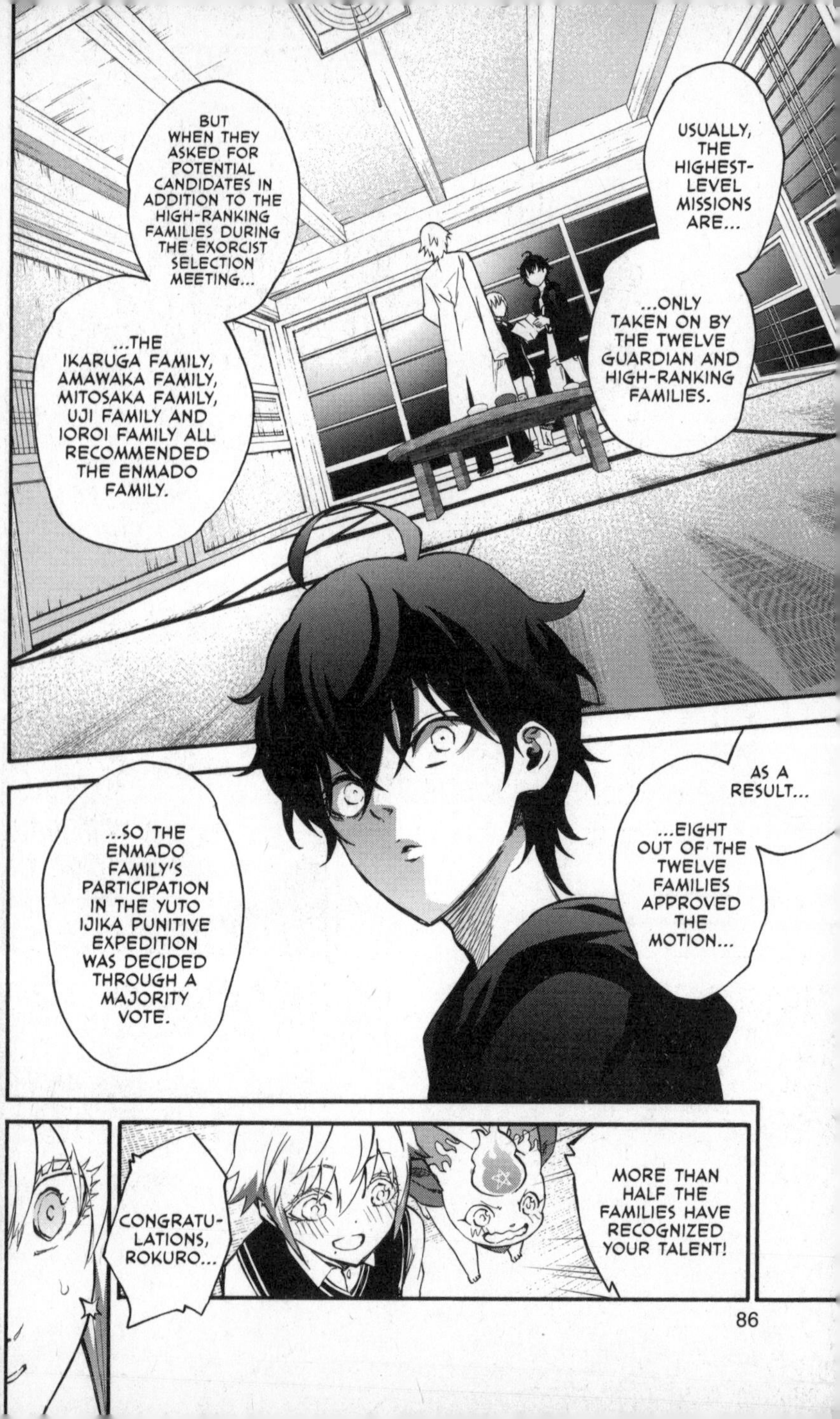
USUALLY, THE HIGHEST-LEVEL MISSIONS ARE...
...ONLY TAKEN ON BY THE TWELVE GUARDIAN AND HIGH-RANKING FAMILIES.
BUT WHEN THEY ASKED FOR POTENTIAL CANDIDATES IN ADDITION TO THE HIGH-RANKING FAMILIES DURING THE EXORCIST SELECTION MEETING...
...THE IKARUGA FAMILY, AMAWAKA FAMILY, MITOSAKA FAMILY, UJI FAMILY AND IOROI FAMILY ALL RECOMMENDED THE ENMADO FAMILY.
AS A RESULT...
...EIGHT OUT OF THE TWELVE FAMILIES APPROVED THE MOTION...
...SO THE ENMADO FAMILY'S PARTICIPATION IN THE YUTO IJIKA PUNITIVE EXPEDITION WAS DECIDED THROUGH A MAJORITY VOTE.
MORE THAN HALF THE FAMILIES HAVE RECOGNIZED YOUR TALENT!
CONGRATU-LATIONS, ROKURO...

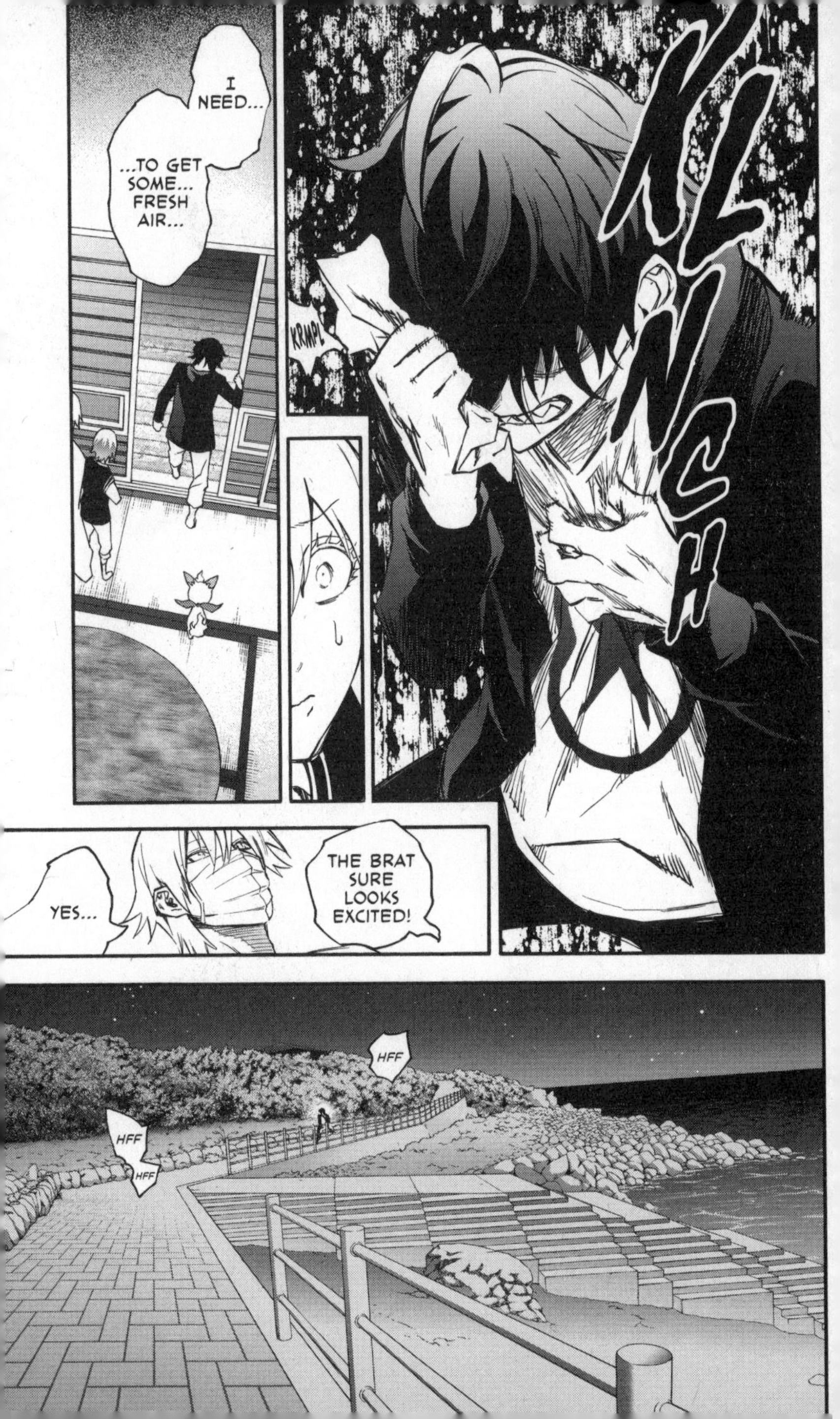
KRMPL
I NEED...
...TO GET SOME... FRESH AIR...
THE BRAT SURE LOOKS EXCITED!
YES...
HFF
HFF
HFF

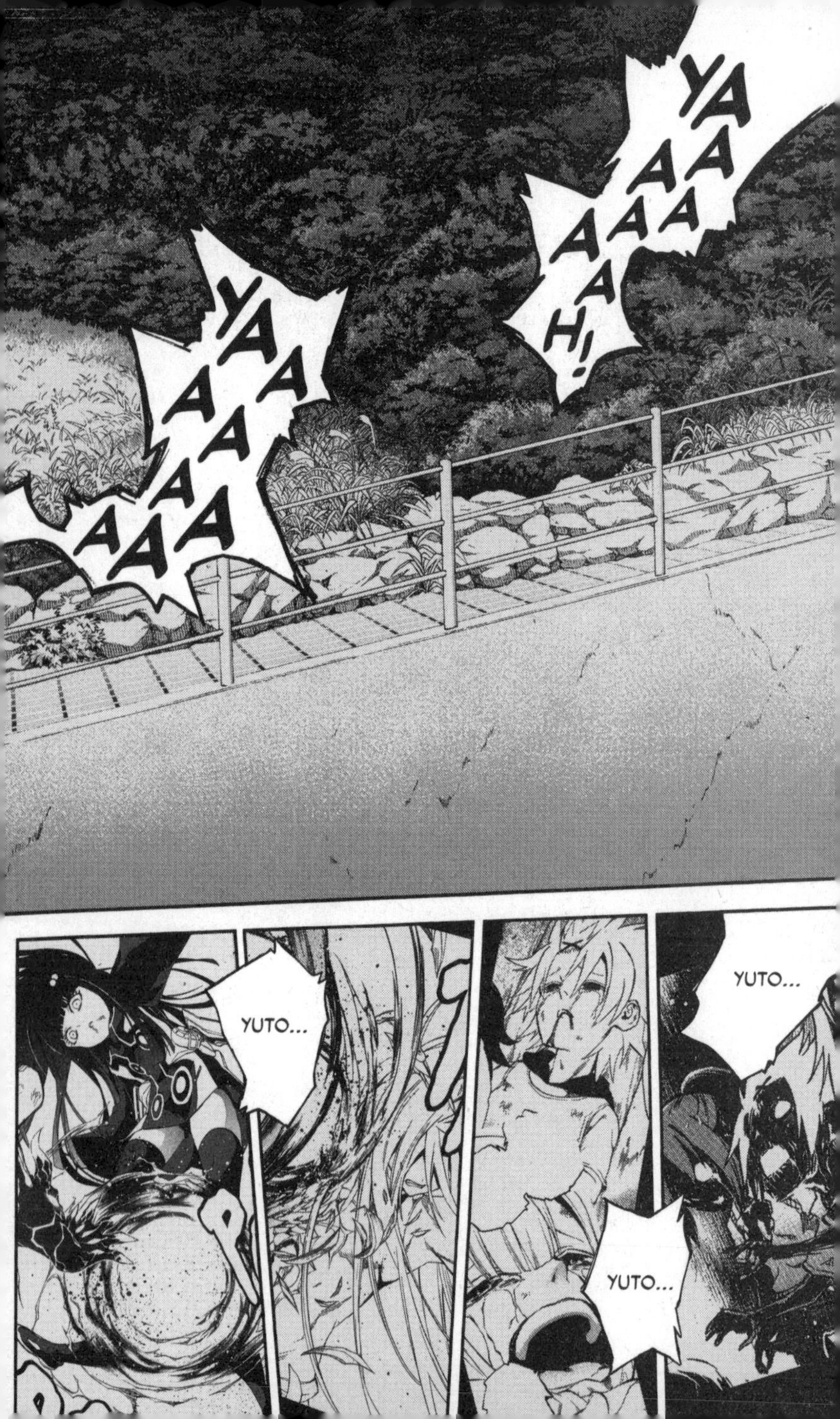
YAAAAAAAH!
YAAAAAAAAA
YUTO...
YUTO...
YUTO...

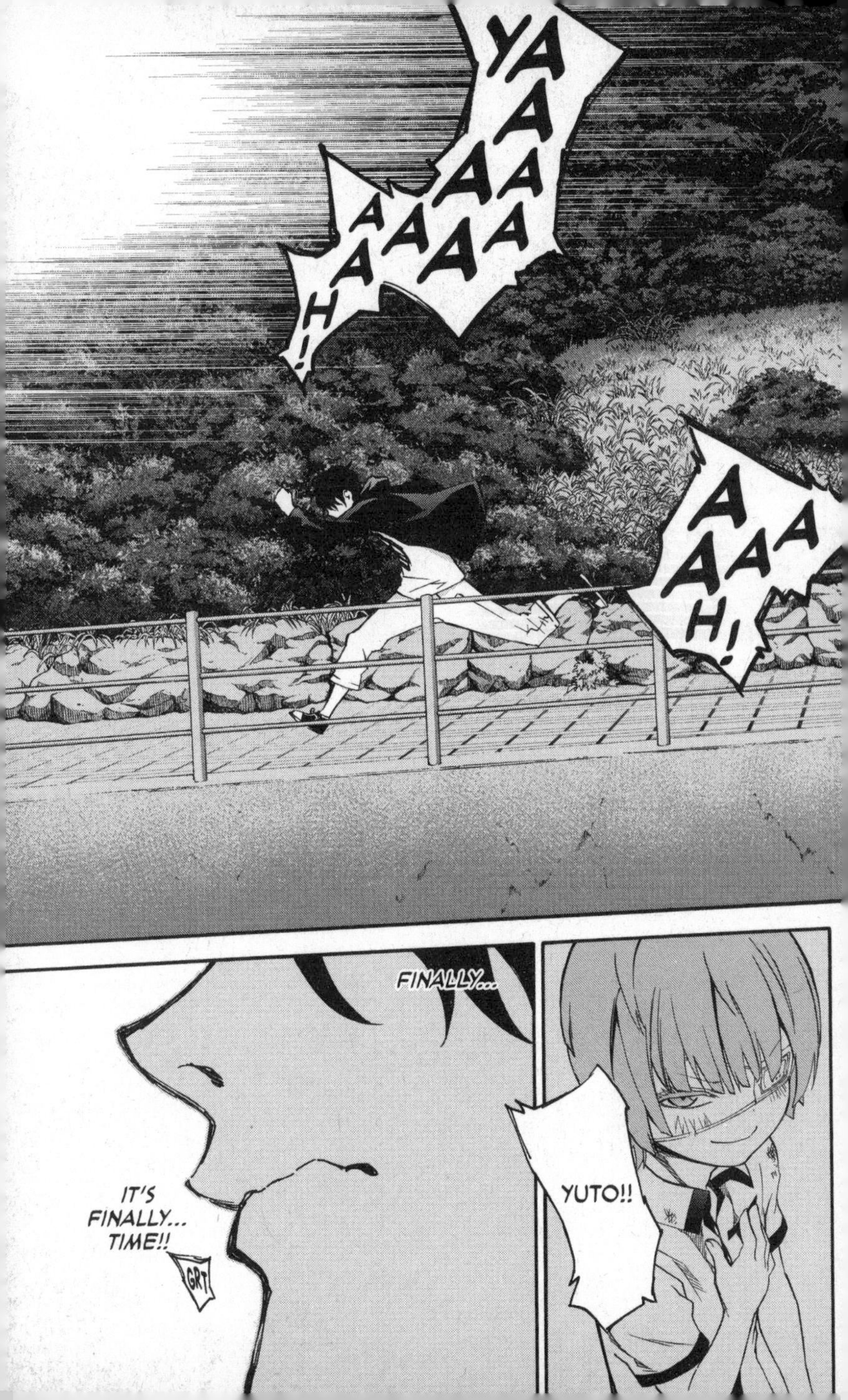

YAAAAAAAAAH!
AAAAH!
YUTO!!
FINALLY...
IT'S FINALLY... TIME!!
GRT

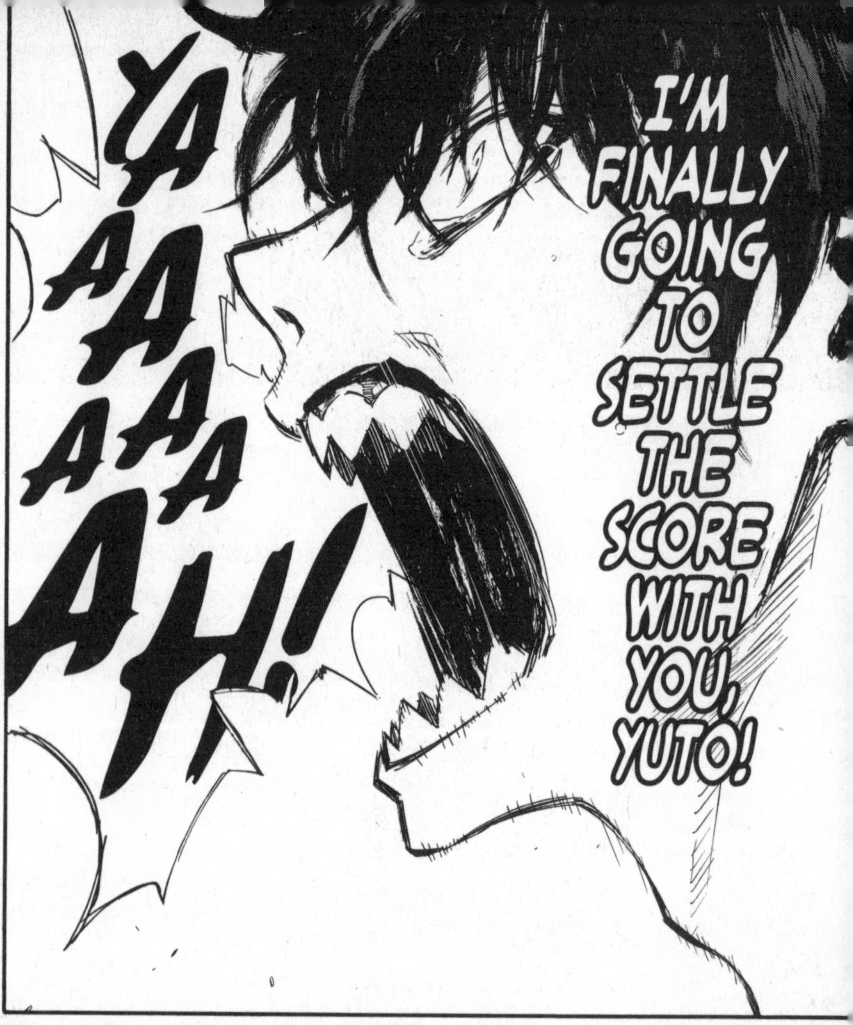
I'M FINALLY GOING TO SETTLE THE SCORE WITH YOU, YUTO!
YAAAAAAAH!
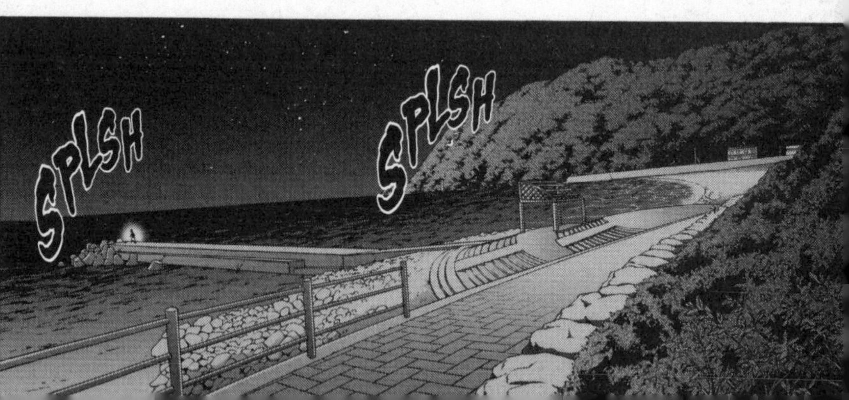
SPLSH
SPLSH

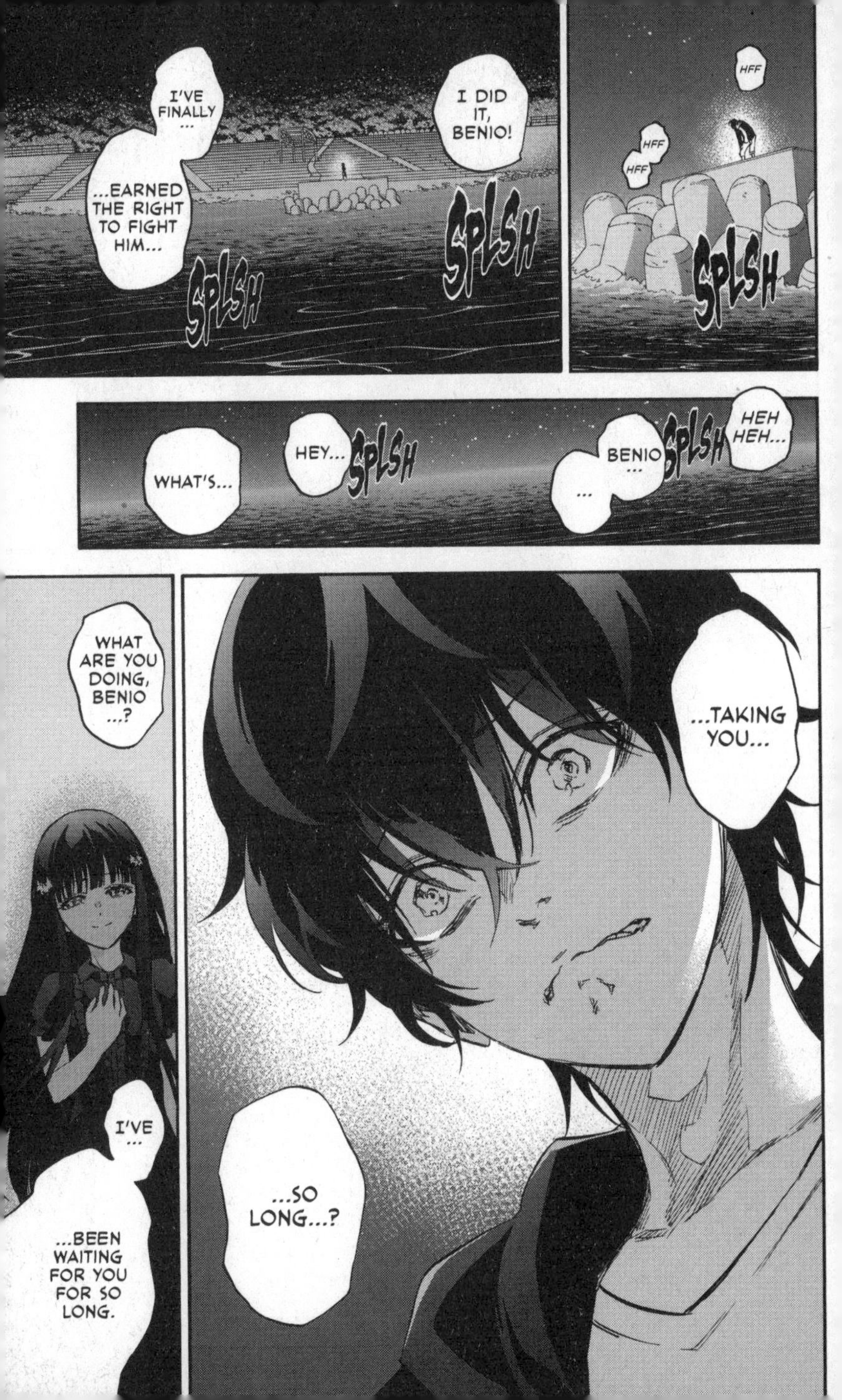
HFF
HFF
HFF
SPLSH
I DID IT, BENIO!
SPLSH
I'VE FINALLY...
...EARNED THE RIGHT TO FIGHT HIM...
SPLSH
HEH HEH...
SPLSH
BENIO...
...
HEY...
SPLSH
WHAT'S...
...TAKING YOU...
...SO LONG...?
WHAT ARE YOU DOING, BENIO...?
I'VE...
...BEEN WAITING FOR YOU FOR SO LONG.

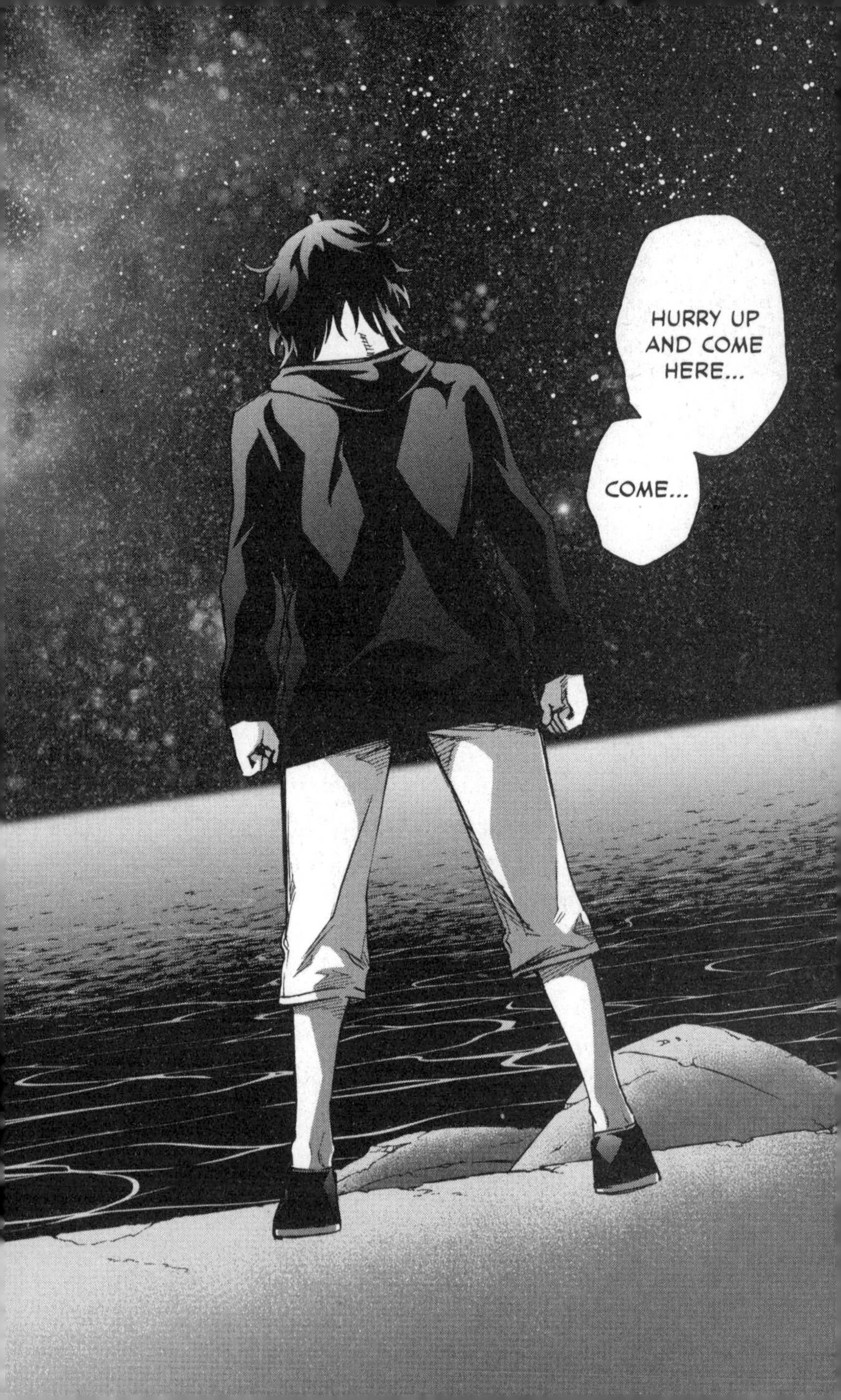
HURRY UP AND COME HERE...
COME...

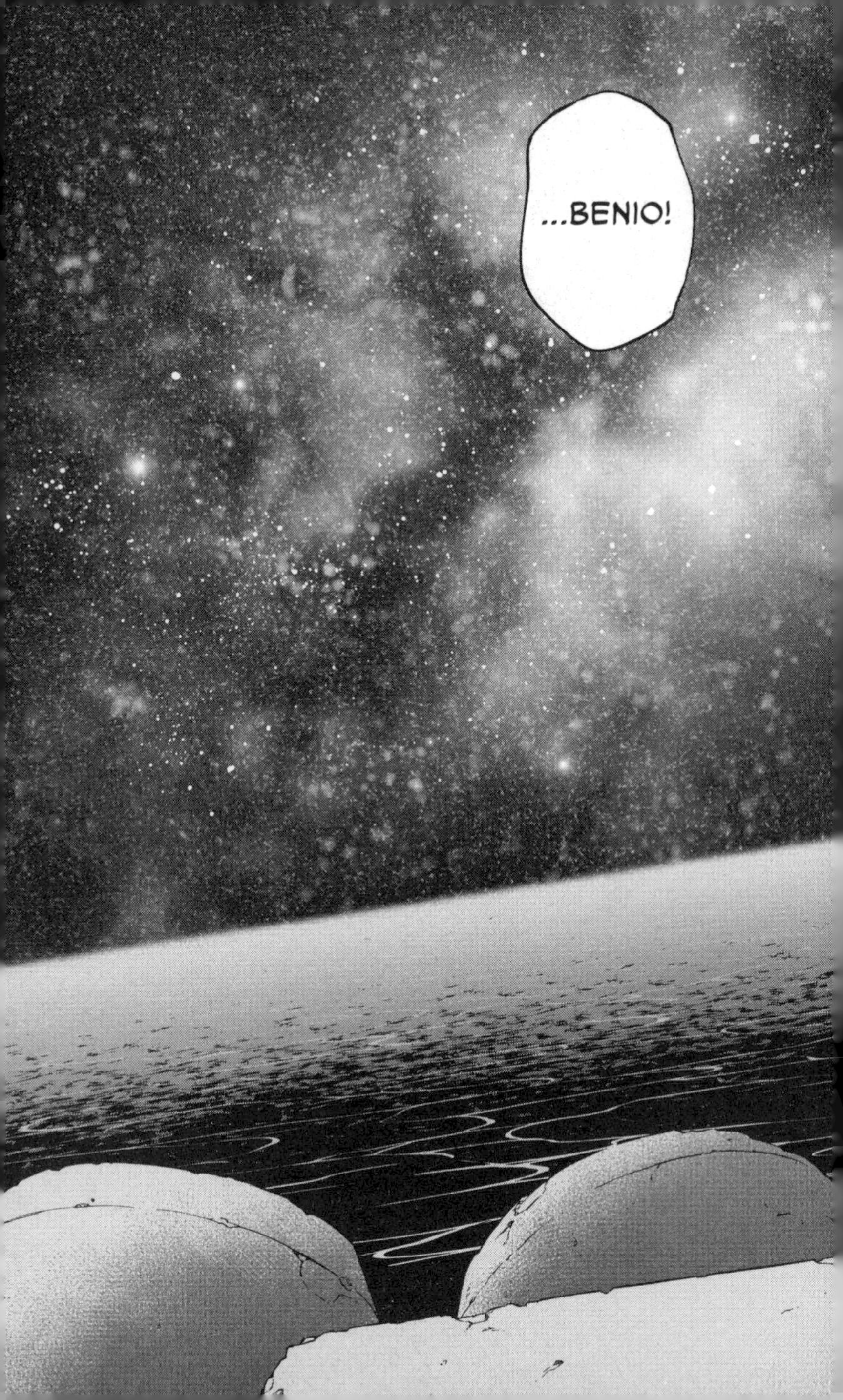
...BENIO!

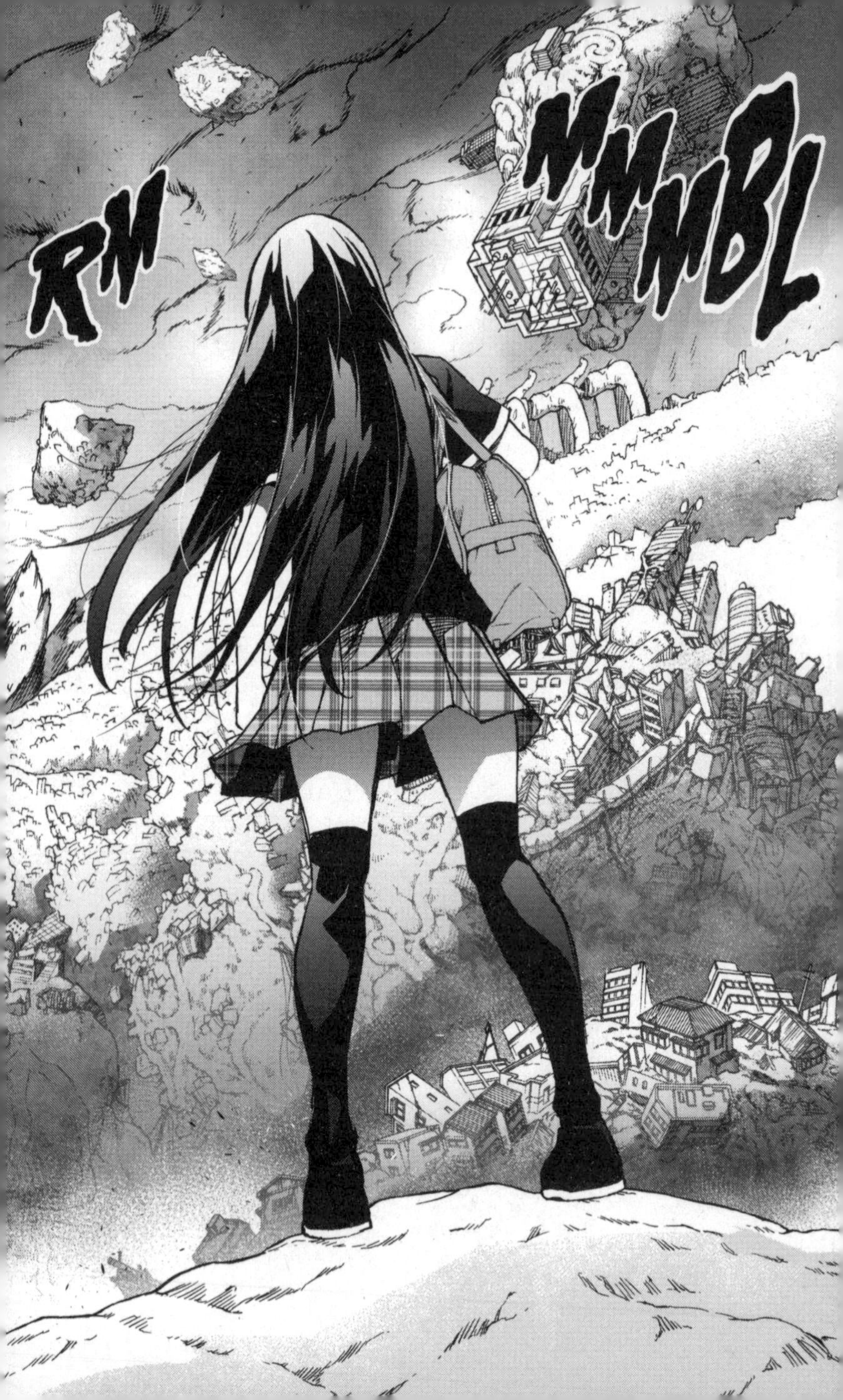
RM
MMMBL

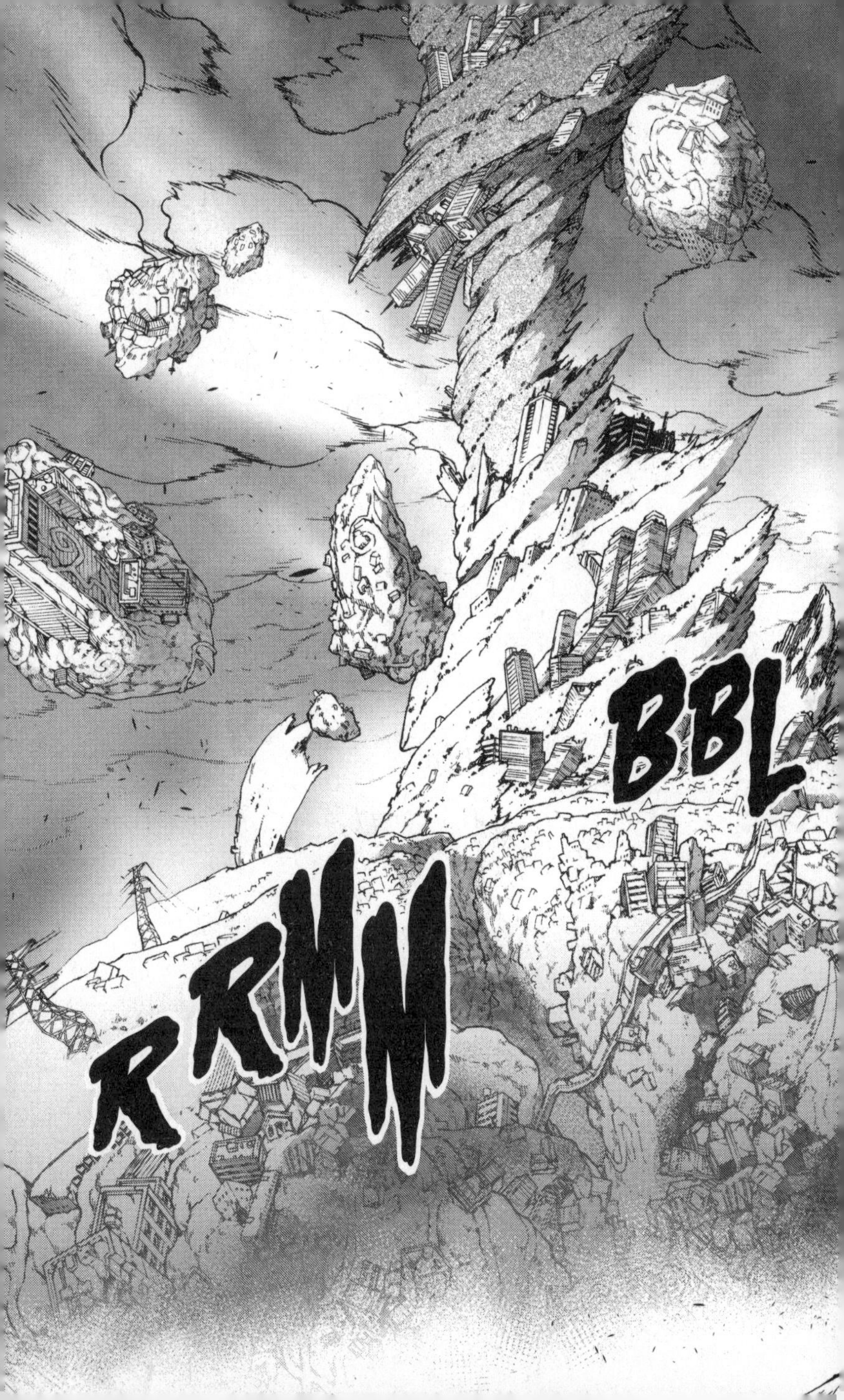
RRMMBBL

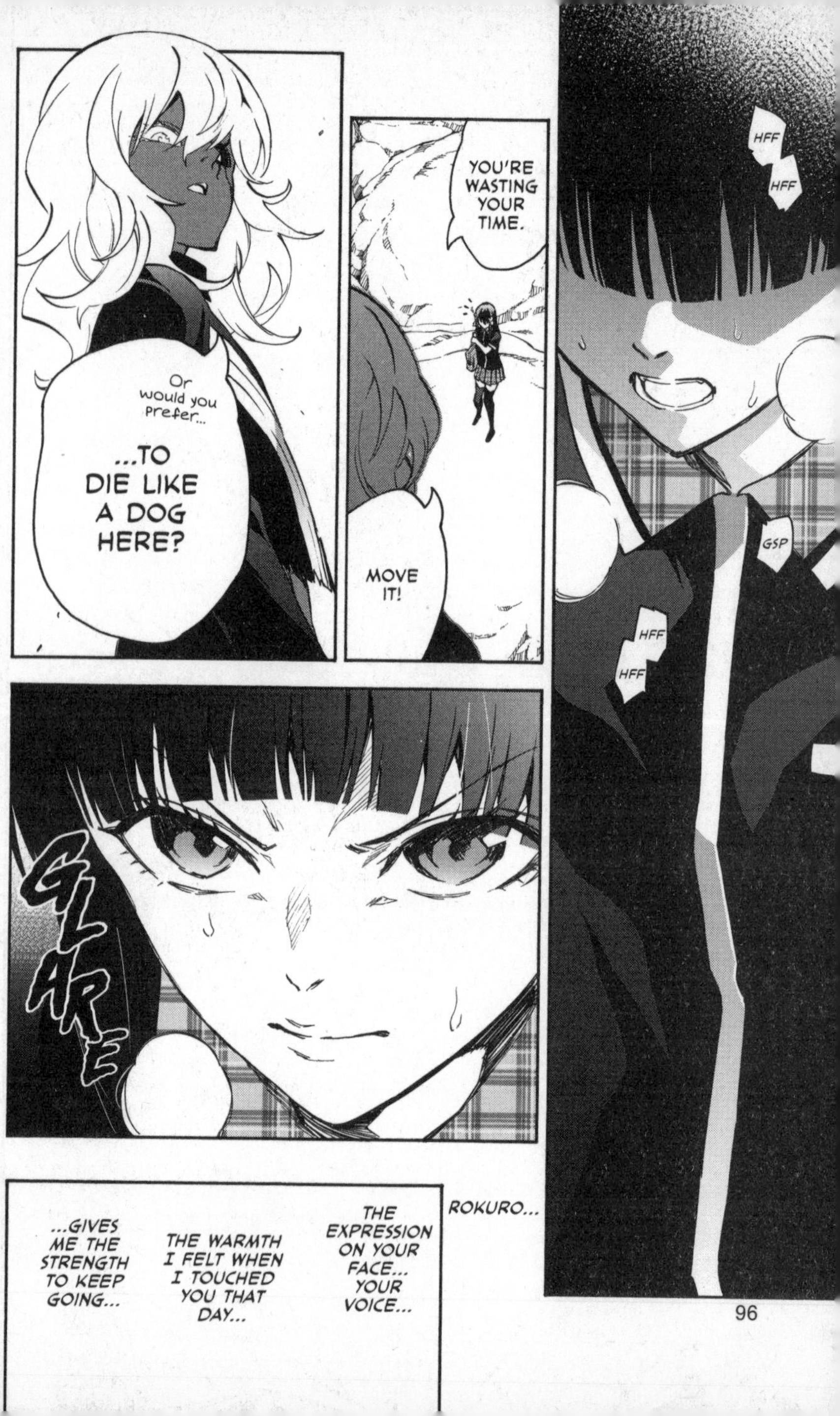
HFF
HFF
GSP
HFF
HFF
YOU'RE WASTING YOUR TIME.
MOVE IT!
Or would you prefer...
...TO DIE LIKE A DOG HERE?
GLARE
ROKURO...
THE EXPRESSION ON YOUR FACE... YOUR VOICE...
THE WARMTH I FELT WHEN I TOUCHED YOU THAT DAY...
...GIVES ME THE STRENGTH TO KEEP GOING...

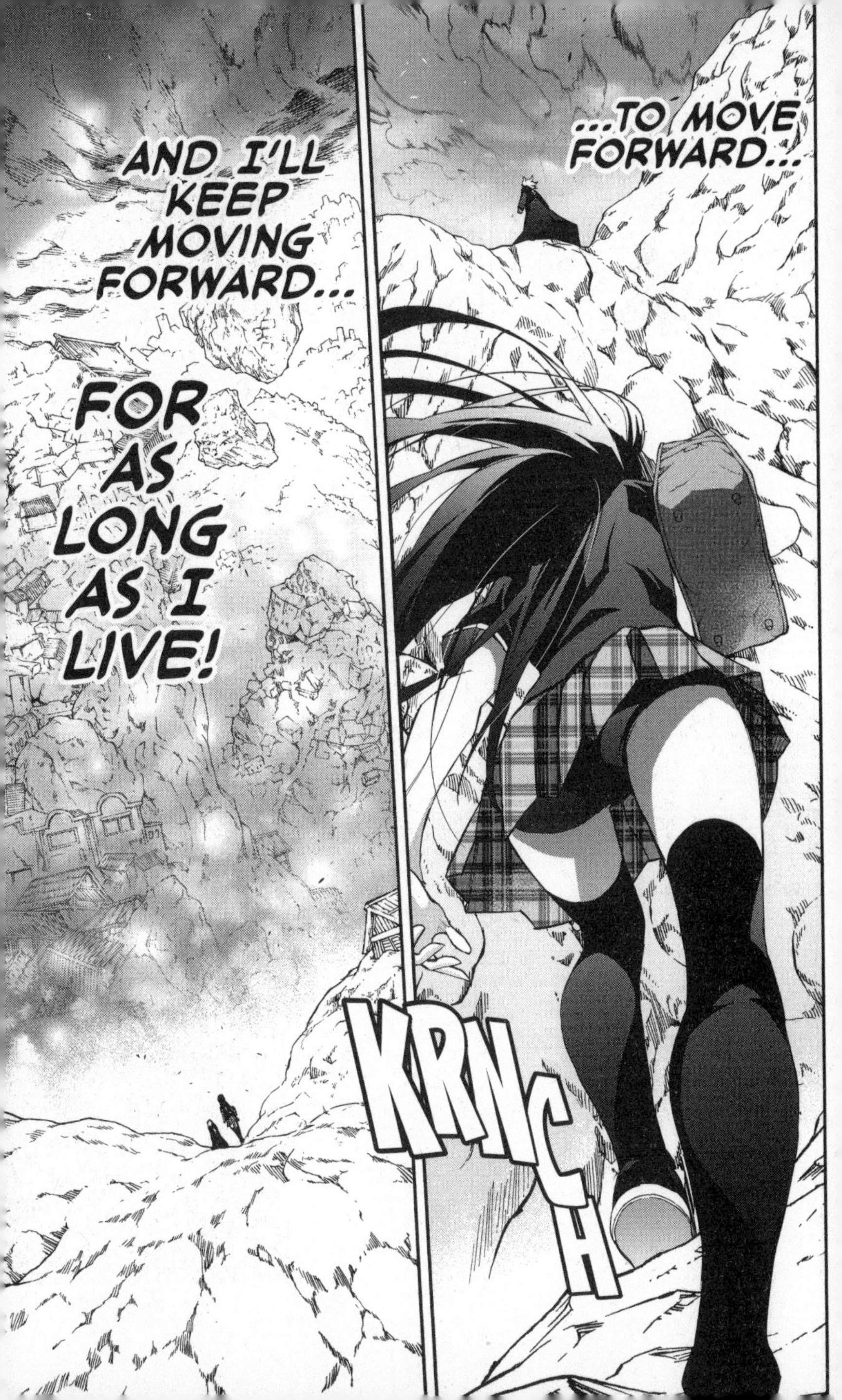
...TO MOVE FORWARD...
KRNCH
AND I'LL KEEP MOVING FORWARD...
FOR AS LONG AS I LIVE!

Twin Star Exorcists
ONMYOJI

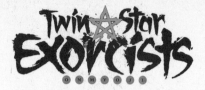

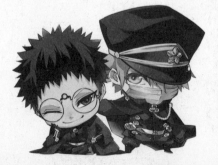

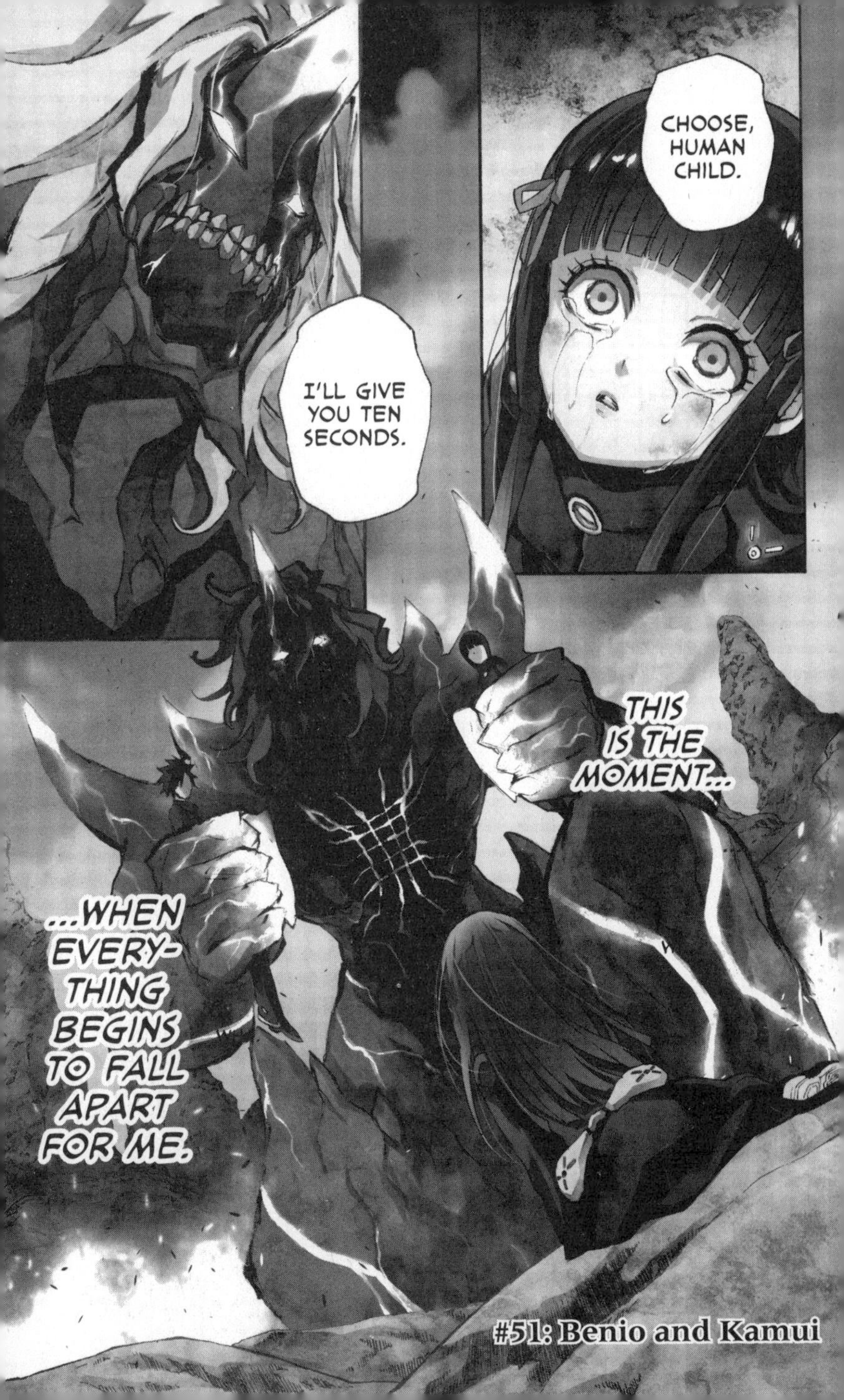
CHOOSE, HUMAN CHILD.
I'LL GIVE YOU TEN SECONDS.
THIS IS THE MOMENT...
...WHEN EVERYTHING BEGINS TO FALL APART FOR ME.

#51: Benio and Kamui

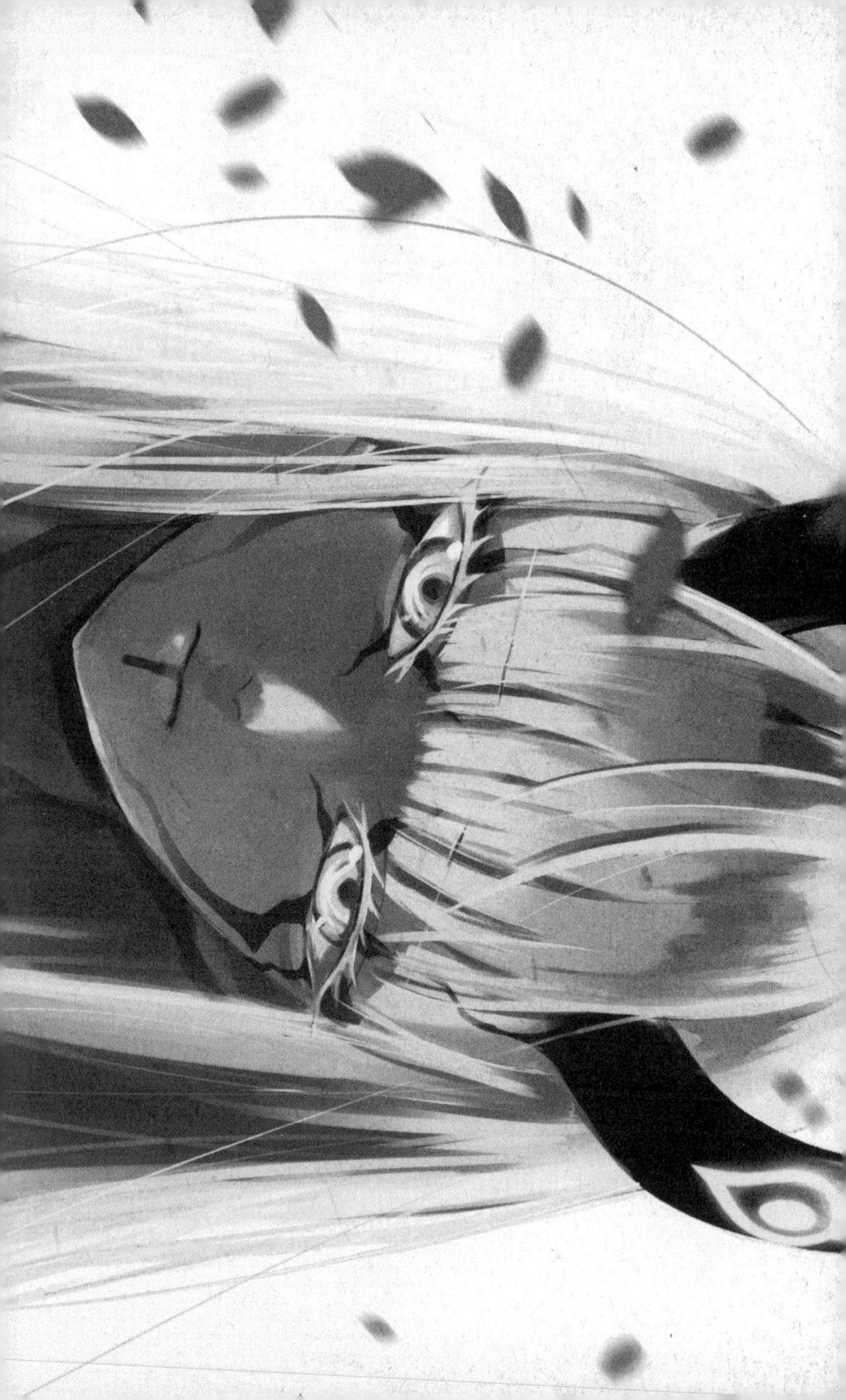

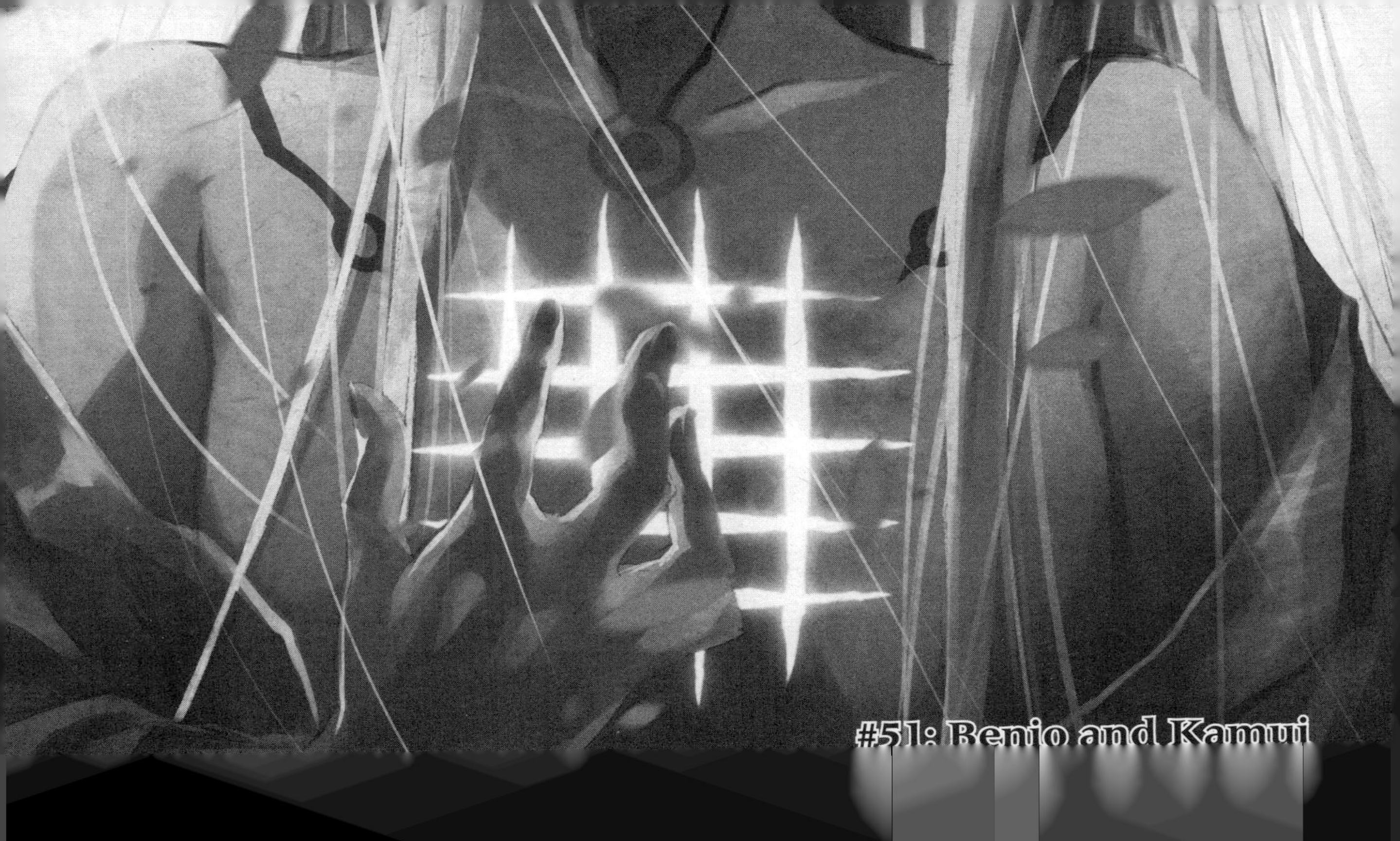

#51: Benio and Kamui

Twin Star Exorcists

O N M Y O J I

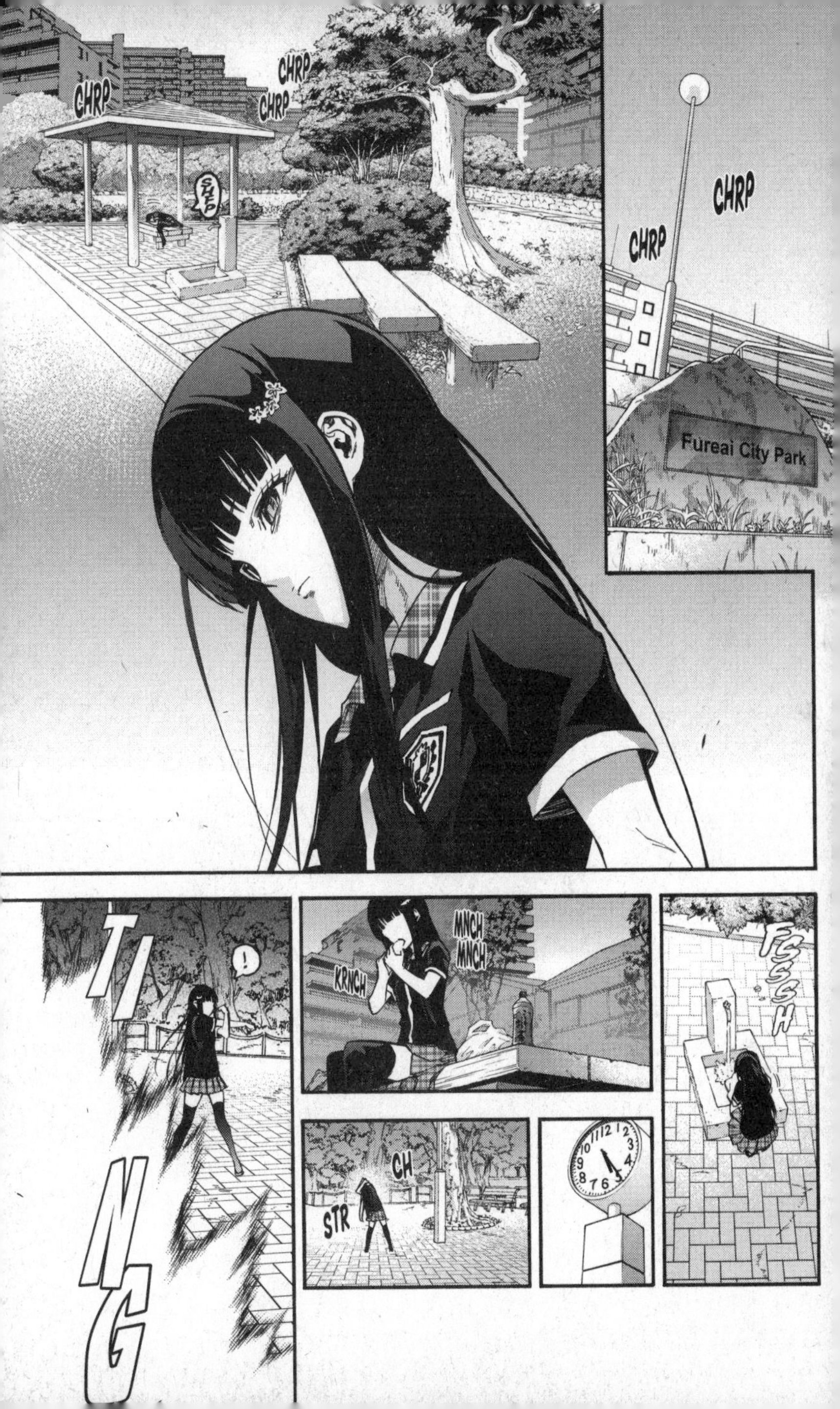
CHRP
CHRP
Fureai City Park
CHRP
CHRP
CHRP
SHFP
FSSH
MNCH MNCH
KRNCH
STR
CH
!
TI
NG

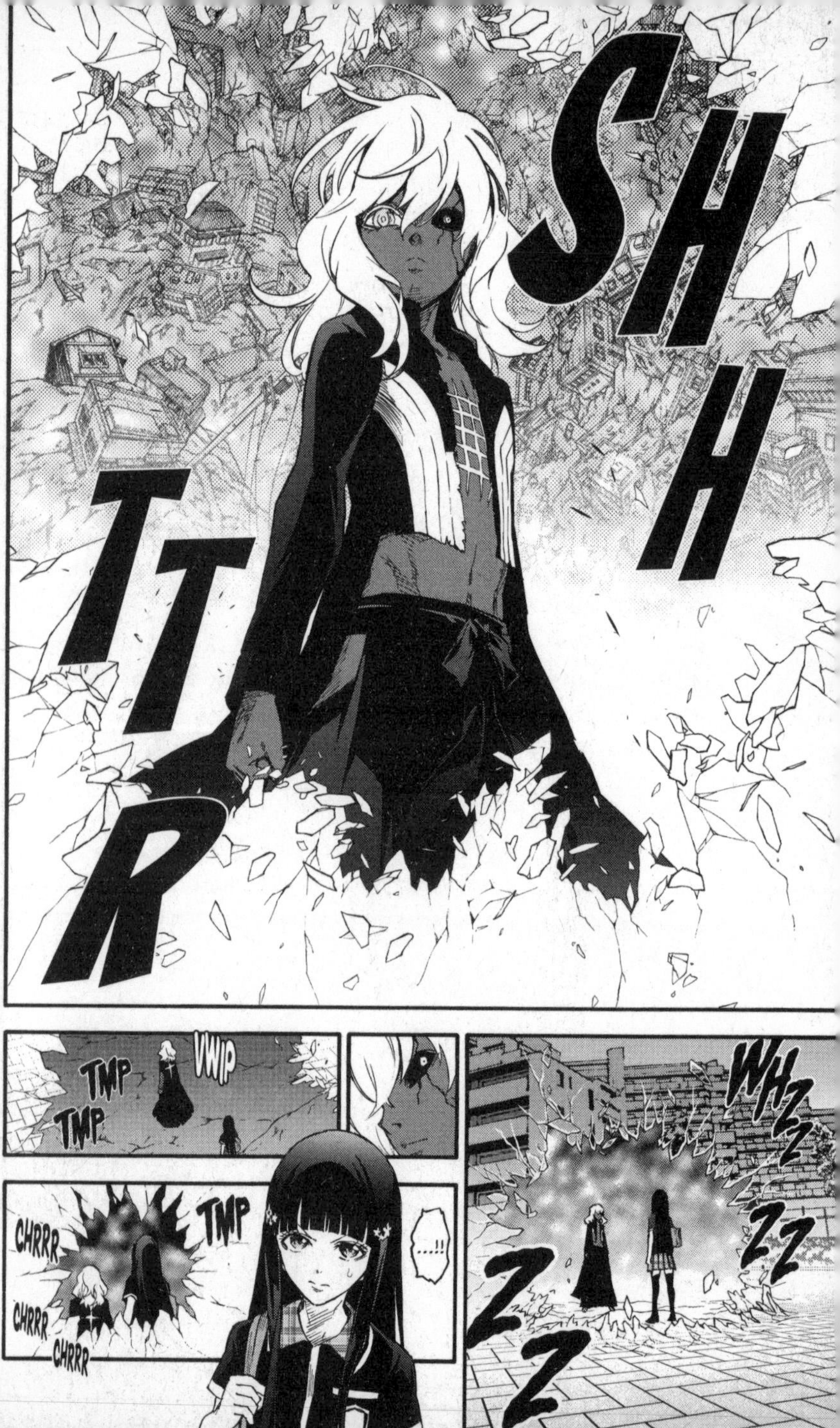

SHHH
TTR
WHZZ
ZZ
ZZZ
VWIP
TMP
TMP
...!!
TMP
CHRRR
CHRRR
CHRRR

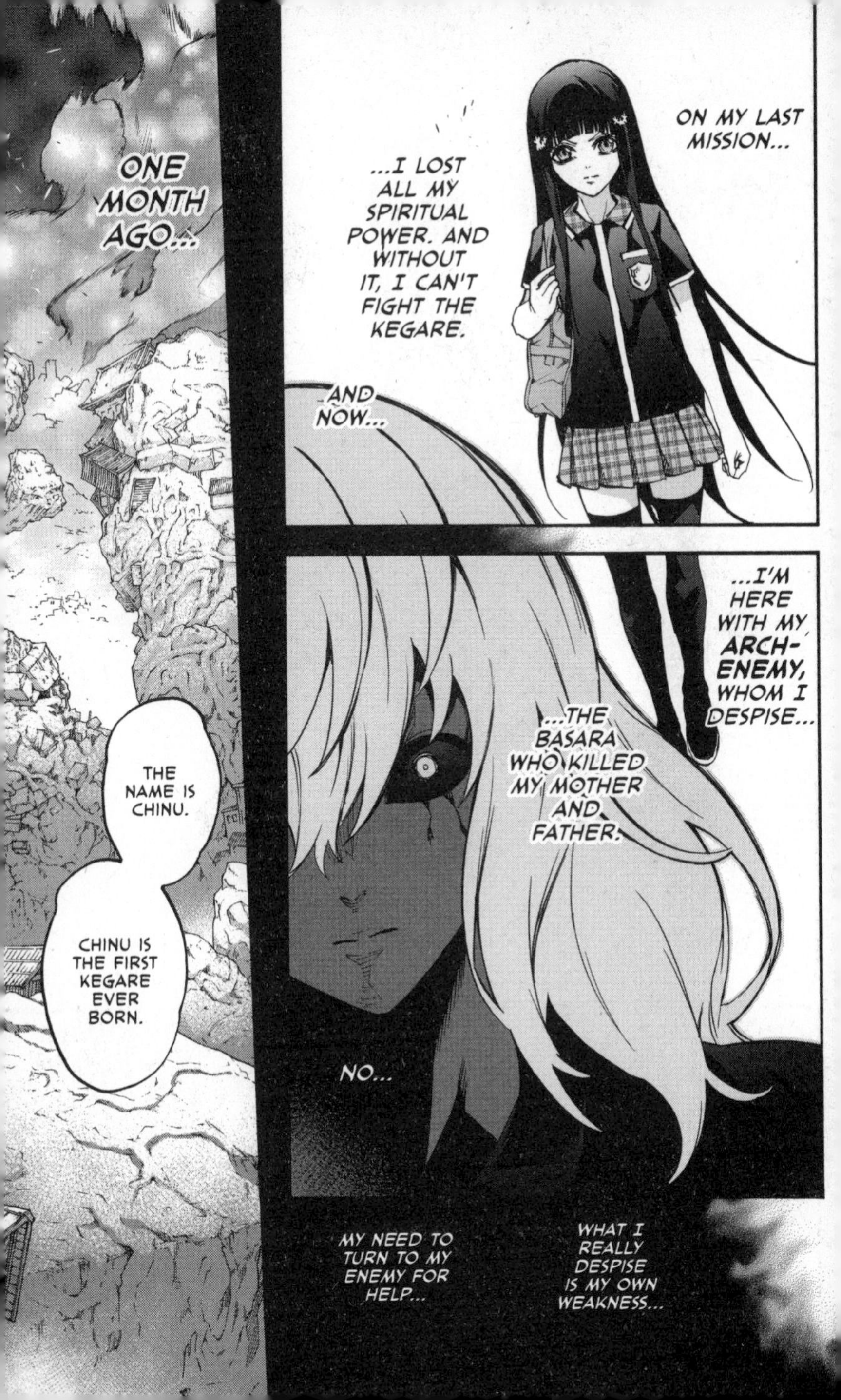

ON MY LAST MISSION...
...I LOST ALL MY SPIRITUAL POWER. AND WITHOUT IT, I CAN'T FIGHT THE KEGARE.
AND NOW...
...I'M HERE WITH MY ARCH-ENEMY, WHOM I DESPISE...
...THE BASARA WHO KILLED MY MOTHER AND FATHER.
NO...
WHAT I REALLY DESPISE IS MY OWN WEAKNESS...
MY NEED TO TURN TO MY ENEMY FOR HELP...
ONE MONTH AGO...
THE NAME IS CHINU.
CHINU IS THE FIRST KEGARE EVER BORN.

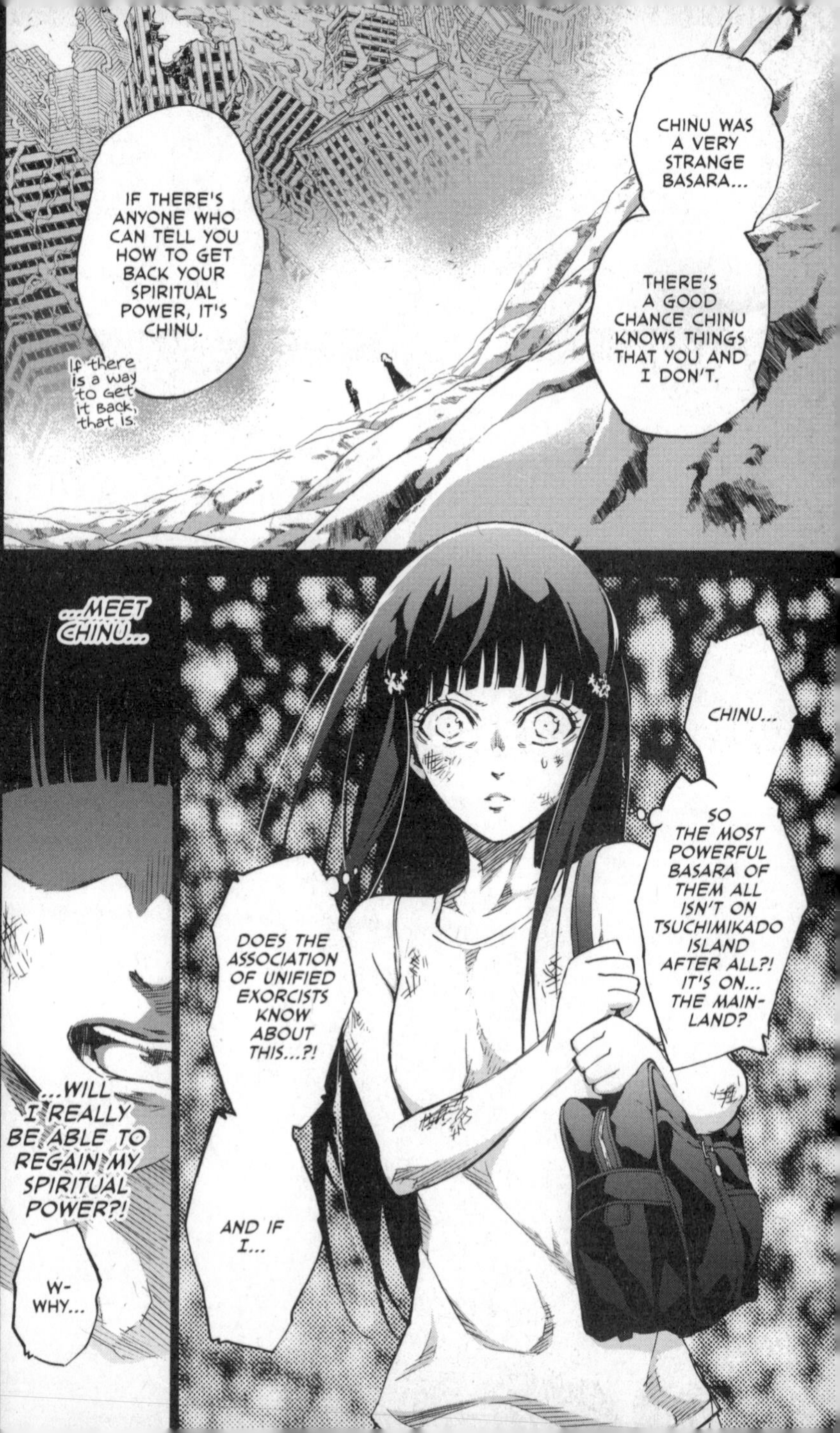

CHINU WAS A VERY STRANGE BASARA...
THERE'S A GOOD CHANCE CHINU KNOWS THINGS THAT YOU AND I DON'T.
IF THERE'S ANYONE WHO CAN TELL YOU HOW TO GET BACK YOUR SPIRITUAL POWER, IT'S CHINU.
If there is a way to get it back, that is.
CHINU...
SO THE MOST POWERFUL BASARA OF THEM ALL ISN'T ON TSUCHIMIKADO ISLAND AFTER ALL?! IT'S ON... THE MAIN-LAND?
DOES THE ASSOCIATION OF UNIFIED EXORCISTS KNOW ABOUT THIS...?!
AND IF I...
...MEET CHINU...
...WILL I REALLY BE ABLE TO REGAIN MY SPIRITUAL POWER?!
W-WHY...

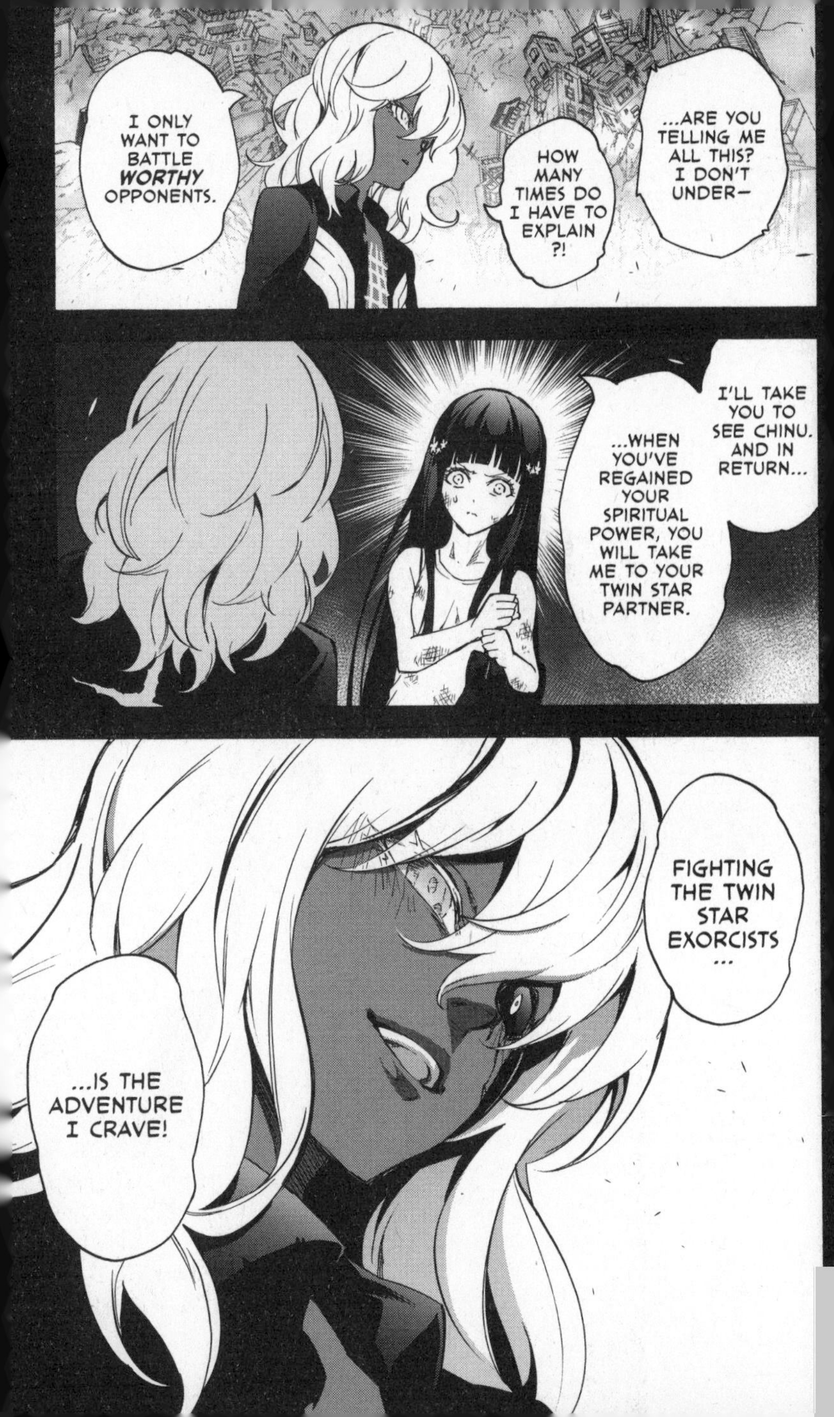
...ARE YOU TELLING ME ALL THIS? I DON'T UNDER—
HOW MANY TIMES DO I HAVE TO EXPLAIN ?!
I ONLY WANT TO BATTLE *WORTHY* OPPONENTS.
I'LL TAKE YOU TO SEE CHINU. AND IN RETURN...
...WHEN YOU'VE REGAINED YOUR SPIRITUAL POWER, YOU WILL TAKE ME TO YOUR TWIN STAR PARTNER.
FIGHTING THE TWIN STAR EXORCISTS ...
...IS THE ADVENTURE I CRAVE!

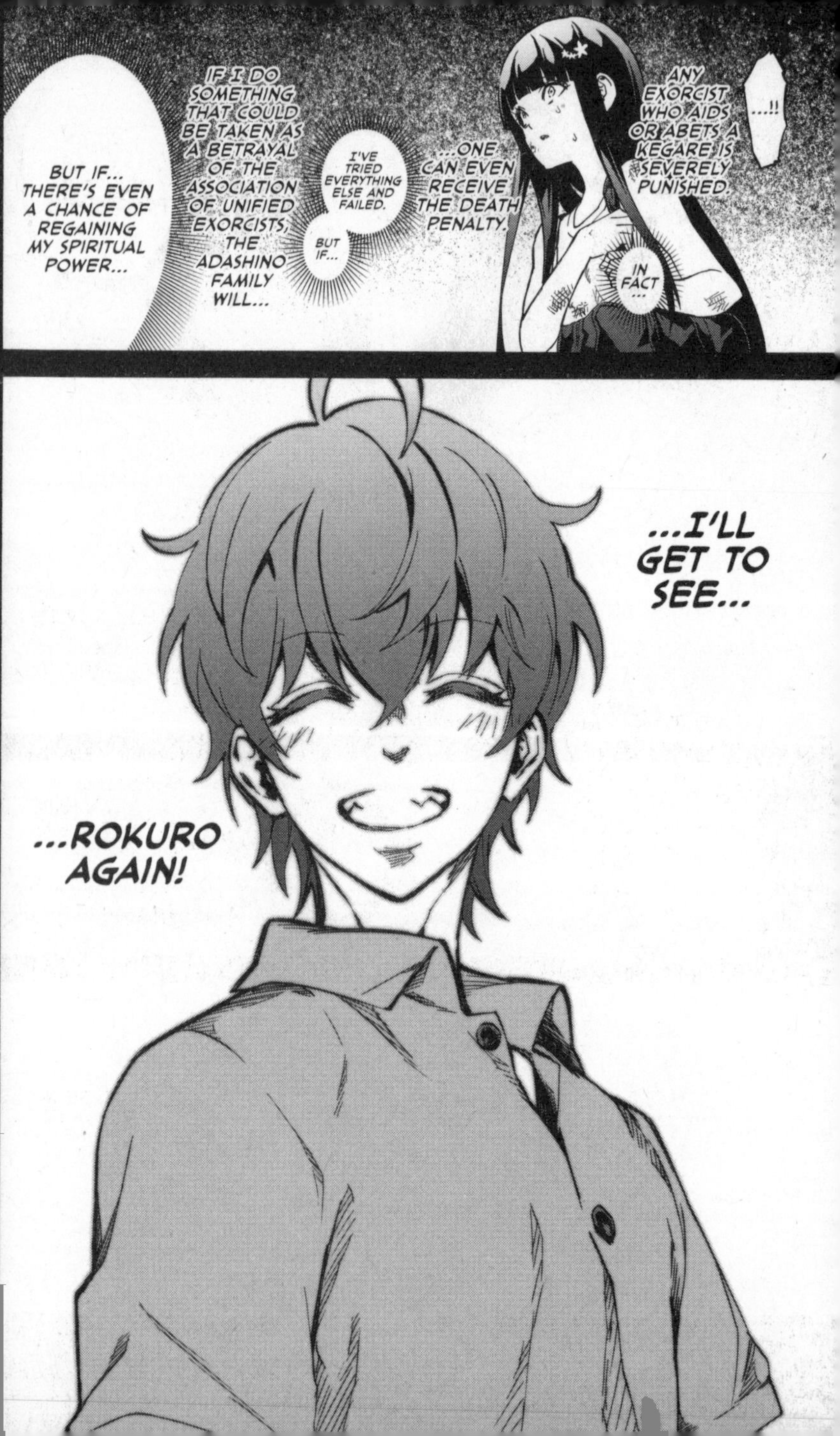
...!!
ANY EXORCIST WHO AIDS OR ABETS A KEGARE IS SEVERELY PUNISHED.
IN FACT...
...ONE CAN EVEN RECEIVE THE DEATH PENALTY.
I'VE TRIED EVERYTHING ELSE AND FAILED.
BUT IF...
IF I DO SOMETHING THAT COULD BE TAKEN AS A BETRAYAL OF THE ASSOCIATION OF UNIFIED EXORCISTS, THE ADASHINO FAMILY WILL...
BUT IF... THERE'S EVEN A CHANCE OF REGAINING MY SPIRITUAL POWER...
...I'LL GET TO SEE...
...ROKURO AGAIN!

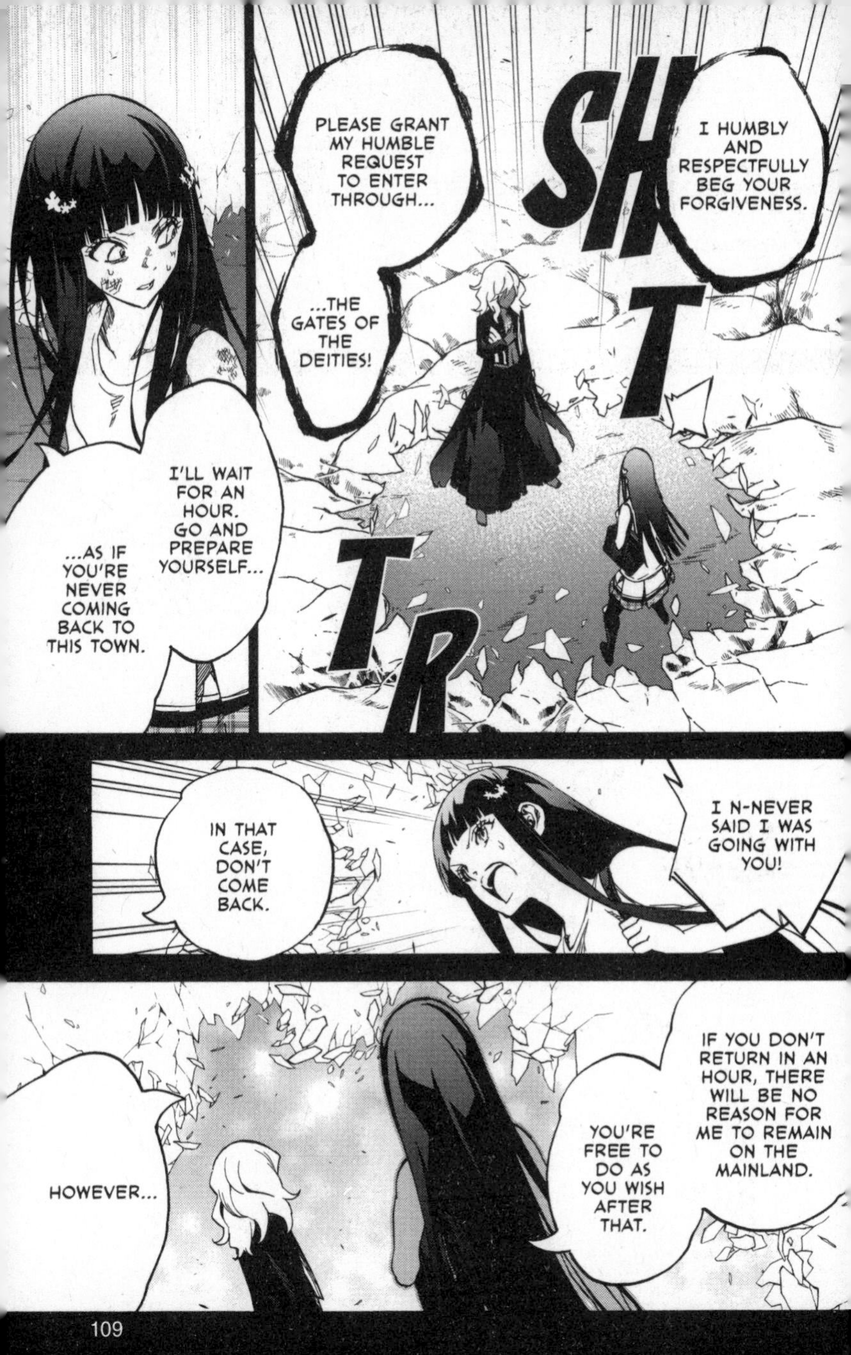
I HUMBLY AND RESPECTFULLY BEG YOUR FORGIVENESS.
PLEASE GRANT MY HUMBLE REQUEST TO ENTER THROUGH...
...THE GATES OF THE DEITIES!
SHTTR
I'LL WAIT FOR AN HOUR. GO AND PREPARE YOURSELF...
...AS IF YOU'RE NEVER COMING BACK TO THIS TOWN.
I N-NEVER SAID I WAS GOING WITH YOU!
IN THAT CASE, DON'T COME BACK.
IF YOU DON'T RETURN IN AN HOUR, THERE WILL BE NO REASON FOR ME TO REMAIN ON THE MAINLAND.
YOU'RE FREE TO DO AS YOU WISH AFTER THAT.
HOWEVER...

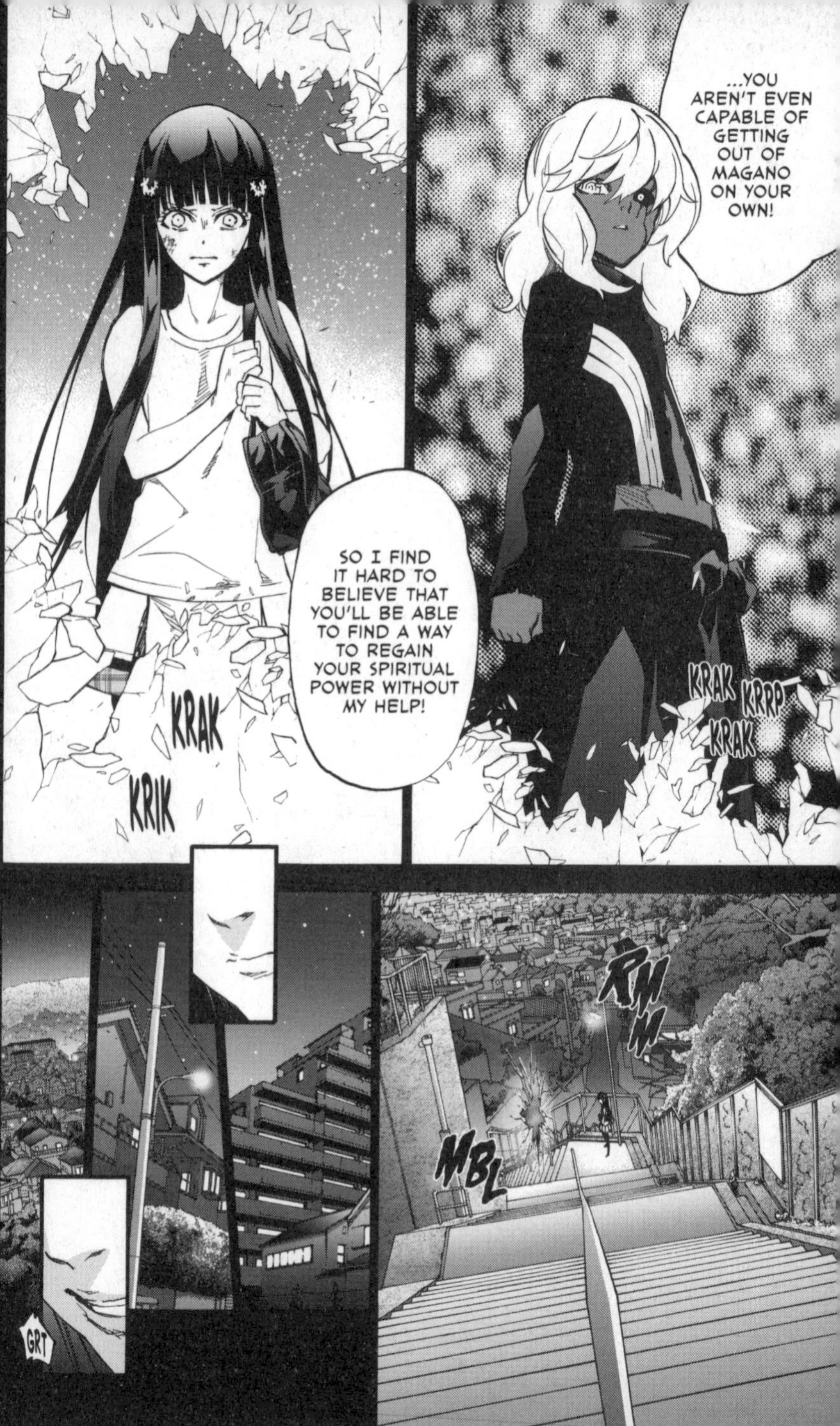
...YOU AREN'T EVEN CAPABLE OF GETTING OUT OF MAGANO ON YOUR OWN!
KRAK KRRP KRAK
SO I FIND IT HARD TO BELIEVE THAT YOU'LL BE ABLE TO FIND A WAY TO REGAIN YOUR SPIRITUAL POWER WITHOUT MY HELP!
KRAK
KRIK
RMM
MBL
GRT

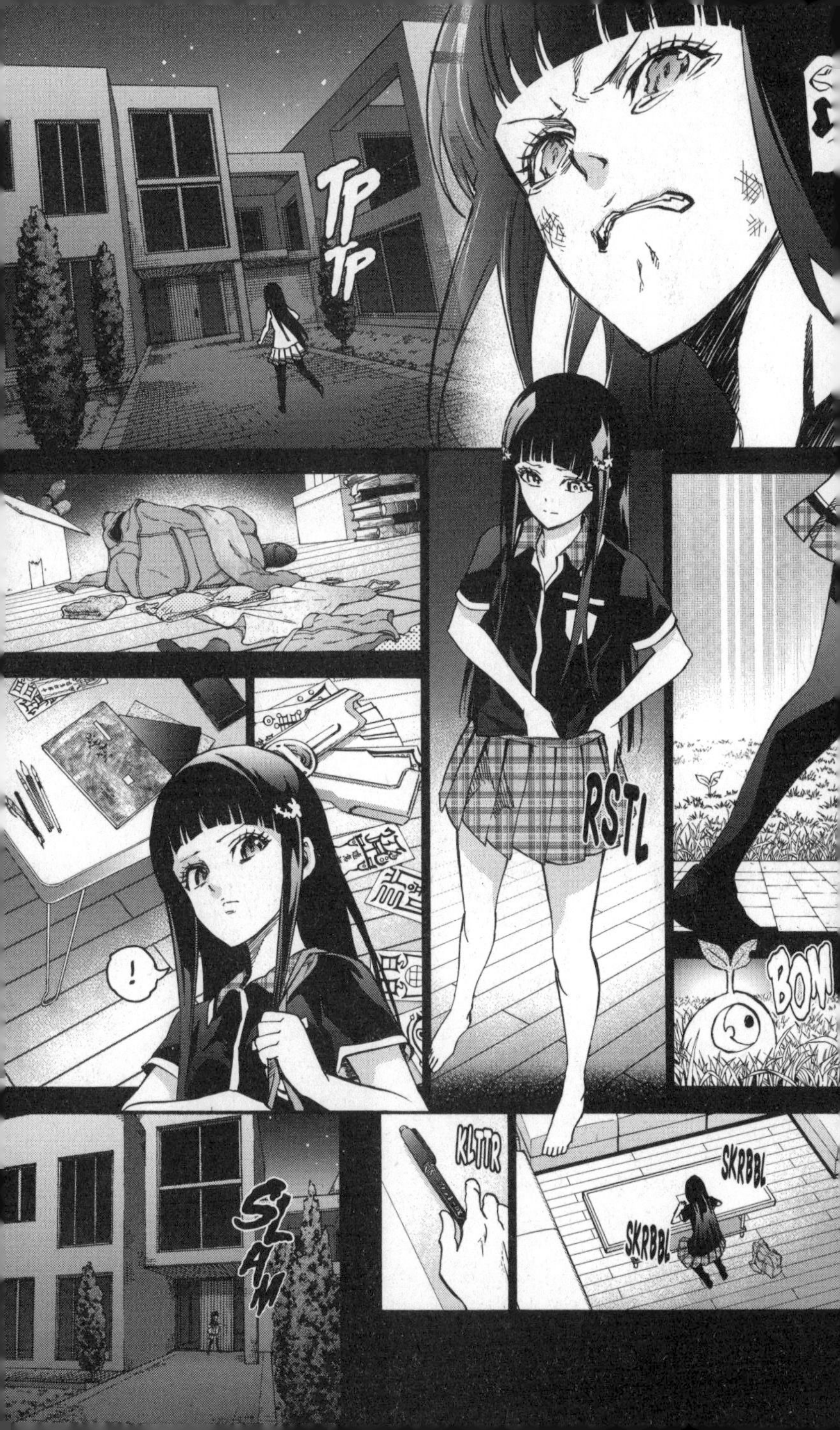
TP
TP
BOM
RSTL
!
SKRBBL
SKRBBL
KLTTR
SLAM

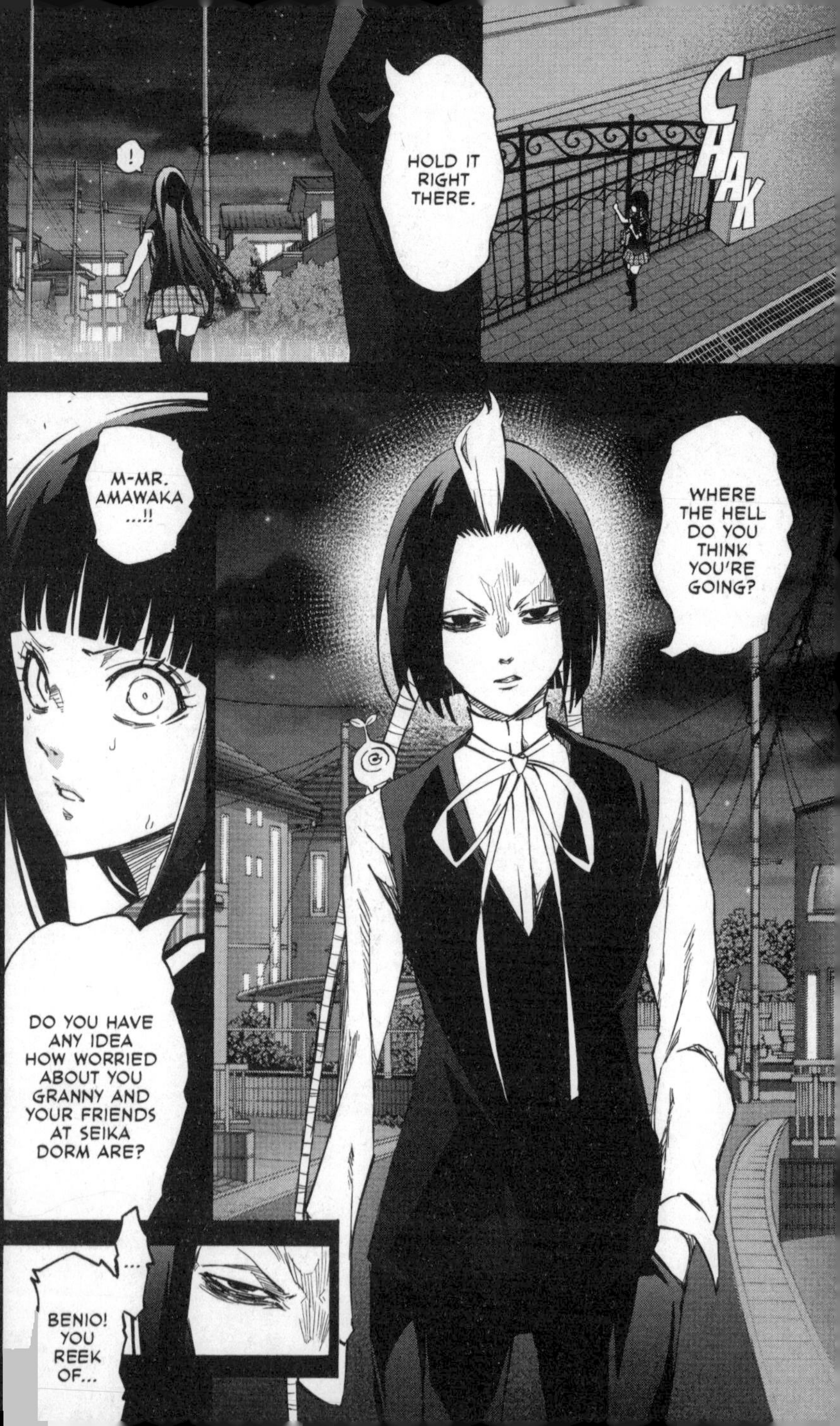
CHAK
HOLD IT RIGHT THERE.
!
WHERE THE HELL DO YOU THINK YOU'RE GOING?
M-MR. AMAWAKA ...!!
DO YOU HAVE ANY IDEA HOW WORRIED ABOUT YOU GRANNY AND YOUR FRIENDS AT SEIKA DORM ARE?
...
BENIO! YOU REEK OF...

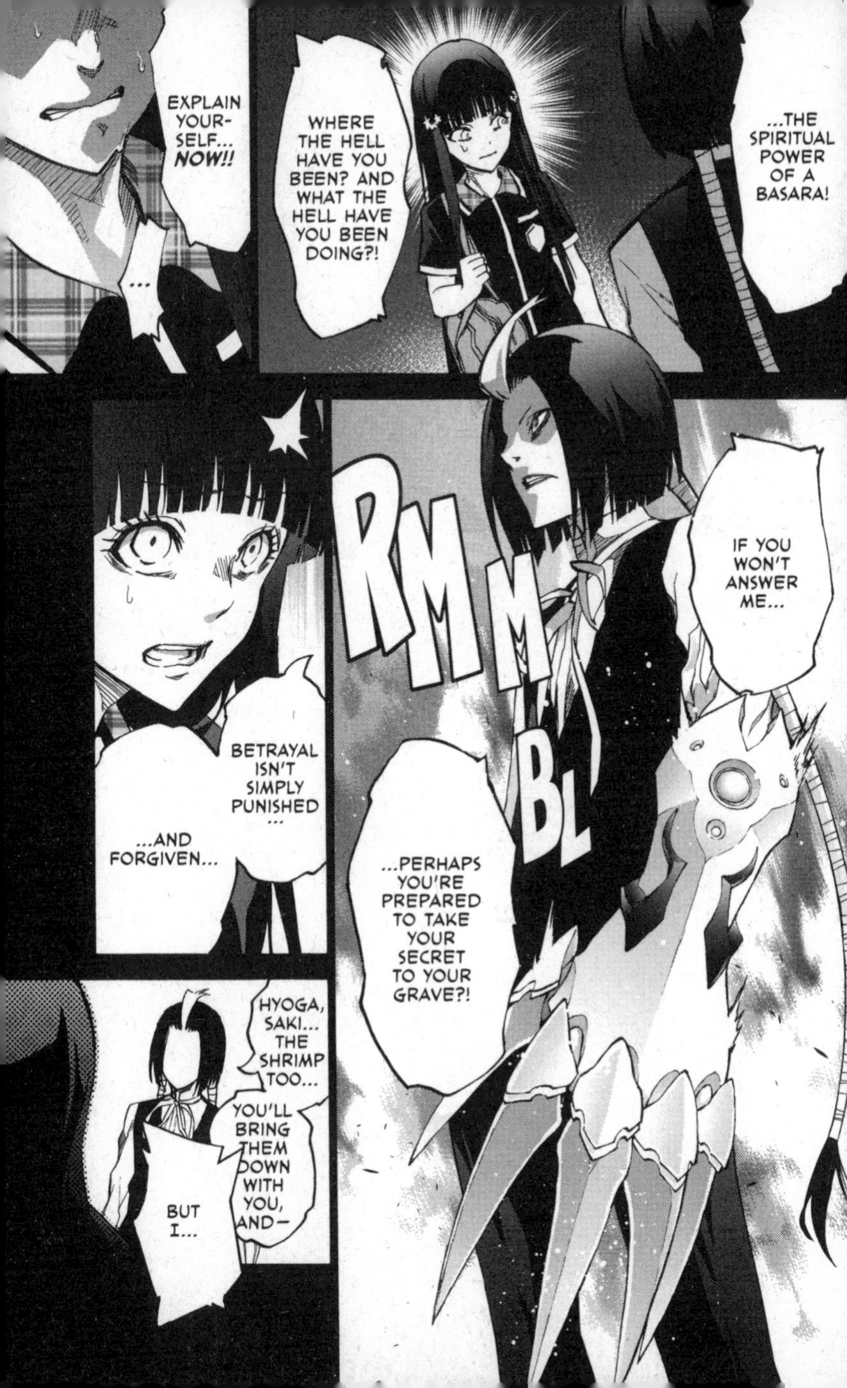
...THE SPIRITUAL POWER OF A BASARA!
WHERE THE HELL HAVE YOU BEEN? AND WHAT THE HELL HAVE YOU BEEN DOING?!
EXPLAIN YOURSELF... ***NOW!!***
...
IF YOU WON'T ANSWER ME...
RMMBL
...PERHAPS YOU'RE PREPARED TO TAKE YOUR SECRET TO YOUR GRAVE?!
BETRAYAL ISN'T SIMPLY PUNISHED...
...AND FORGIVEN...
HYOGA, SAKI... THE SHRIMP TOO...
YOU'LL BRING THEM DOWN WITH YOU, AND—
BUT I...

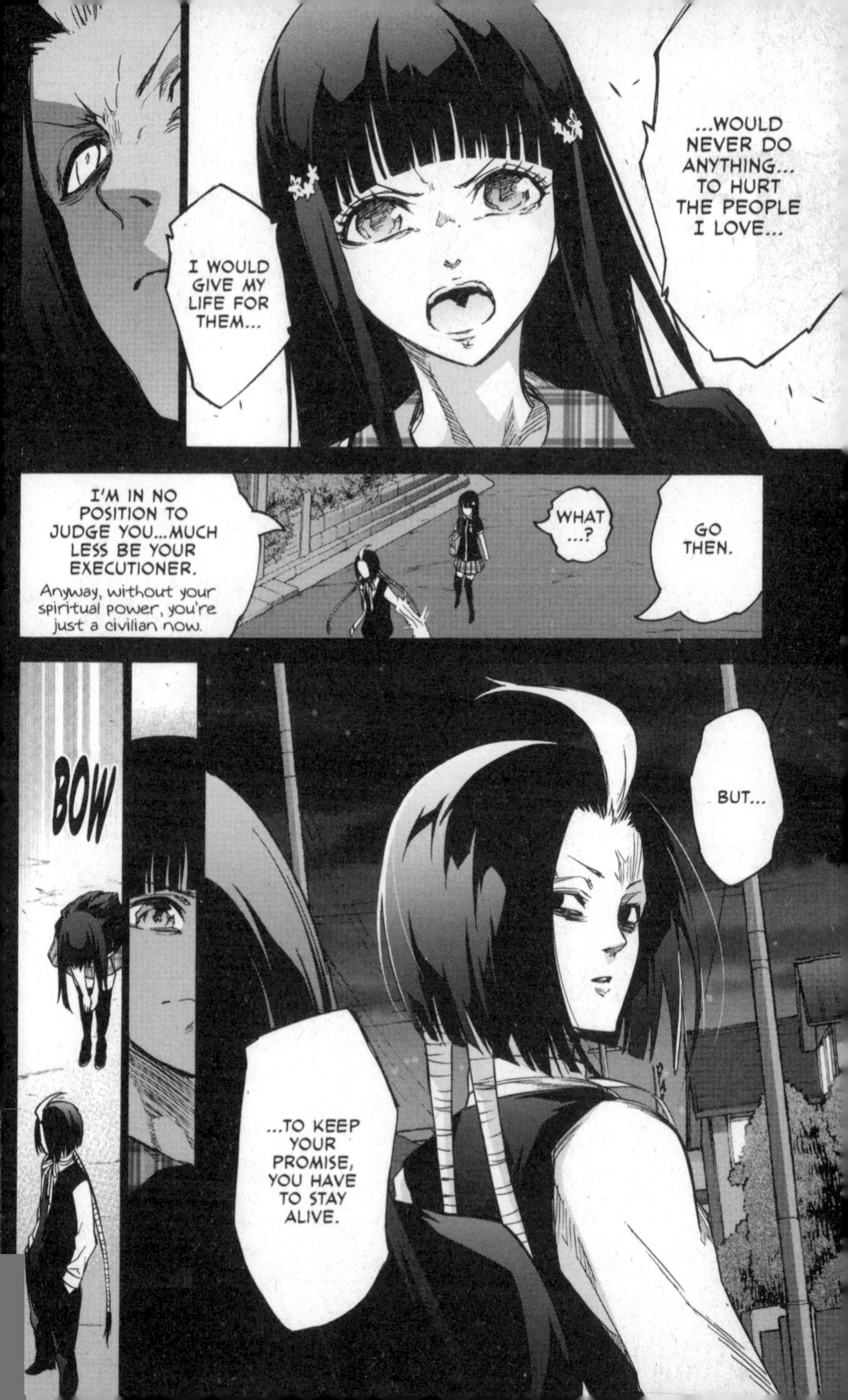
...WOULD NEVER DO ANYTHING... TO HURT THE PEOPLE I LOVE...
I WOULD GIVE MY LIFE FOR THEM...
GO THEN.
WHAT ...?
I'M IN NO POSITION TO JUDGE YOU...MUCH LESS BE YOUR EXECUTIONER.
Anyway, without your spiritual power, you're just a civilian now.
BUT...
...TO KEEP YOUR PROMISE, YOU HAVE TO STAY ALIVE.
BOW

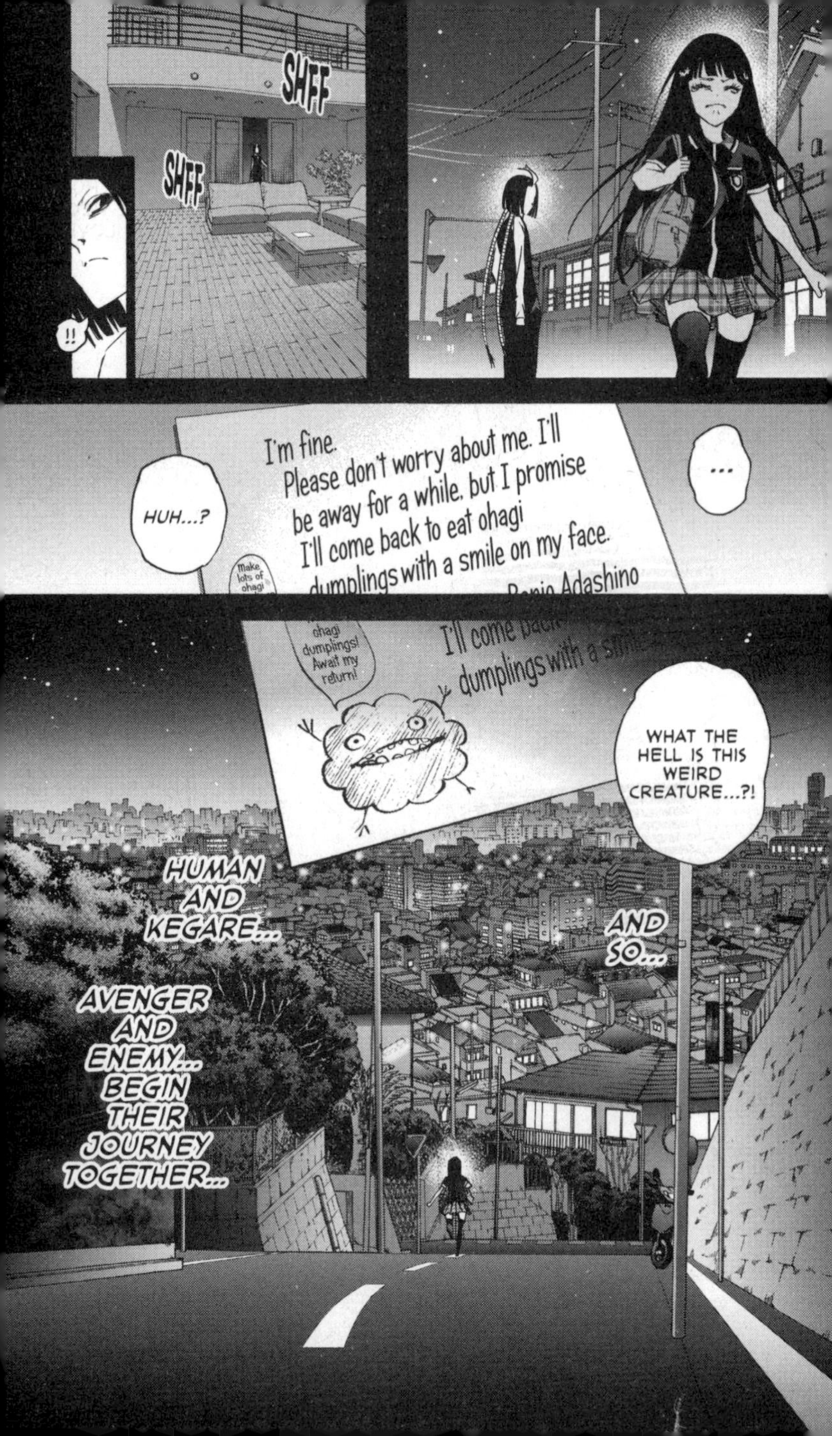
SHFF
SHFF
!!
...
I'm fine.
Please don't worry about me. I'll be away for a while, but I promise I'll come back to eat ohagi dumplings with a smile on my face.
Adashino
HUH...?
Make lots of ohagi
WHAT THE HELL IS THIS WEIRD CREATURE...?!
I'll come back
dumplings with a
ohagi dumplings! Await my return!
AND SO...
HUMAN AND KEGARE...
AVENGER AND ENEMY... BEGIN THEIR JOURNEY TOGETHER...

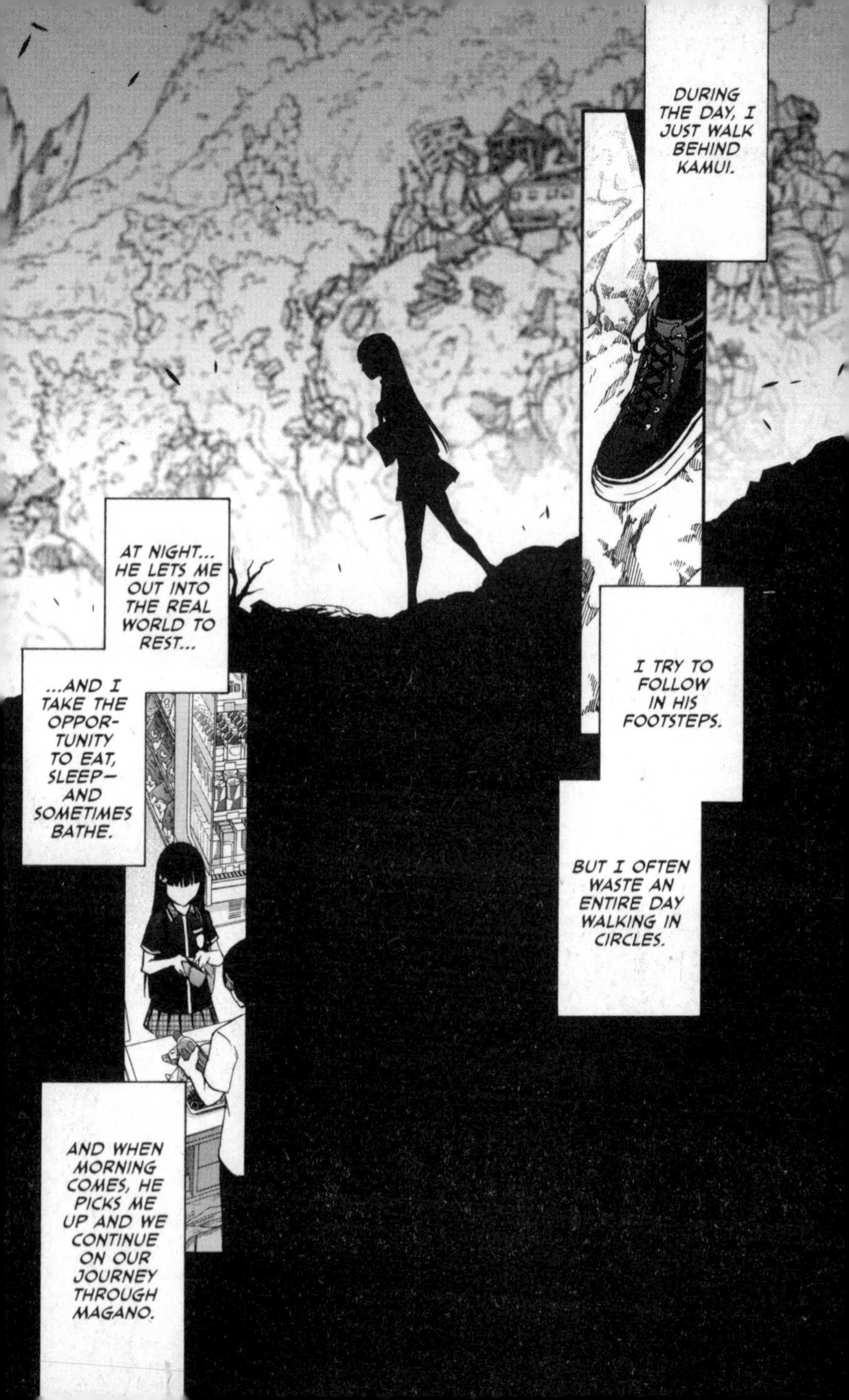
DURING THE DAY, I JUST WALK BEHIND KAMUI.
I TRY TO FOLLOW IN HIS FOOTSTEPS.
BUT I OFTEN WASTE AN ENTIRE DAY WALKING IN CIRCLES.
AT NIGHT... HE LETS ME OUT INTO THE REAL WORLD TO REST...
...AND I TAKE THE OPPOR-TUNITY TO EAT, SLEEP—AND SOMETIMES BATHE.
AND WHEN MORNING COMES, HE PICKS ME UP AND WE CONTINUE ON OUR JOURNEY THROUGH MAGANO.

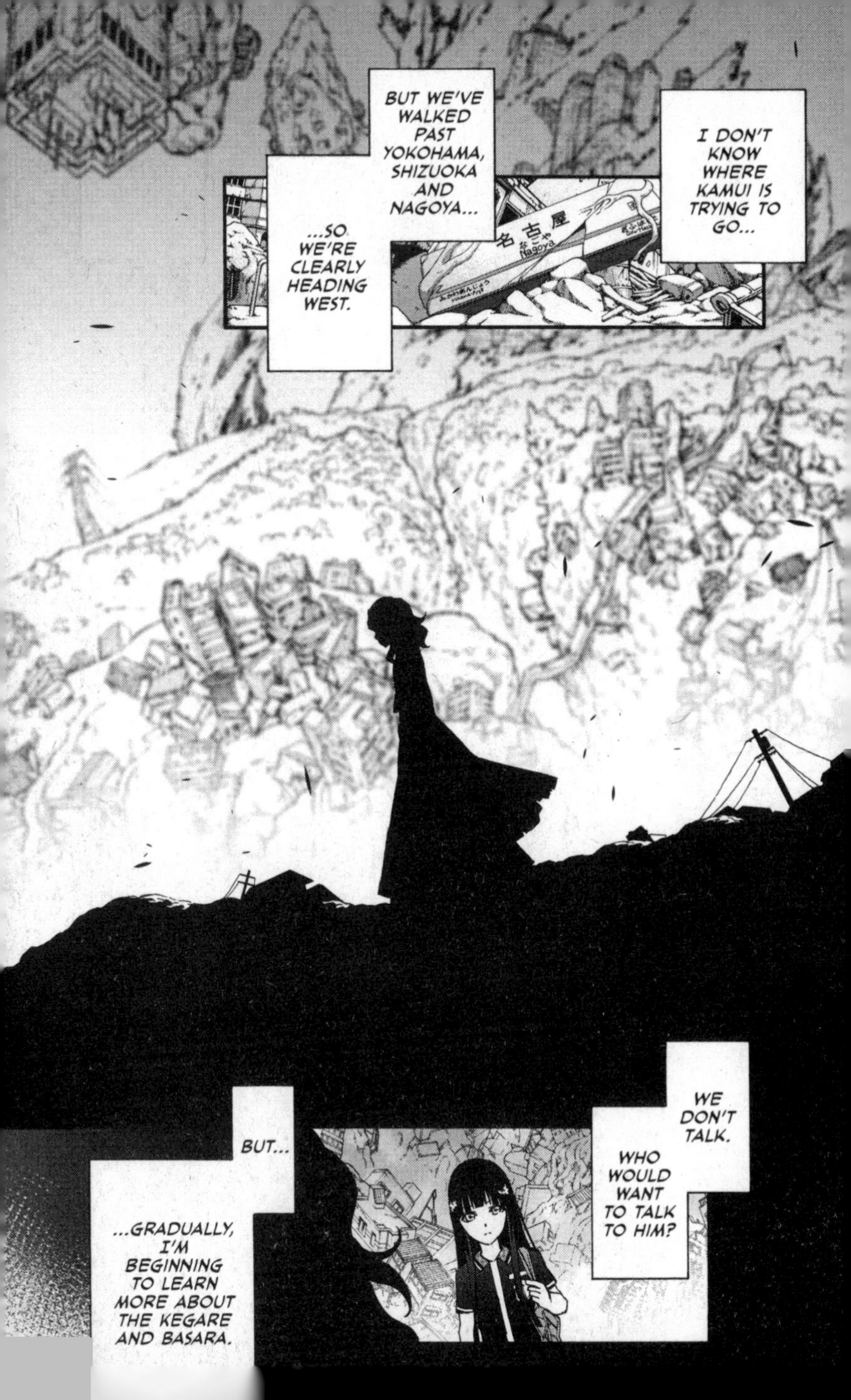
I DON'T KNOW WHERE KAMUI IS TRYING TO GO...
BUT WE'VE WALKED PAST YOKOHAMA, SHIZUOKA AND NAGOYA...
名古屋
なごや
Nagoya
...SO WE'RE CLEARLY HEADING WEST.
WE DON'T TALK.
WHO WOULD WANT TO TALK TO HIM?
BUT...
...GRADUALLY, I'M BEGINNING TO LEARN MORE ABOUT THE KEGARE AND BASARA.

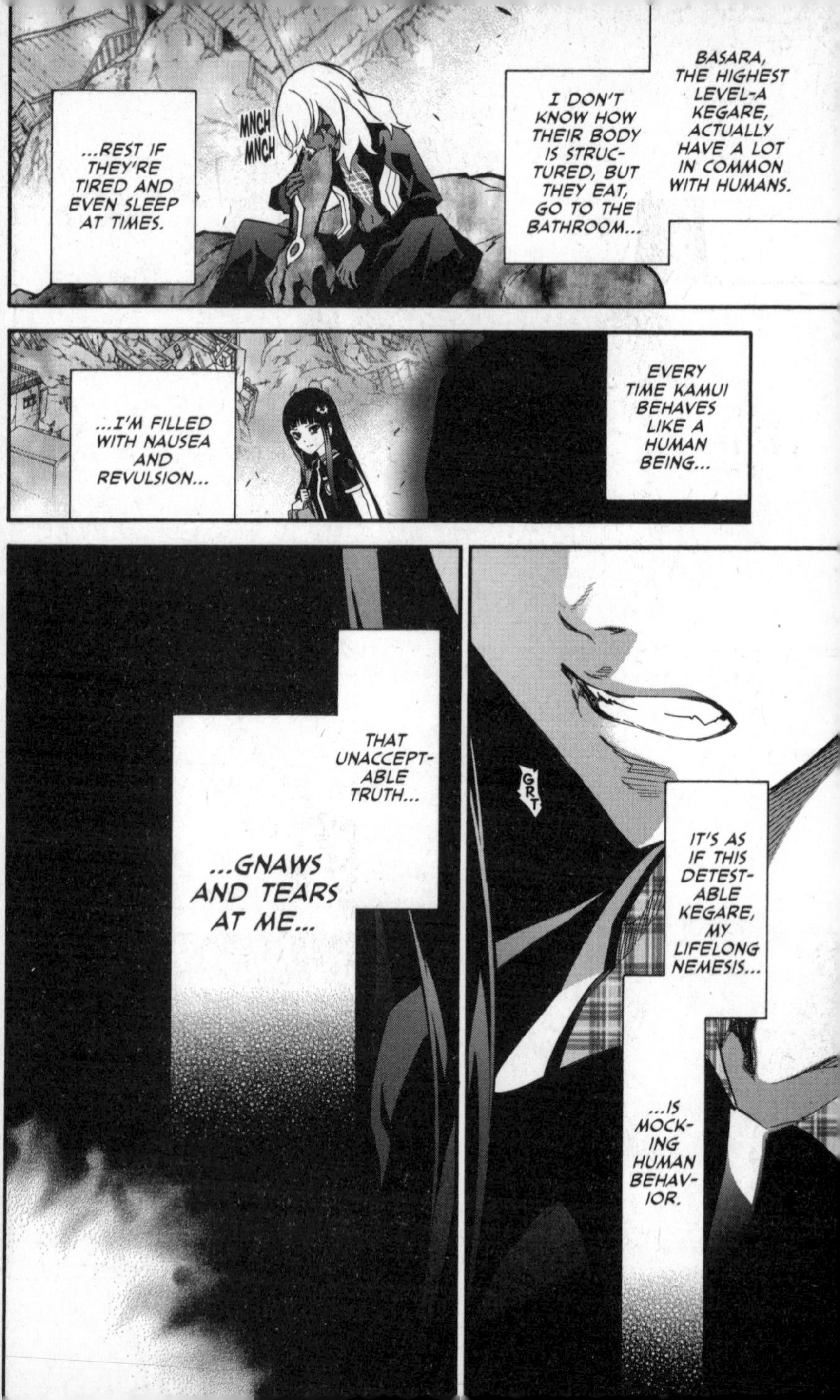
BASARA, THE HIGHEST LEVEL-A KEGARE, ACTUALLY HAVE A LOT IN COMMON WITH HUMANS.
I DON'T KNOW HOW THEIR BODY IS STRUCTURED, BUT THEY EAT, GO TO THE BATHROOM...
MNCH MNCH
...REST IF THEY'RE TIRED AND EVEN SLEEP AT TIMES.
EVERY TIME KAMUI BEHAVES LIKE A HUMAN BEING...
...I'M FILLED WITH NAUSEA AND REVULSION...
GRT
IT'S AS IF THIS DETESTABLE KEGARE, MY LIFELONG NEMESIS...
...IS MOCKING HUMAN BEHAVIOR.
THAT UNACCEPTABLE TRUTH...
...GNAWS AND TEARS AT ME...

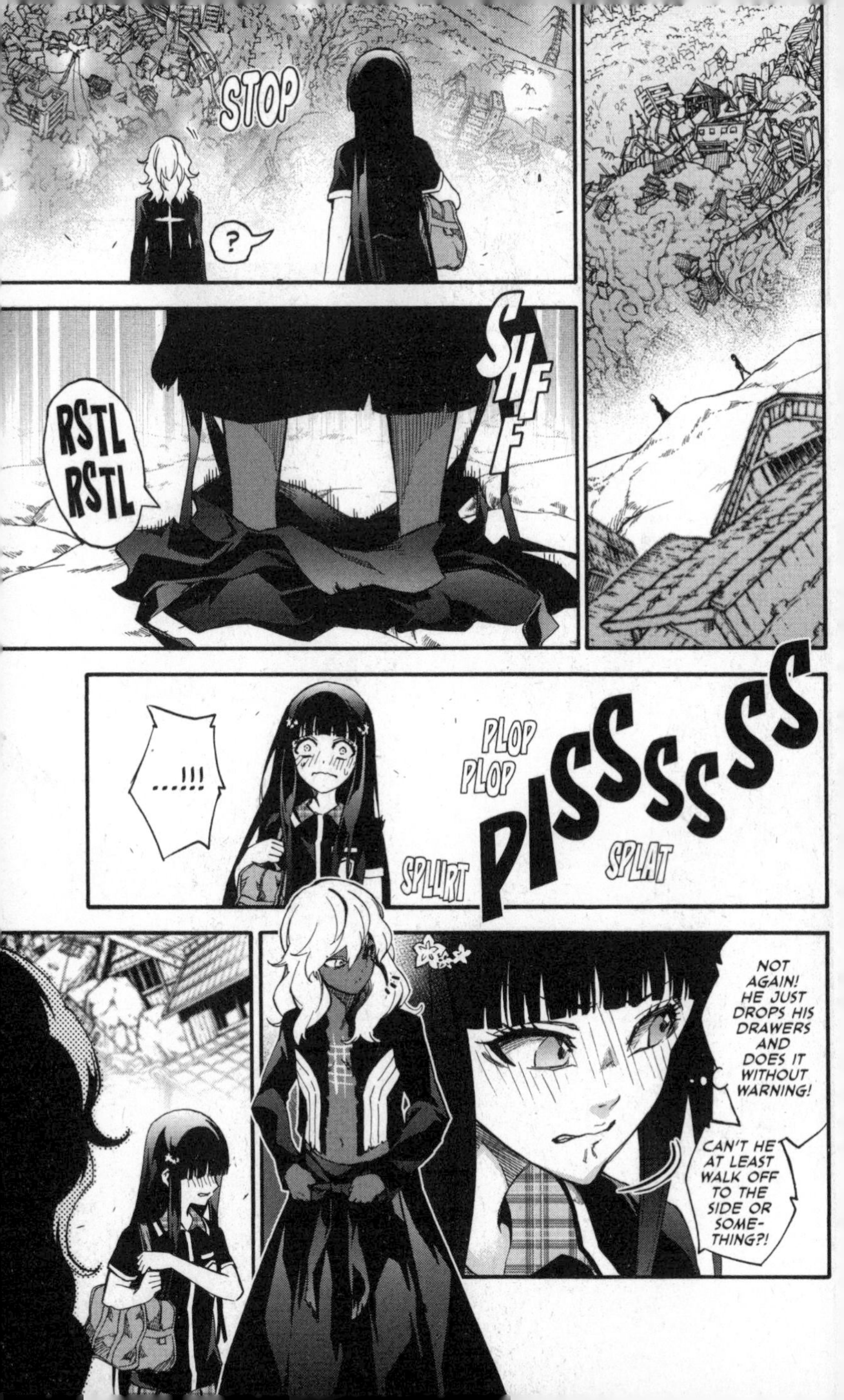

STOP
?
SHFF
RSTL RSTL
PISSSSSS
PLOP PLOP
...!!!
SPLAT
SPLURT
NOT AGAIN! HE JUST DROPS HIS DRAWERS AND DOES IT WITHOUT WARNING!
CAN'T HE AT LEAST WALK OFF TO THE SIDE OR SOME-THING?!

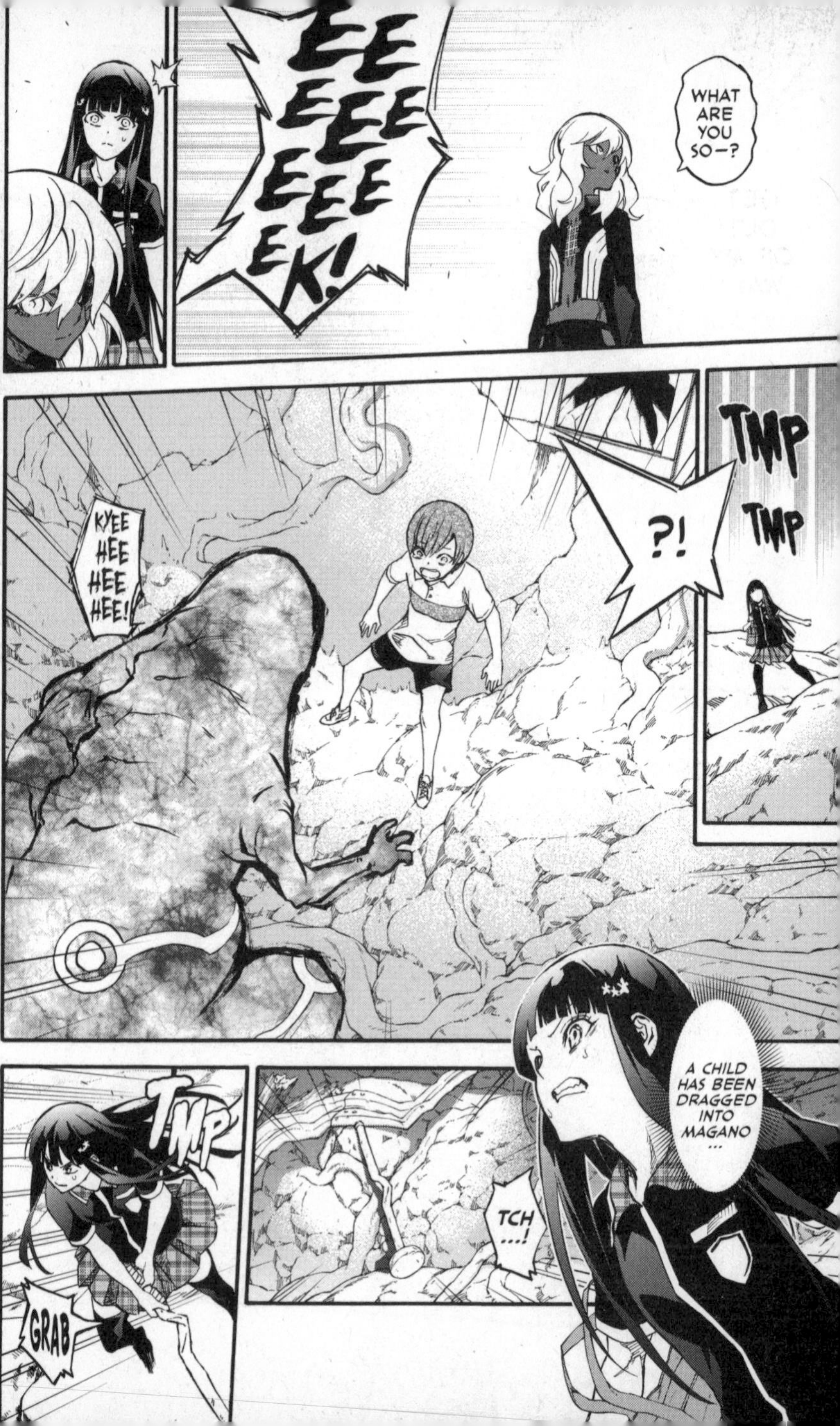
WHAT ARE YOU SO—?
EEEEEEEEEEEEEK!
TMP TMP
?!
KYEE HEE HEE HEE!
A CHILD HAS BEEN DRAGGED INTO MAGANO...
TCH...!
TMP
GRAB

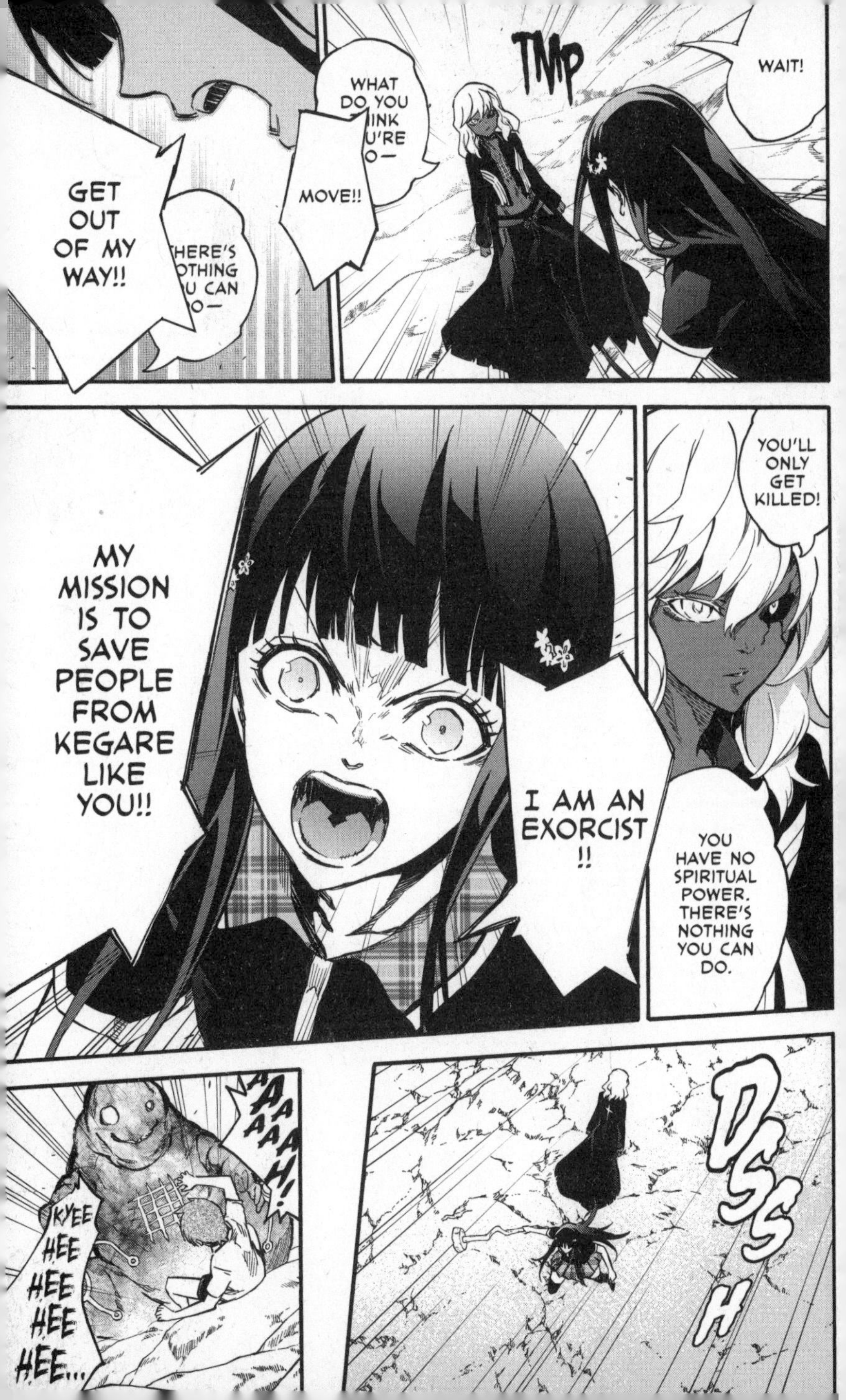
TMP
WAIT!
WHAT DO YOU INK U'RE O—
MOVE!!
HERE'S OTHING U CAN O—
GET OUT OF MY WAY!!
YOU'LL ONLY GET KILLED!
YOU HAVE NO SPIRITUAL POWER. THERE'S NOTHING YOU CAN DO.
I AM AN EXORCIST!!
MY MISSION IS TO SAVE PEOPLE FROM KEGARE LIKE YOU!!
DSSH
AAAAAAH!
KYEE HEE HEE HEE HEE...

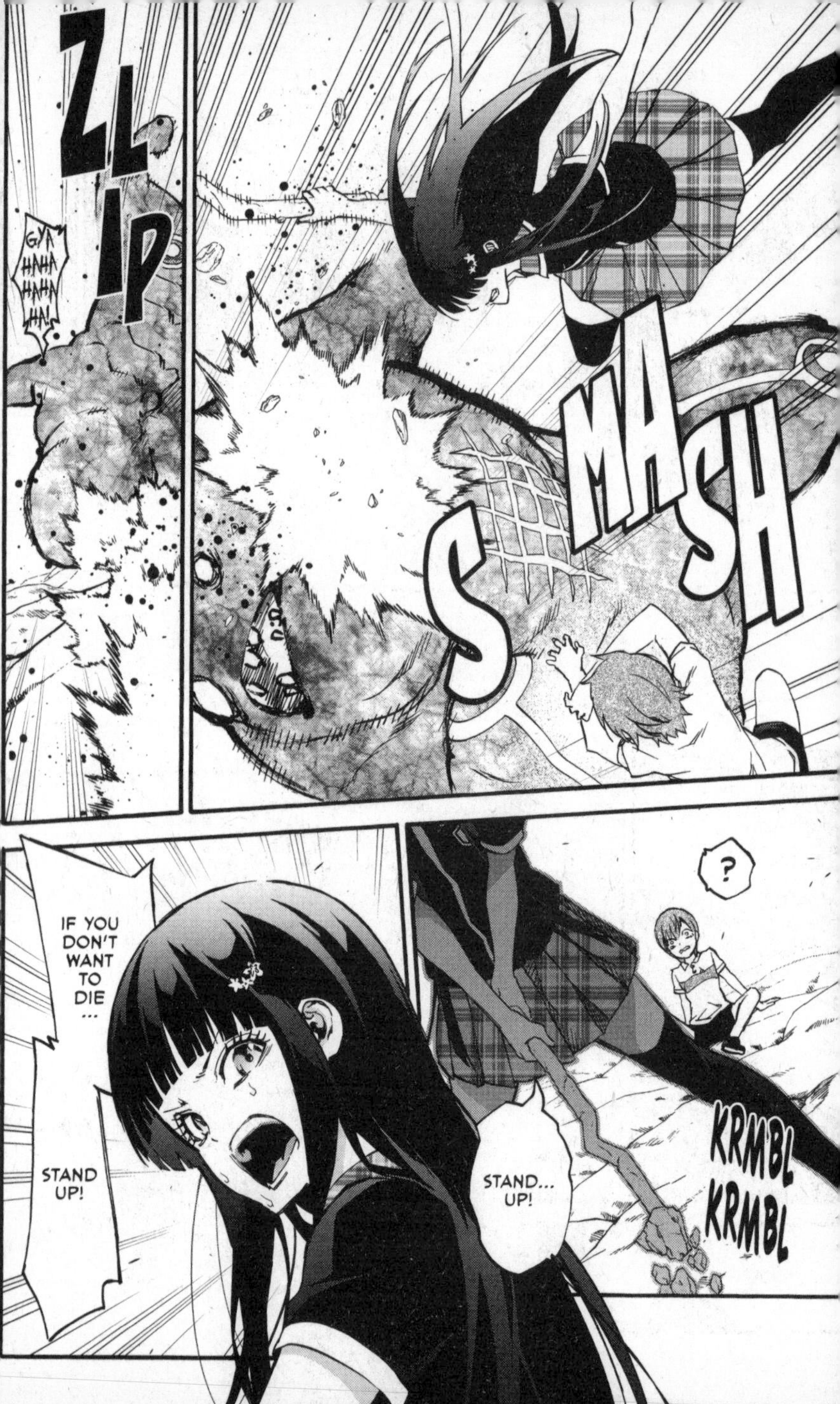
SMASH
ZLIP
GYAHAHAHAHAHA!
?
STAND... UP!
KRMBL KRMBL
IF YOU DON'T WANT TO DIE...
STAND UP!

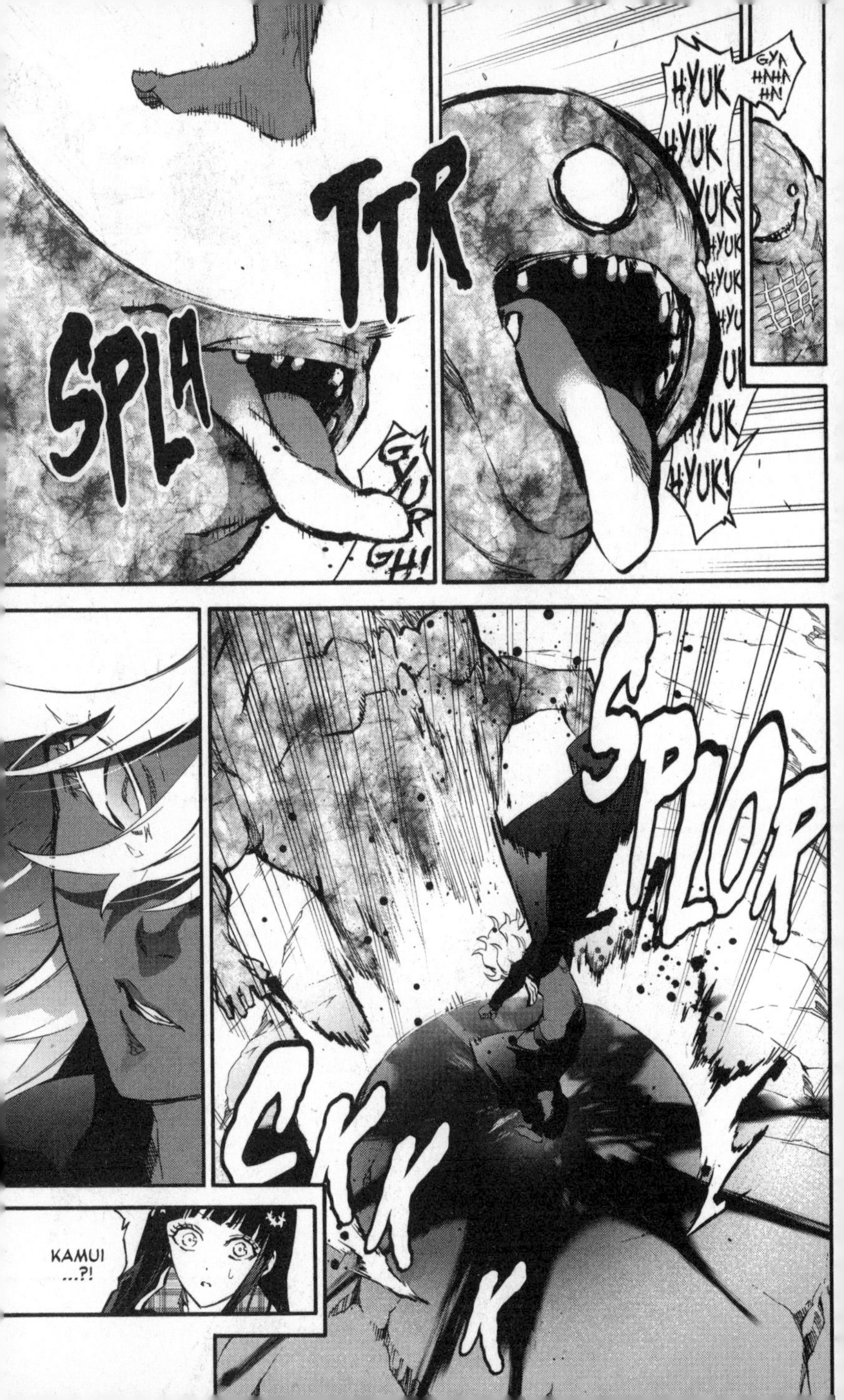
GYAHNHAHN!
HYUK HYUK HYUK HYUK HYUK HYUK HYUK HYUK HYUK!
SPLATTR
GYURGH!
SPLOP
CKKK
KAMUI ...?!

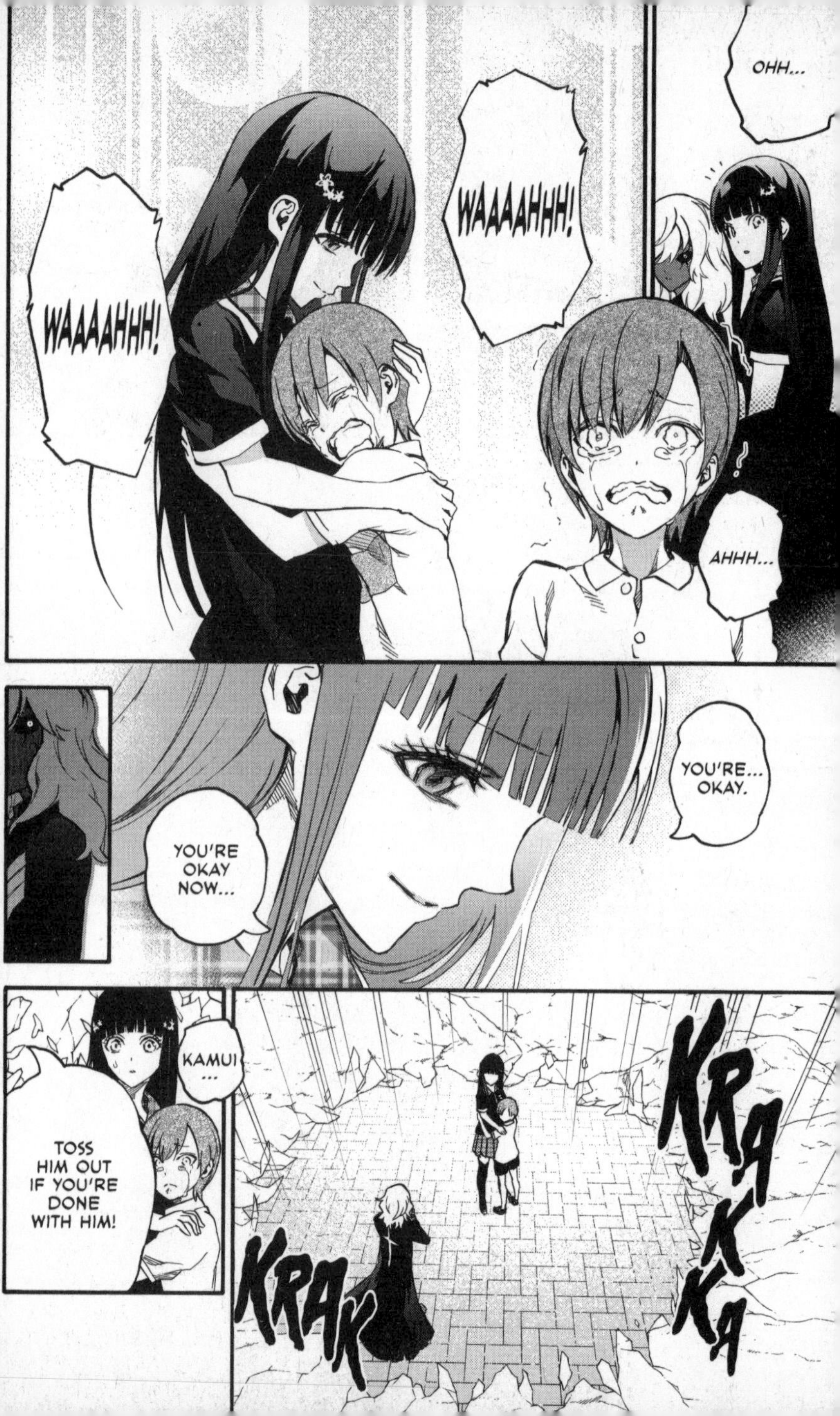
OHH...
AHHH...
WAAAAHHH!
WAAAAHHH!
YOU'RE... OKAY.
YOU'RE OKAY NOW...
KRAKKA
KRAK
KAMUI...
TOSS HIM OUT IF YOU'RE DONE WITH HIM!

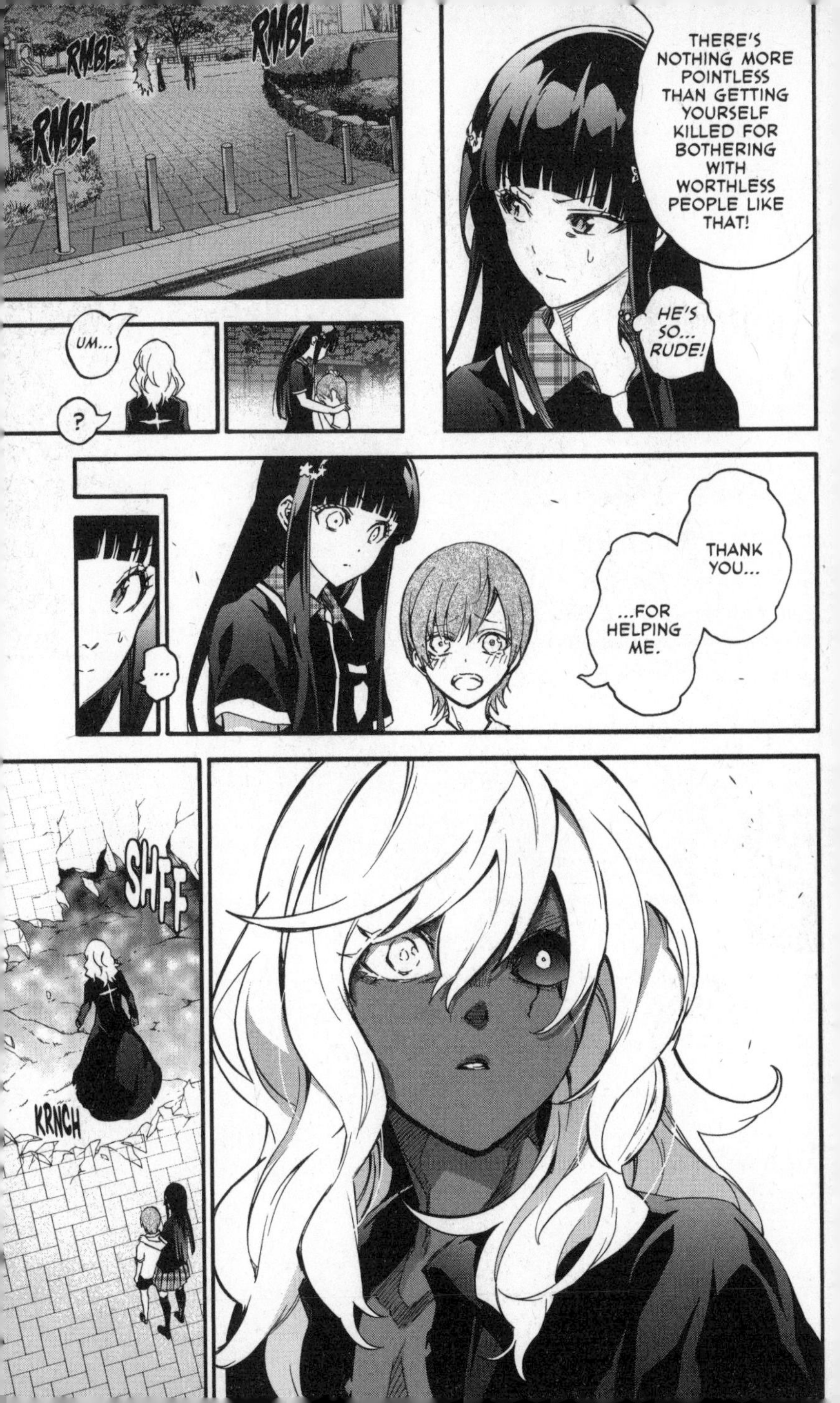
THERE'S NOTHING MORE POINTLESS THAN GETTING YOURSELF KILLED FOR BOTHERING WITH WORTHLESS PEOPLE LIKE THAT!
HE'S SO... RUDE!
RMBL
RMBL
RMBL
UM...
?
THANK YOU...
...FOR HELPING ME.
...
SHFF
KRNCH

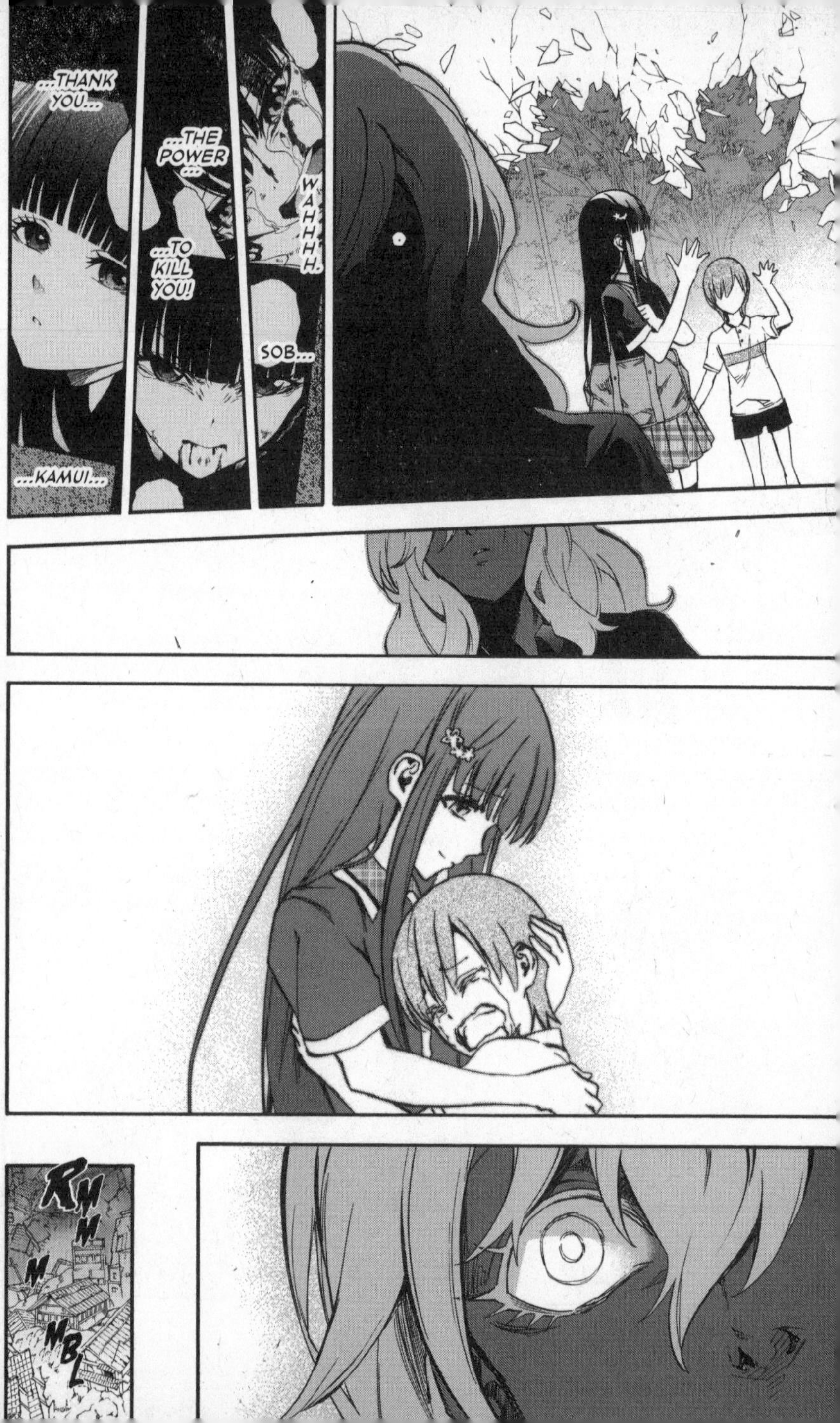

WAHHHH.
SOB...
...THE POWER...
...TO KILL YOU!
...THANK YOU...
...KAMUI...
RMMMMMBL

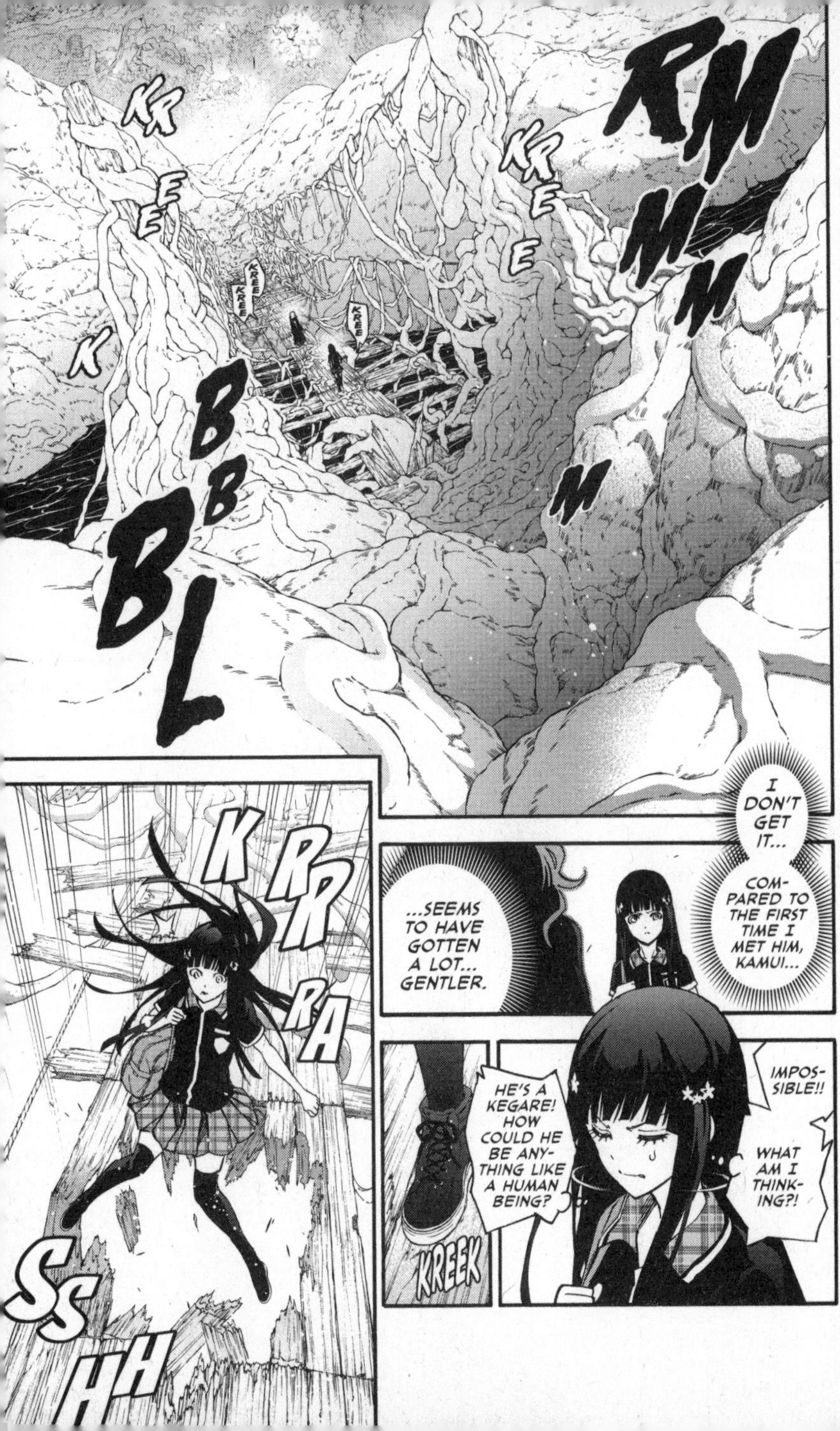
RMMMM
KREEE
KREE
KREE
KREE
KREEK
BBBL
M
I DON'T GET IT...
COMPARED TO THE FIRST TIME I MET HIM, KAMUI...
...SEEMS TO HAVE GOTTEN A LOT... GENTLER.
IMPOSSIBLE!!
WHAT AM I THINKING?!
HE'S A KEGARE! HOW COULD HE BE ANYTHING LIKE A HUMAN BEING?
KREEK
KRRRA
SSHH

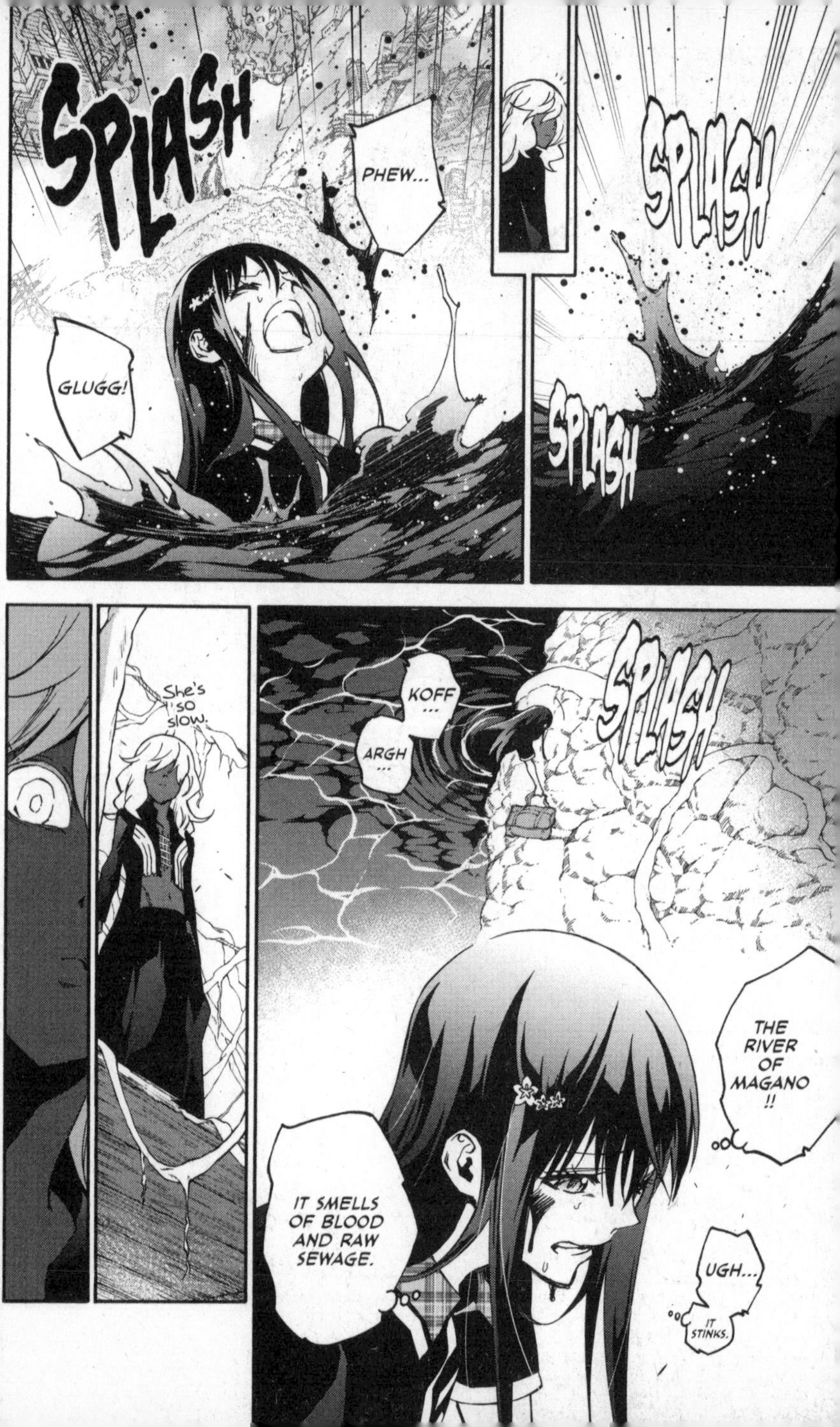
SPLASH
SPLASH
SPLASH
PHEW...
GLUGG!
SPLASH
KOFF...
ARGH...
THE RIVER OF MAGANO!!
UGH...
IT STINKS.
IT SMELLS OF BLOOD AND RAW SEWAGE.
She's so slow.

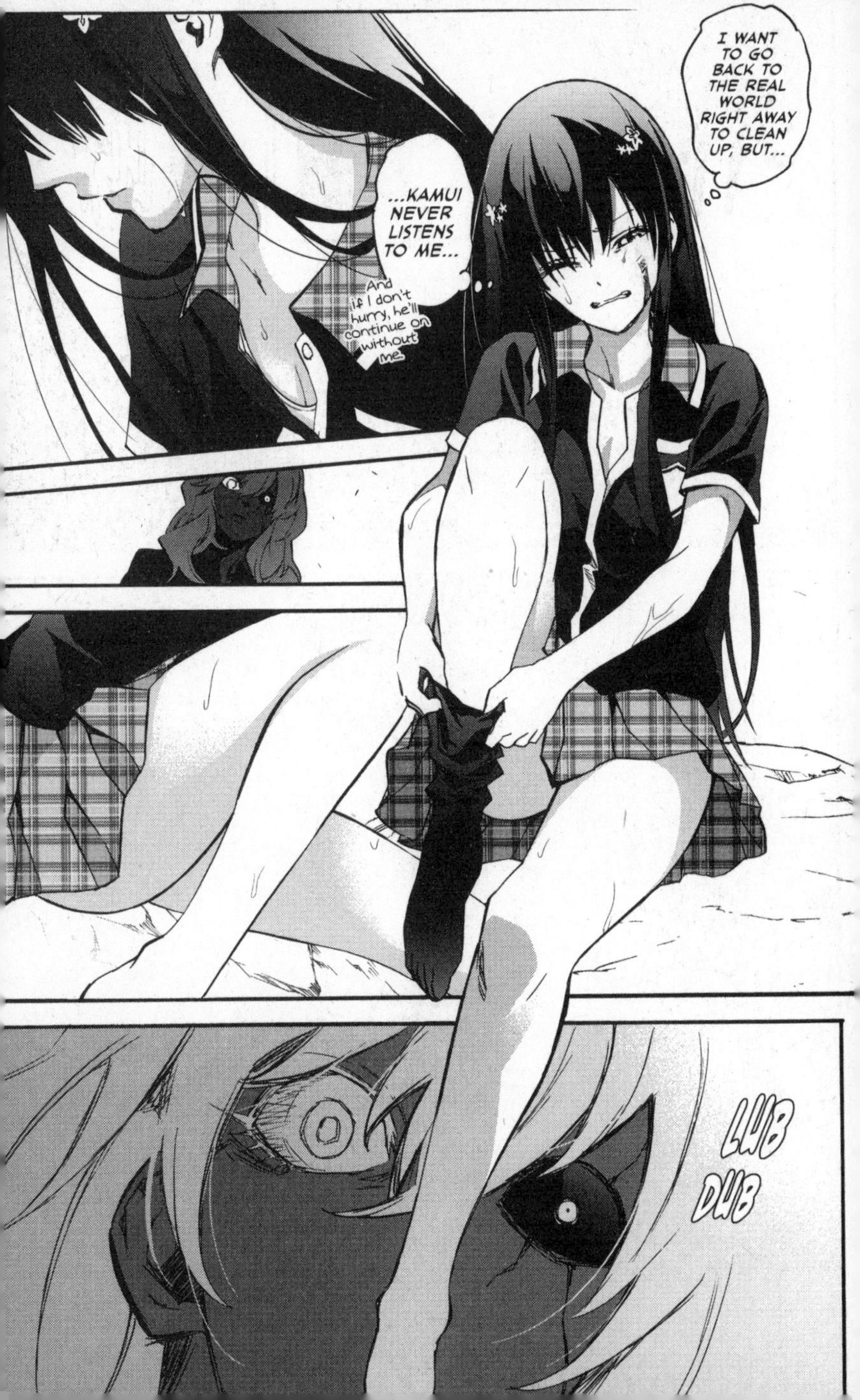
I WANT TO GO BACK TO THE REAL WORLD RIGHT AWAY TO CLEAN UP, BUT...
...KAMUI NEVER LISTENS TO ME...
And if I don't hurry, he'll continue on without me.
LUB
DUB

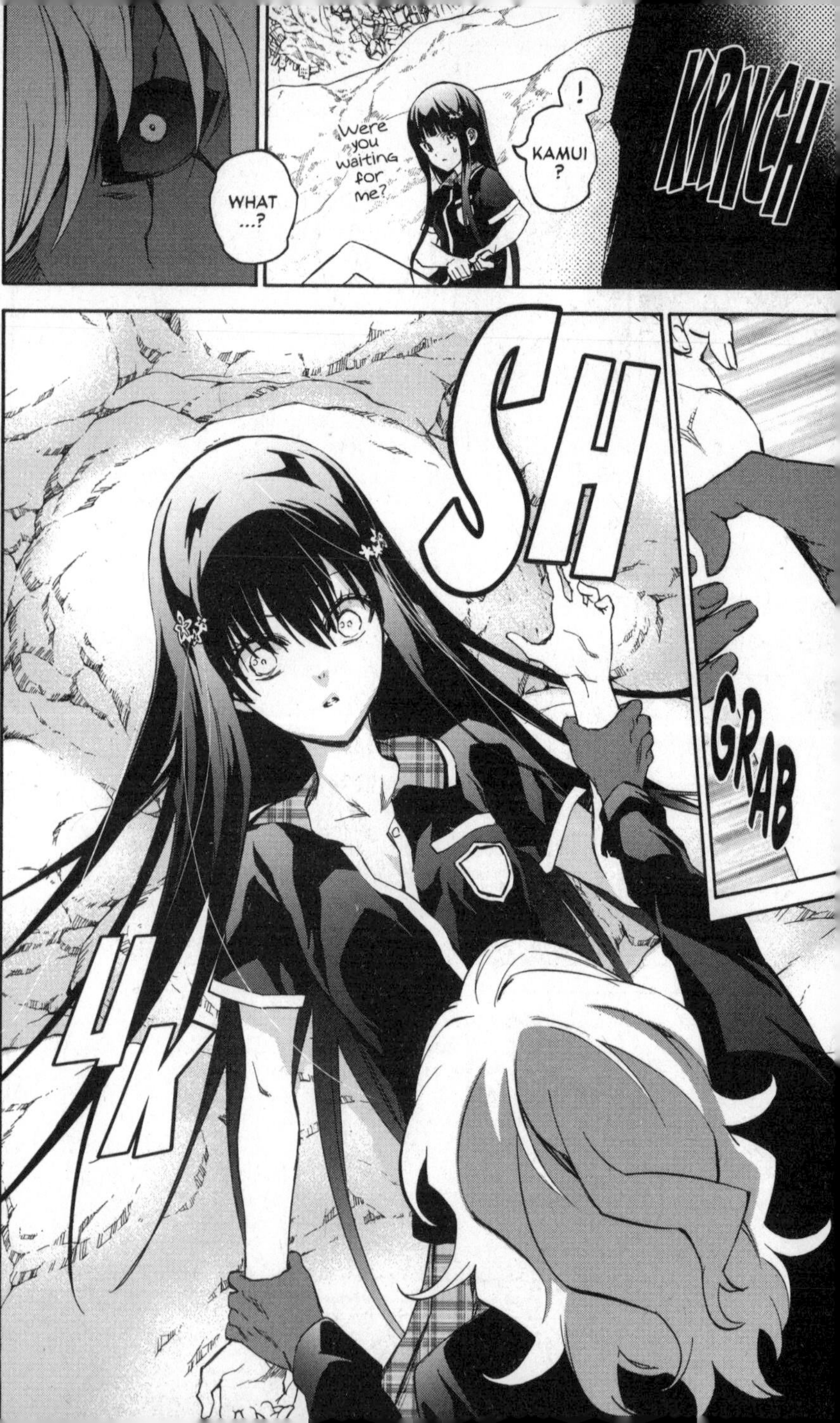
KRNCH
!
KAMUI?
Were you waiting for me?
WHAT ...?
GRAB
SH
UNK

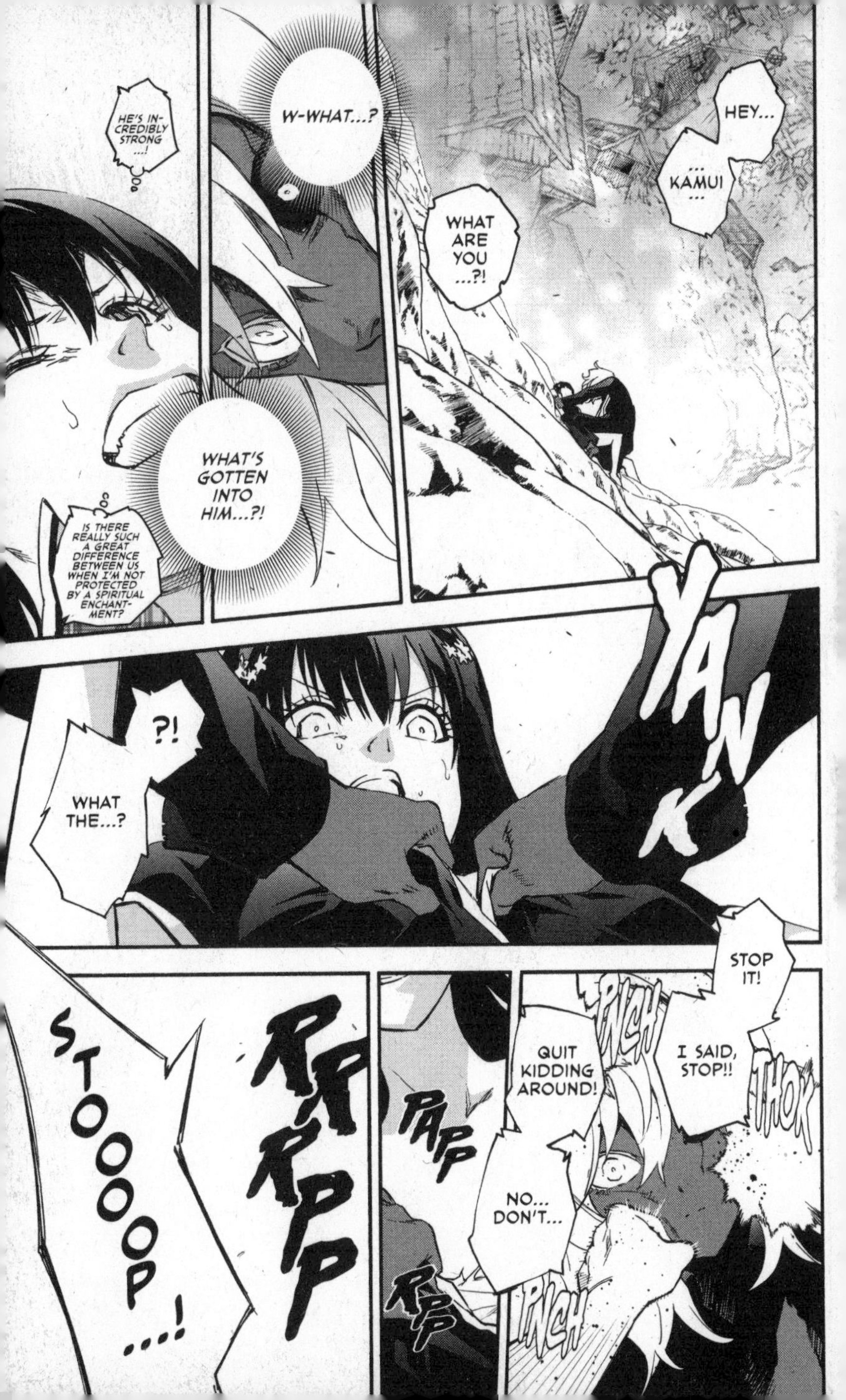

HEY... ...KAMUI...
WHAT ARE YOU ...?!
W-WHAT...?
WHAT'S GOTTEN INTO HIM...?!
HE'S INCREDIBLY STRONG...!
IS THERE REALLY SUCH A GREAT DIFFERENCE BETWEEN US WHEN I'M NOT PROTECTED BY A SPIRITUAL ENCHANTMENT?
YANK
?!
WHAT THE...?
STOP IT!
PINCH
I SAID, STOP!!
THOK
QUIT KIDDING AROUND!
NO... DON'T...
PINCH
RRRIP
PAPP
RRP
STOOOOP...!

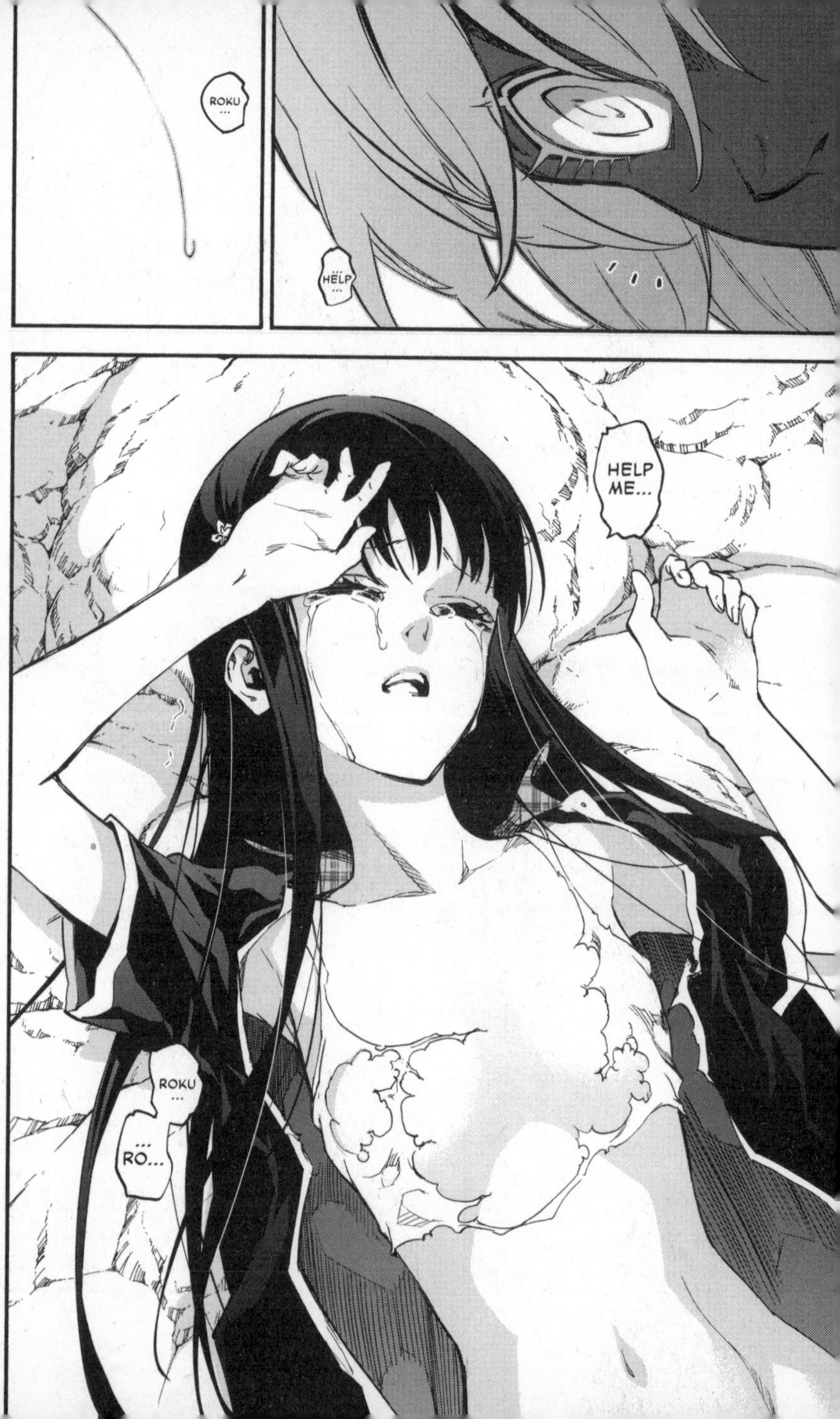
... HELP ...
ROKU ...
HELP ME...
ROKU ...
... RO...

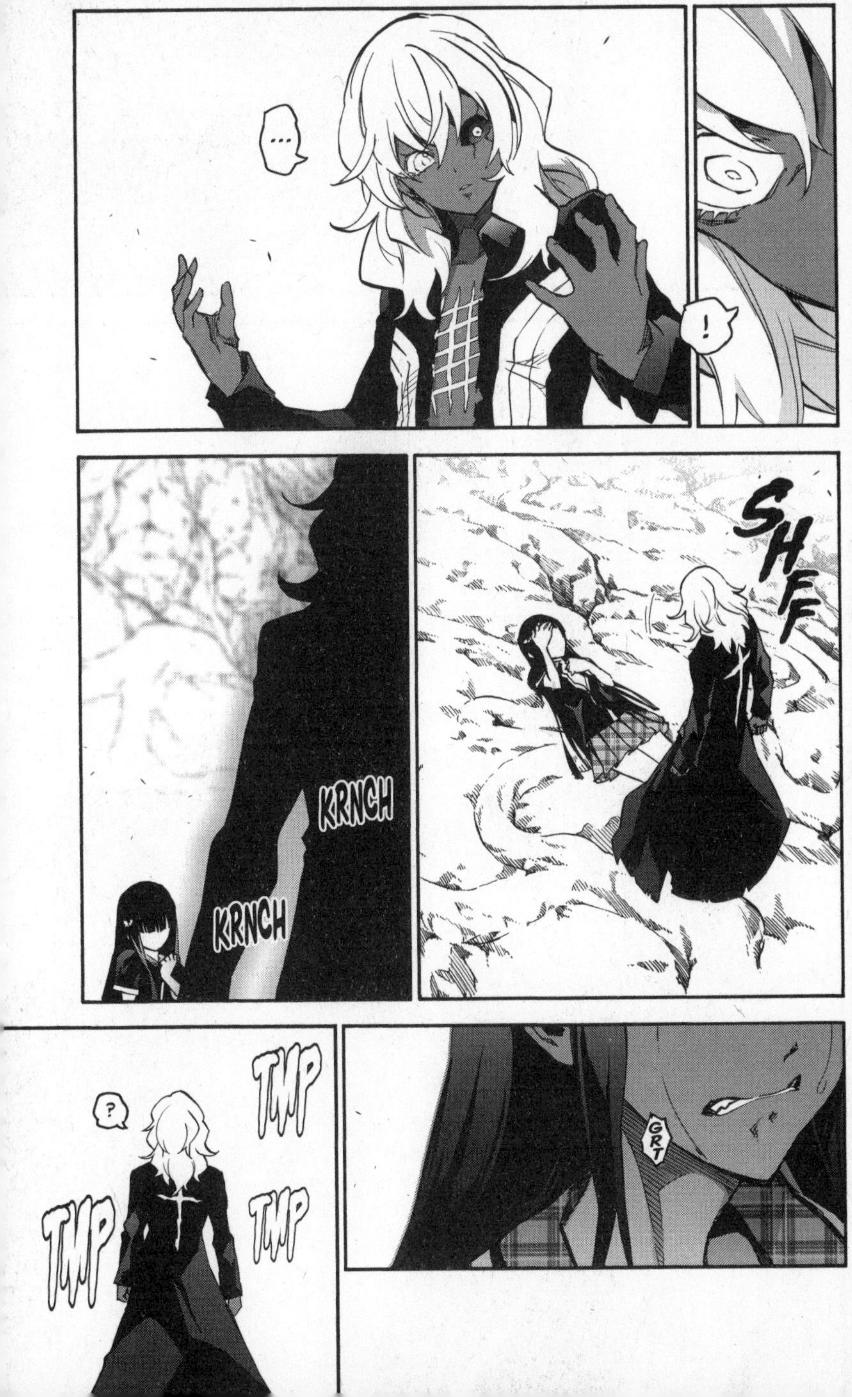
!
...
SHFF
KRNCH
KRNCH
GRT
TMP
?
TMP
TMP

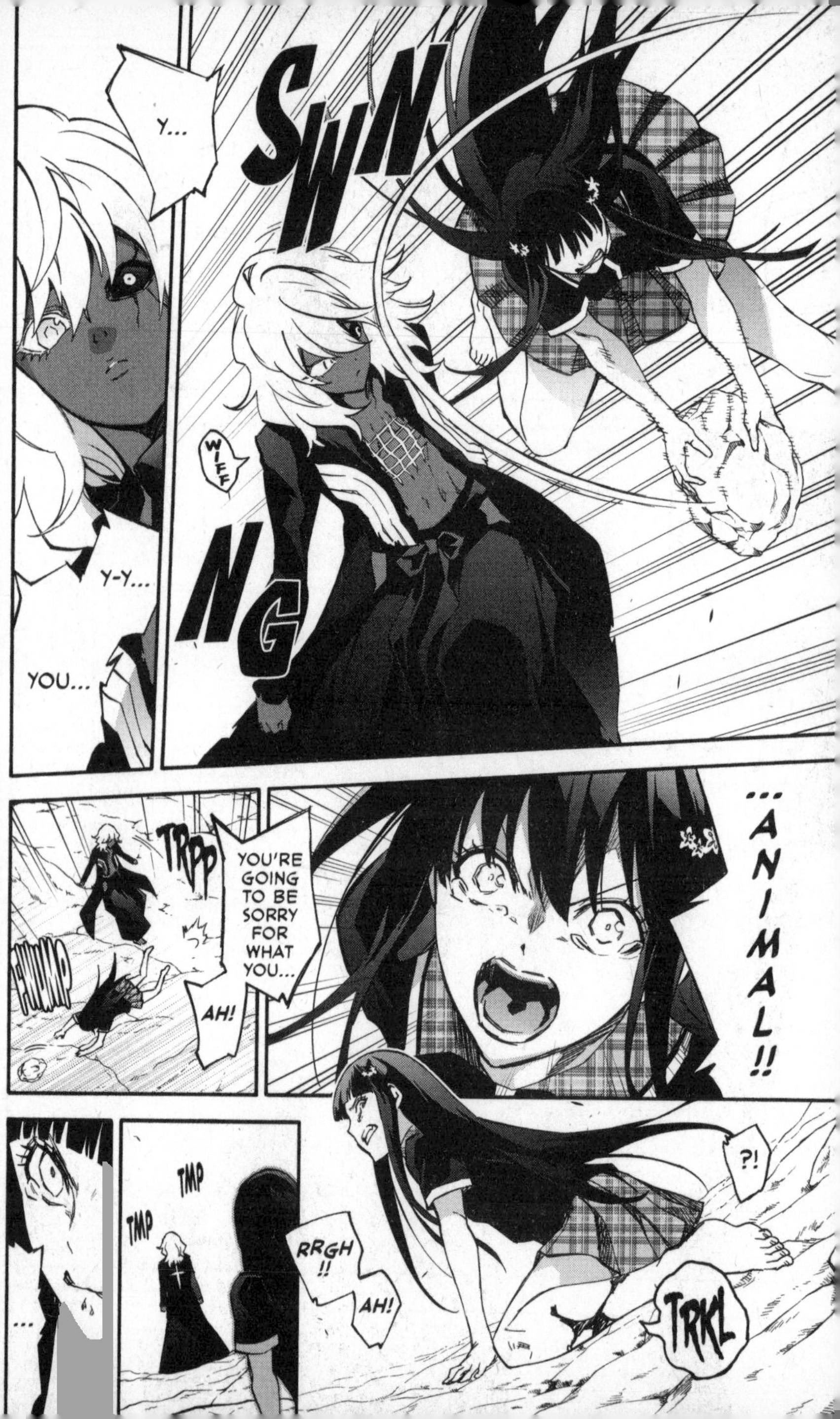
SWING
WIFF
Y...
Y-Y...
YOU...
...ANIMAL!!
YOU'RE GOING TO BE SORRY FOR WHAT YOU...
TRPP
AH!
?!
TRKL
RRGH!!
AH!
TMP
TMP
...

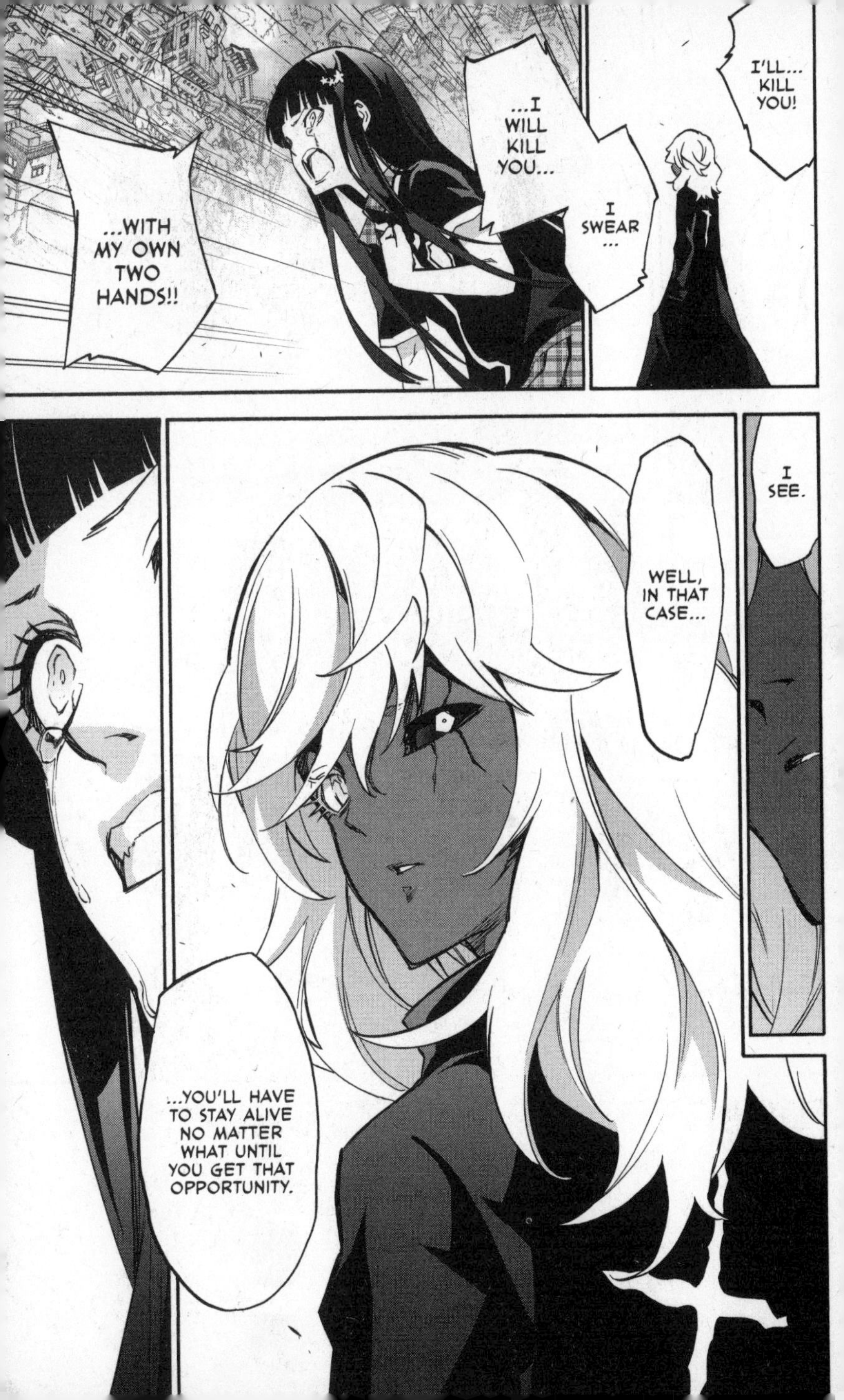
I'LL... KILL YOU!
...I WILL KILL YOU...
I SWEAR ...
...WITH MY OWN TWO HANDS!!
I SEE.
WELL, IN THAT CASE...
...YOU'LL HAVE TO STAY ALIVE NO MATTER WHAT UNTIL YOU GET THAT OPPORTUNITY.

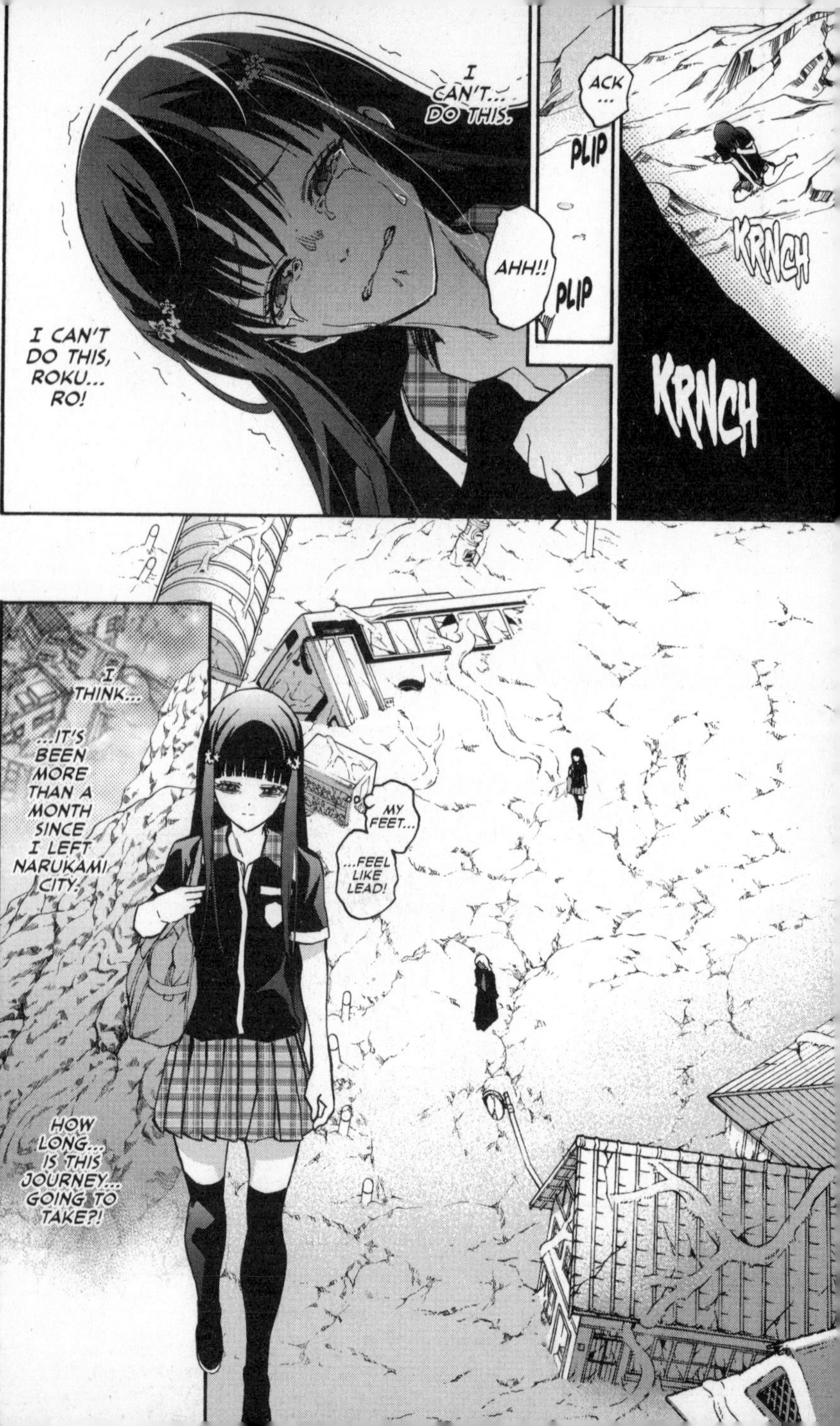
ACK...
KRNCH
KRNCH
PLIP
PLIP
I CAN'T... DO THIS.
AHH!!
I CAN'T DO THIS, ROKU... RO!
I THINK...
...IT'S BEEN MORE THAN A MONTH SINCE I LEFT NARUKAMI CITY.
MY FEET...
...FEEL LIKE LEAD!
HOW LONG... IS THIS JOURNEY... GOING TO TAKE?!

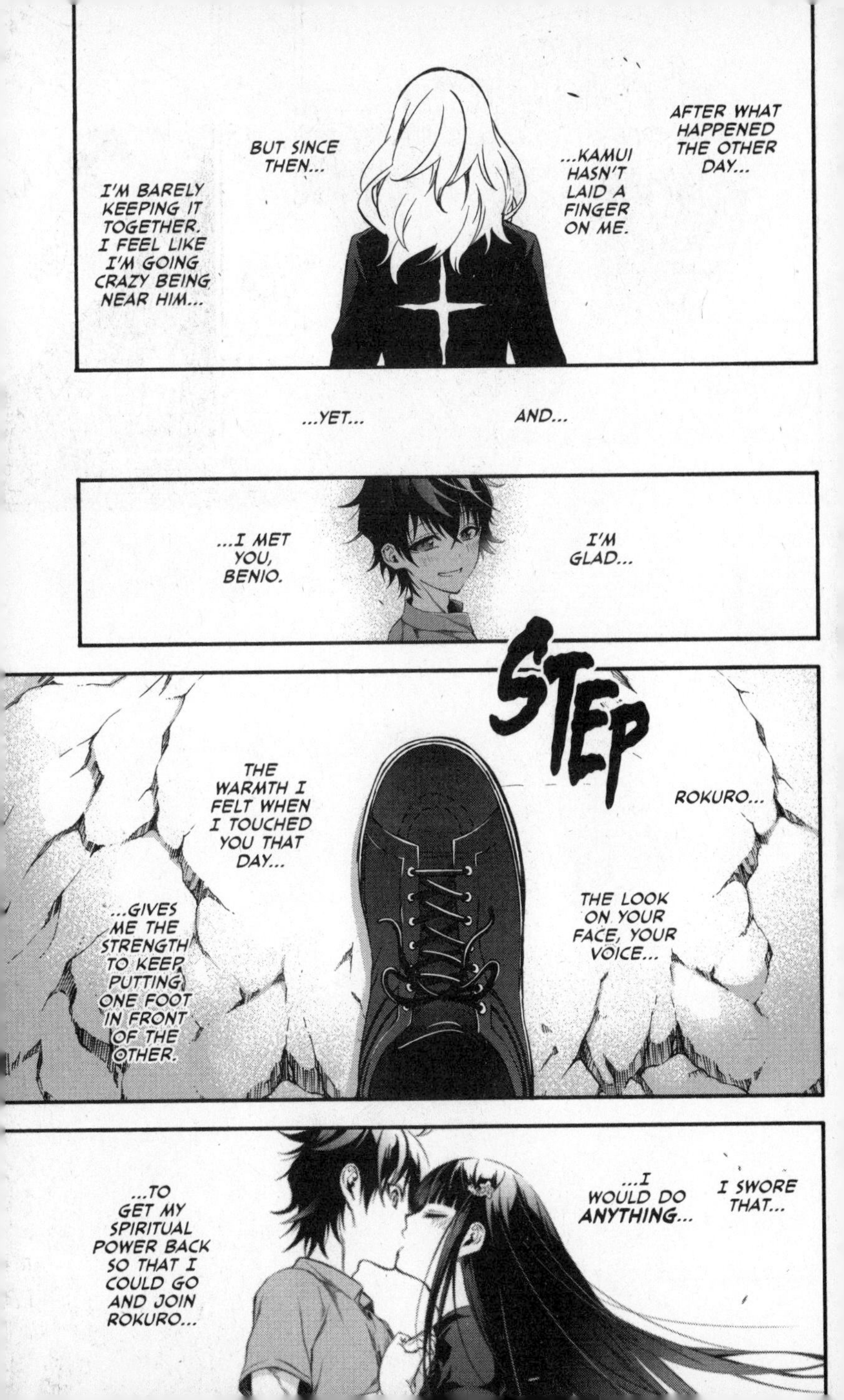
AFTER WHAT HAPPENED THE OTHER DAY...
...KAMUI HASN'T LAID A FINGER ON ME.
BUT SINCE THEN...
I'M BARELY KEEPING IT TOGETHER. I FEEL LIKE I'M GOING CRAZY BEING NEAR HIM...
AND...
...YET...
I'M GLAD...
...I MET YOU, BENIO.
STEP
ROKURO...
THE LOOK ON YOUR FACE, YOUR VOICE...
THE WARMTH I FELT WHEN I TOUCHED YOU THAT DAY...
...GIVES ME THE STRENGTH TO KEEP PUTTING ONE FOOT IN FRONT OF THE OTHER.
I SWORE THAT...
...I WOULD DO **ANYTHING**...
...TO GET MY SPIRITUAL POWER BACK SO THAT I COULD GO AND JOIN ROKURO...

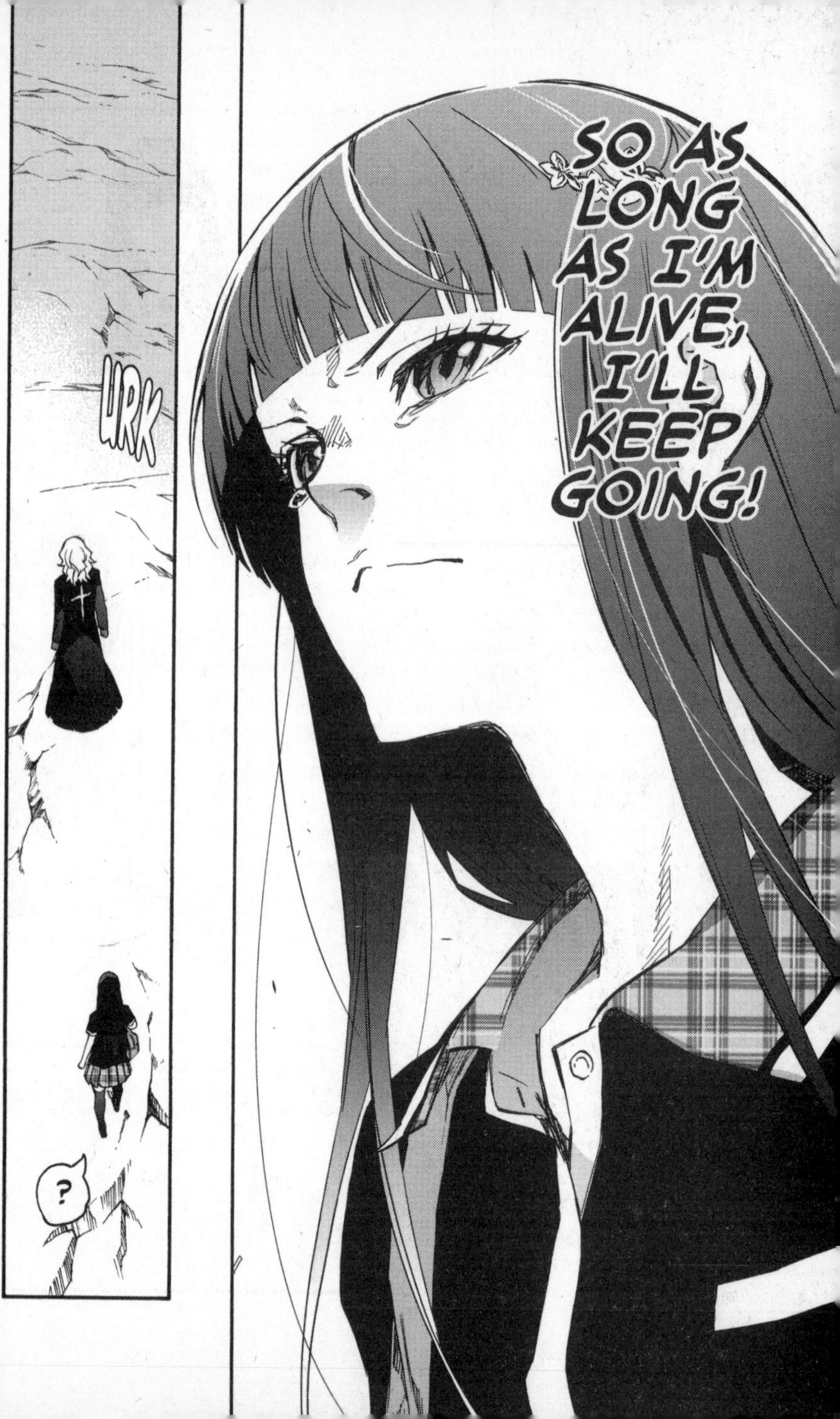
SO AS LONG AS I'M ALIVE, I'LL KEEP GOING!
URK
?

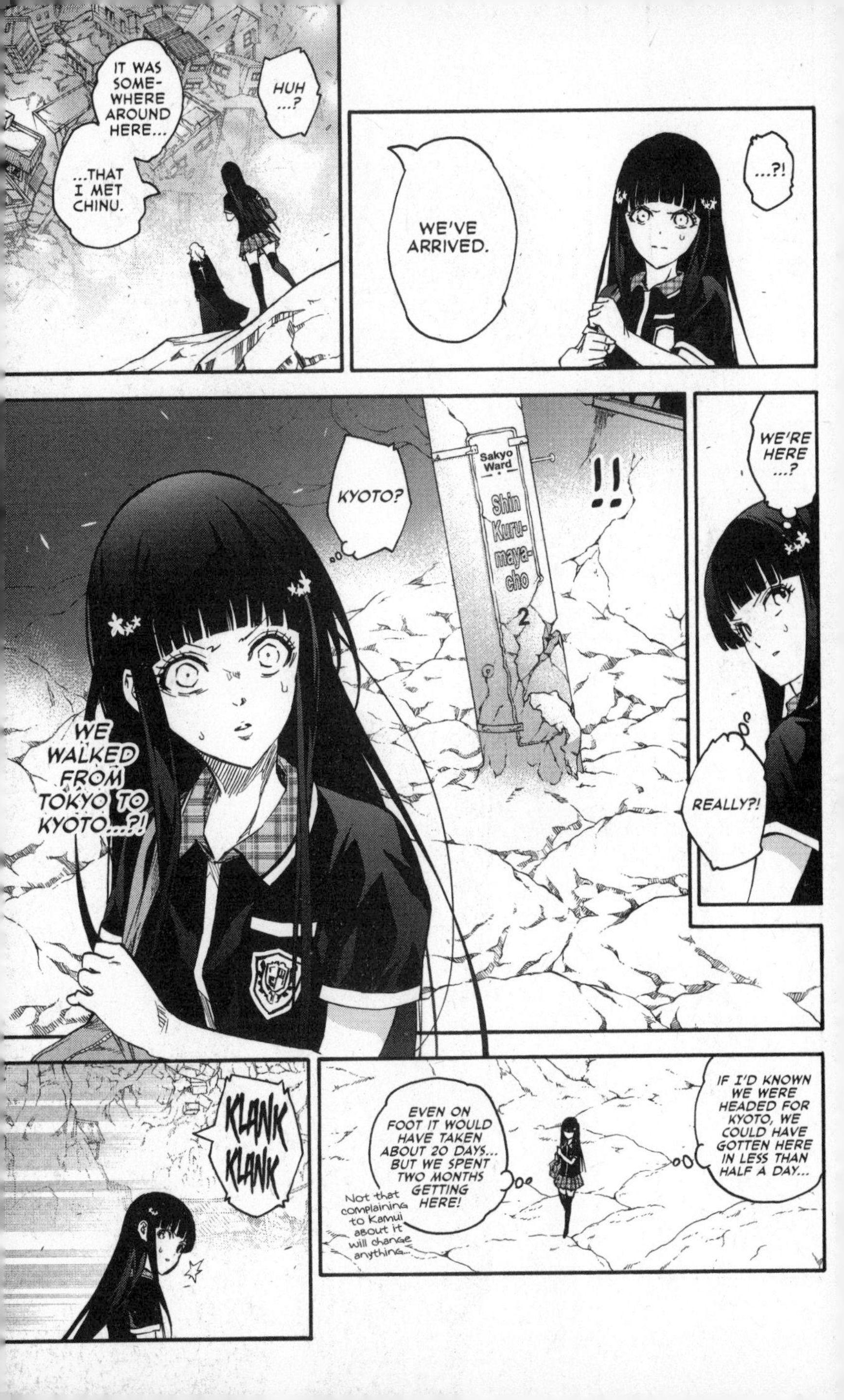
...?!
WE'VE ARRIVED.
HUH ...?
IT WAS SOMEWHERE AROUND HERE...
...THAT I MET CHINU.
WE'RE HERE ...?
REALLY?!
!!
Sakyo Ward
Shin Kurumaya-cho 2
KYOTO?
WE WALKED FROM TOKYO TO KYOTO...?!
IF I'D KNOWN WE WERE HEADED FOR KYOTO, WE COULD HAVE GOTTEN HERE IN LESS THAN HALF A DAY...
EVEN ON FOOT IT WOULD HAVE TAKEN ABOUT 20 DAYS... BUT WE SPENT TWO MONTHS GETTING HERE!
Not that complaining to Kamui about it will change anything...
KLANK KLANK

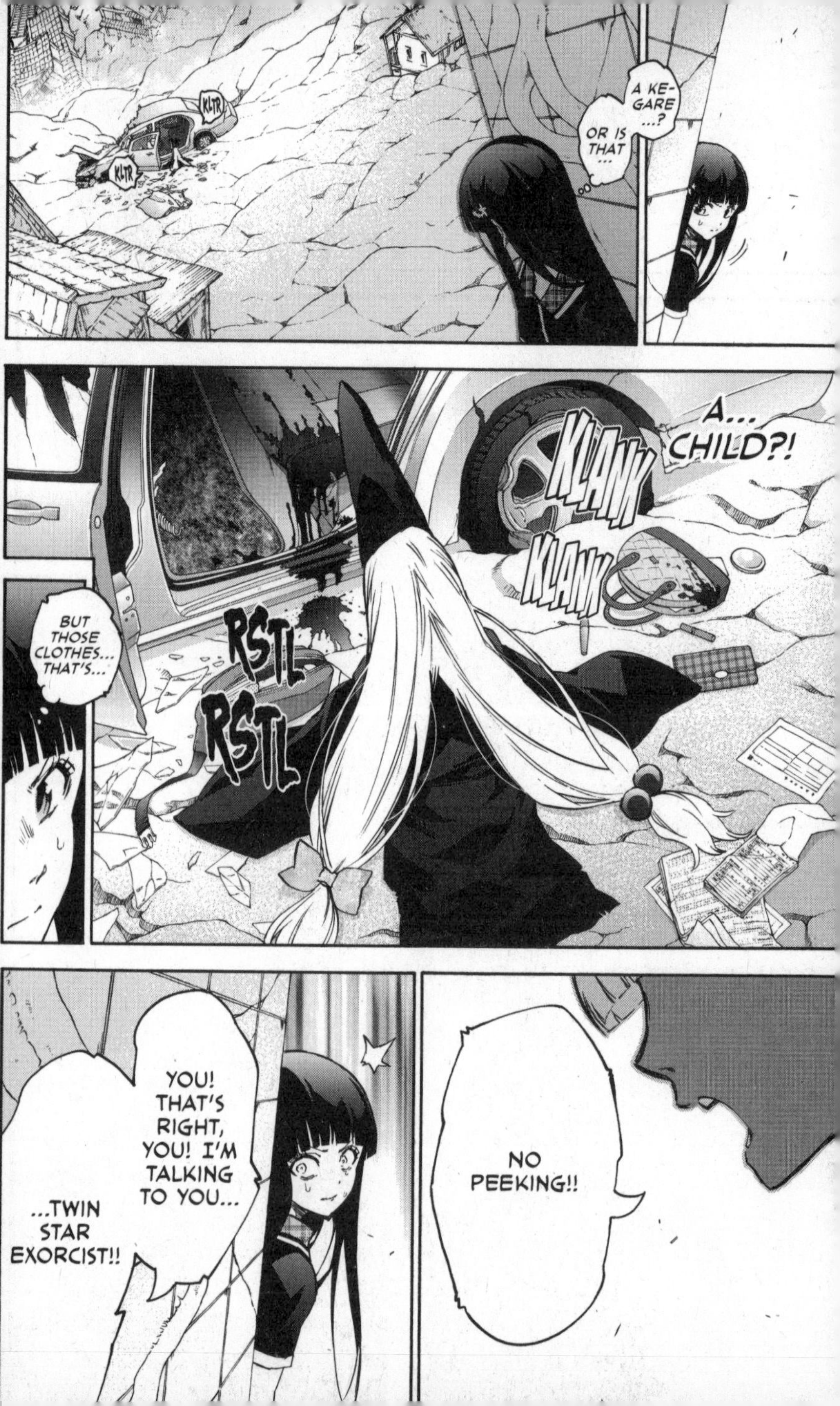
A KE-GARE ...?
OR IS THAT ...
KLTR
KLTR
A... CHILD?!
KLANK
KLANK
RSTL
RSTL
BUT THOSE CLOTHES... THAT'S...
NO PEEKING!!
YOU! THAT'S RIGHT, YOU! I'M TALKING TO YOU...
...TWIN STAR EXORCIST!!

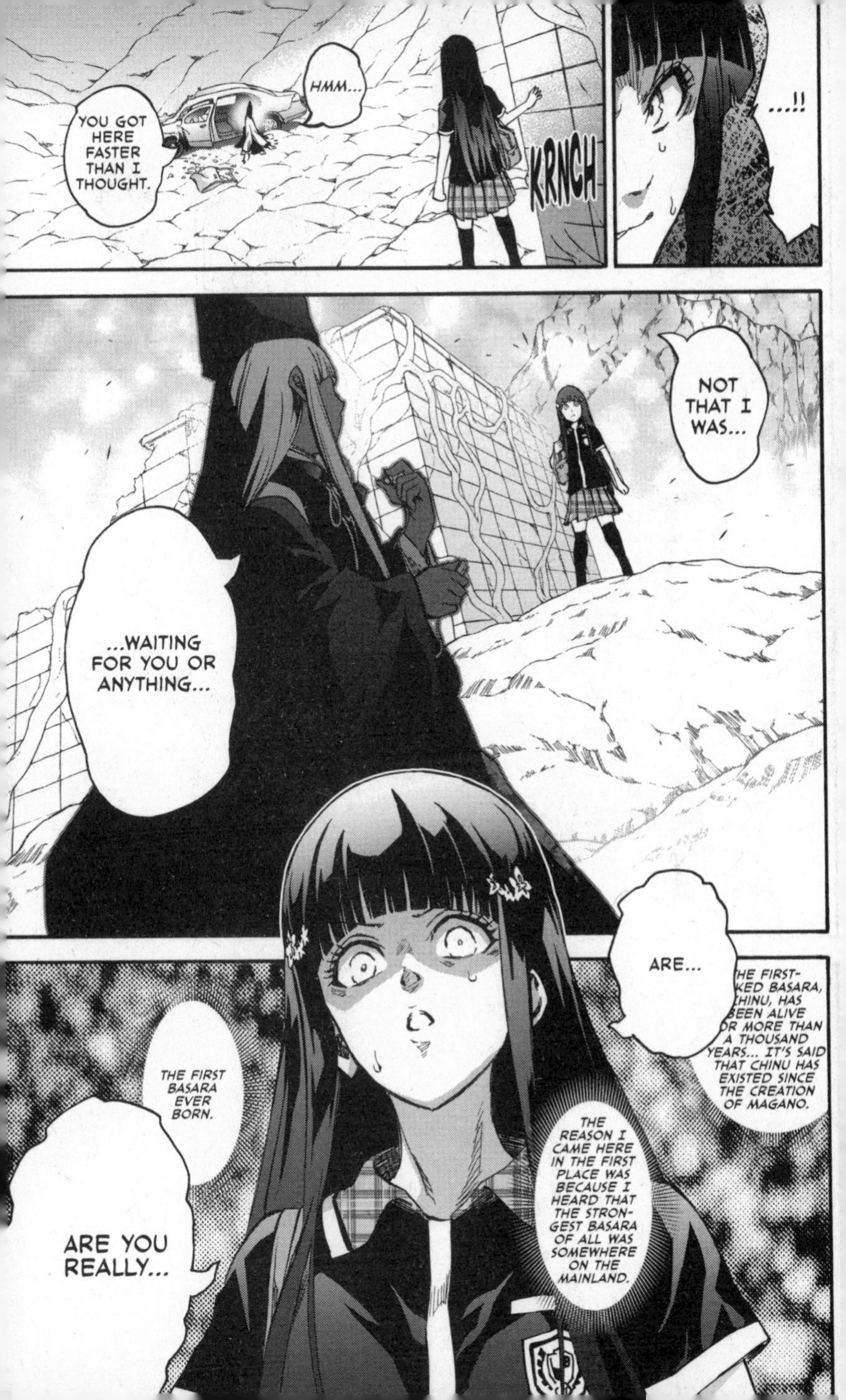
...!!
KRNCH
HMM...
YOU GOT HERE FASTER THAN I THOUGHT.
NOT THAT I WAS...
...WAITING FOR YOU OR ANYTHING...
ARE...
THE FIRST- KED BASARA, HINU, HAS BEEN ALIVE R MORE THAN A THOUSAND YEARS... IT'S SAID THAT CHINU HAS EXISTED SINCE THE CREATION OF MAGANO.
THE REASON I CAME HERE IN THE FIRST PLACE WAS BECAUSE I HEARD THAT THE STRONGEST BASARA OF ALL WAS SOMEWHERE ON THE MAINLAND.
THE FIRST BASARA EVER BORN.
ARE YOU REALLY...

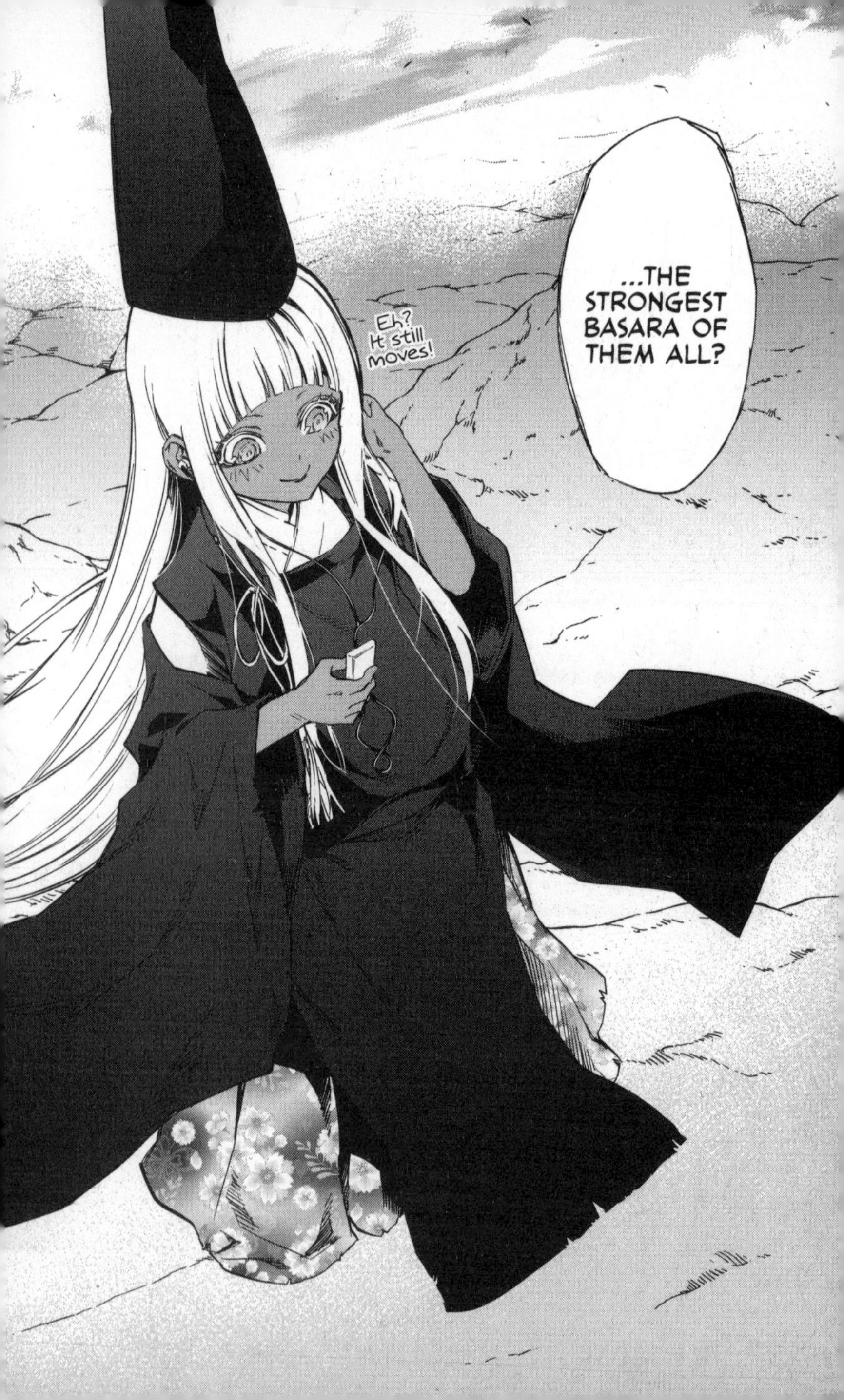
...THE STRONGEST BASARA OF THEM ALL?
Eh? It still moves!

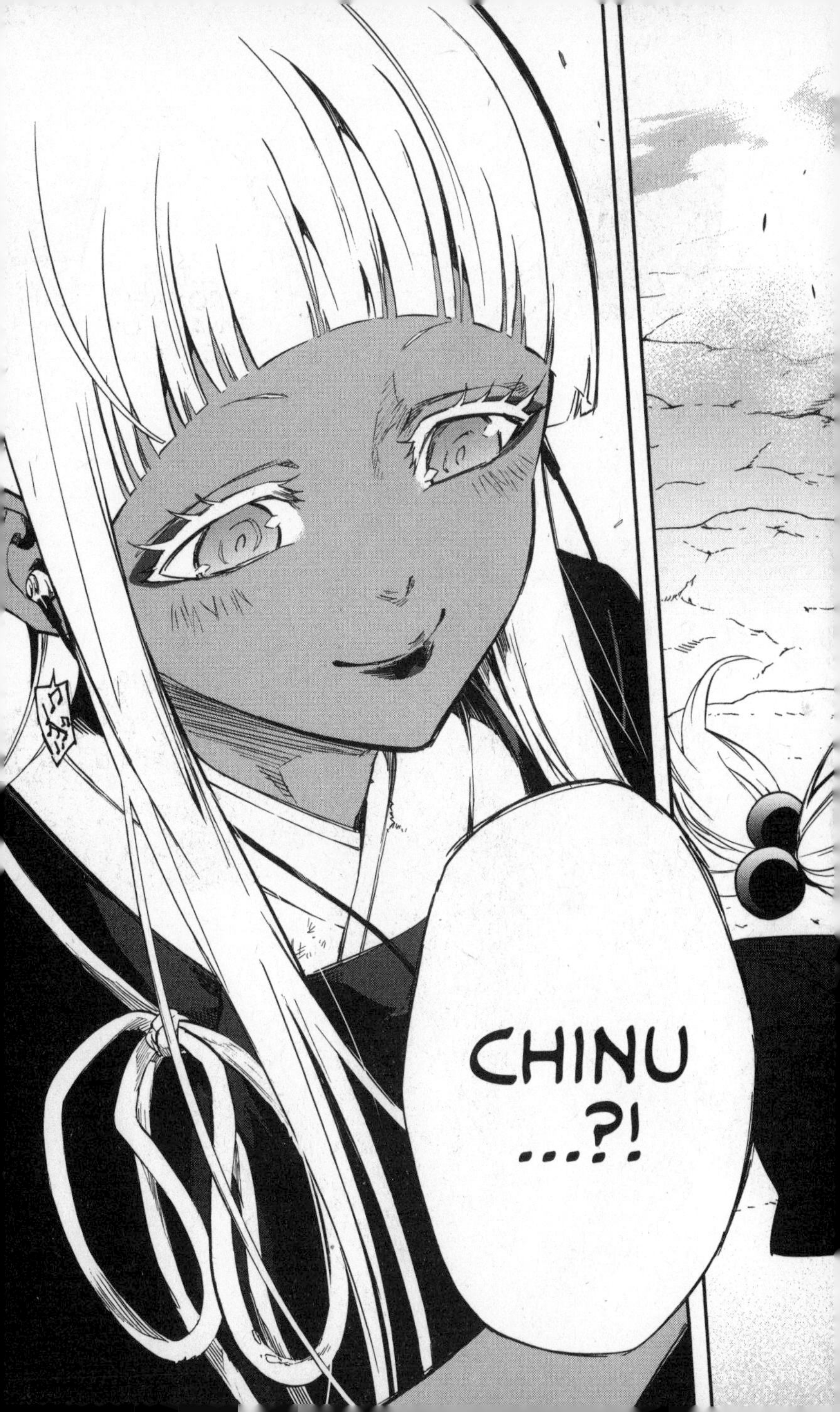
CHINU ...?!

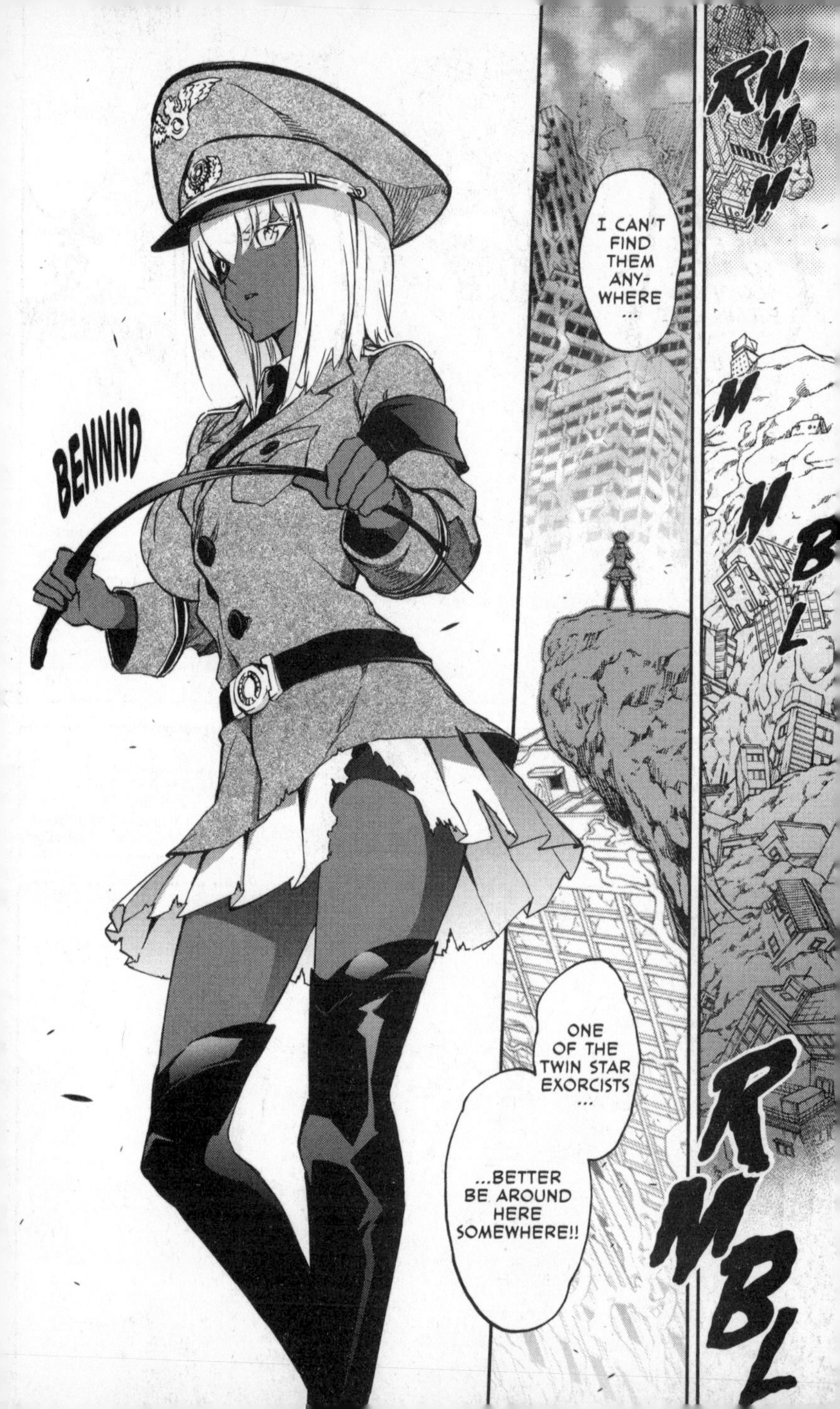
RMMMMMBL
RMMBL
I CAN'T FIND THEM ANYWHERE...
ONE OF THE TWIN STAR EXORCISTS...
...BETTER BE AROUND HERE SOMEWHERE!!
BENNND

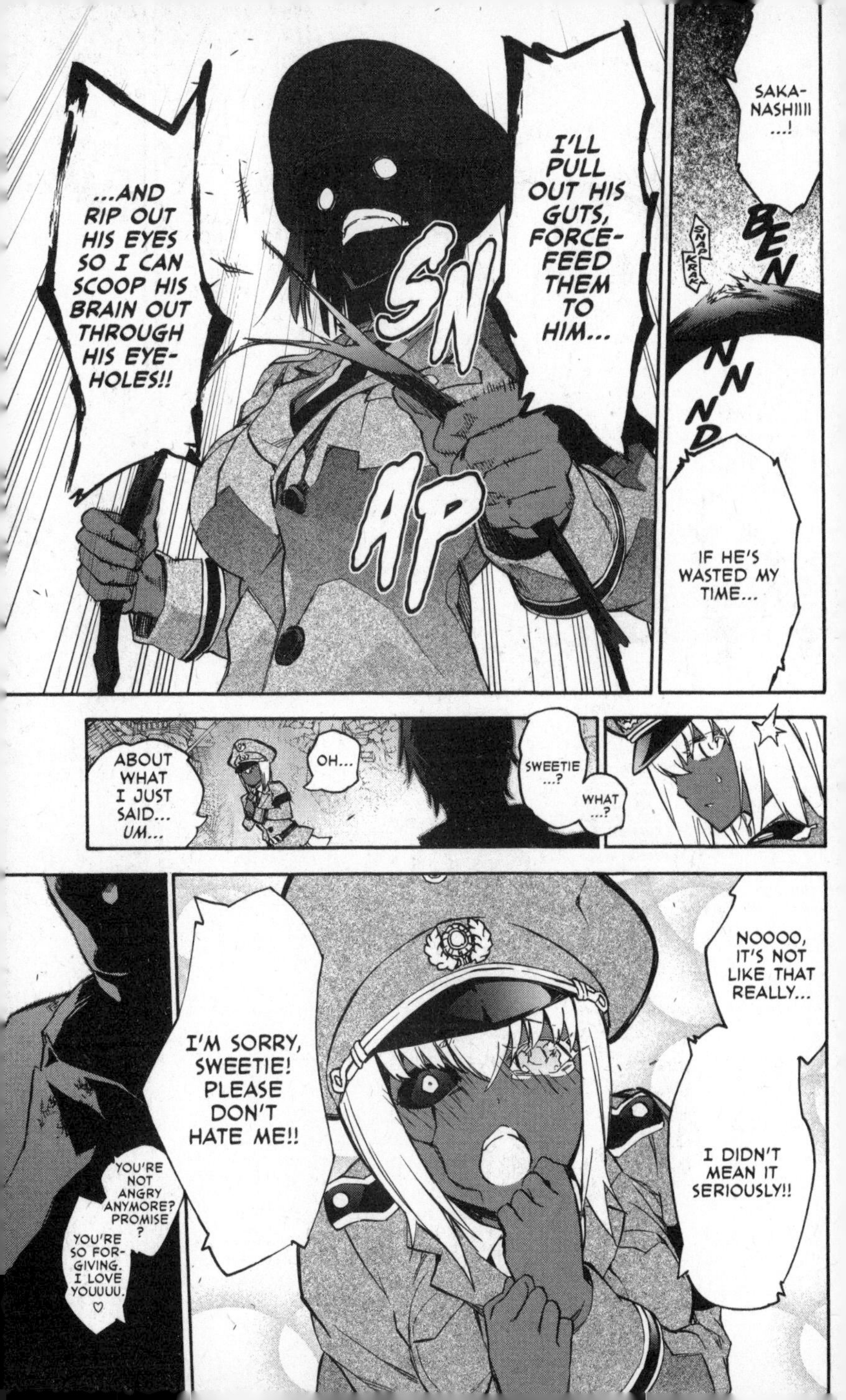
SAKA-NASHIIIII ...!
BENNNND
SNAP KRAK
IF HE'S WASTED MY TIME...
I'LL PULL OUT HIS GUTS, FORCE-FEED THEM TO HIM...
...AND RIP OUT HIS EYES SO I CAN SCOOP HIS BRAIN OUT THROUGH HIS EYE-HOLES!!
SNAP
SWEETIE ...?
WHAT ...?
OH...
ABOUT WHAT I JUST SAID... UM...
NOOOO, IT'S NOT LIKE THAT REALLY...
I DIDN'T MEAN IT SERIOUSLY!!
I'M SORRY, SWEETIE! PLEASE DON'T HATE ME!!
YOU'RE NOT ANGRY ANYMORE? PROMISE?
YOU'RE SO FOR-GIVING. I LOVE YOUUUU. ♡

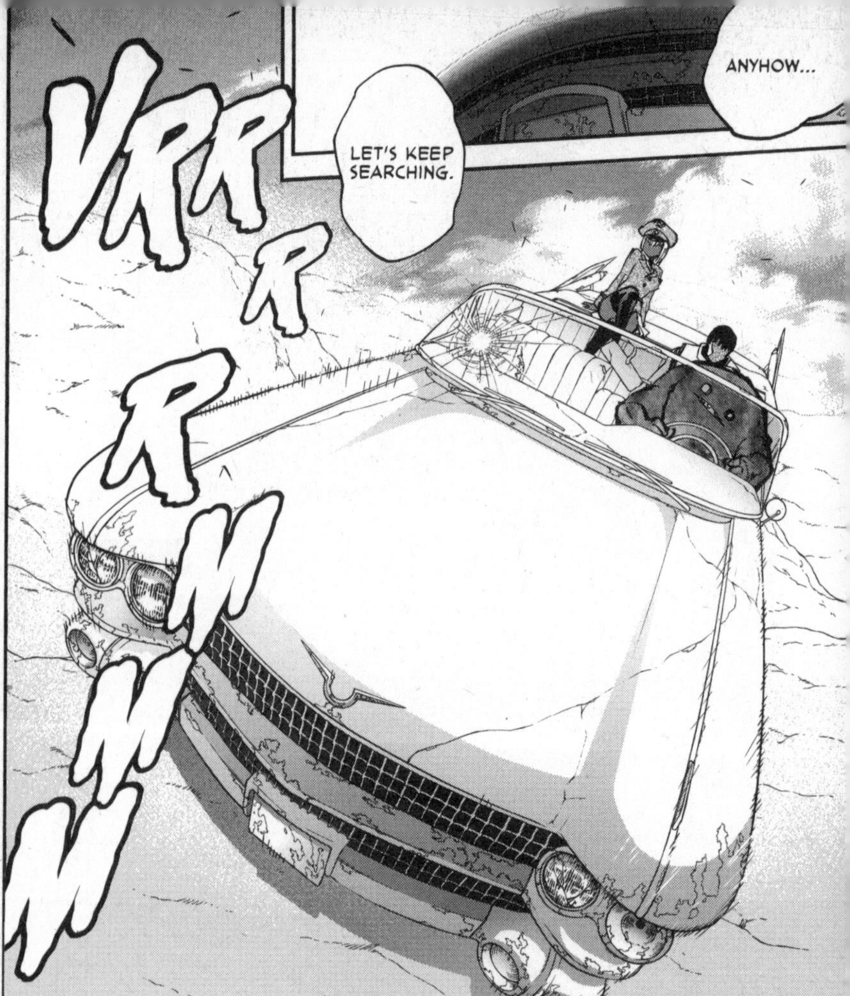
ANYHOW...
LET'S KEEP SEARCHING.
VRRRRMMM

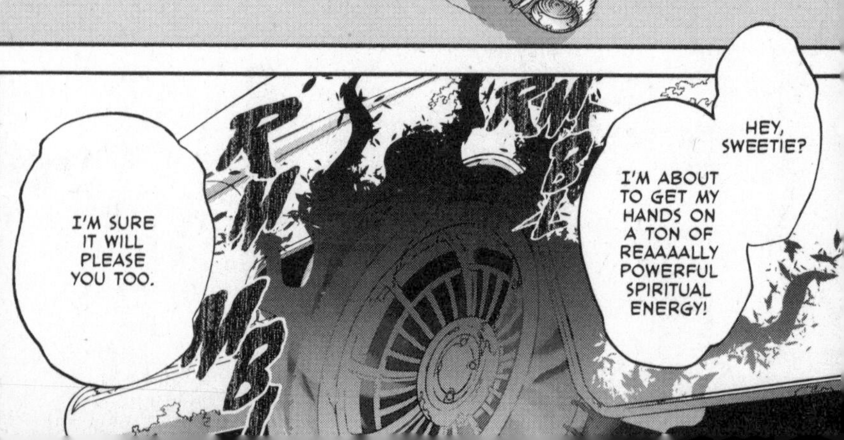
HEY, SWEETIE?
I'M ABOUT TO GET MY HANDS ON A TON OF REAAAALLY POWERFUL SPIRITUAL ENERGY!
I'M SURE IT WILL PLEASE YOU TOO.

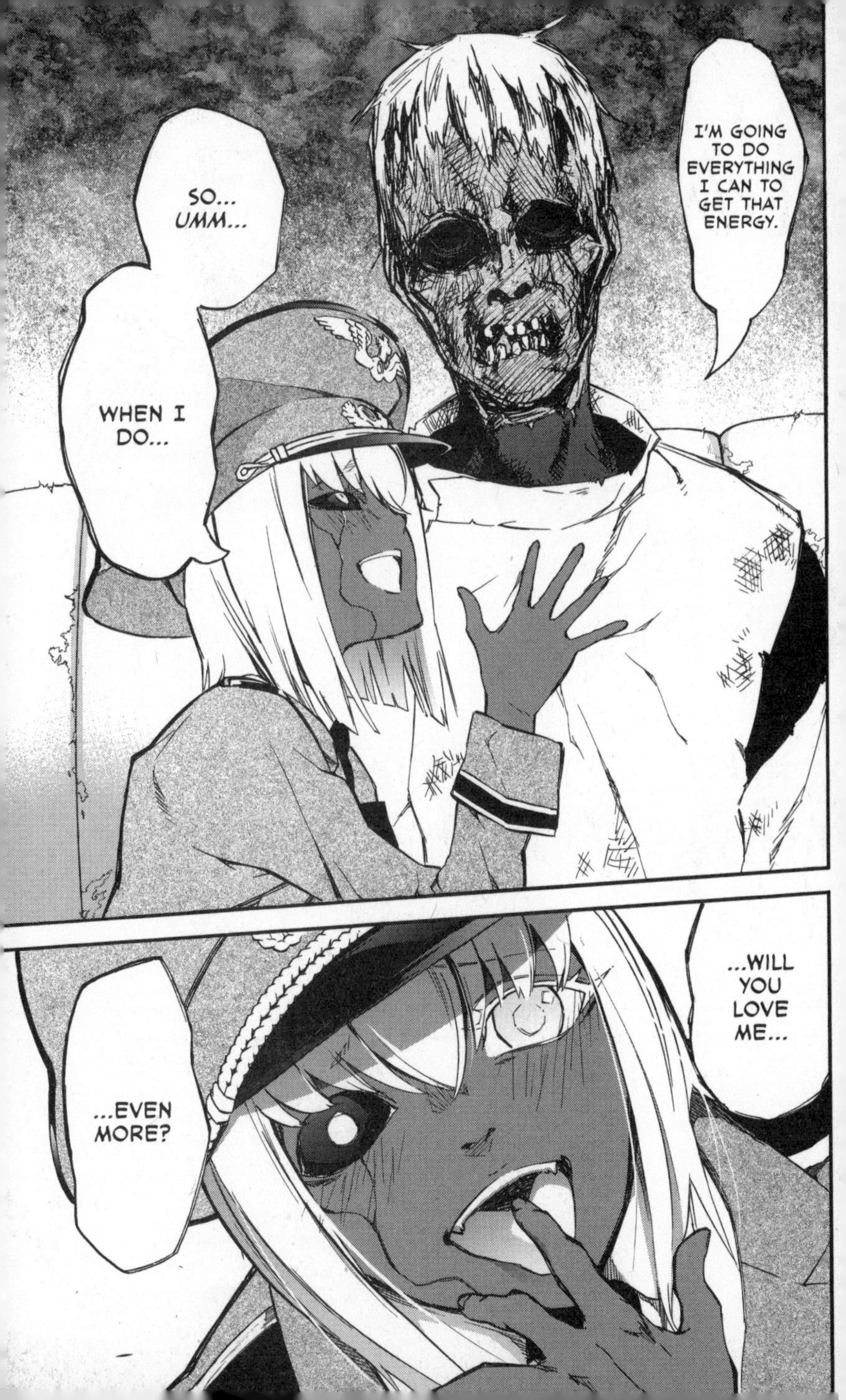
I'M GOING TO DO EVERYTHING I CAN TO GET THAT ENERGY.
SO... UMM...
WHEN I DO...
...WILL YOU LOVE ME...
...EVEN MORE?

Twin Star Exorcists

O N M Y O J I

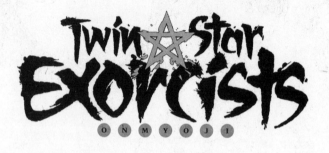

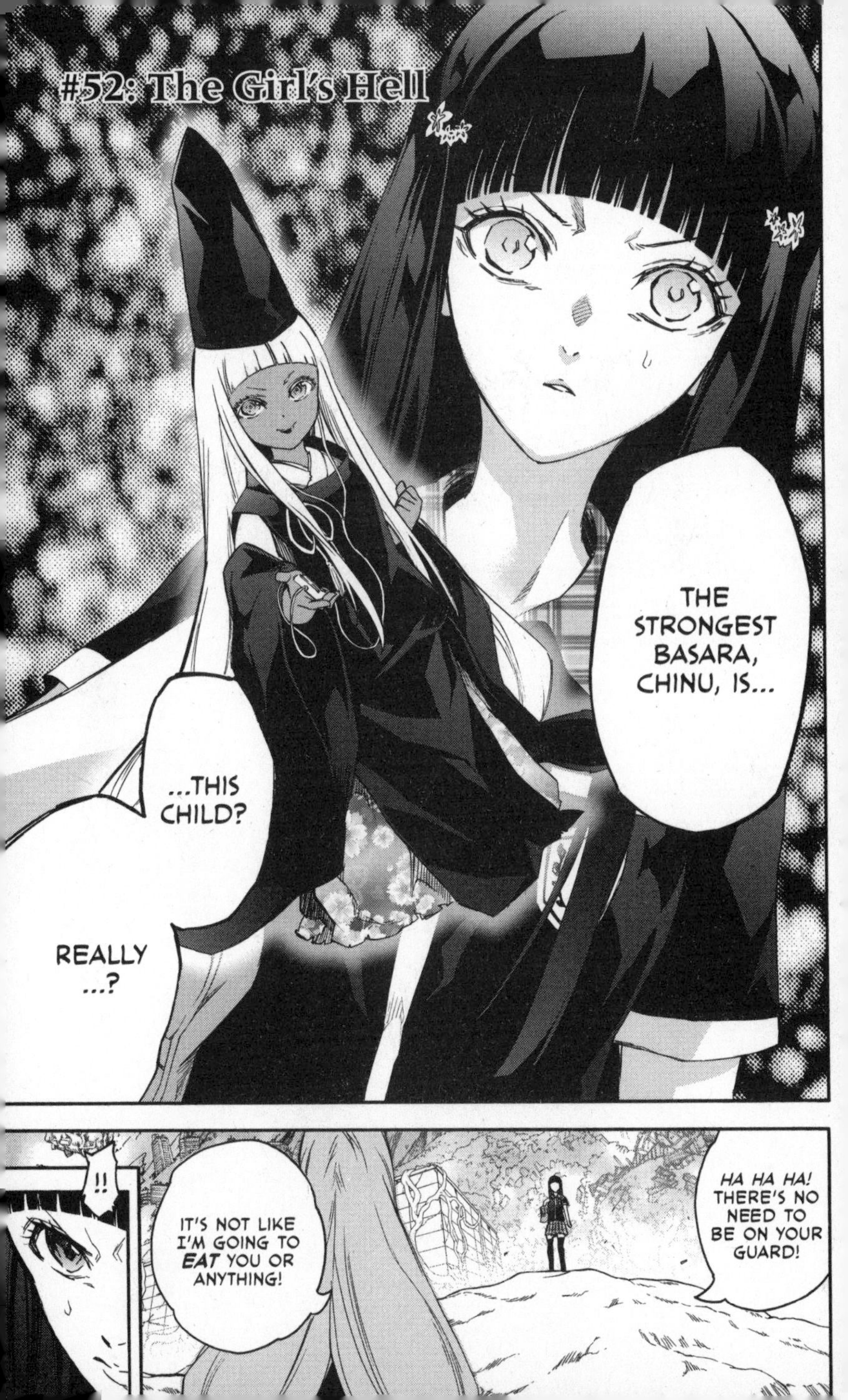
#52: The Girl's Hell
THE STRONGEST BASARA, CHINU, IS...
...THIS CHILD?
REALLY ...?
HA HA HA! THERE'S NO NEED TO BE ON YOUR GUARD!
IT'S NOT LIKE I'M GOING TO ***EAT*** YOU OR ANYTHING!
!!

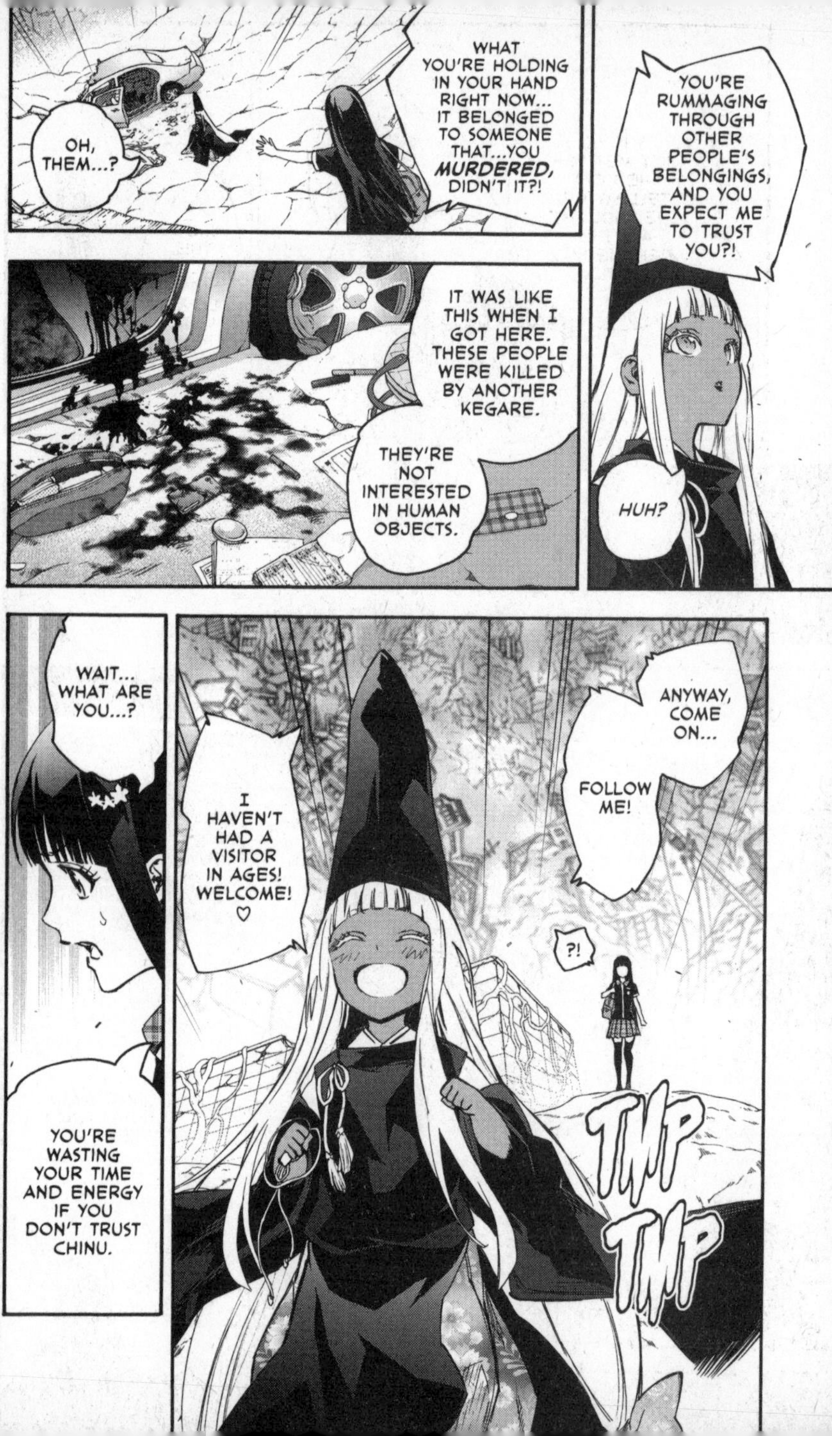
YOU'RE RUMMAGING THROUGH OTHER PEOPLE'S BELONGINGS, AND YOU EXPECT ME TO TRUST YOU?!
HUH?
WHAT YOU'RE HOLDING IN YOUR HAND RIGHT NOW... IT BELONGED TO SOMEONE THAT...YOU ***MURDERED,*** DIDN'T IT?!
OH, THEM...?
IT WAS LIKE THIS WHEN I GOT HERE. THESE PEOPLE WERE KILLED BY ANOTHER KEGARE.
THEY'RE NOT INTERESTED IN HUMAN OBJECTS.
ANYWAY, COME ON...
FOLLOW ME!
I HAVEN'T HAD A VISITOR IN AGES! WELCOME! ♡
?!
TMP TMP
WAIT... WHAT ARE YOU...?
YOU'RE WASTING YOUR TIME AND ENERGY IF YOU DON'T TRUST CHINU.

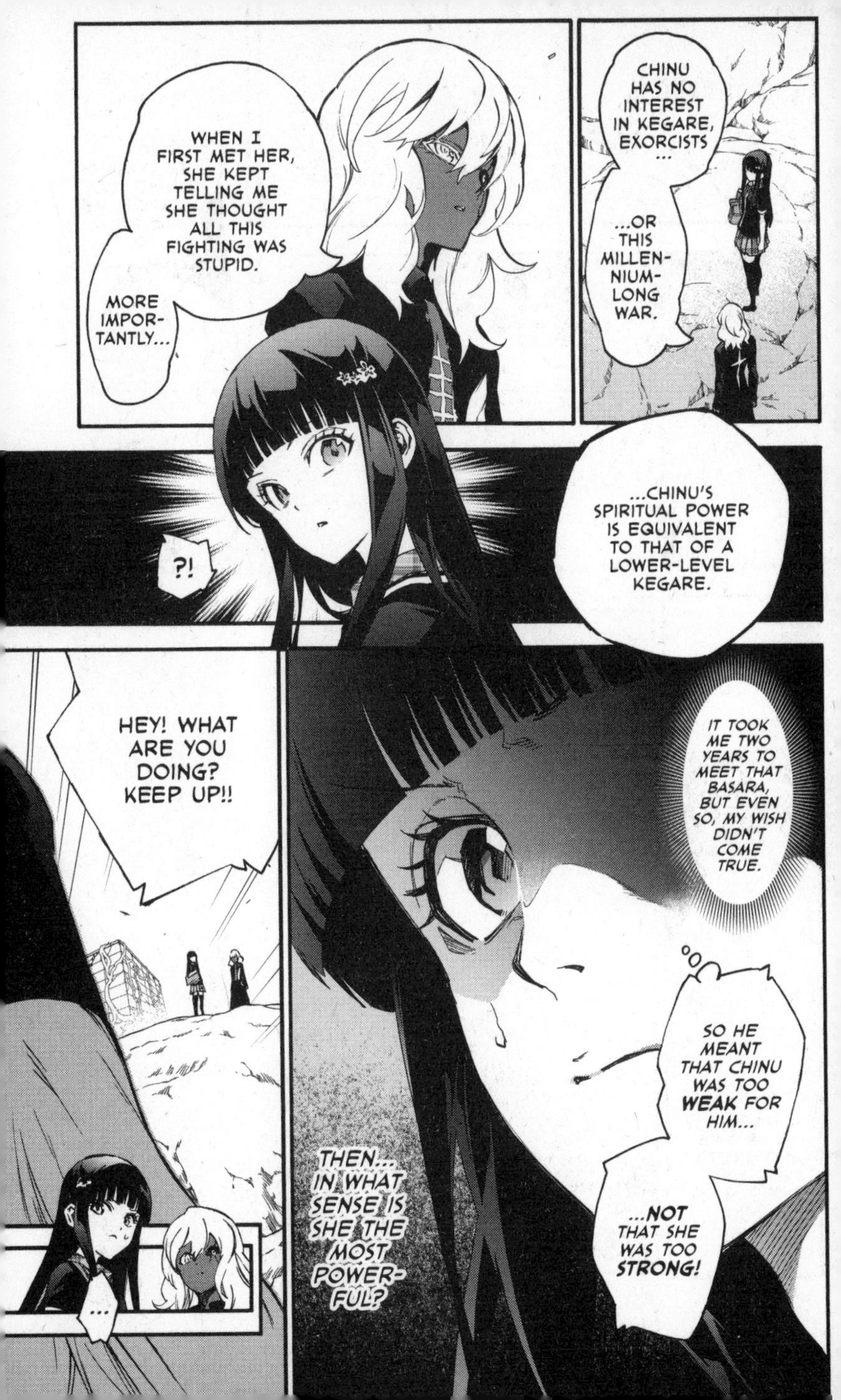
CHINU HAS NO INTEREST IN KEGARE, EXORCISTS ...
...OR THIS MILLEN-NIUM-LONG WAR.
WHEN I FIRST MET HER, SHE KEPT TELLING ME SHE THOUGHT ALL THIS FIGHTING WAS STUPID.
MORE IMPOR-TANTLY...
...CHINU'S SPIRITUAL POWER IS EQUIVALENT TO THAT OF A LOWER-LEVEL KEGARE.
?!
IT TOOK ME TWO YEARS TO MEET THAT BASARA, BUT EVEN SO, MY WISH DIDN'T COME TRUE.
SO HE MEANT THAT CHINU WAS TOO **WEAK** FOR HIM...
...**NOT** THAT SHE WAS TOO **STRONG!**
THEN... IN WHAT SENSE IS SHE THE MOST POWER-FUL?
HEY! WHAT ARE YOU DOING? KEEP UP!!
...

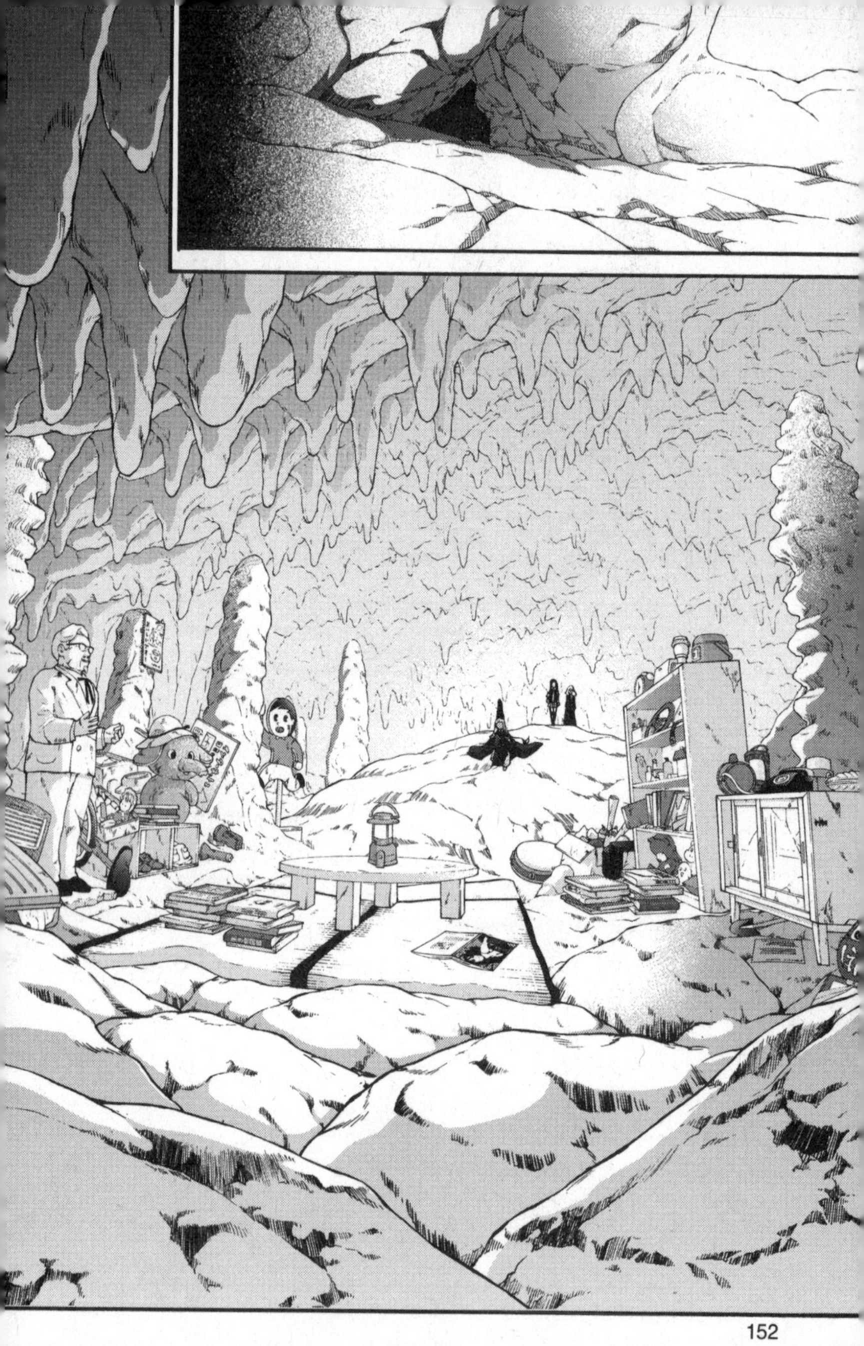

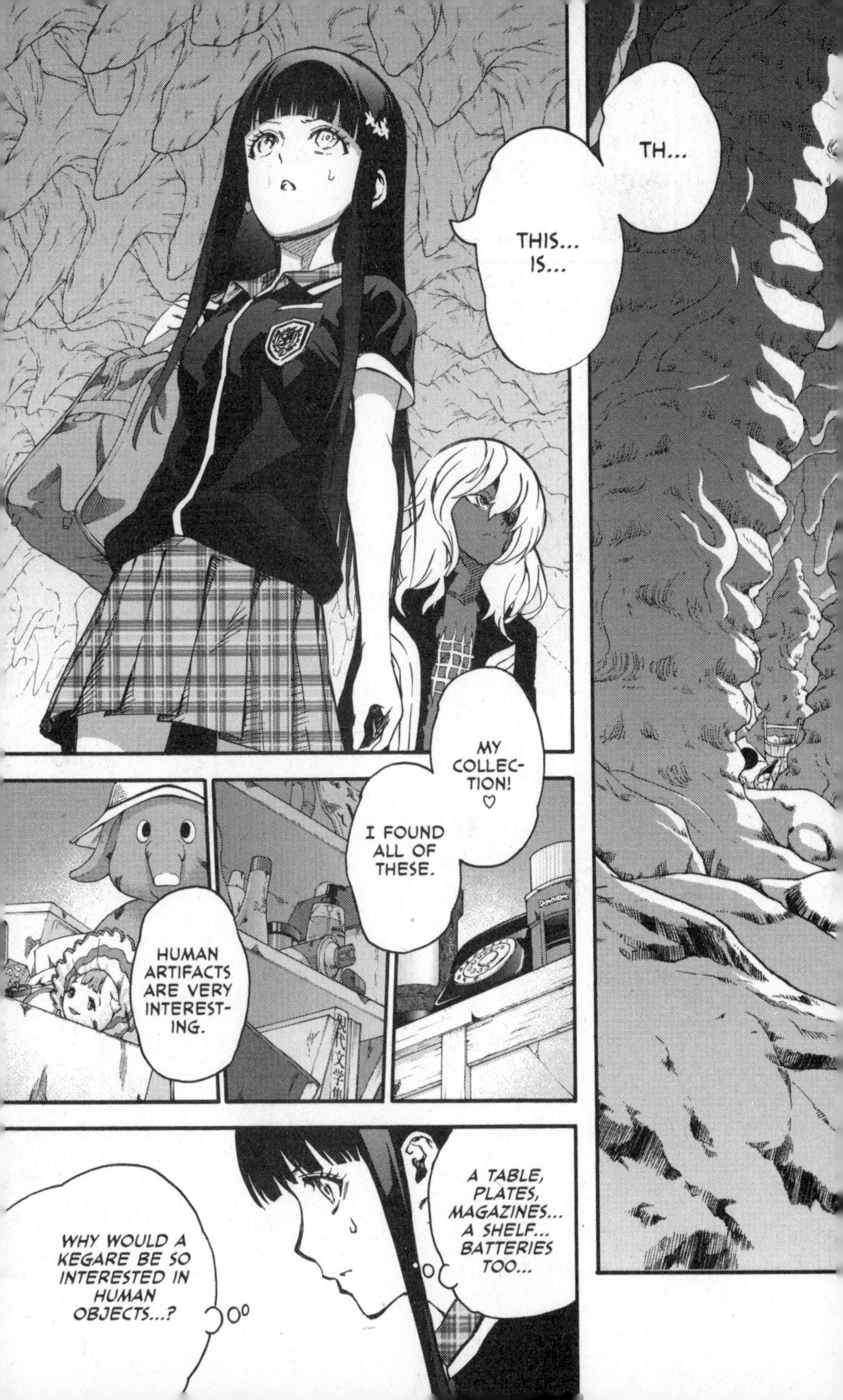
TH...
THIS... IS...
MY COLLEC-TION! ♡
I FOUND ALL OF THESE.
HUMAN ARTIFACTS ARE VERY INTEREST-ING.
A TABLE, PLATES, MAGAZINES... A SHELF... BATTERIES TOO...
WHY WOULD A KEGARE BE SO INTERESTED IN HUMAN OBJECTS...?

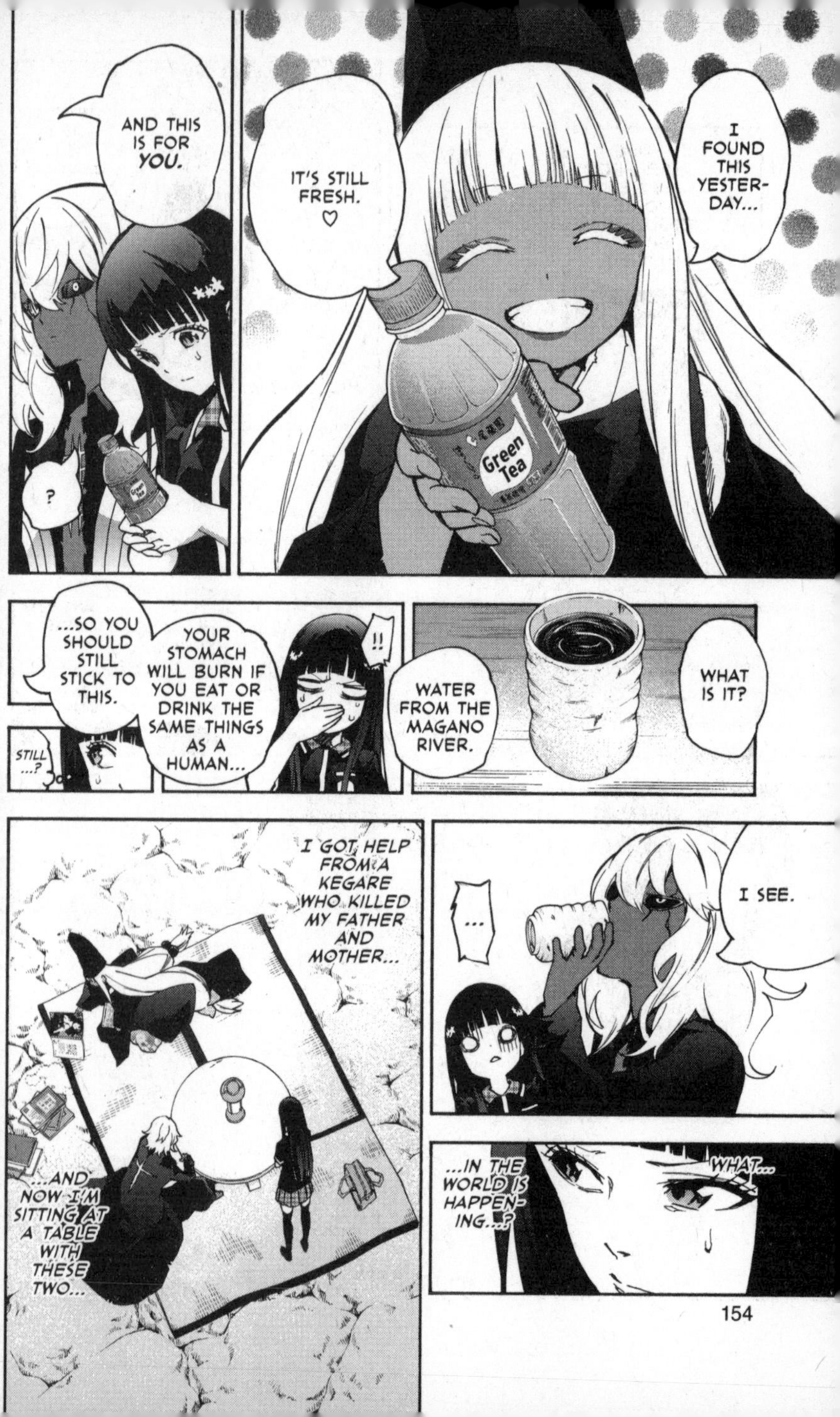
I FOUND THIS YESTER-DAY...
IT'S STILL FRESH. ♡
AND THIS IS FOR *YOU.*
?
WHAT IS IT?
WATER FROM THE MAGANO RIVER.
!!
YOUR STOMACH WILL BURN IF YOU EAT OR DRINK THE SAME THINGS AS A HUMAN...
...SO YOU SHOULD STILL STICK TO THIS.
STILL ...?
I SEE.
...
WHAT...
...IN THE WORLD IS HAPPEN-ING...?
I GOT HELP FROM A KEGARE WHO KILLED MY FATHER AND MOTHER...
...AND NOW I'M SITTING AT A TABLE WITH THESE TWO...

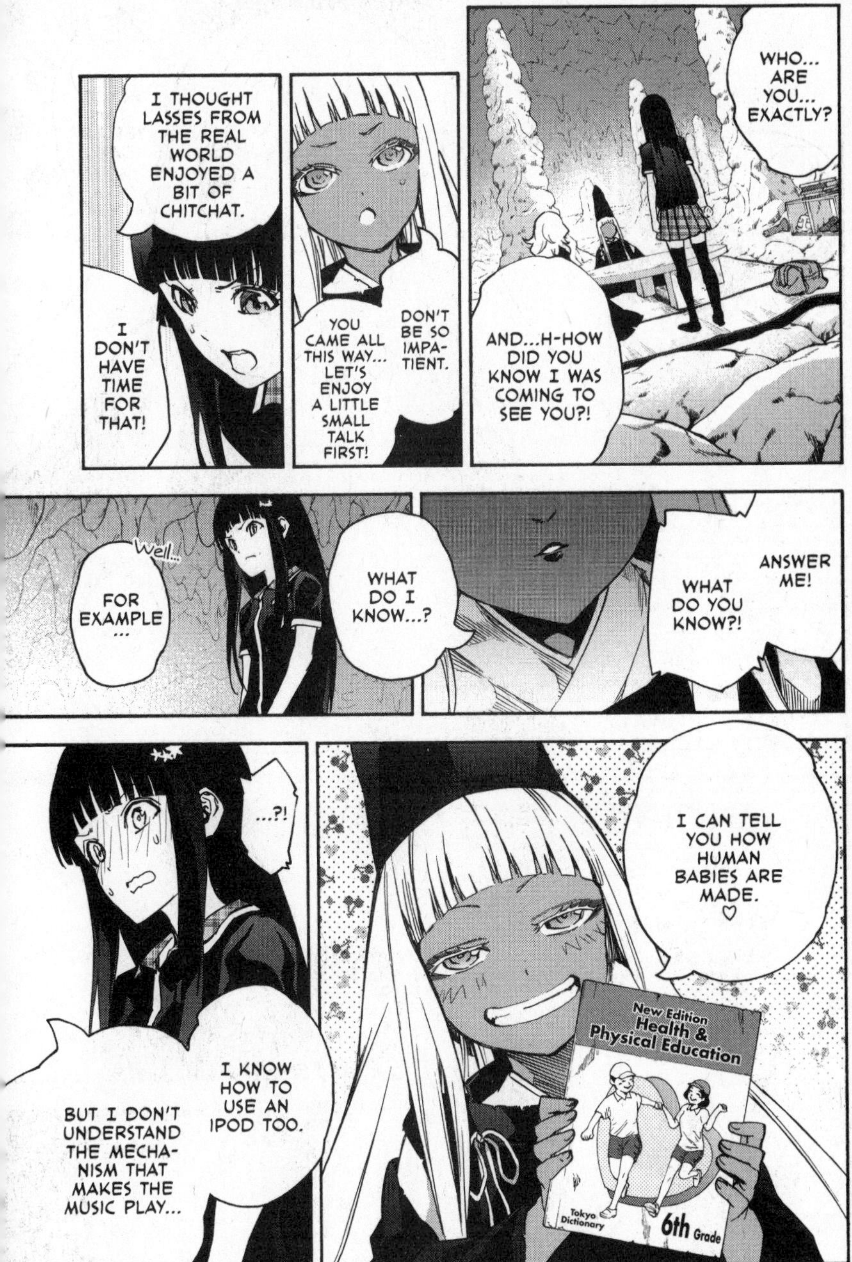
WHO... ARE YOU... EXACTLY?
AND...H-HOW DID YOU KNOW I WAS COMING TO SEE YOU?!
DON'T BE SO IMPA-TIENT.
YOU CAME ALL THIS WAY... LET'S ENJOY A LITTLE SMALL TALK FIRST!
I THOUGHT LASSES FROM THE REAL WORLD ENJOYED A BIT OF CHITCHAT.
I DON'T HAVE TIME FOR THAT!
ANSWER ME!
WHAT DO YOU KNOW?!
WHAT DO I KNOW...?
Well...
FOR EXAMPLE...
I CAN TELL YOU HOW HUMAN BABIES ARE MADE. ♡
New Edition Health & Physical Education
Tokyo Dictionary
6th Grade
...?!
I KNOW HOW TO USE AN IPOD TOO.
BUT I DON'T UNDERSTAND THE MECHA-NISM THAT MAKES THE MUSIC PLAY...

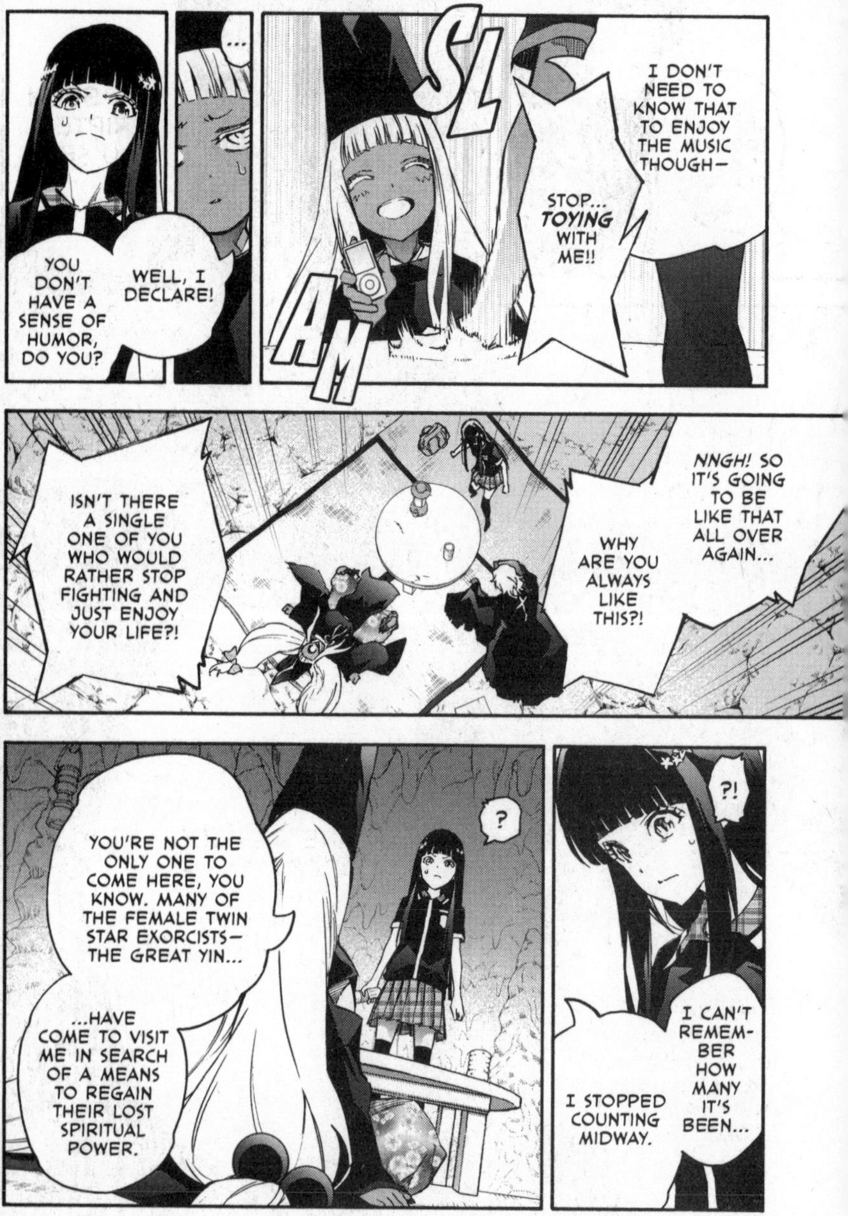
I DON'T NEED TO KNOW THAT TO ENJOY THE MUSIC THOUGH—
STOP... *TOYING* WITH ME!!
SL
AM
...
WELL, I DECLARE!
YOU DON'T HAVE A SENSE OF HUMOR, DO YOU?
NNGH! SO IT'S GOING TO BE LIKE THAT ALL OVER AGAIN...
WHY ARE YOU ALWAYS LIKE THIS?!
ISN'T THERE A SINGLE ONE OF YOU WHO WOULD RATHER STOP FIGHTING AND JUST ENJOY YOUR LIFE?!
?!
I CAN'T REMEM-BER HOW MANY IT'S BEEN...
I STOPPED COUNTING MIDWAY.
?
YOU'RE NOT THE ONLY ONE TO COME HERE, YOU KNOW. MANY OF THE FEMALE TWIN STAR EXORCISTS— THE GREAT YIN...
...HAVE COME TO VISIT ME IN SEARCH OF A MEANS TO REGAIN THEIR LOST SPIRITUAL POWER.

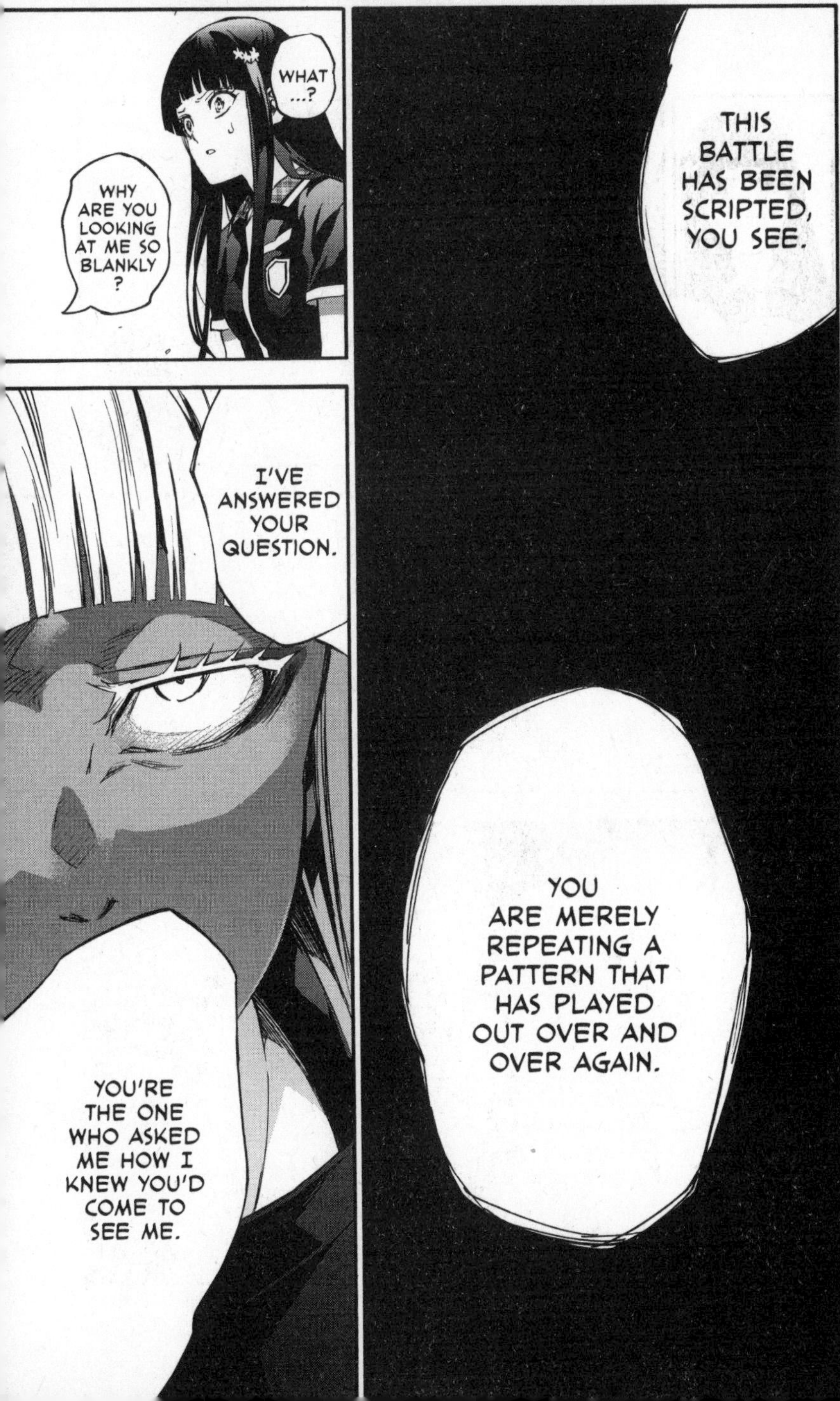
THIS BATTLE HAS BEEN SCRIPTED, YOU SEE.
YOU ARE MERELY REPEATING A PATTERN THAT HAS PLAYED OUT OVER AND OVER AGAIN.
WHAT ...?
WHY ARE YOU LOOKING AT ME SO BLANKLY?
I'VE ANSWERED YOUR QUESTION.
YOU'RE THE ONE WHO ASKED ME HOW I KNEW YOU'D COME TO SEE ME.

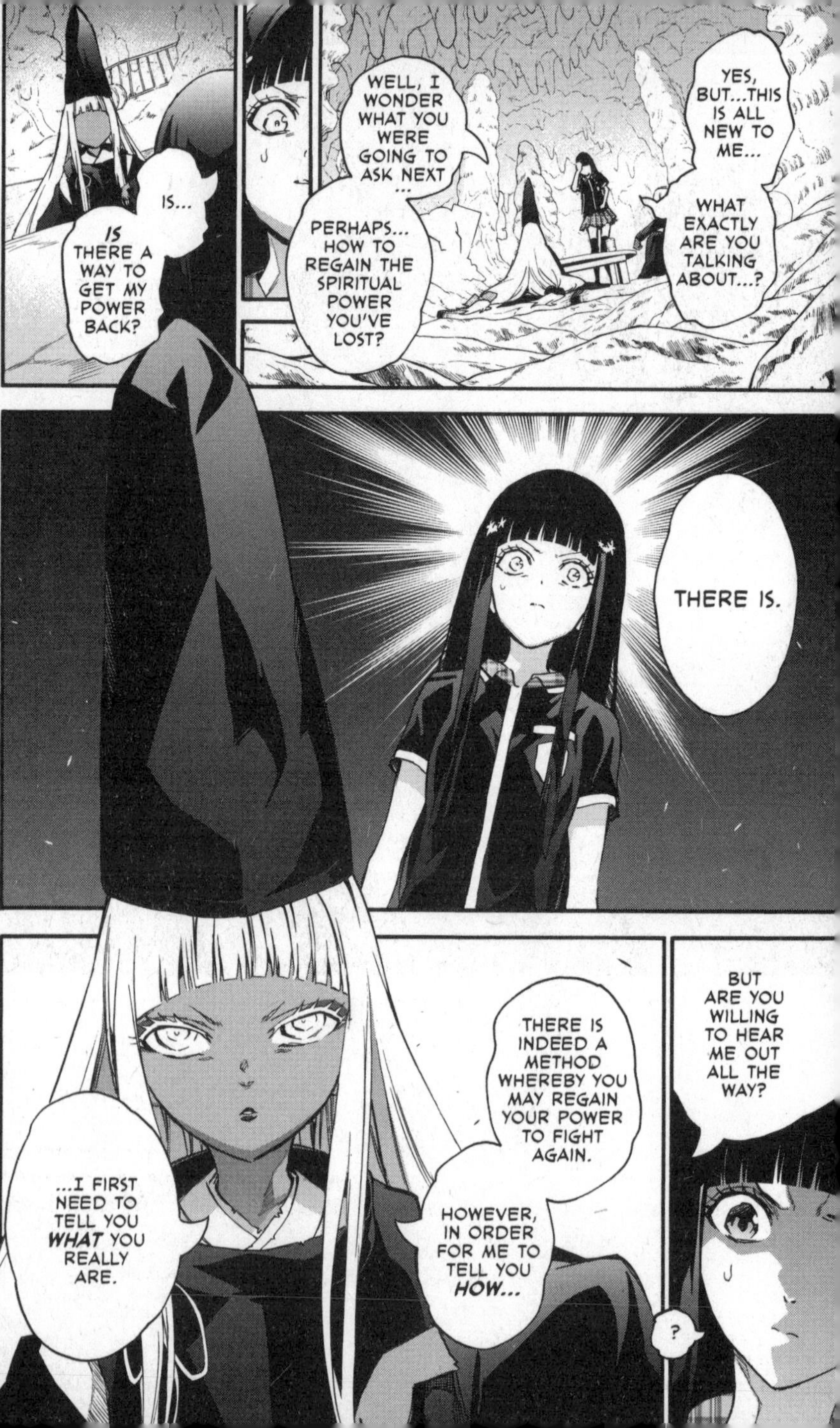
YES, BUT...THIS IS ALL NEW TO ME...
WHAT EXACTLY ARE YOU TALKING ABOUT...?
WELL, I WONDER WHAT YOU WERE GOING TO ASK NEXT...
PERHAPS... HOW TO REGAIN THE SPIRITUAL POWER YOU'VE LOST?
IS...
IS THERE A WAY TO GET MY POWER BACK?
THERE IS.
BUT ARE YOU WILLING TO HEAR ME OUT ALL THE WAY?
?
THERE IS INDEED A METHOD WHEREBY YOU MAY REGAIN YOUR POWER TO FIGHT AGAIN.
HOWEVER, IN ORDER FOR ME TO TELL YOU *HOW*...
...I FIRST NEED TO TELL YOU *WHAT* YOU REALLY ARE.

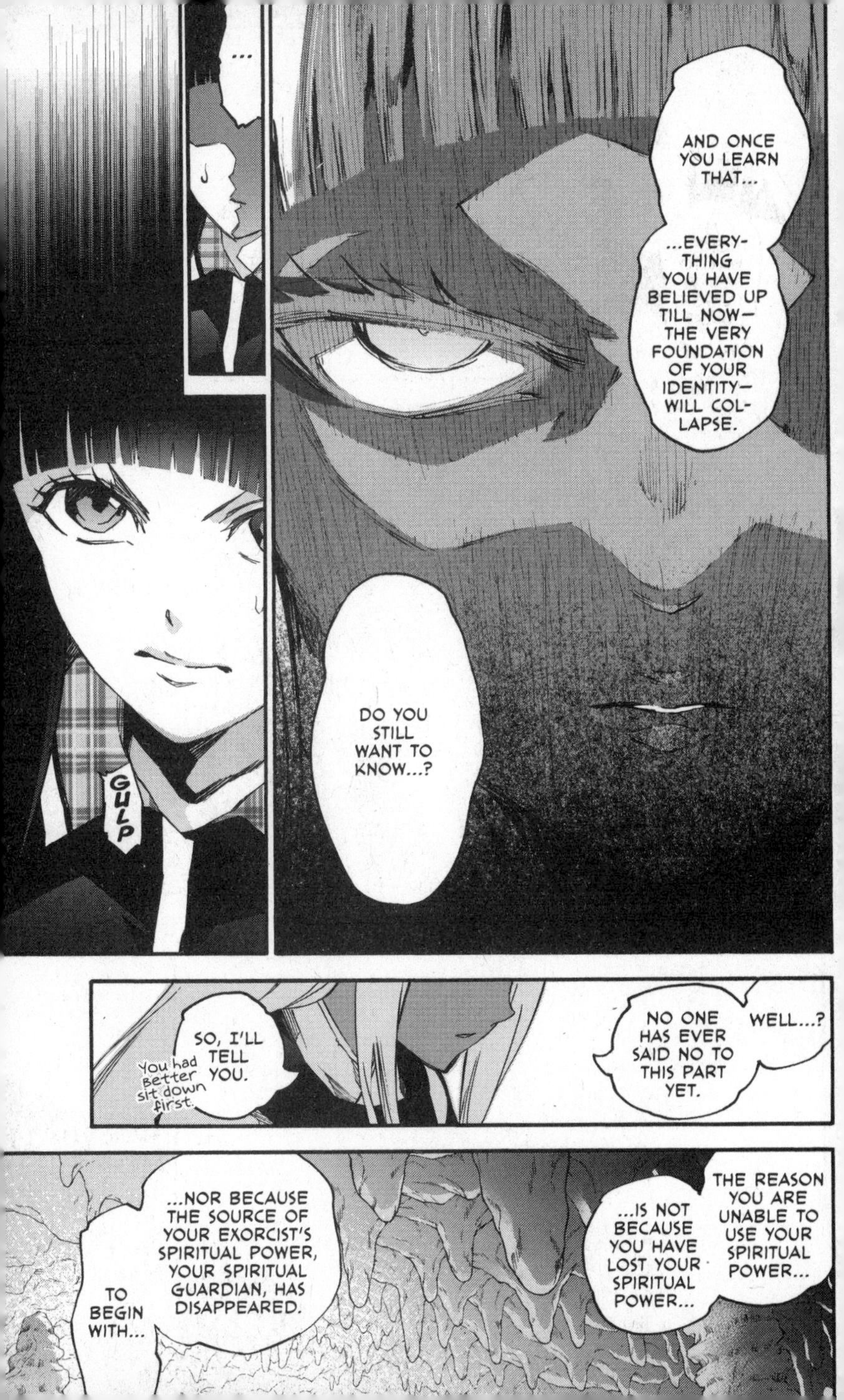
AND ONCE YOU LEARN THAT...
...EVERY-THING YOU HAVE BELIEVED UP TILL NOW—THE VERY FOUNDATION OF YOUR IDENTITY—WILL COL-LAPSE.
DO YOU STILL WANT TO KNOW...?
...
GULP
WELL...?
NO ONE HAS EVER SAID NO TO THIS PART YET.
SO, I'LL TELL YOU.
You had Better sit down first.
THE REASON YOU ARE UNABLE TO USE YOUR SPIRITUAL POWER...
...IS NOT BECAUSE YOU HAVE LOST YOUR SPIRITUAL POWER...
...NOR BECAUSE THE SOURCE OF YOUR EXORCIST'S SPIRITUAL POWER, YOUR SPIRITUAL GUARDIAN, HAS DISAPPEARED.
TO BEGIN WITH...

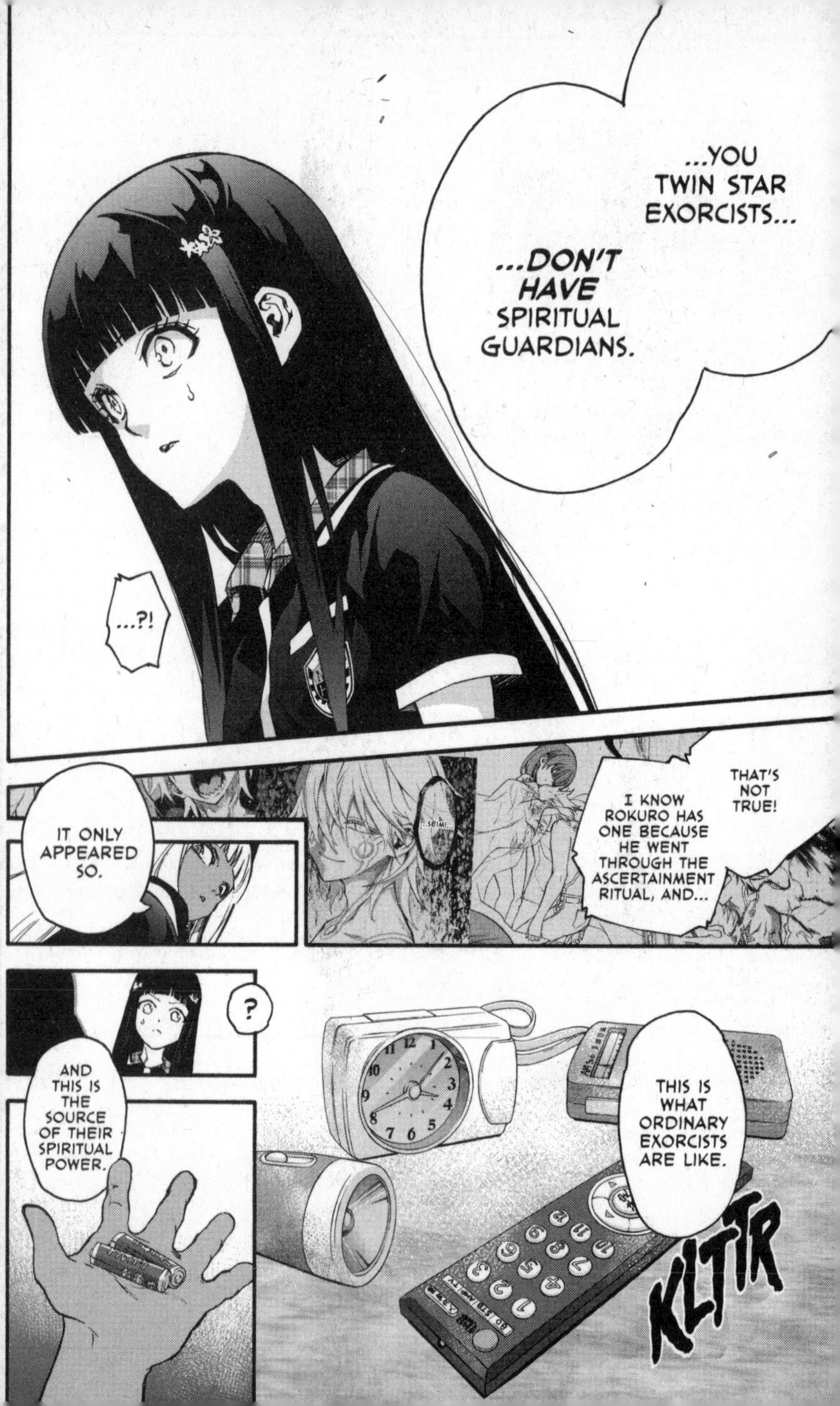
...YOU TWIN STAR EXORCISTS...
...DON'T HAVE SPIRITUAL GUARDIANS.
...?!
THAT'S NOT TRUE!
I KNOW ROKURO HAS ONE BECAUSE HE WENT THROUGH THE ASCERTAINMENT RITUAL, AND...
...SEIMI...
IT ONLY APPEARED SO.
THIS IS WHAT ORDINARY EXORCISTS ARE LIKE.
KLTTR
?
AND THIS IS THE SOURCE OF THEIR SPIRITUAL POWER.

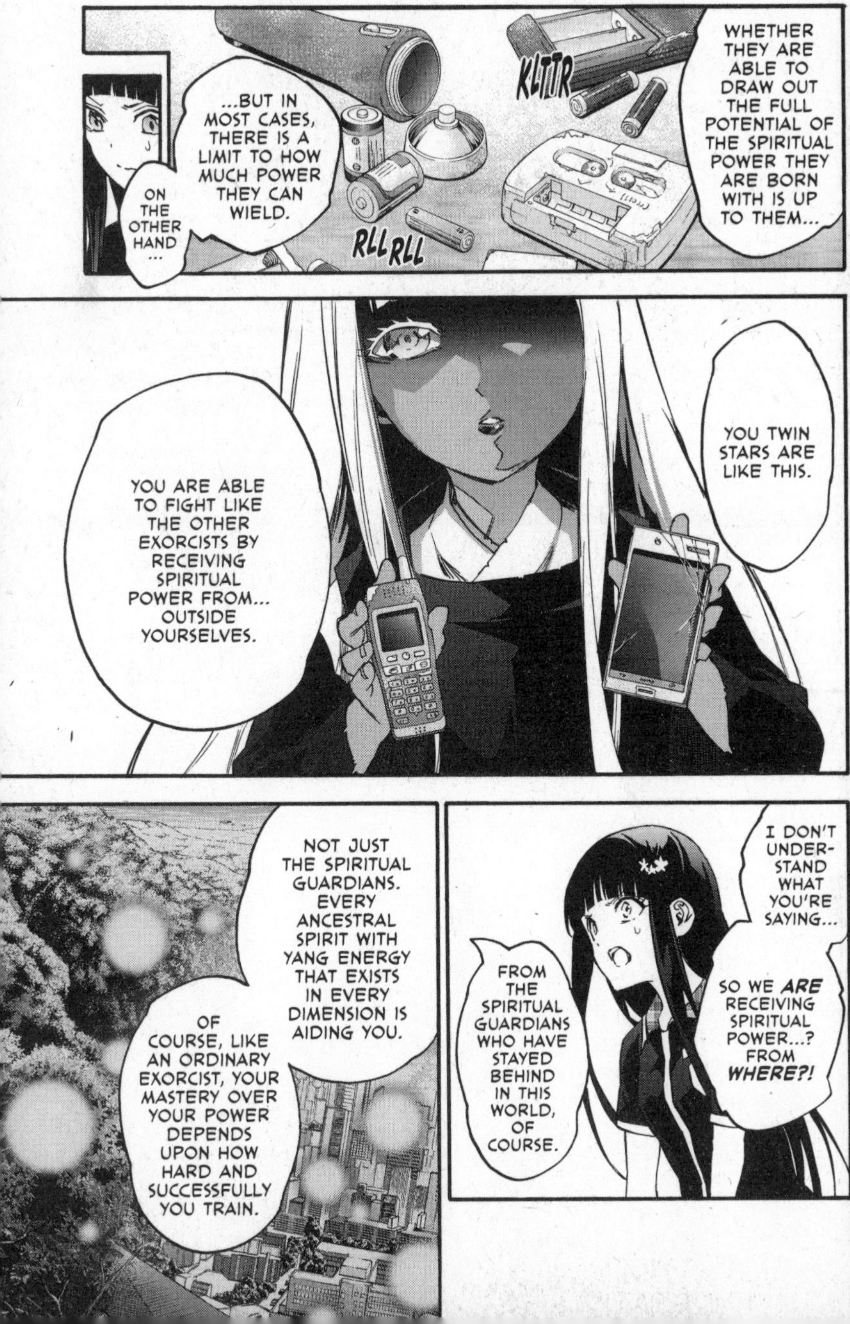
WHETHER THEY ARE ABLE TO DRAW OUT THE FULL POTENTIAL OF THE SPIRITUAL POWER THEY ARE BORN WITH IS UP TO THEM...
KLTTR
...BUT IN MOST CASES, THERE IS A LIMIT TO HOW MUCH POWER THEY CAN WIELD.
ON THE OTHER HAND ...
RLL RLL
YOU TWIN STARS ARE LIKE THIS.
YOU ARE ABLE TO FIGHT LIKE THE OTHER EXORCISTS BY RECEIVING SPIRITUAL POWER FROM... OUTSIDE YOURSELVES.
I DON'T UNDER-STAND WHAT YOU'RE SAYING...
SO WE *ARE* RECEIVING SPIRITUAL POWER...? FROM ***WHERE?!***
FROM THE SPIRITUAL GUARDIANS WHO HAVE STAYED BEHIND IN THIS WORLD, OF COURSE.
NOT JUST THE SPIRITUAL GUARDIANS. EVERY ANCESTRAL SPIRIT WITH YANG ENERGY THAT EXISTS IN EVERY DIMENSION IS AIDING YOU.
OF COURSE, LIKE AN ORDINARY EXORCIST, YOUR MASTERY OVER YOUR POWER DEPENDS UPON HOW HARD AND SUCCESSFULLY YOU TRAIN.

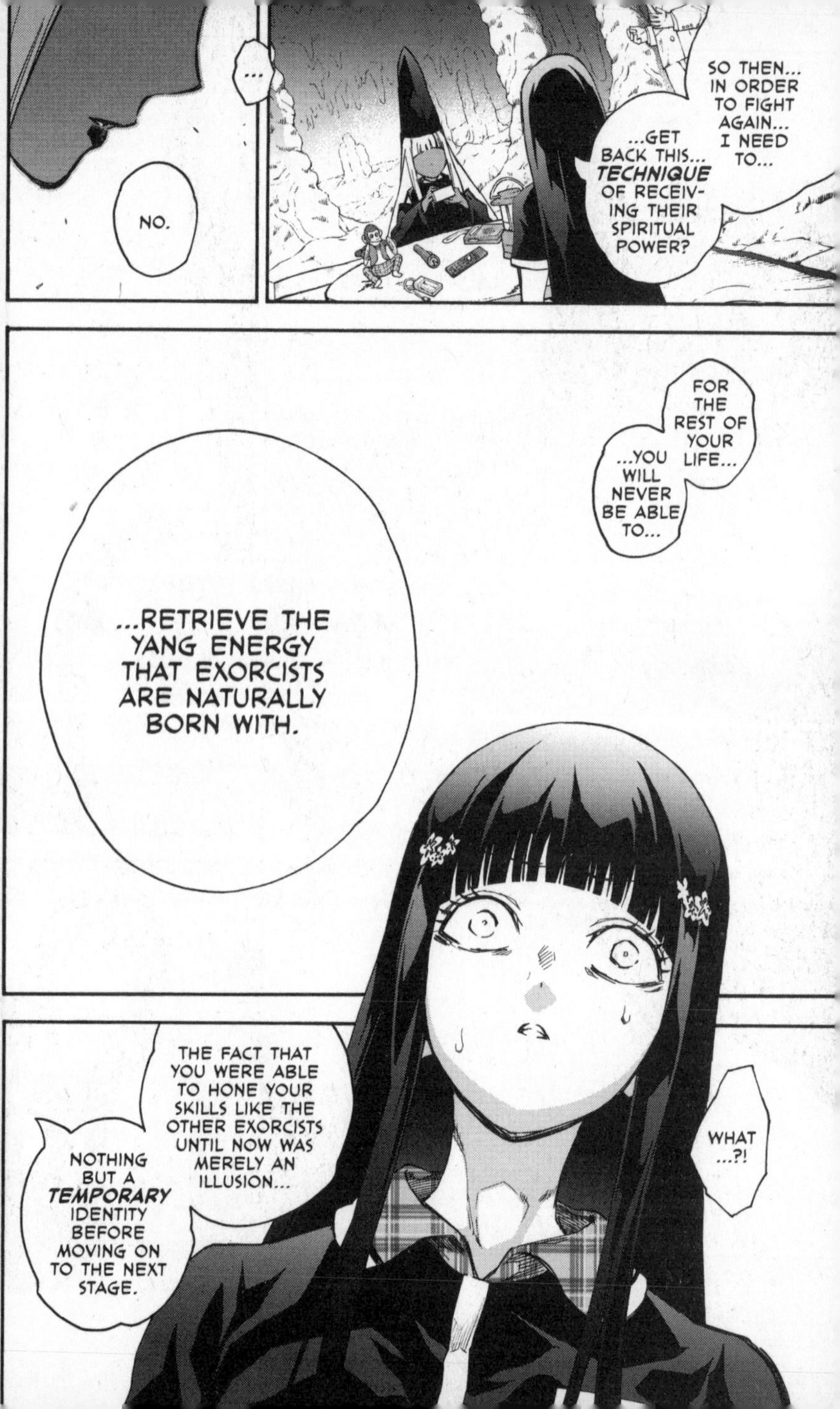
SO THEN... IN ORDER TO FIGHT AGAIN... I NEED TO...
...GET BACK THIS... TECHNIQUE OF RECEIVING THEIR SPIRITUAL POWER?
...
NO.
FOR THE REST OF YOUR LIFE...
...YOU WILL NEVER BE ABLE TO...
...RETRIEVE THE YANG ENERGY THAT EXORCISTS ARE NATURALLY BORN WITH.
WHAT ...?!
THE FACT THAT YOU WERE ABLE TO HONE YOUR SKILLS LIKE THE OTHER EXORCISTS UNTIL NOW WAS MERELY AN ILLUSION...
NOTHING BUT A TEMPORARY IDENTITY BEFORE MOVING ON TO THE NEXT STAGE.

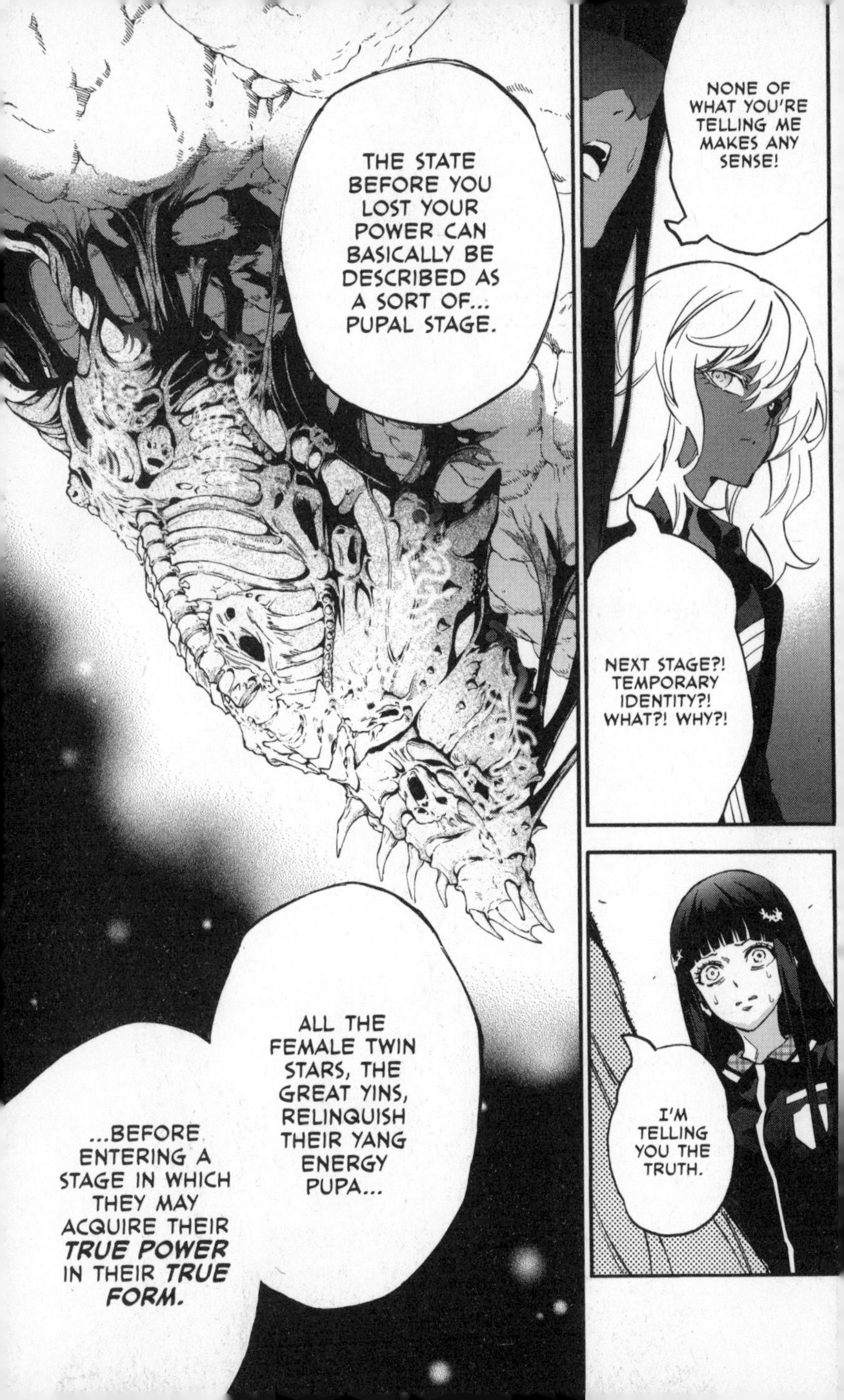
NONE OF WHAT YOU'RE TELLING ME MAKES ANY SENSE!
NEXT STAGE?! TEMPORARY IDENTITY?! WHAT?! WHY?!
I'M TELLING YOU THE TRUTH.
THE STATE BEFORE YOU LOST YOUR POWER CAN BASICALLY BE DESCRIBED AS A SORT OF... PUPAL STAGE.
ALL THE FEMALE TWIN STARS, THE GREAT YINS, RELINQUISH THEIR YANG ENERGY PUPA...
...BEFORE ENTERING A STAGE IN WHICH THEY MAY ACQUIRE THEIR *TRUE POWER* IN THEIR *TRUE FORM.*

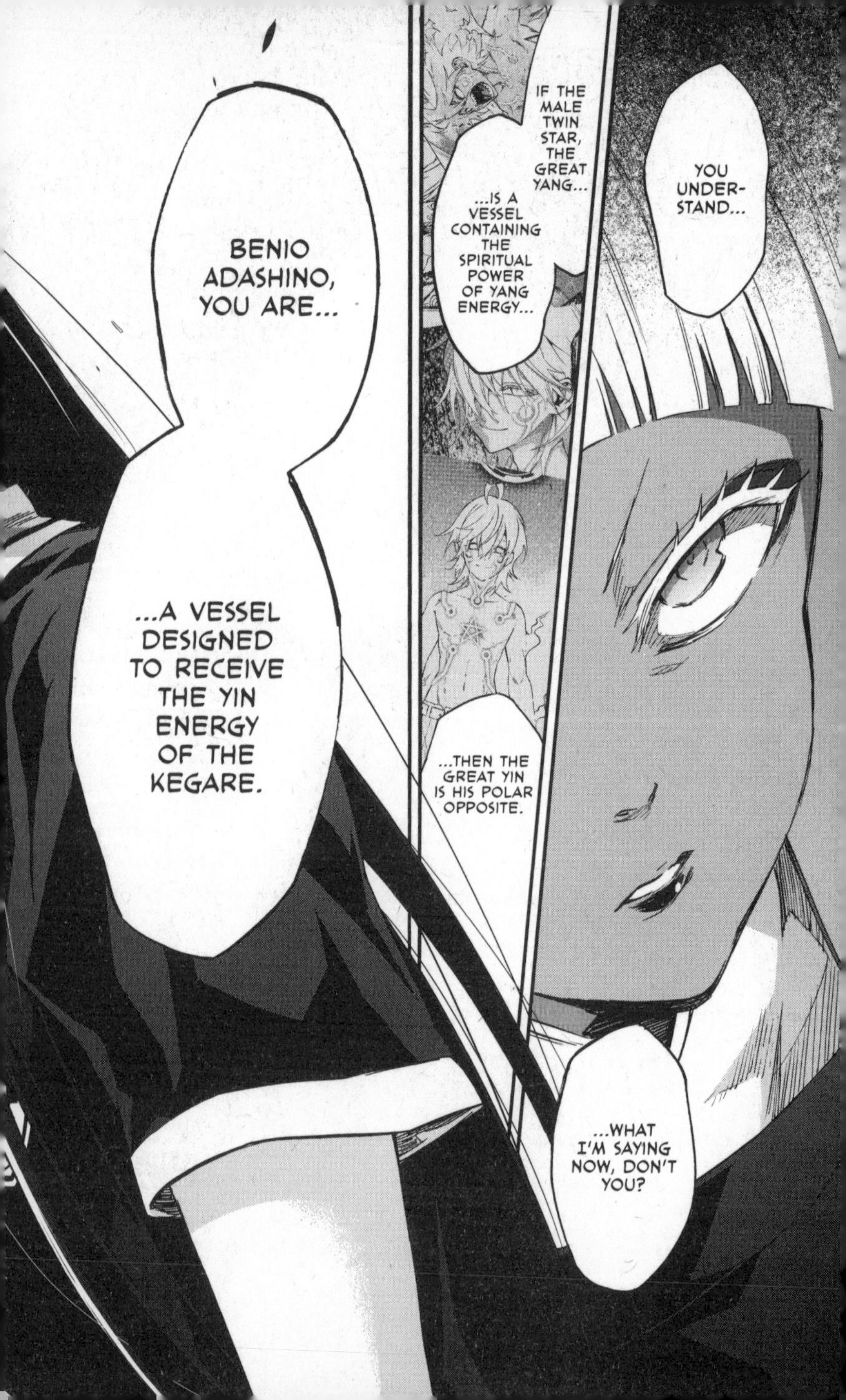
YOU UNDER-STAND...
...WHAT I'M SAYING NOW, DON'T YOU?
IF THE MALE TWIN STAR, THE GREAT YANG...
...IS A VESSEL CONTAINING THE SPIRITUAL POWER OF YANG ENERGY...
...THEN THE GREAT YIN IS HIS POLAR OPPOSITE.
BENIO ADASHINO, YOU ARE...
...A VESSEL DESIGNED TO RECEIVE THE YIN ENERGY OF THE KEGARE.

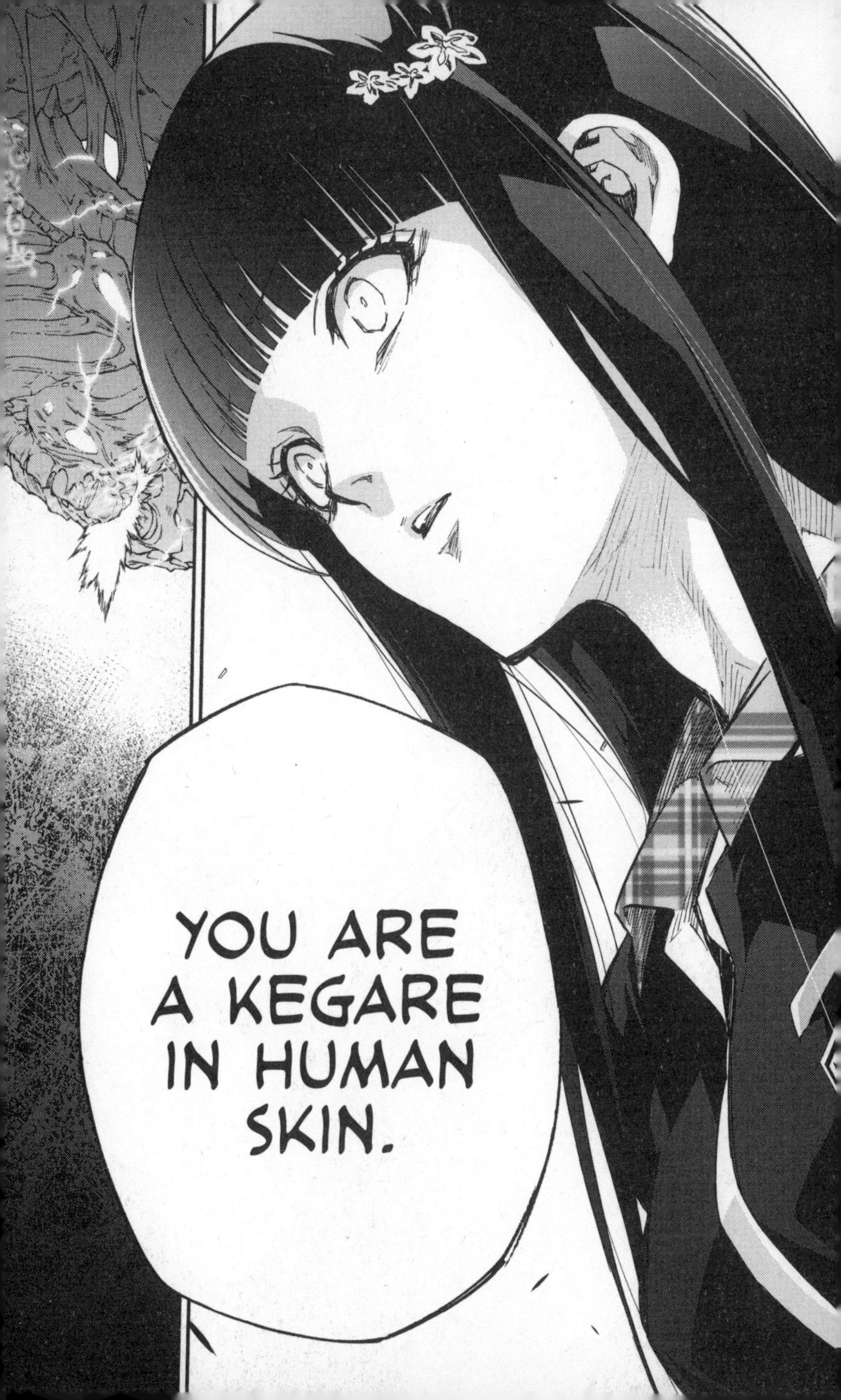
YOU ARE A KEGARE IN HUMAN SKIN.

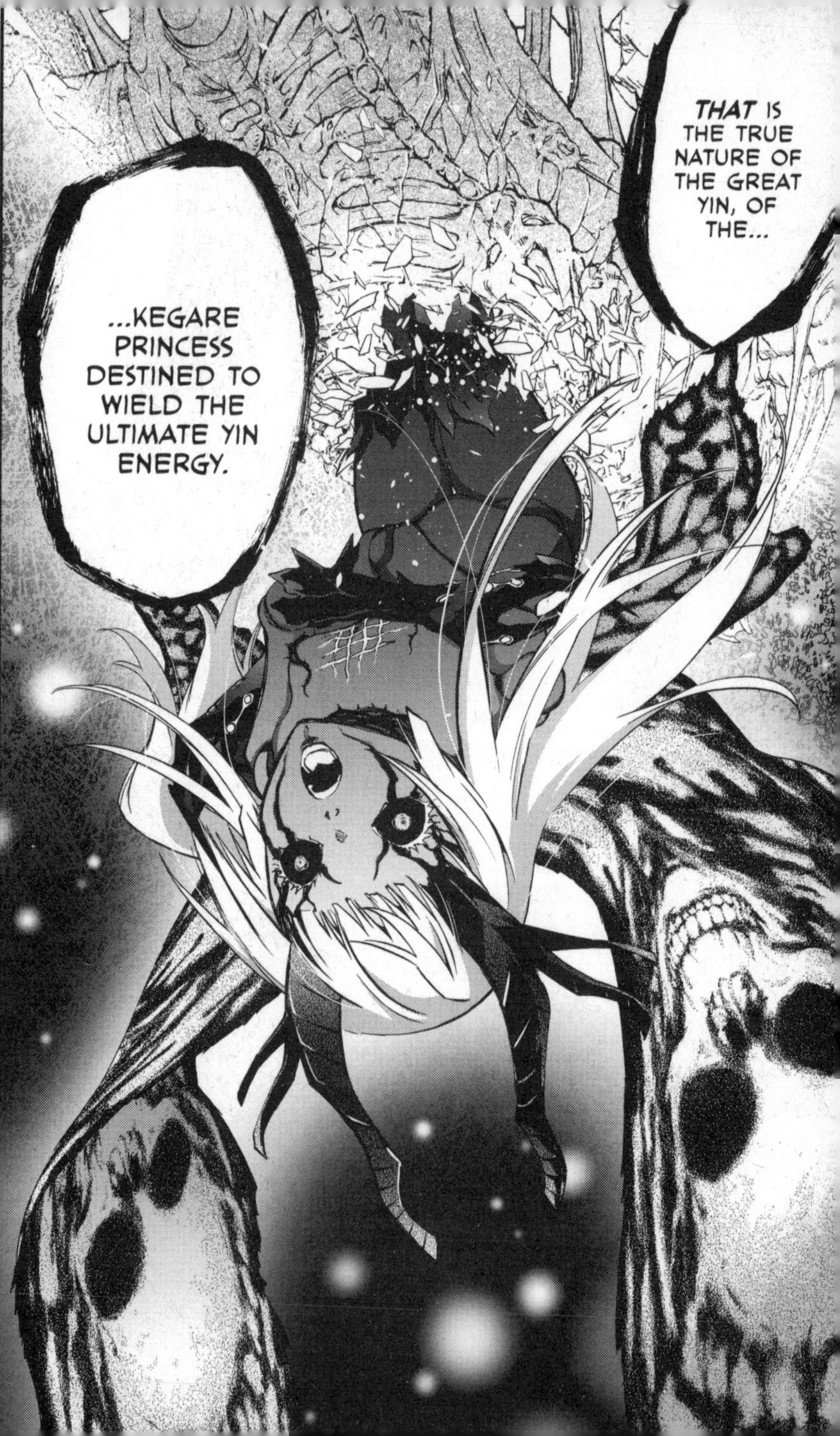
THAT IS THE TRUE NATURE OF THE GREAT YIN, OF THE...
...KEGARE PRINCESS DESTINED TO WIELD THE ULTIMATE YIN ENERGY.

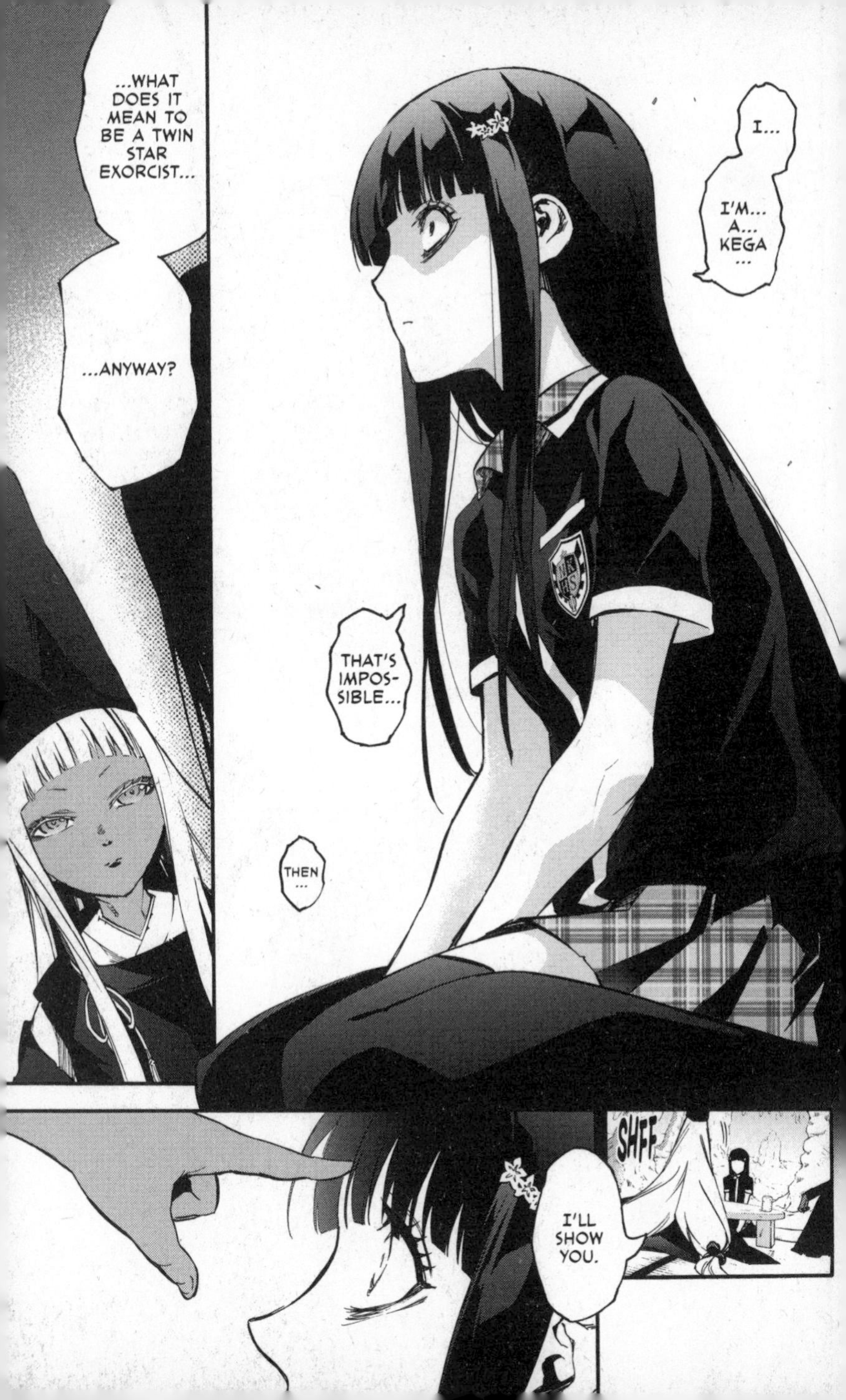
I...
I'M... A... KEGA...
THAT'S IMPOSSIBLE...
THEN...
...WHAT DOES IT MEAN TO BE A TWIN STAR EXORCIST...
...ANYWAY?
SHFF
I'LL SHOW YOU.

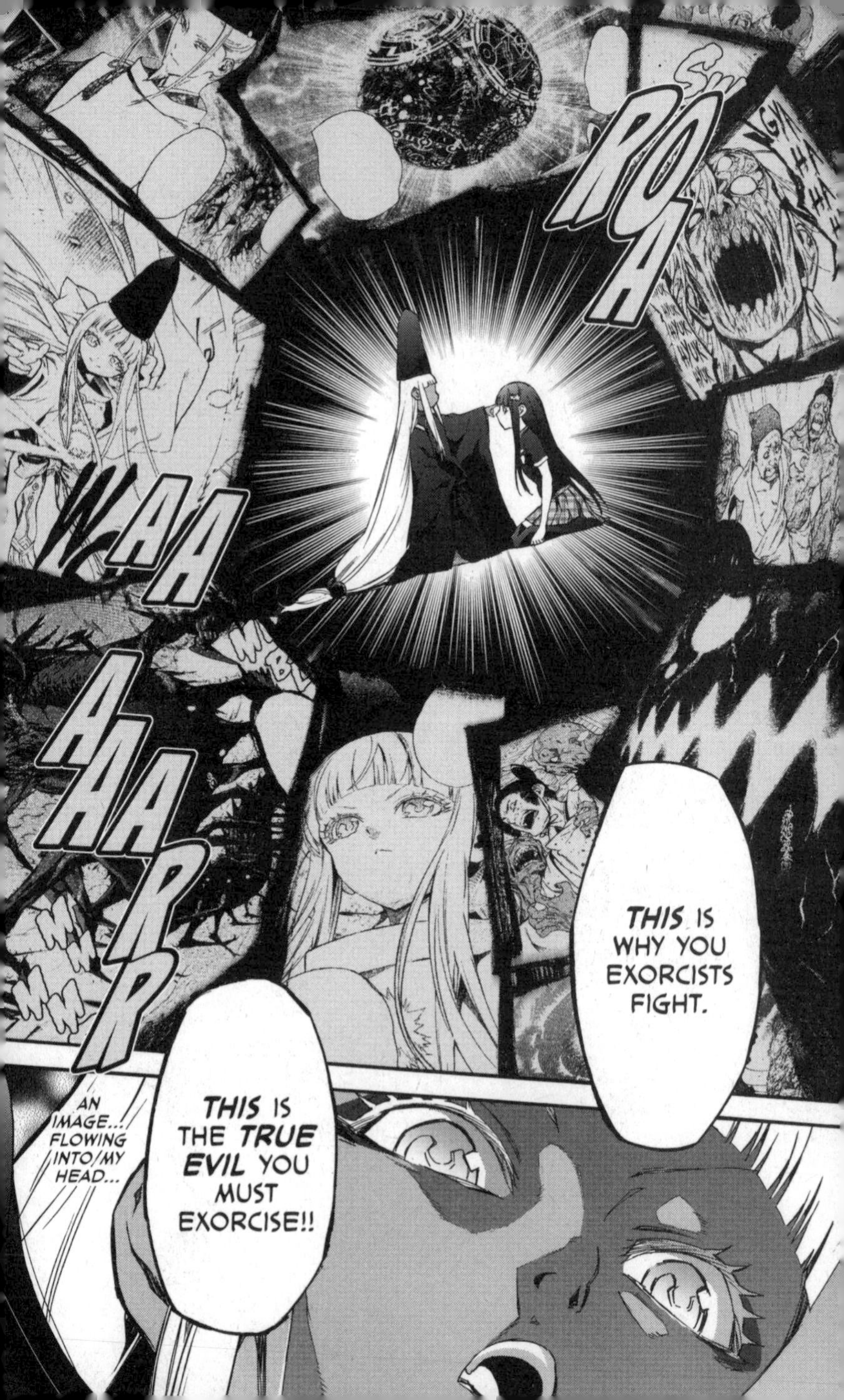
THIS IS WHY YOU EXORCISTS FIGHT.
THIS IS THE TRUE EVIL YOU MUST EXORCISE!!
AN IMAGE... FLOWING INTO MY HEAD...

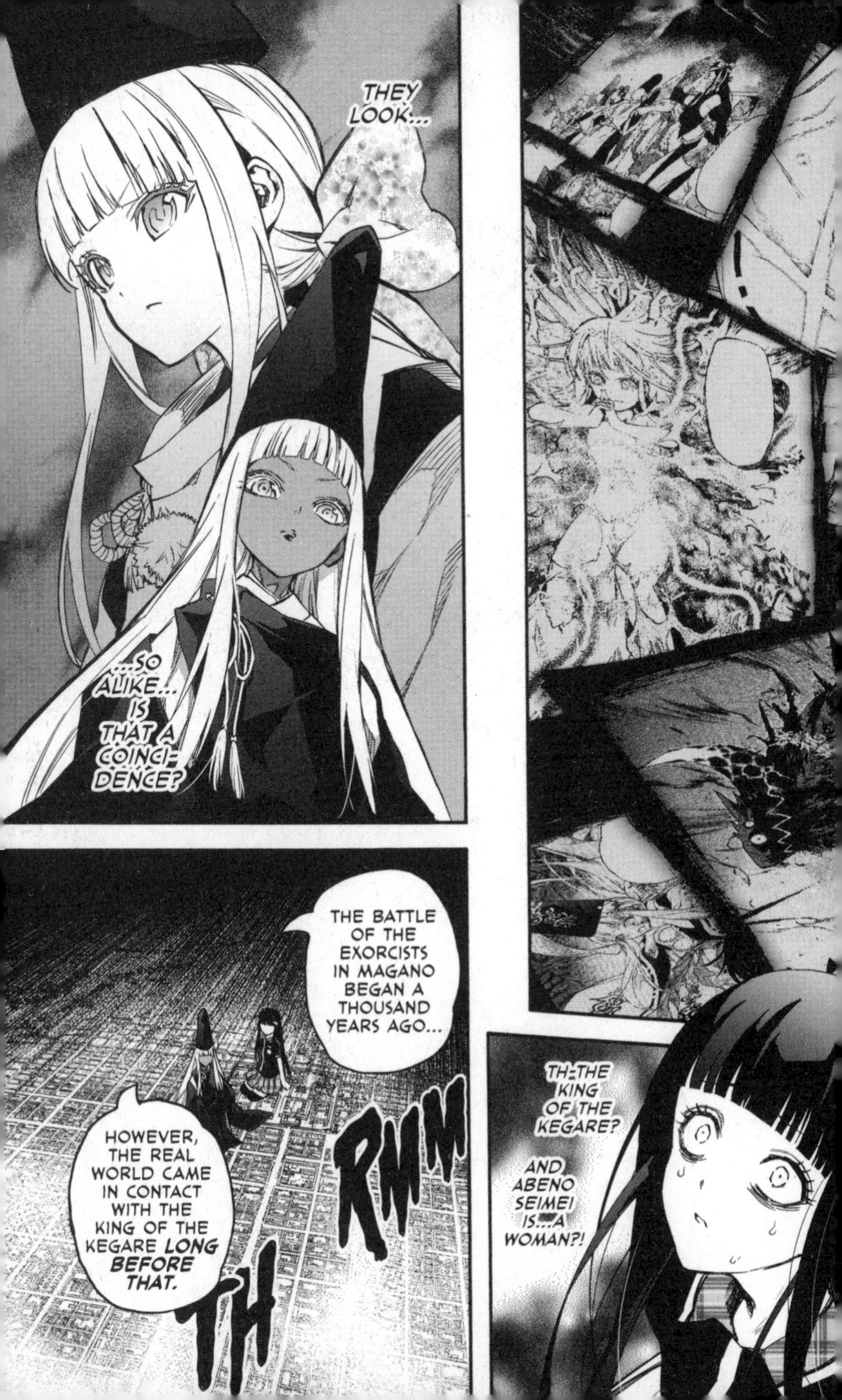
THEY LOOK...
...SO ALIKE... IS THAT A COINCI-DENCE?
TH-THE KING OF THE KEGARE?
AND ABENO SEIMEI IS...A WOMAN?!
THE BATTLE OF THE EXORCISTS IN MAGANO BEGAN A THOUSAND YEARS AGO...
HOWEVER, THE REAL WORLD CAME IN CONTACT WITH THE KING OF THE KEGARE ***LONG BEFORE THAT.***
THRMM

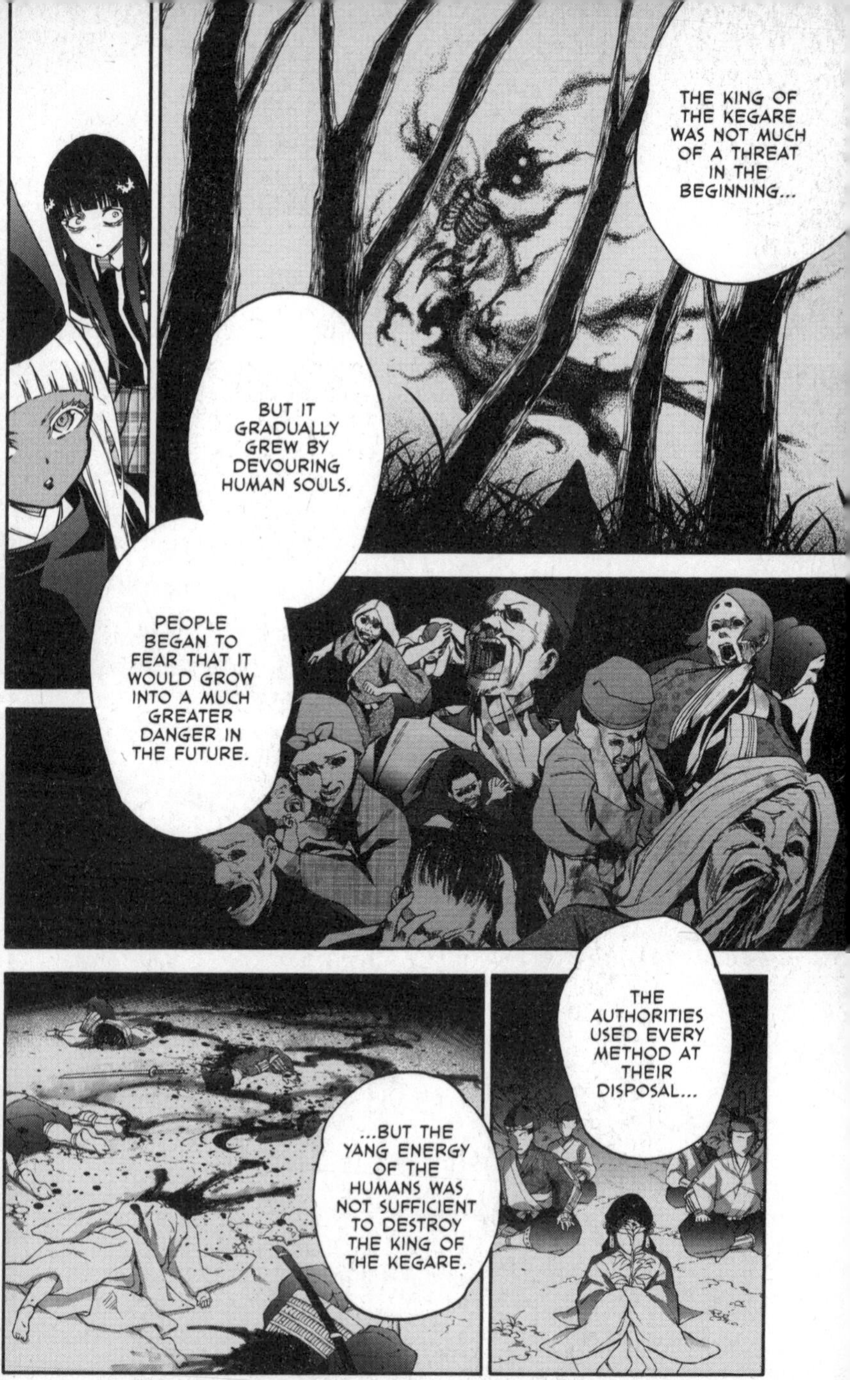
THE KING OF THE KEGARE WAS NOT MUCH OF A THREAT IN THE BEGINNING...
BUT IT GRADUALLY GREW BY DEVOURING HUMAN SOULS.
PEOPLE BEGAN TO FEAR THAT IT WOULD GROW INTO A MUCH GREATER DANGER IN THE FUTURE.
THE AUTHORITIES USED EVERY METHOD AT THEIR DISPOSAL...
...BUT THE YANG ENERGY OF THE HUMANS WAS NOT SUFFICIENT TO DESTROY THE KING OF THE KEGARE.

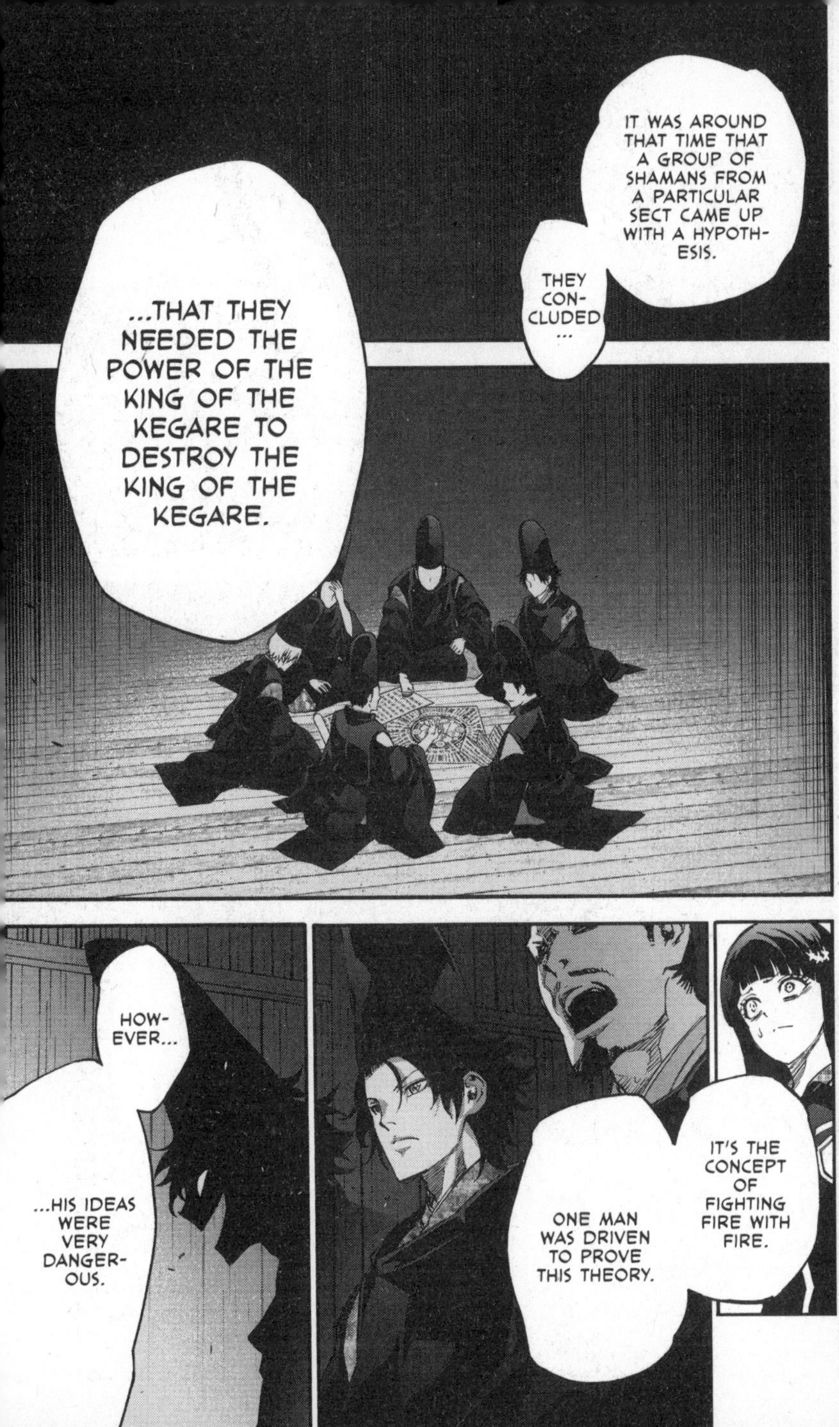
IT WAS AROUND THAT TIME THAT A GROUP OF SHAMANS FROM A PARTICULAR SECT CAME UP WITH A HYPOTH-ESIS.
THEY CON-CLUDED...
...THAT THEY NEEDED THE POWER OF THE KING OF THE KEGARE TO DESTROY THE KING OF THE KEGARE.
IT'S THE CONCEPT OF FIGHTING FIRE WITH FIRE.
ONE MAN WAS DRIVEN TO PROVE THIS THEORY.
HOW-EVER...
...HIS IDEAS WERE VERY DANGER-OUS.

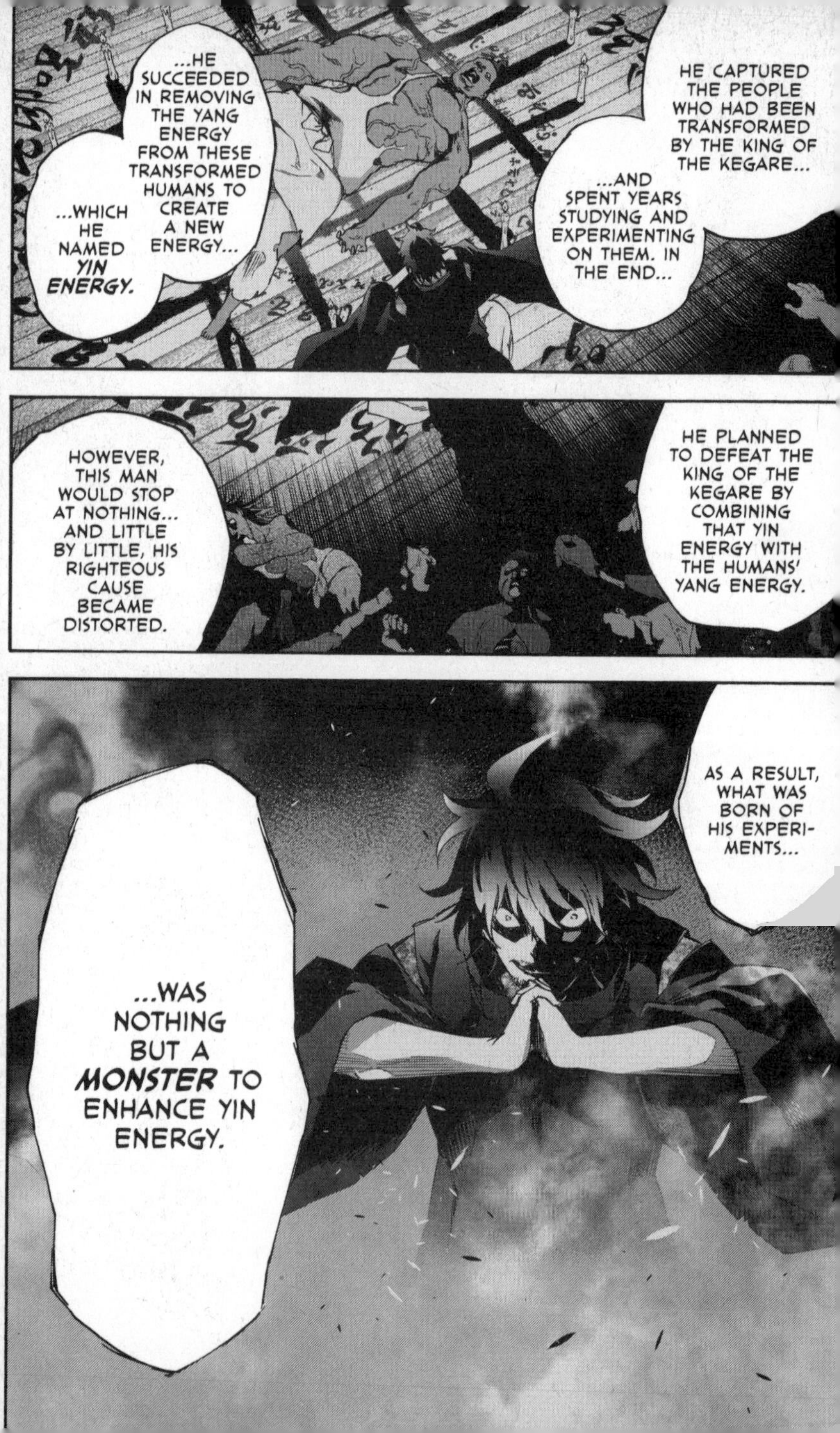
HE CAPTURED THE PEOPLE WHO HAD BEEN TRANSFORMED BY THE KING OF THE KEGARE...
...AND SPENT YEARS STUDYING AND EXPERIMENTING ON THEM. IN THE END...
...HE SUCCEEDED IN REMOVING THE YANG ENERGY FROM THESE TRANSFORMED HUMANS TO CREATE A NEW ENERGY...
...WHICH HE NAMED *YIN ENERGY.*
HE PLANNED TO DEFEAT THE KING OF THE KEGARE BY COMBINING THAT YIN ENERGY WITH THE HUMANS' YANG ENERGY.
HOWEVER, THIS MAN WOULD STOP AT NOTHING... AND LITTLE BY LITTLE, HIS RIGHTEOUS CAUSE BECAME DISTORTED.
AS A RESULT, WHAT WAS BORN OF HIS EXPERIMENTS...
...WAS NOTHING BUT A *MONSTER* TO ENHANCE YIN ENERGY.

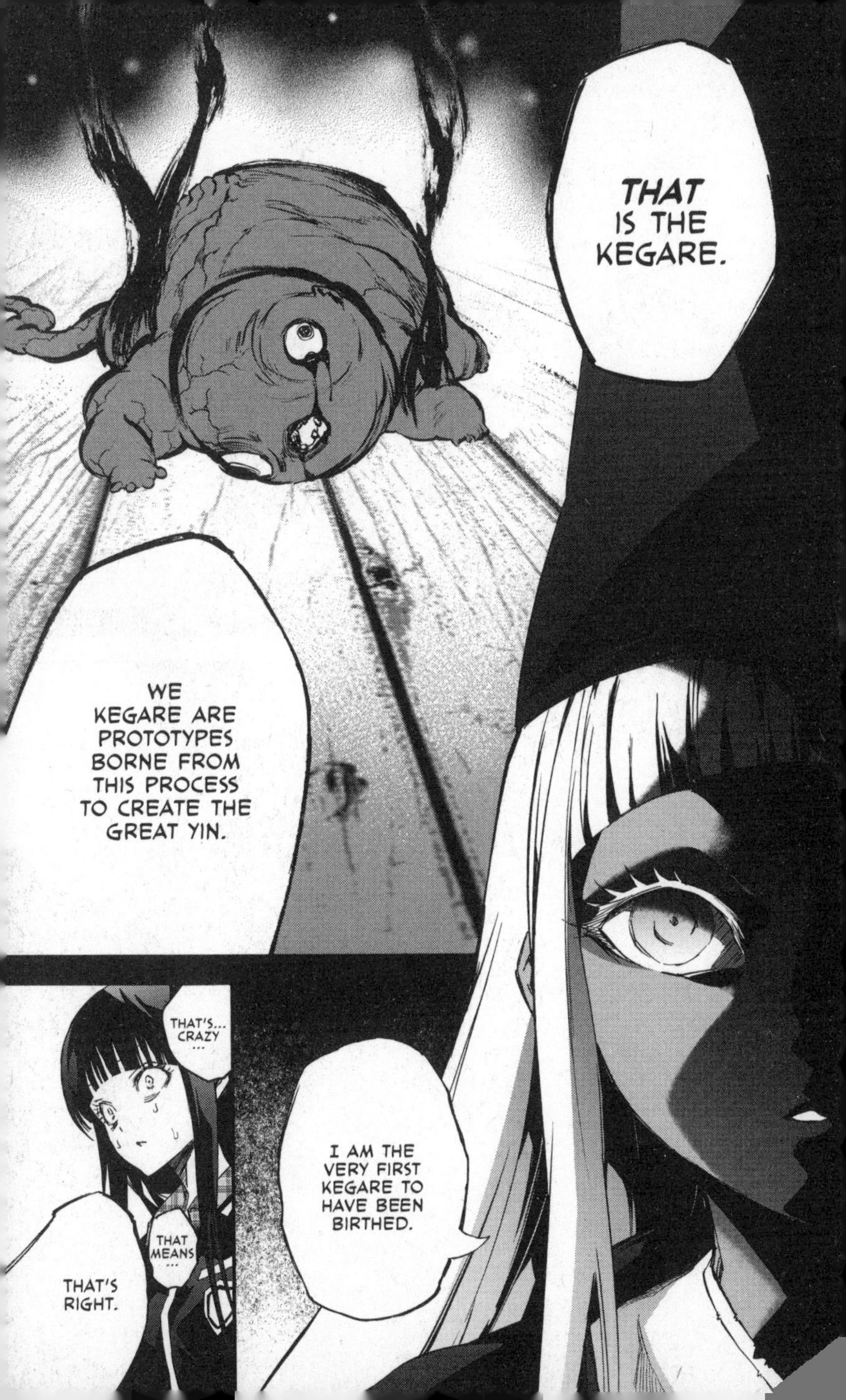
THAT IS THE KEGARE.
WE KEGARE ARE PROTOTYPES BORNE FROM THIS PROCESS TO CREATE THE GREAT YIN.
THAT'S... CRAZY ...
THAT MEANS ...
THAT'S RIGHT.
I AM THE VERY FIRST KEGARE TO HAVE BEEN BIRTHED.

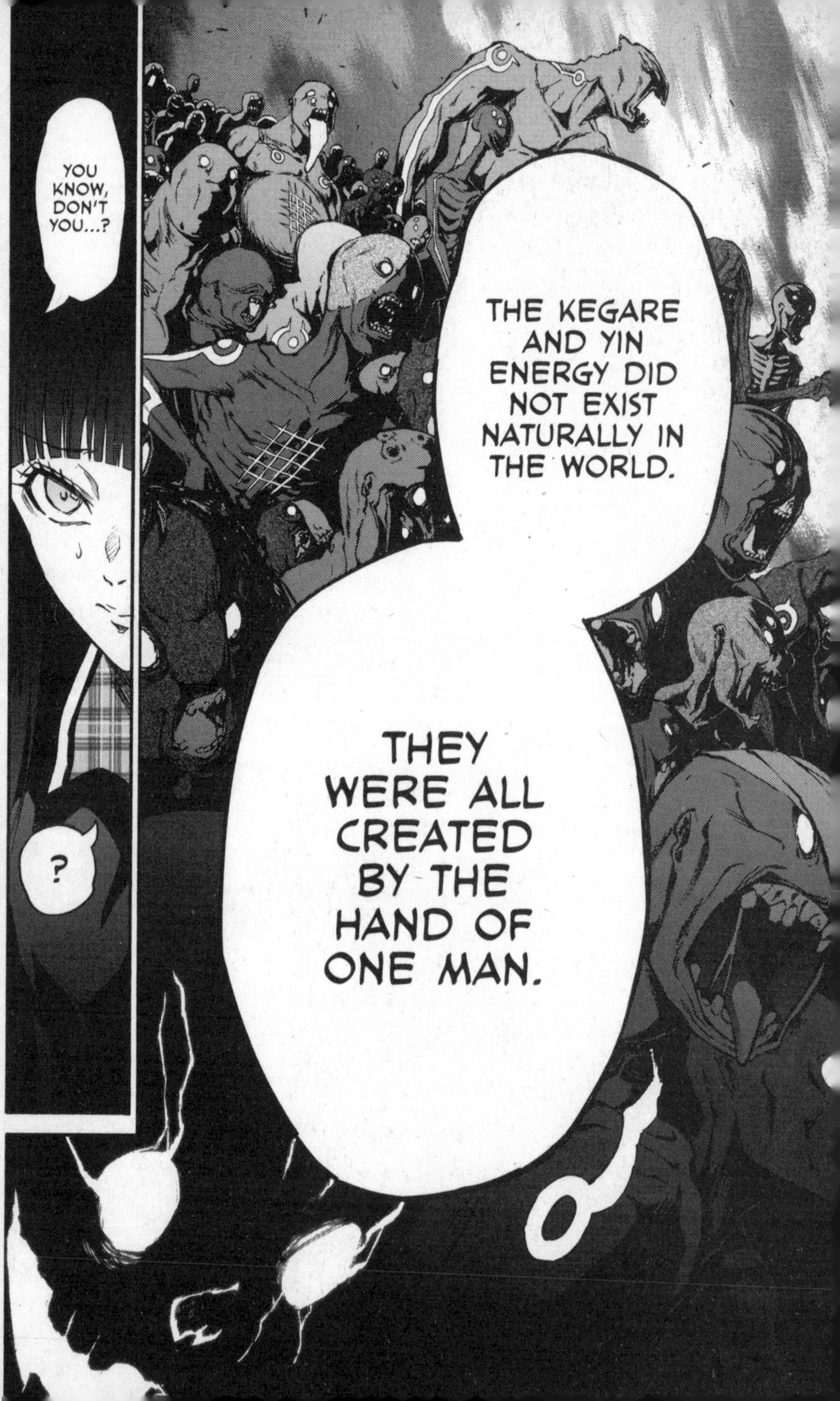
THE KEGARE AND YIN ENERGY DID NOT EXIST NATURALLY IN THE WORLD.
THEY WERE ALL CREATED BY THE HAND OF ONE MAN.
YOU KNOW, DON'T YOU...?
?

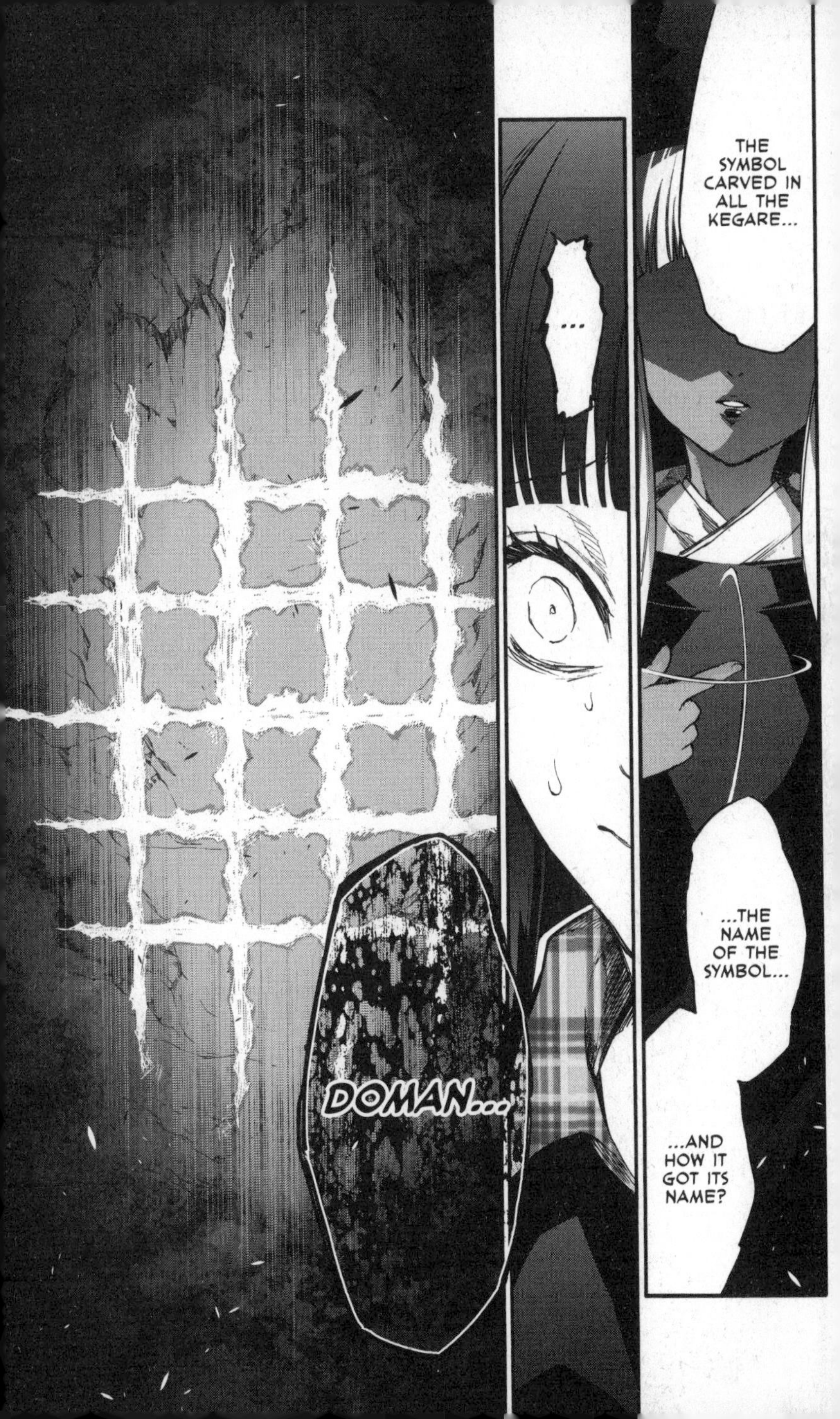
THE SYMBOL CARVED IN ALL THE KEGARE...
...THE NAME OF THE SYMBOL...
...AND HOW IT GOT ITS NAME?
...
DOMAN...

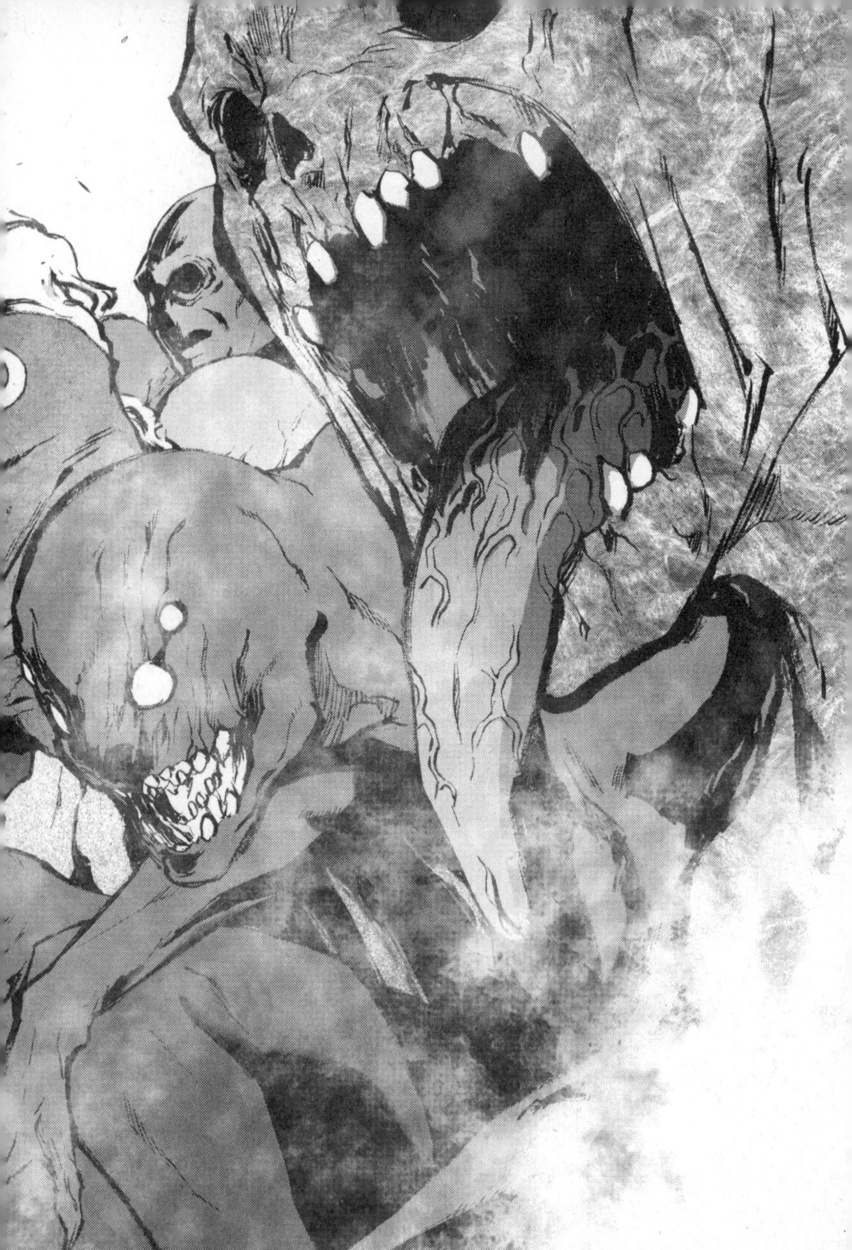

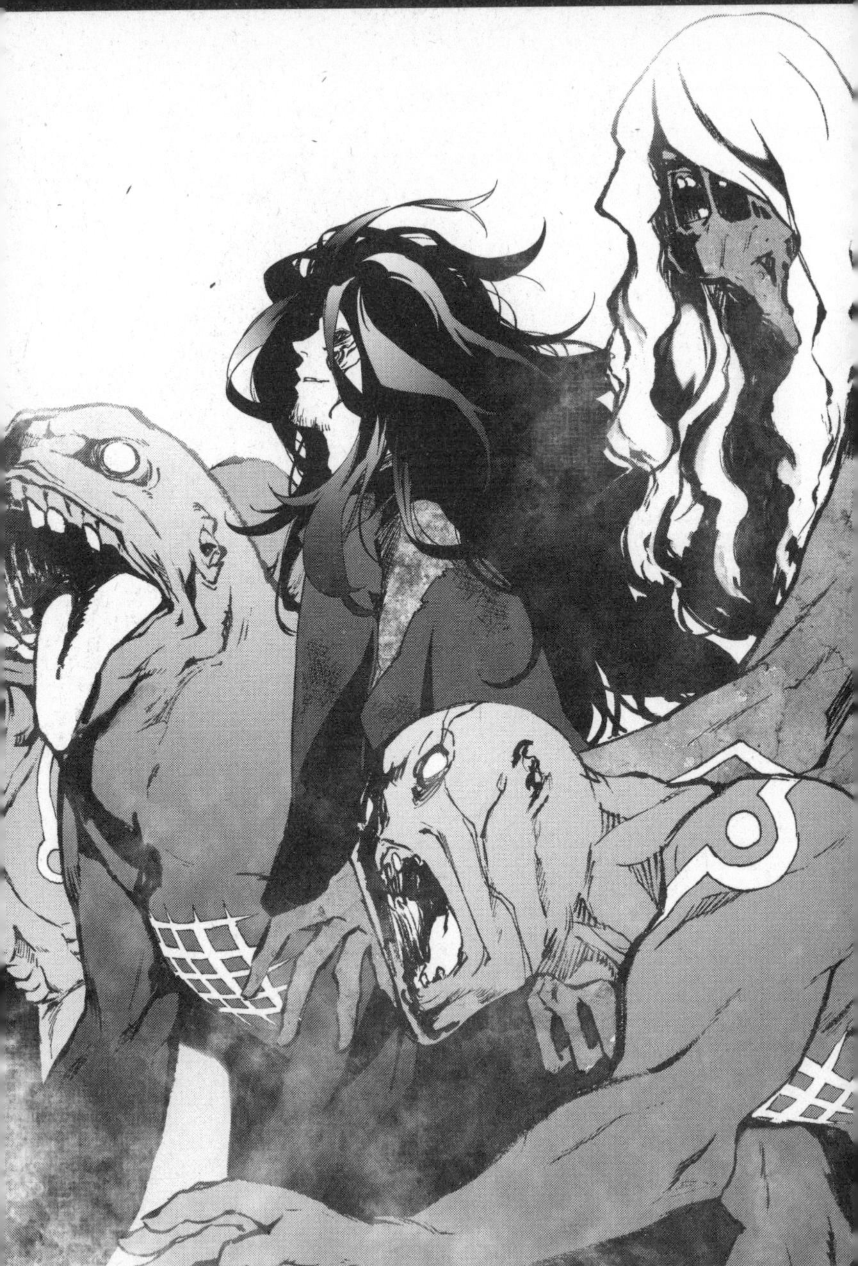

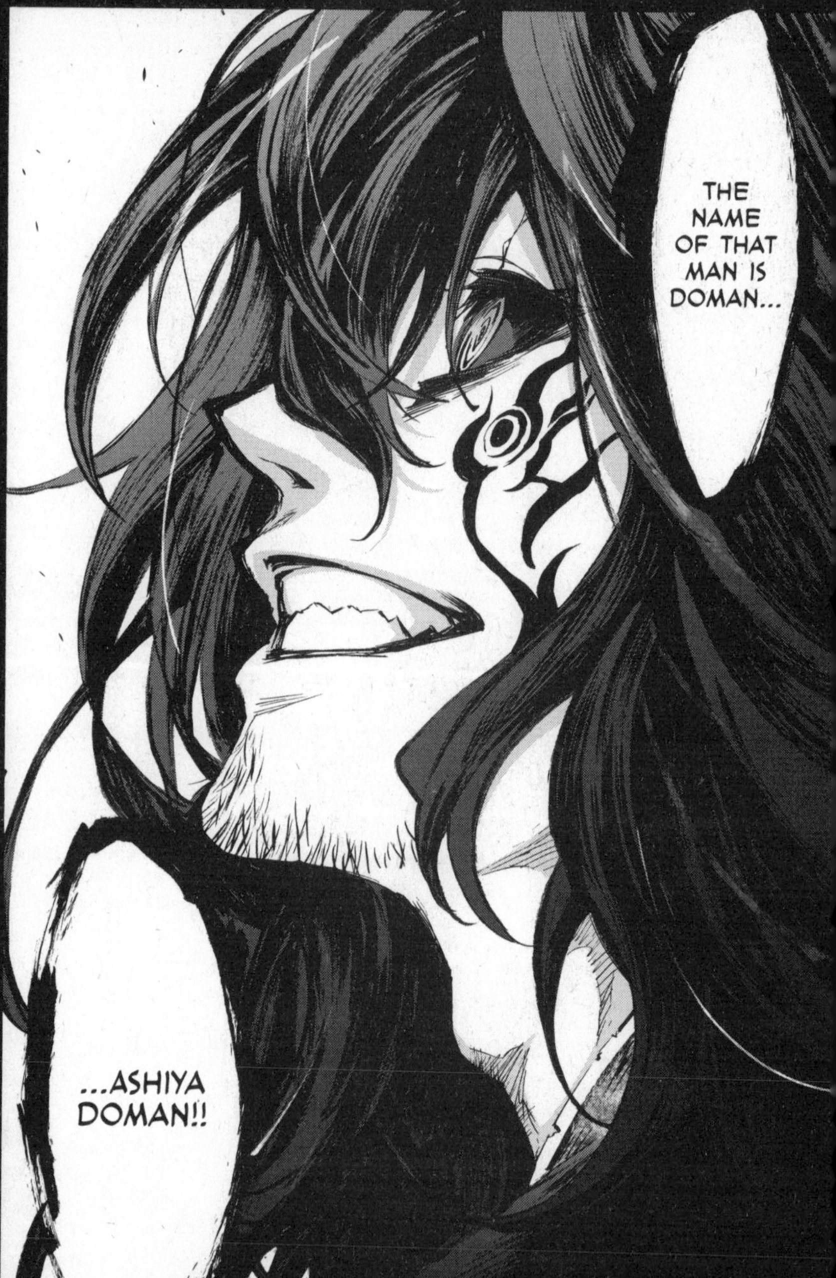
THE NAME OF THAT MAN IS DOMAN...
...ASHIYA DOMAN!!

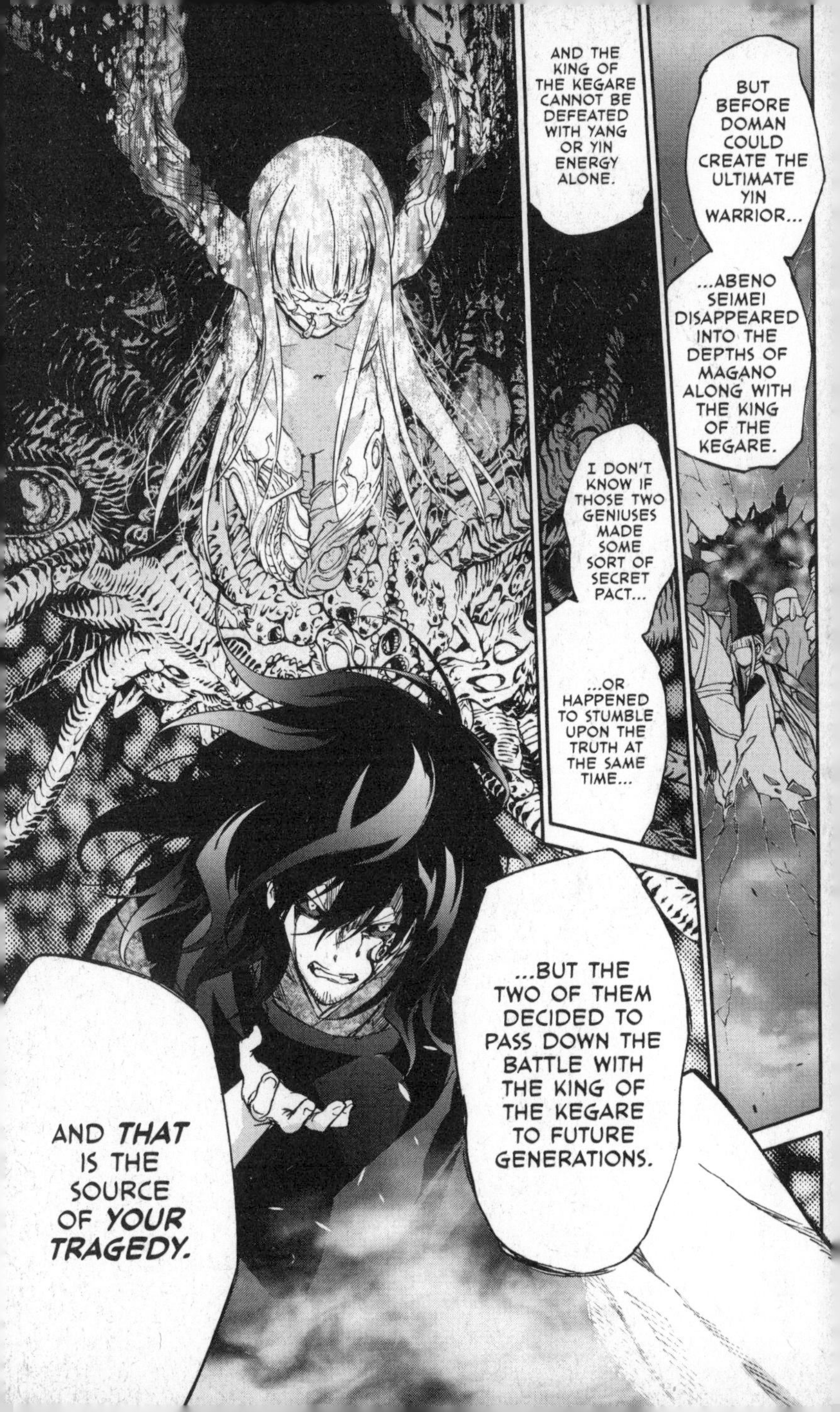
BUT BEFORE DOMAN COULD CREATE THE ULTIMATE YIN WARRIOR...
...ABENO SEIMEI DISAPPEARED INTO THE DEPTHS OF MAGANO ALONG WITH THE KING OF THE KEGARE.
AND THE KING OF THE KEGARE CANNOT BE DEFEATED WITH YANG OR YIN ENERGY ALONE.
I DON'T KNOW IF THOSE TWO GENIUSES MADE SOME SORT OF SECRET PACT...
...OR HAPPENED TO STUMBLE UPON THE TRUTH AT THE SAME TIME...
...BUT THE TWO OF THEM DECIDED TO PASS DOWN THE BATTLE WITH THE KING OF THE KEGARE TO FUTURE GENERATIONS.
AND *THAT* IS THE SOURCE OF *YOUR TRAGEDY.*

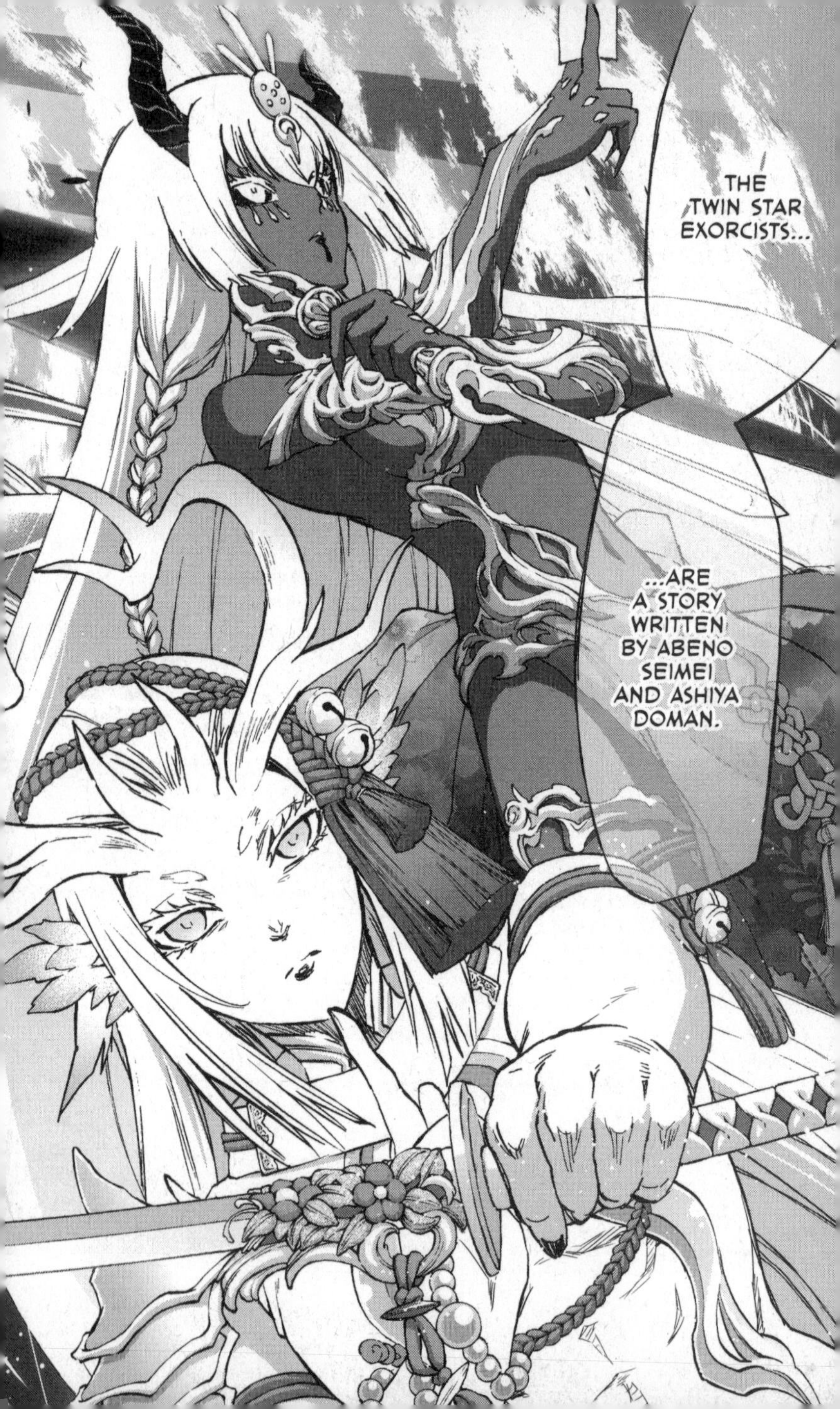
THE TWIN STAR EXORCISTS...
...ARE A STORY WRITTEN BY ABENO SEIMEI AND ASHIYA DOMAN.

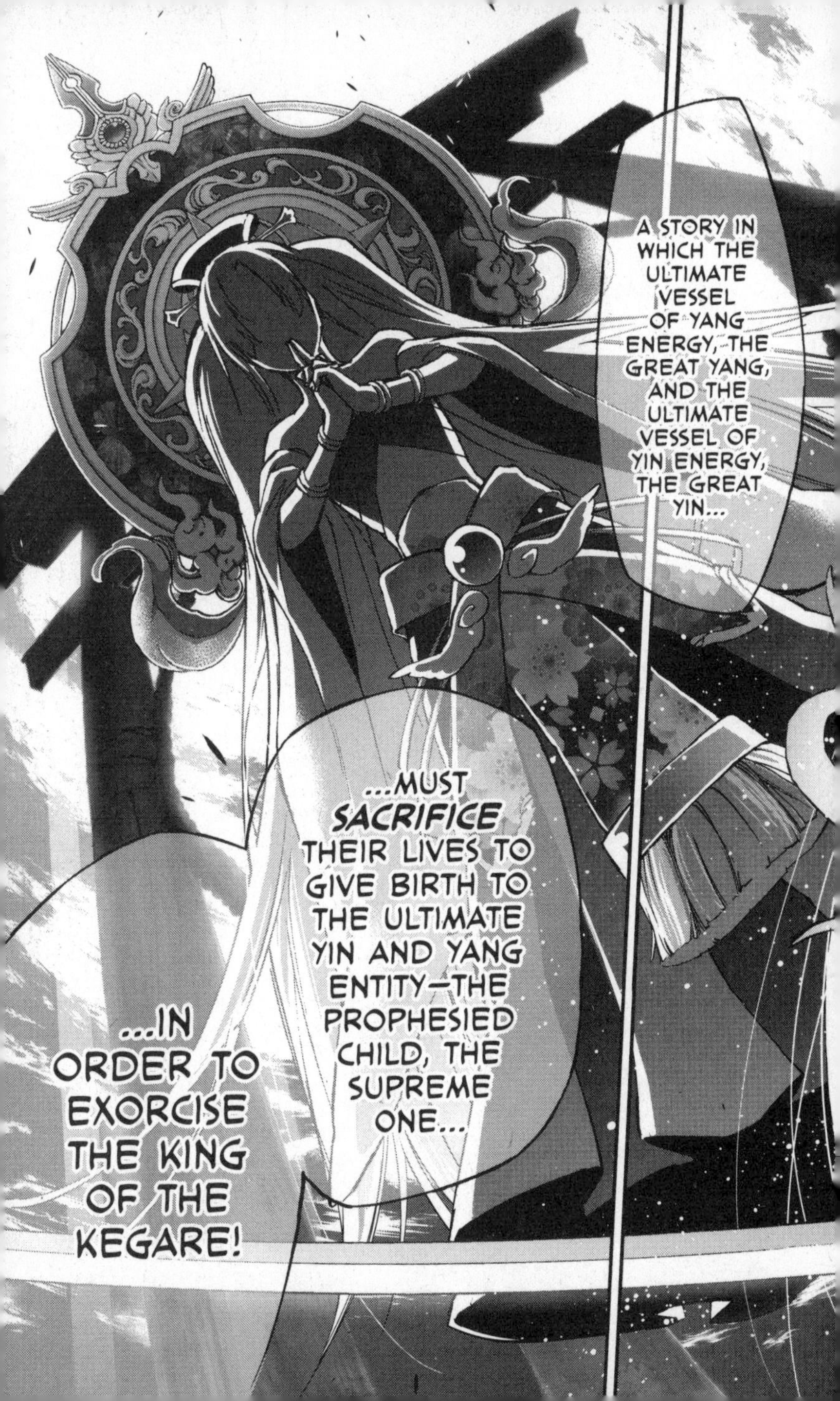
A STORY IN WHICH THE ULTIMATE VESSEL OF YANG ENERGY, THE GREAT YANG, AND THE ULTIMATE VESSEL OF YIN ENERGY, THE GREAT YIN...
...MUST SACRIFICE THEIR LIVES TO GIVE BIRTH TO THE ULTIMATE YIN AND YANG ENTITY—THE PROPHESIED CHILD, THE SUPREME ONE...
...IN ORDER TO EXORCISE THE KING OF THE KEGARE!

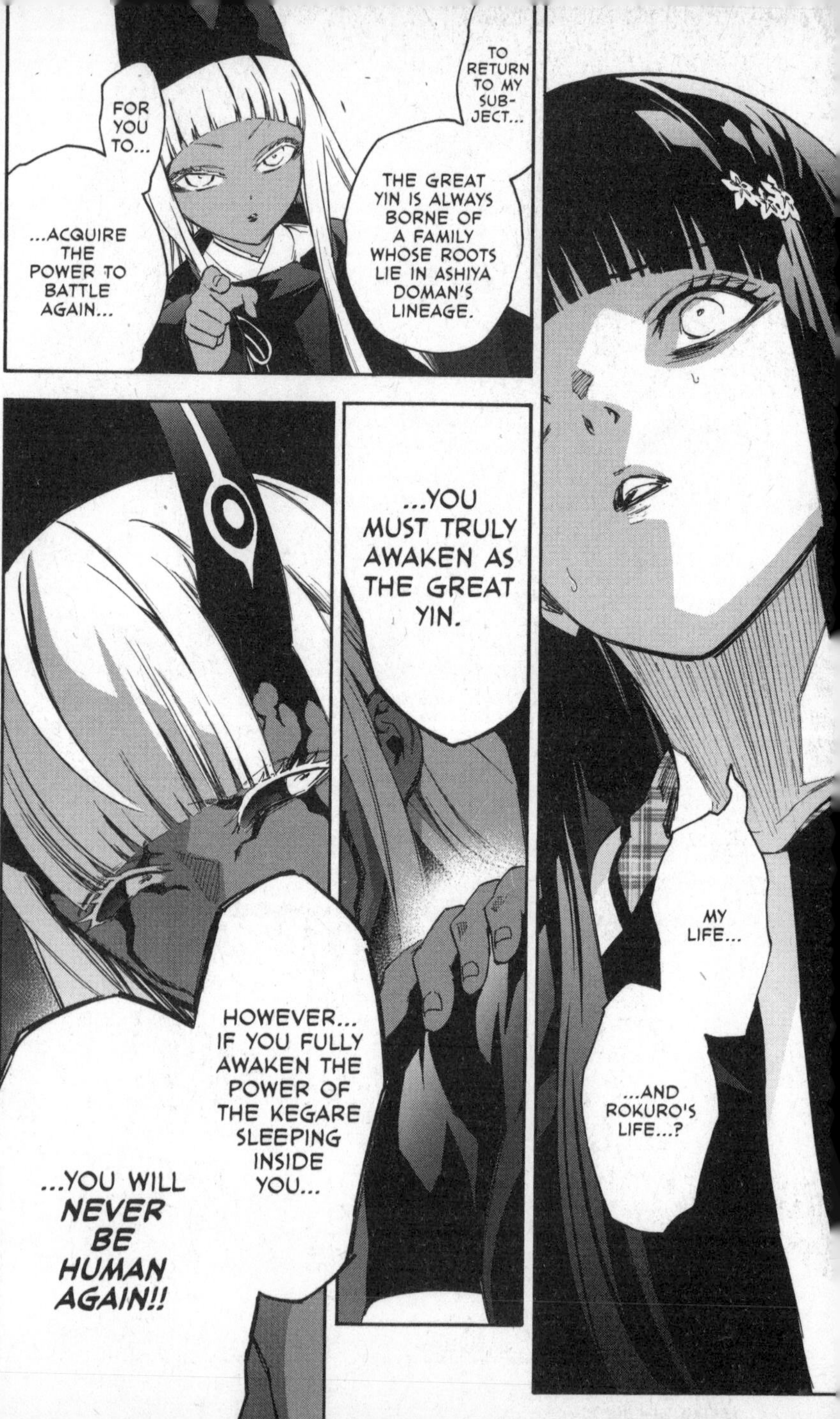
MY LIFE...
...AND ROKURO'S LIFE...?
TO RETURN TO MY SUBJECT...
THE GREAT YIN IS ALWAYS BORNE OF A FAMILY WHOSE ROOTS LIE IN ASHIYA DOMAN'S LINEAGE.
FOR YOU TO...
...ACQUIRE THE POWER TO BATTLE AGAIN...
...YOU MUST TRULY AWAKEN AS THE GREAT YIN.
HOWEVER... IF YOU FULLY AWAKEN THE POWER OF THE KEGARE SLEEPING INSIDE YOU...
...YOU WILL ***NEVER* BE HUMAN AGAIN!!**

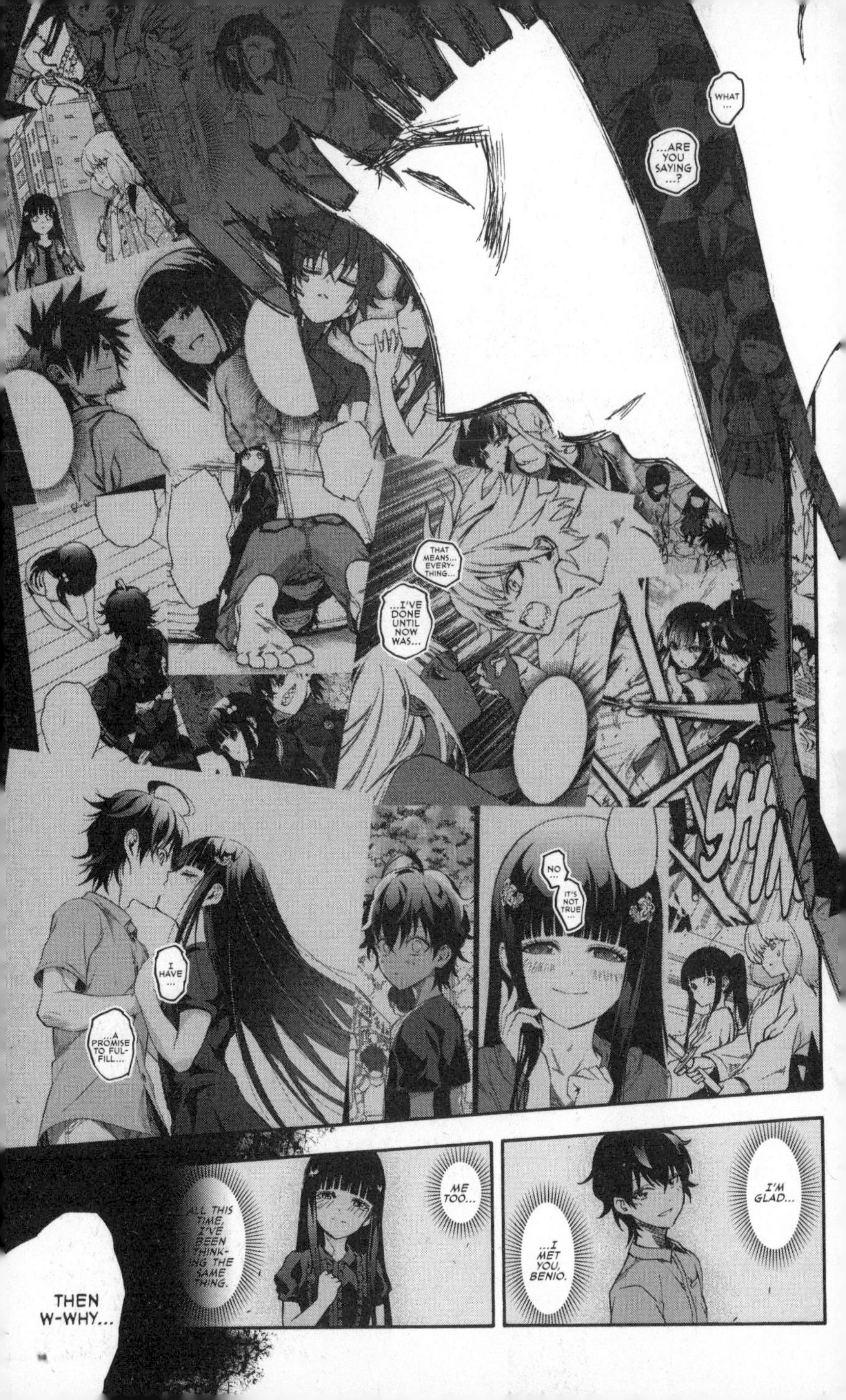
WHAT...
...ARE YOU SAYING...?
THAT MEANS... EVERYTHING...
...I'VE DONE UNTIL NOW WAS...
NO...
IT'S NOT TRUE...
I HAVE...
...A PROMISE TO FULFILL...
I'M GLAD...
...I MET YOU, BENIO.
ME TOO...
ALL THIS TIME, I'VE BEEN THINKING THE SAME THING.
THEN W-WHY...

...WAS...

...I...
...BORN?!

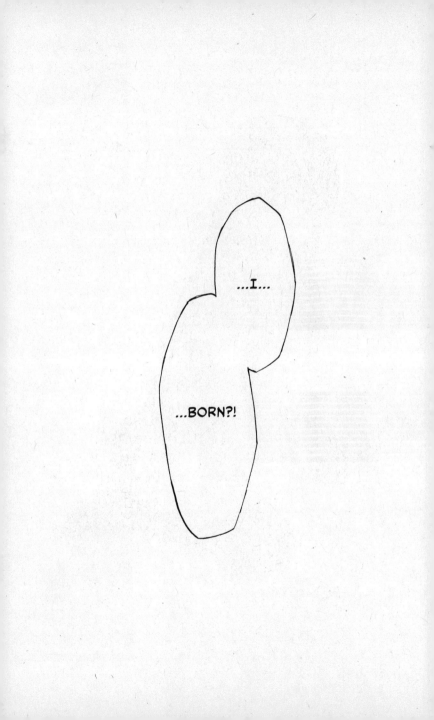

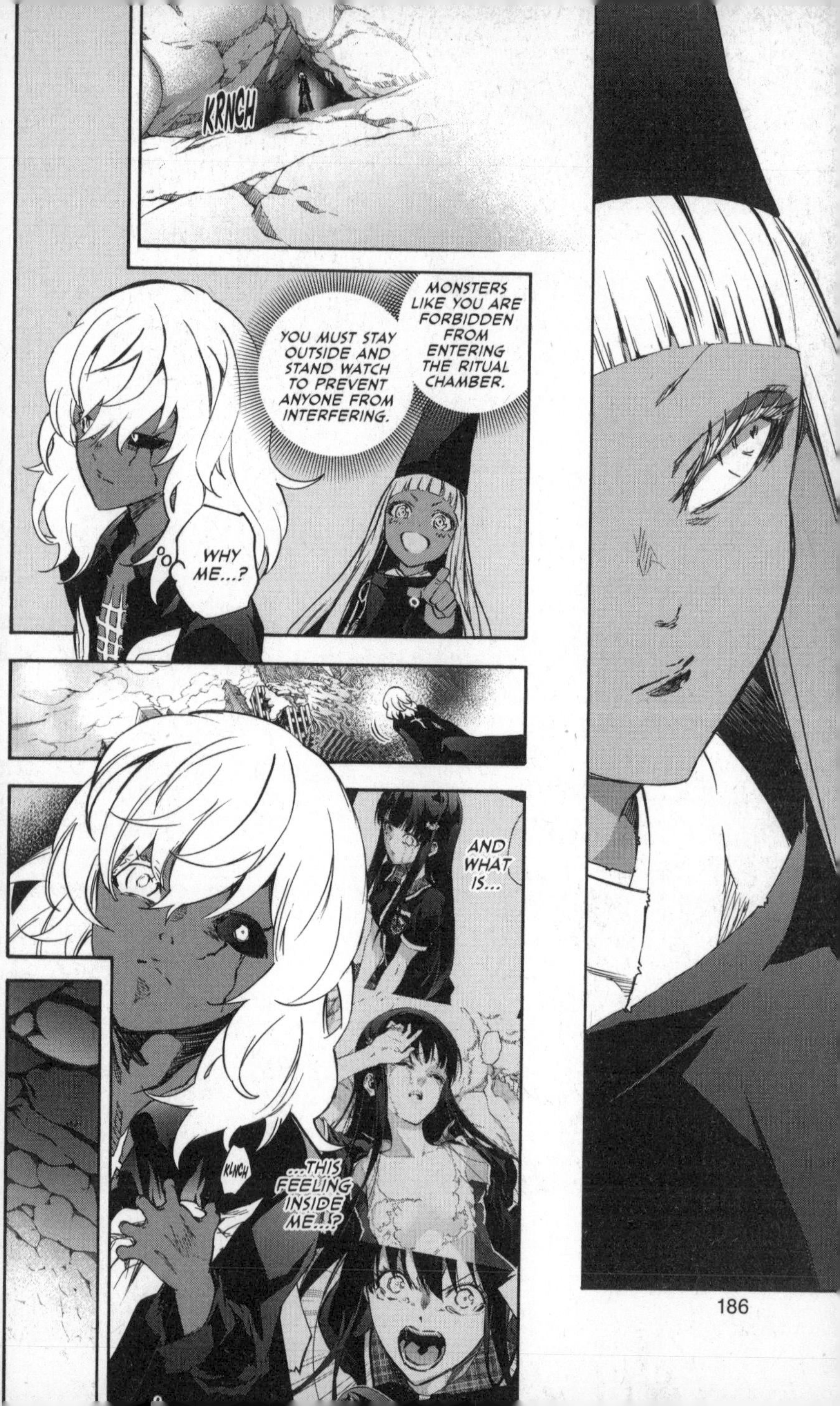
KRNCH
MONSTERS LIKE YOU ARE FORBIDDEN FROM ENTERING THE RITUAL CHAMBER.
YOU MUST STAY OUTSIDE AND STAND WATCH TO PREVENT ANYONE FROM INTERFERING.
WHY ME...?
AND WHAT IS...
KLNCH
...THIS FEELING INSIDE ME...!?

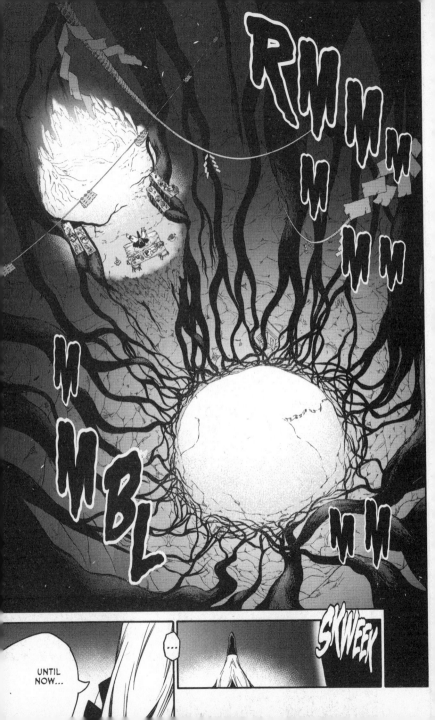

RMMMM
M
MM
M
MM
M
MBL

MM

SKWEEK

UNTIL
NOW...

...

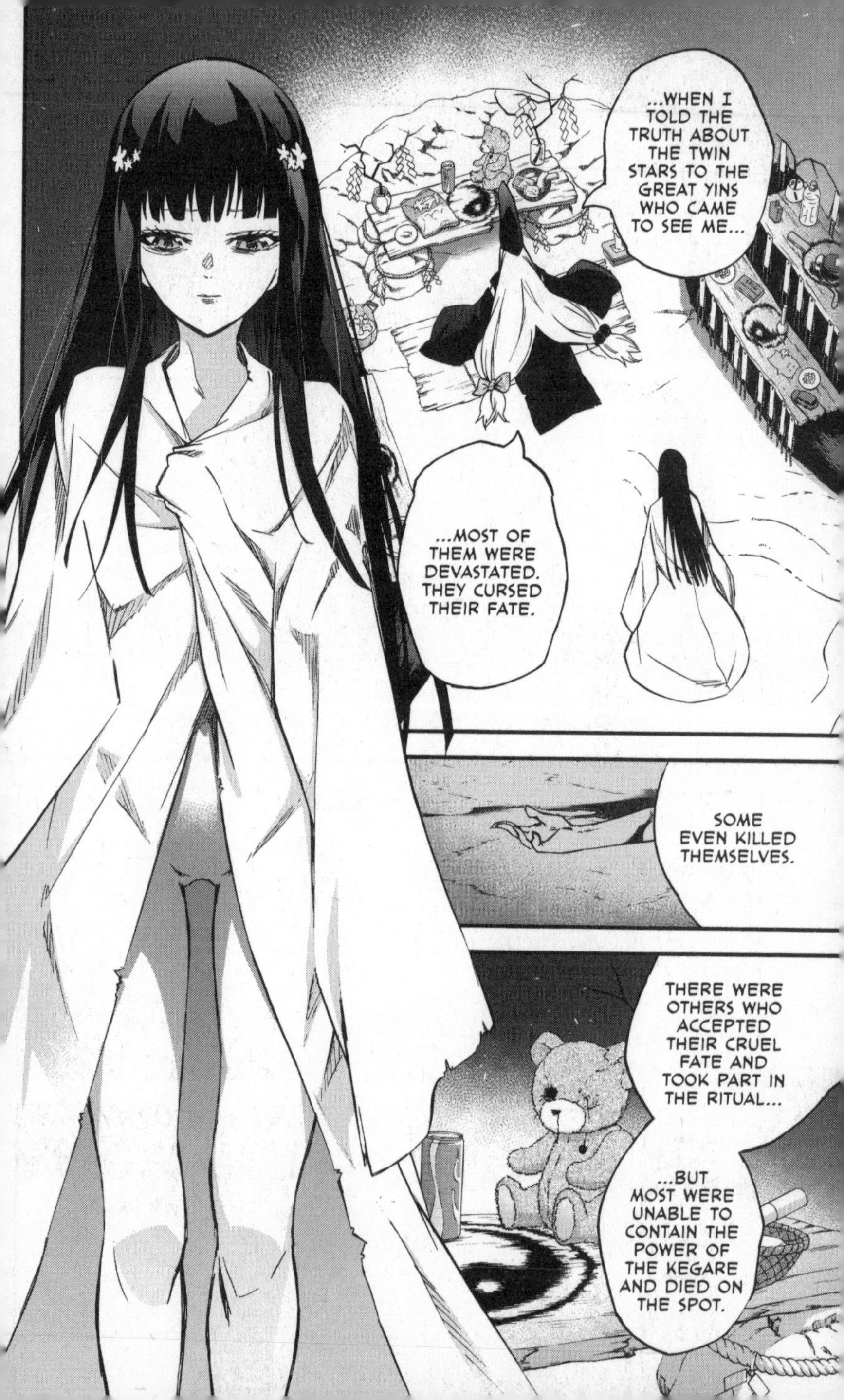
...WHEN I TOLD THE TRUTH ABOUT THE TWIN STARS TO THE GREAT YINS WHO CAME TO SEE ME...
...MOST OF THEM WERE DEVASTATED. THEY CURSED THEIR FATE.
SOME EVEN KILLED THEMSELVES.
THERE WERE OTHERS WHO ACCEPTED THEIR CRUEL FATE AND TOOK PART IN THE RITUAL...
...BUT MOST WERE UNABLE TO CONTAIN THE POWER OF THE KEGARE AND DIED ON THE SPOT.

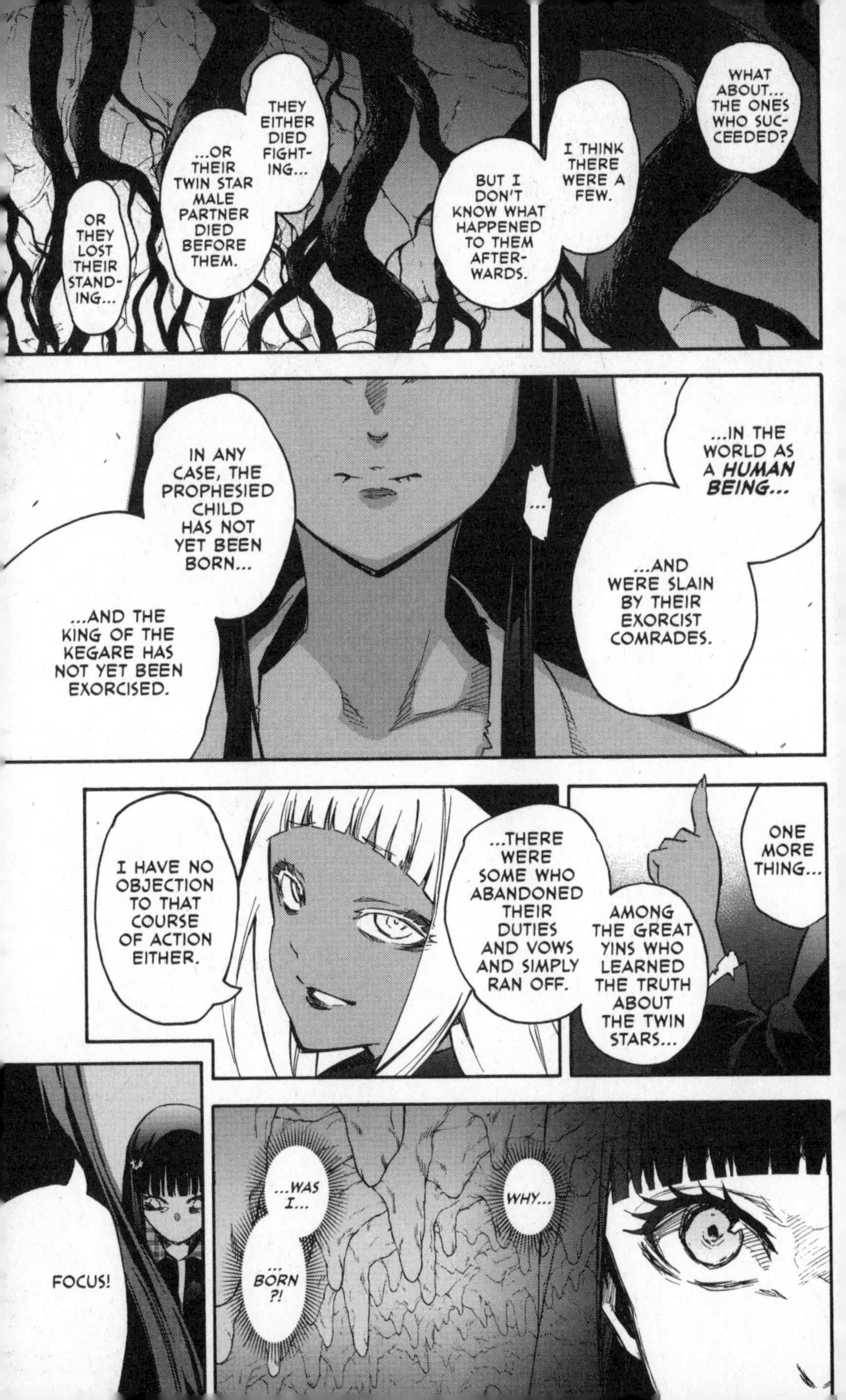
WHAT ABOUT... THE ONES WHO SUCCEEDED?
I THINK THERE WERE A FEW.
BUT I DON'T KNOW WHAT HAPPENED TO THEM AFTERWARDS.
THEY EITHER DIED FIGHTING...
...OR THEIR TWIN STAR MALE PARTNER DIED BEFORE THEM.
OR THEY LOST THEIR STANDING...
...IN THE WORLD AS A *HUMAN BEING...*
...
...AND WERE SLAIN BY THEIR EXORCIST COMRADES.
IN ANY CASE, THE PROPHESIED CHILD HAS NOT YET BEEN BORN...
...AND THE KING OF THE KEGARE HAS NOT YET BEEN EXORCISED.
ONE MORE THING...
AMONG THE GREAT YINS WHO LEARNED THE TRUTH ABOUT THE TWIN STARS...
...THERE WERE SOME WHO ABANDONED THEIR DUTIES AND VOWS AND SIMPLY RAN OFF.
I HAVE NO OBJECTION TO THAT COURSE OF ACTION EITHER.
WHY...
...WAS I...
...BORN?!
FOCUS!

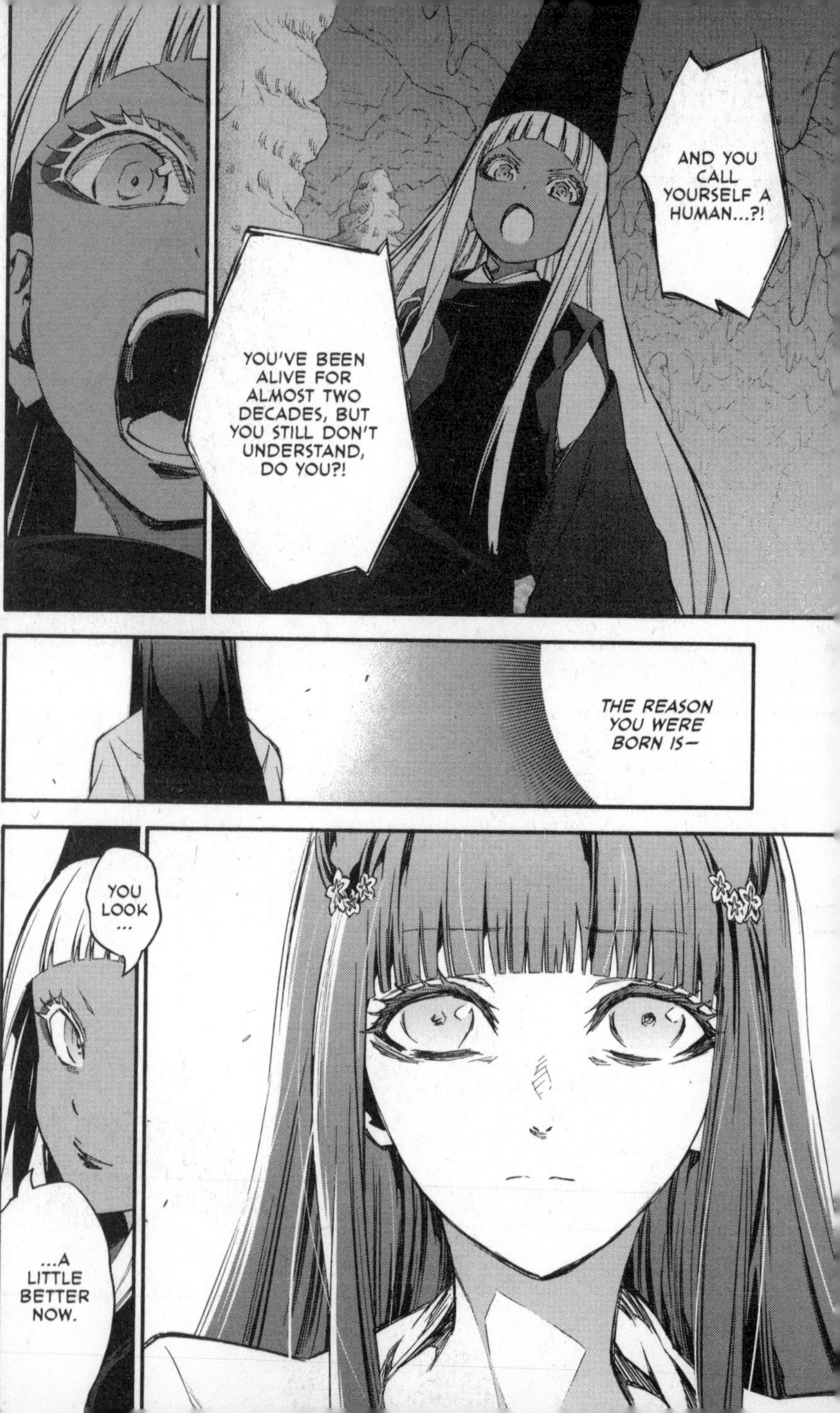
AND YOU CALL YOURSELF A HUMAN...?!
YOU'VE BEEN ALIVE FOR ALMOST TWO DECADES, BUT YOU STILL DON'T UNDERSTAND, DO YOU?!
THE REASON YOU WERE BORN IS—
YOU LOOK...
...A LITTLE BETTER NOW.

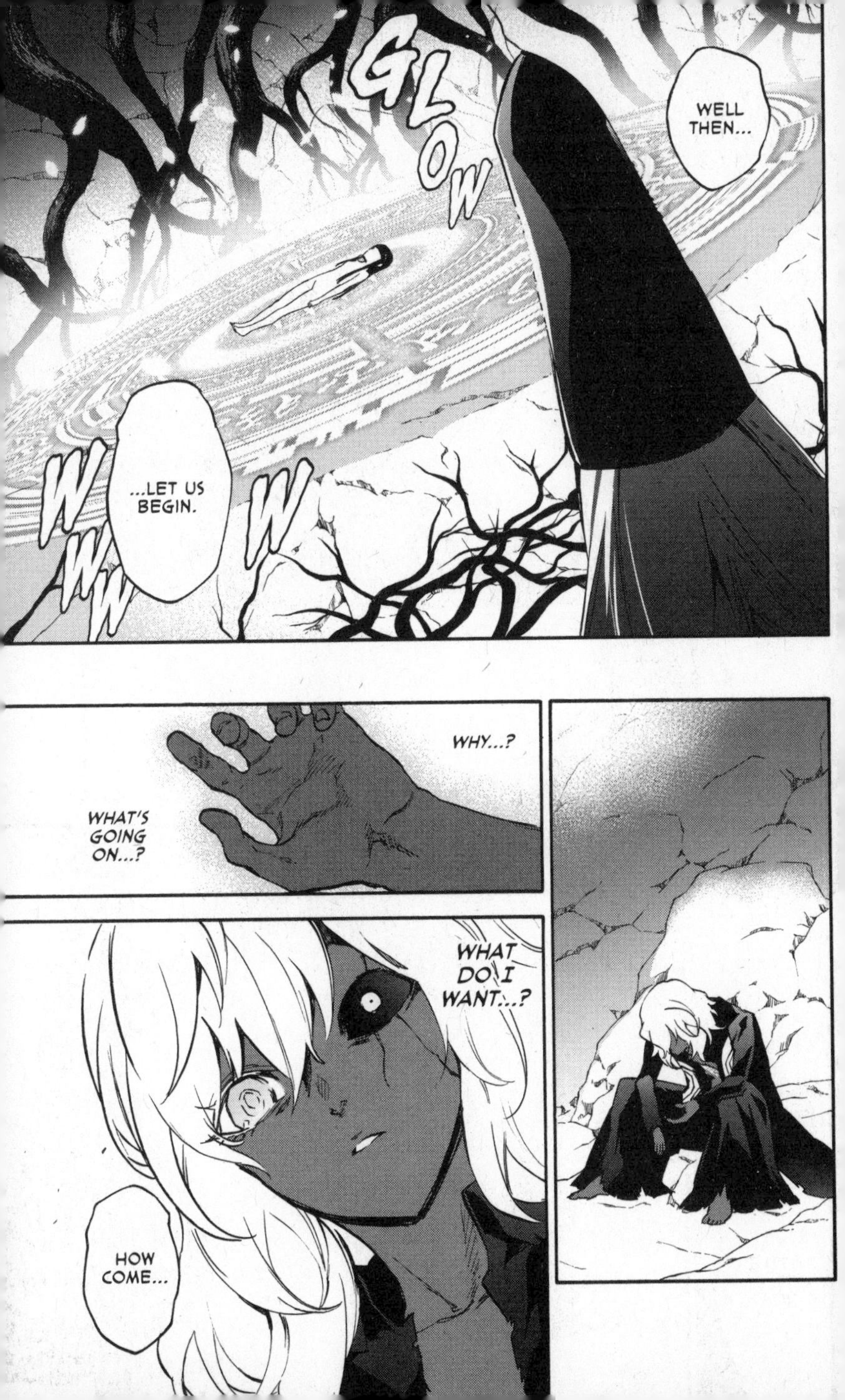
WELL THEN...
GLOW
...LET US BEGIN.
WWWWW
WHY...?
WHAT'S GOING ON...?
WHAT DO I WANT...?
HOW COME...

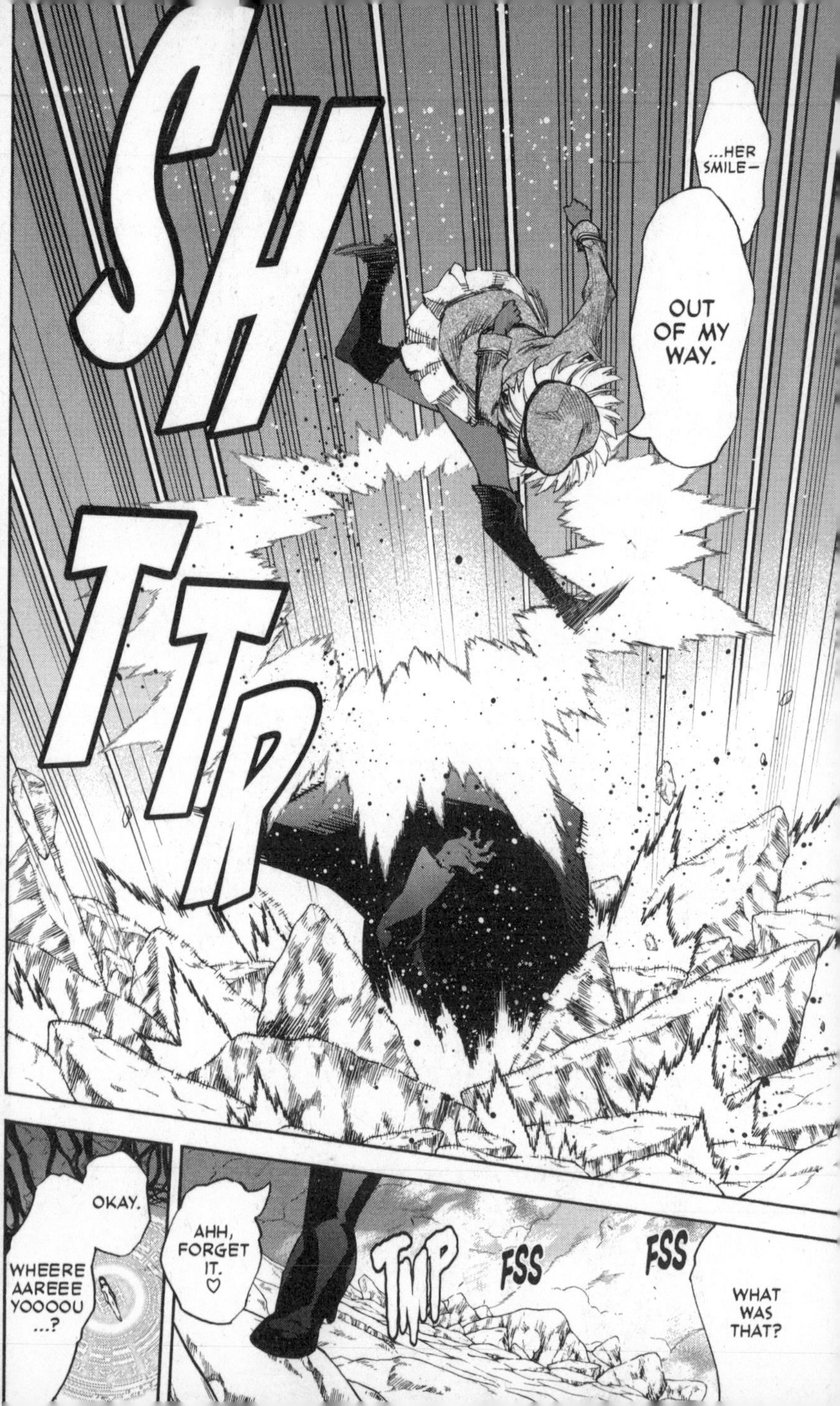

...HER SMILE—
OUT OF MY WAY.
SHTTR
WHAT WAS THAT?
FSS
FSS
TMP
AHH, FORGET IT. ♡
OKAY.
WHEERE AAREEE YOOOOU ...?

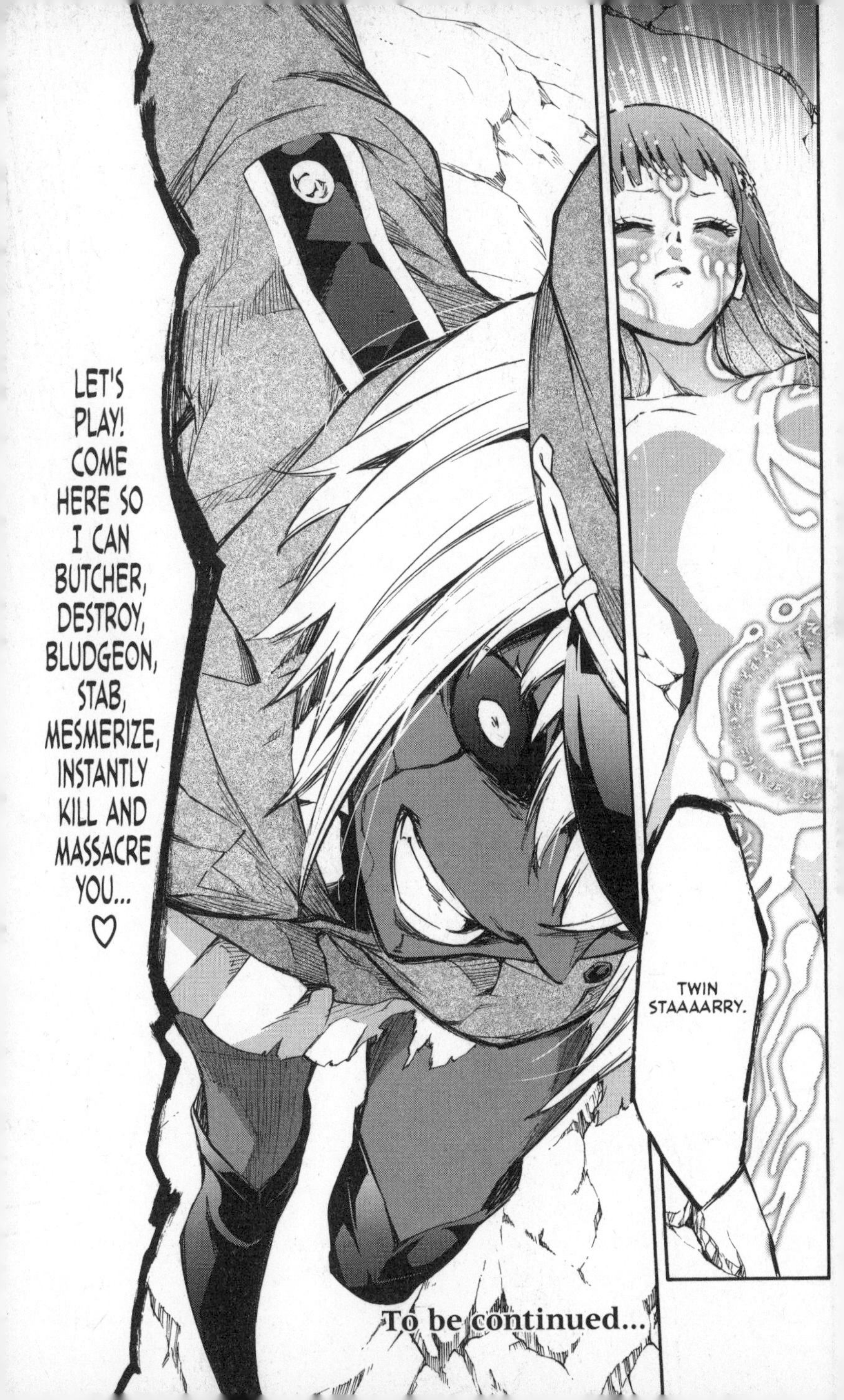
TWIN STAAAARRY.
LET'S PLAY! COME HERE SO I CAN BUTCHER, DESTROY, BLUDGEON, STAB, MESMERIZE, INSTANTLY KILL AND MASSACRE YOU... ♡
To be continued...

Hunting Gear Specifications

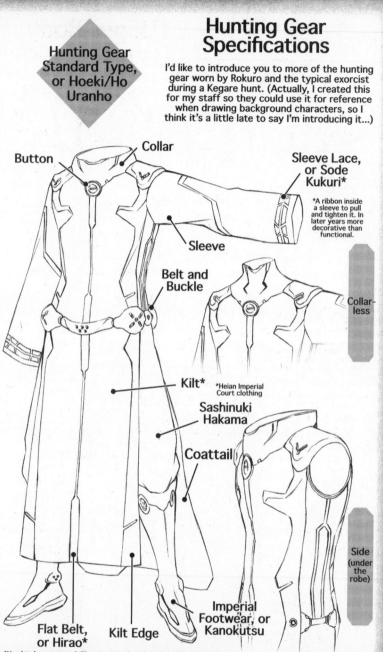

Hunting Gear Standard Type, or Hoeki/Ho Uranho

I'd like to introduce you to more of the hunting gear worn by Rokuro and the typical exorcist during a Kegare hunt. (Actually, I created this for my staff so they could use it for reference when drawing background characters, so I think it's a little late to say I'm introducing it...)

Button

Collar

Sleeve Lace, or Sode Kukuri*

*A ribbon inside a sleeve to pull and tighten it. In later years more decorative than functional.

Sleeve

Belt and Buckle

Collar-less

Kilt*

*Heian Imperial Court clothing

Sashinuki Hakama

Coattail

Side (under the robe)

Imperial Footwear, or Kanokutsu

Flat Belt, or Hirao*

Kilt Edge

*Used to hang a sword. The remaining length is decoratively draped.

Upper Body

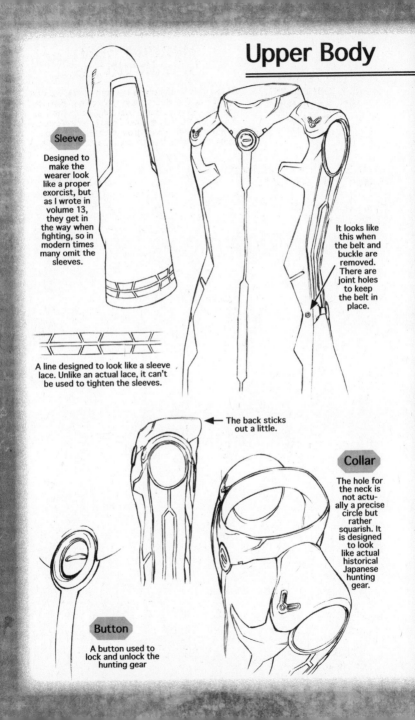

Sleeve

Designed to make the wearer look like a proper exorcist, but as I wrote in volume 13, they get in the way when fighting, so in modern times many omit the sleeves.

It looks like this when the belt and buckle are removed. There are joint holes to keep the belt in place.

A line designed to look like a sleeve lace. Unlike an actual lace, it can't be used to tighten the sleeves.

The back sticks out a little.

Collar

The hole for the neck is not actually a precise circle but rather squarish. It is designed to look like actual historical Japanese hunting gear.

Button

A button used to lock and unlock the hunting gear

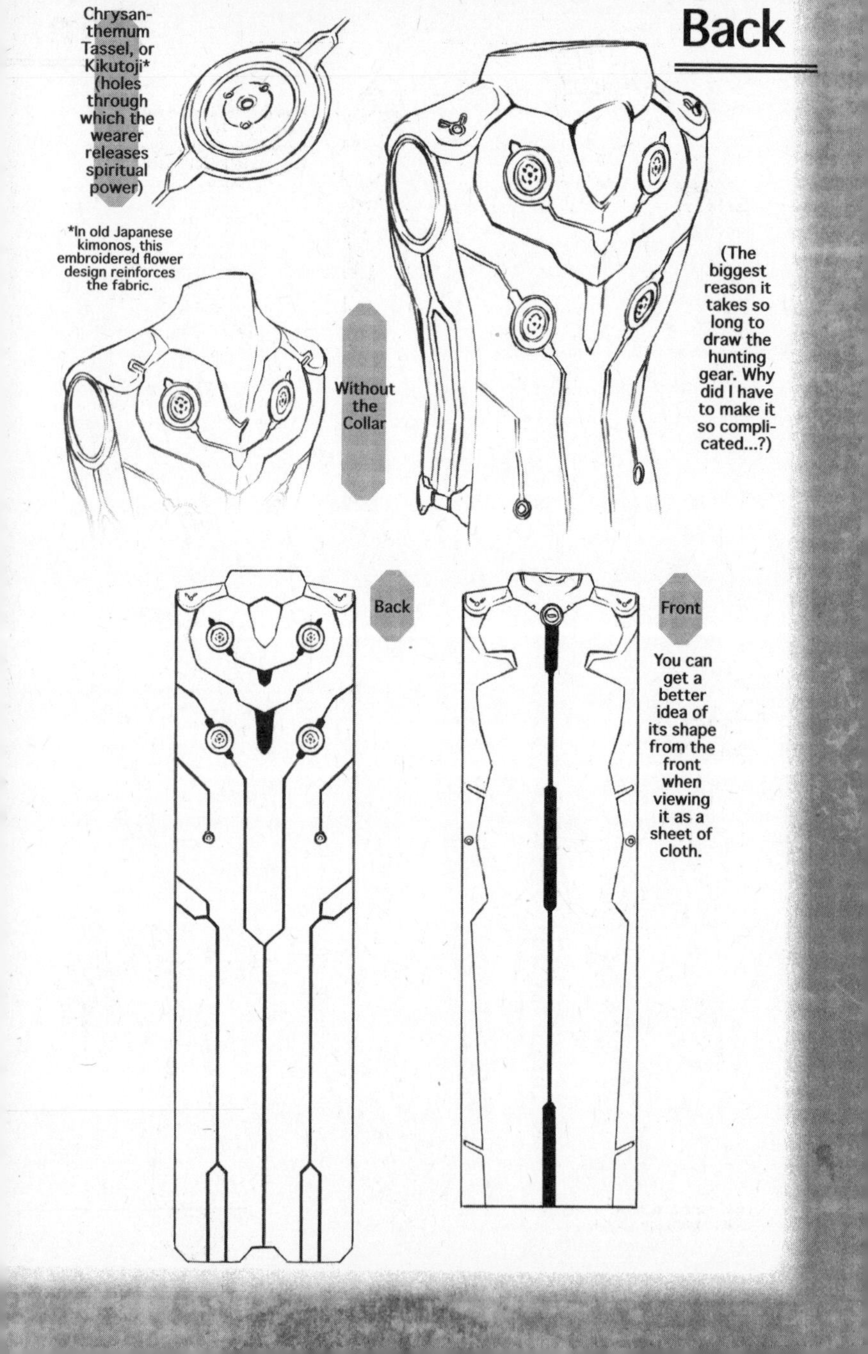
Back
(The biggest reason it takes so long to draw the hunting gear. Why did I have to make it so complicated...?)
Chrysanthemum Tassel, or Kikutoji* (holes through which the wearer releases spiritual power)
*In old Japanese kimonos, this embroidered flower design reinforces the fabric.
Without the Collar
Front
You can get a better idea of its shape from the front when viewing it as a sheet of cloth.
Back

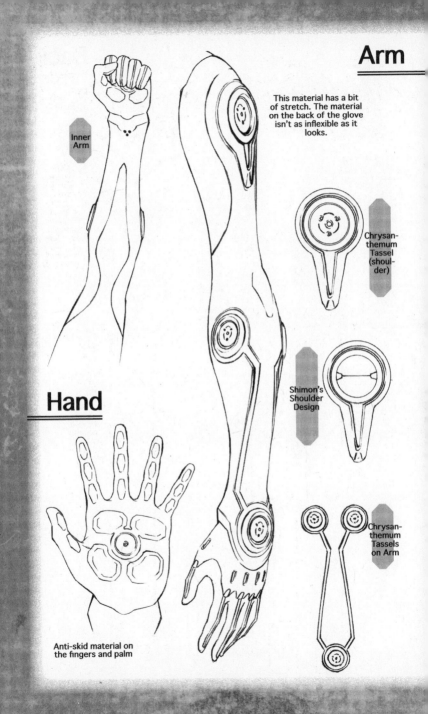

Arm

Inner Arm

This material has a bit of stretch. The material on the back of the glove isn't as inflexible as it looks.

Chrysanthemum Tassel (shoulder)

Shimon's Shoulder Design

Chrysanthemum Tassels on Arm

Hand

Anti-skid material on the fingers and palm

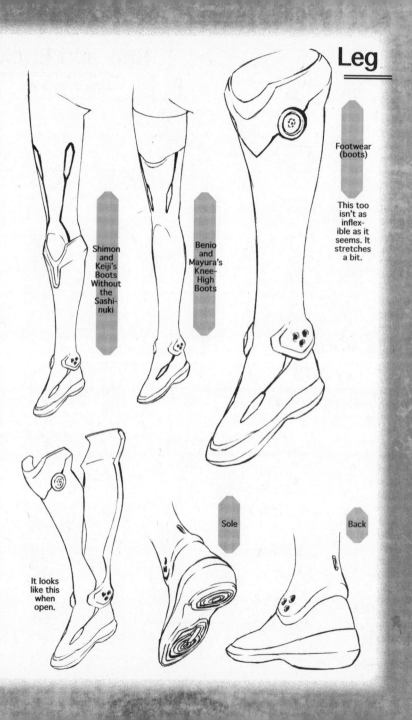

Leg

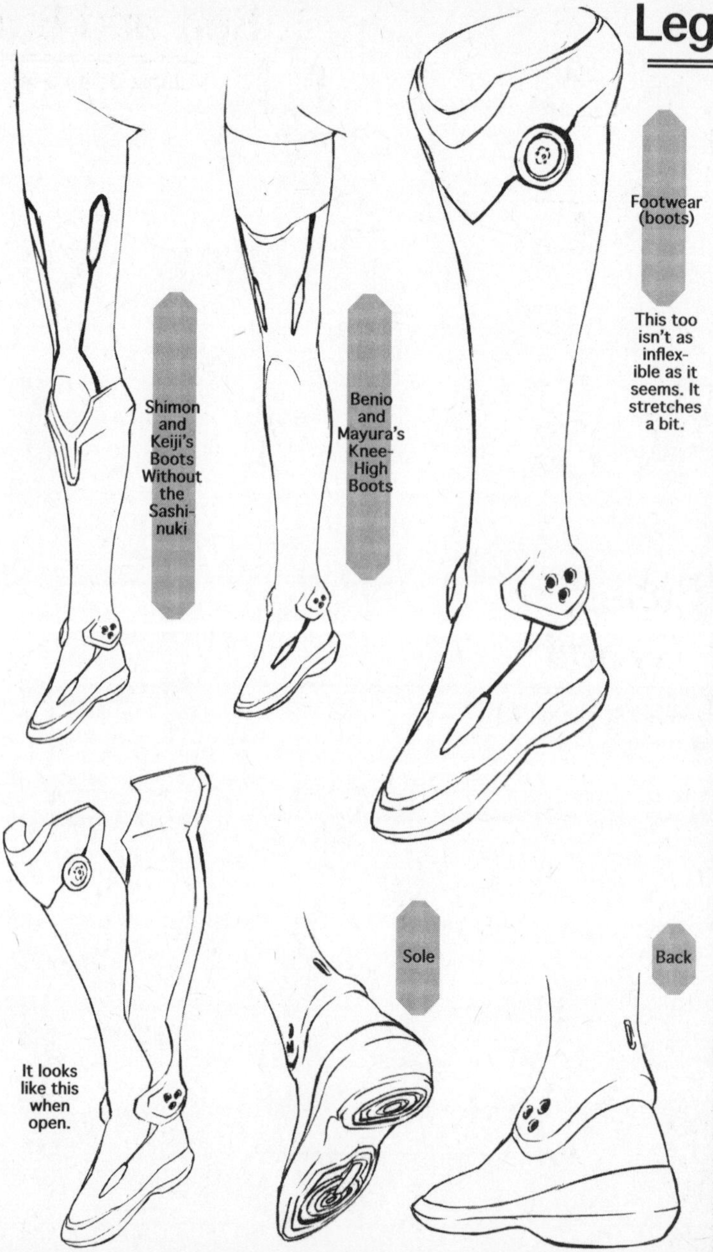
Footwear (boots)
This too isn't as inflexible as it seems. It stretches a bit.
Benio and Mayura's Knee-High Boots
Shimon and Keiji's Boots Without the Sashinuki
It looks like this when open.
Sole
Back

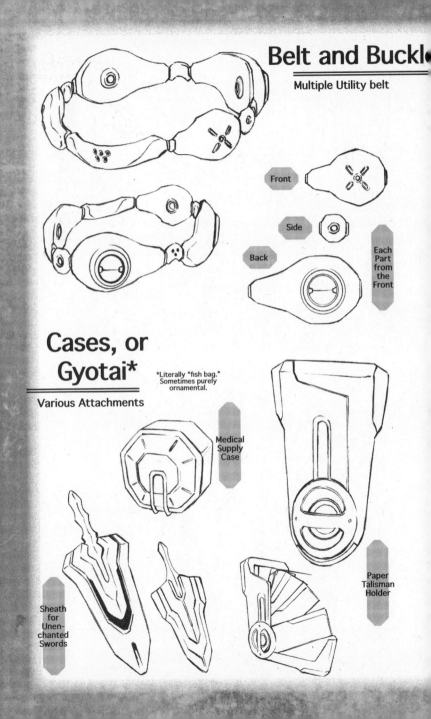

Belt and Buckle

Multiple Utility belt

Front

Side

Back

Each Part from the Front

Cases, or Gyotai*

*Literally "fish bag." Sometimes purely ornamental.

Various Attachments

Medical Supply Case

Paper Talisman Holder

Sheath for Unenchanted Swords

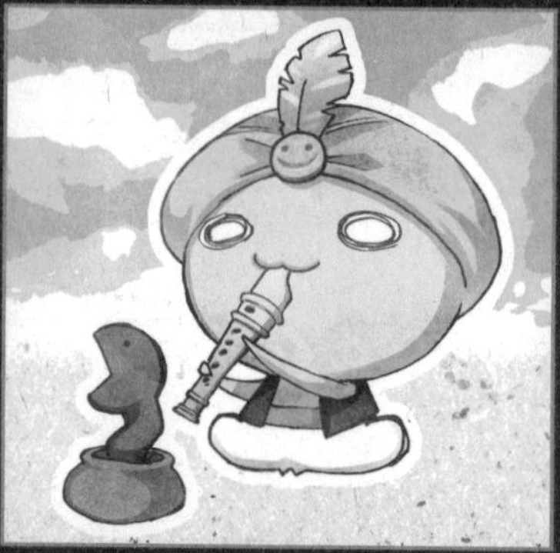

I am privileged to have made so many new discoveries in the world of manga and anime through this series. That feeling you get when you're broadening your horizons by stepping into an unknown new world that is so familiar yet so different...it's a mixture of both trepidation and excitement!

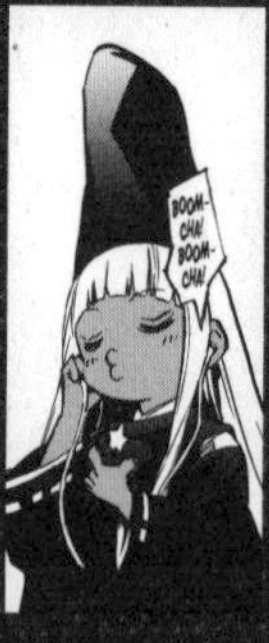
BOOM-CHA! BOOM-CHA!

YOSHIAKI SUKENO was born July 23, 1981, in Wakayama, Japan. He graduated from Kyoto Seika University, where he studied manga. In 2006, he won the Tezuka Award for Best Newcomer Shonen Manga Artist. In 2008, he began his previous work, the supernatural comedy *Binbougami ga!*, which was adapted into the anime *Good Luck Girl!* in 2012.

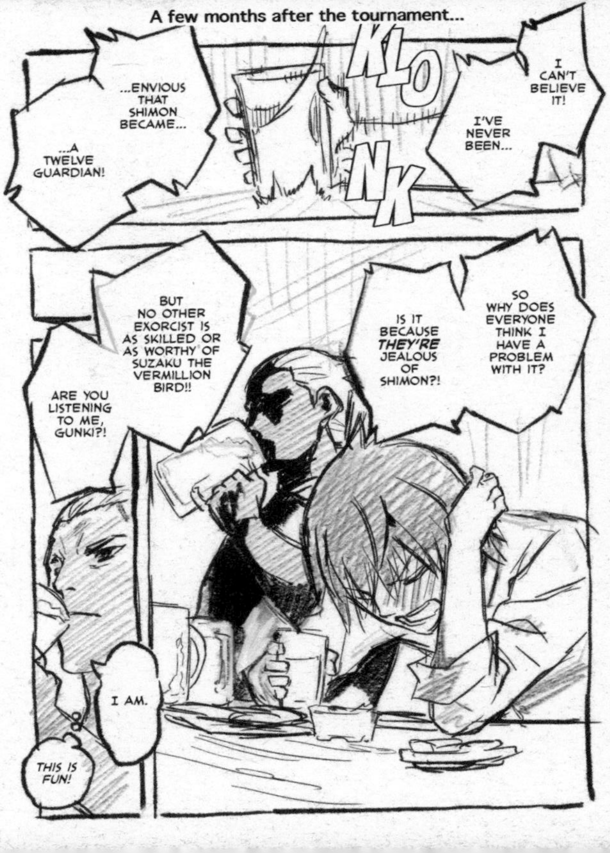
A few months after the tournament...
I CAN'T BELIEVE IT!
I'VE NEVER BEEN...
KLONK
...ENVIOUS THAT SHIMON BECAME...
...A TWELVE GUARDIAN!
SO WHY DOES EVERYONE THINK I HAVE A PROBLEM WITH IT?
IS IT BECAUSE *THEY'RE* JEALOUS OF SHIMON?!
BUT NO OTHER EXORCIST IS AS SKILLED OR AS WORTHY OF SUZAKU THE VERMILLION BIRD!!
ARE YOU LISTENING TO ME, GUNKI!?!
I AM.
THIS IS FUN!
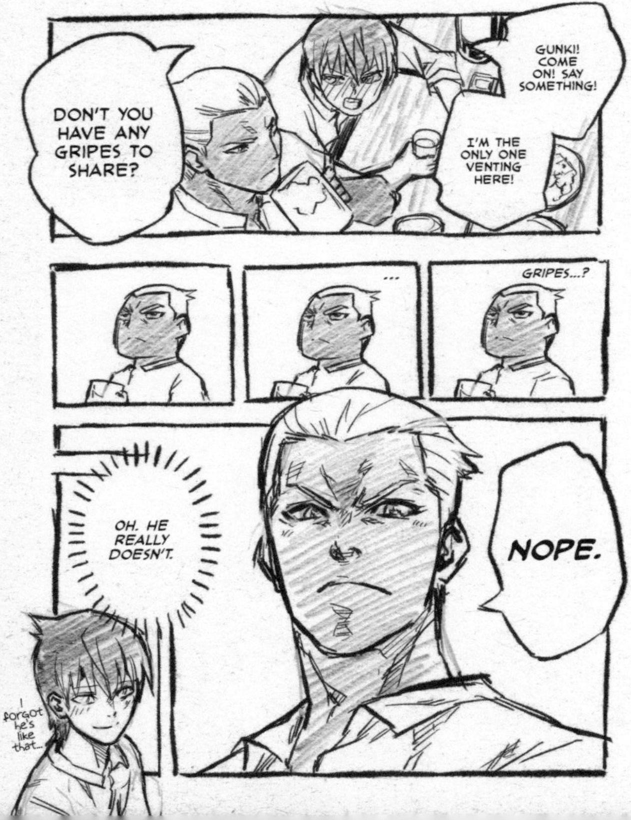
GUNKI! COME ON! SAY SOMETHING!
I'M THE ONLY ONE VENTING HERE!
DON'T YOU HAVE ANY GRIPES TO SHARE?
GRIPES...?
...
NOPE.
OH. HE REALLY DOESN'T.
I forgot he's like that...

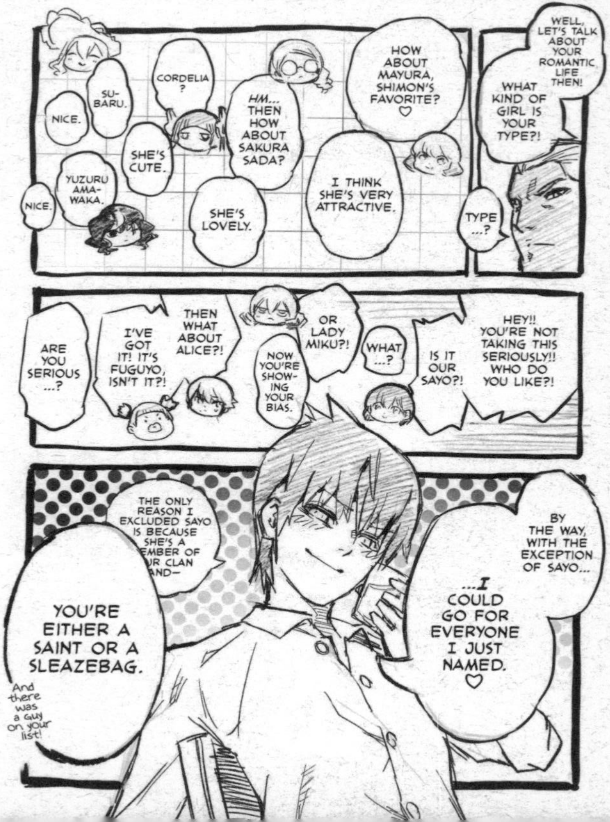
WELL, LET'S TALK ABOUT YOUR ROMANTIC LIFE THEN!
WHAT KIND OF GIRL IS YOUR TYPE?!
TYPE ...?
HOW ABOUT MAYURA, SHIMON'S FAVORITE? ♡
I THINK SHE'S VERY ATTRACTIVE.
HM... THEN HOW ABOUT SAKURA SADA?
SHE'S LOVELY.
CORDELIA ?
SHE'S CUTE.
SU-BARU.
NICE.
YUZURU AMA-WAKA.
NICE.
HEY!! YOU'RE NOT TAKING THIS SERIOUSLY!! WHO DO YOU LIKE?!
IS IT OUR SAYO?!
WHAT ...?
OR LADY MIKU?!
NOW YOU'RE SHOW-ING YOUR BIAS.
THEN WHAT ABOUT ALICE?!
I'VE GOT IT! IT'S FUGUYO, ISN'T IT?!
ARE YOU SERIOUS ...?
BY THE WAY, WITH THE EXCEPTION OF SAYO...
...I COULD GO FOR EVERYONE I JUST NAMED. ♡
THE ONLY REASON I EXCLUDED SAYO IS BECAUSE SHE'S A
YOU'RE EITHER A SAINT OR A SLEAZEBAG.
And there was a guy on your list!
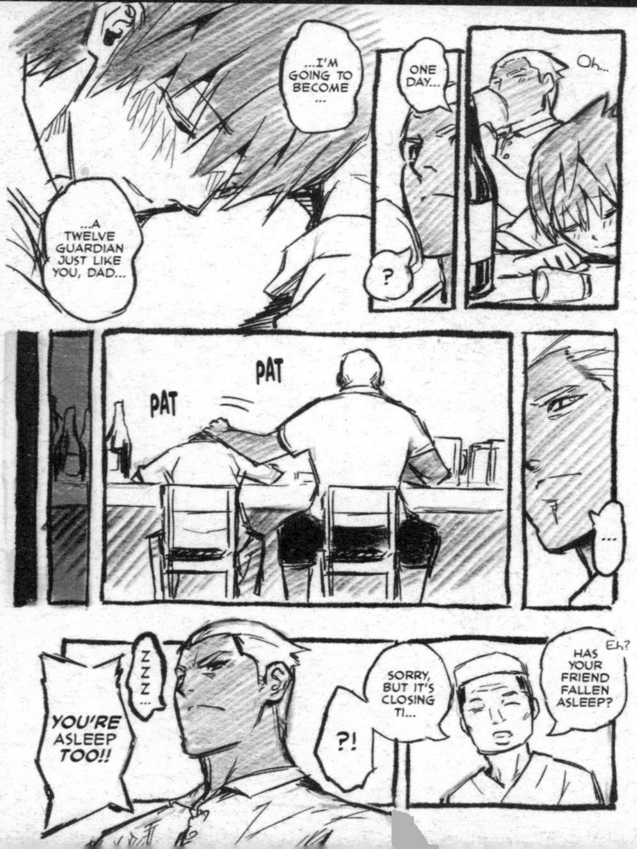
...I'M GOING TO BECOME ...
...A TWELVE GUARDIAN JUST LIKE YOU, DAD...
ONE DAY...
?
Oh...
...
PAT
PAT
Eh?
HAS YOUR FRIEND FALLEN ASLEEP?
SORRY, BUT IT'S CLOSING TI...
?!
Z Z Z ...
YOU'RE ASLEEP TOO!!

—SHONEN JUMP Manga Edition—

STORY & ART **Yoshiaki Sukeno**

TRANSLATION **Tetsuichiro Miyaki**
ENGLISH ADAPTATION **Bryant Turnage**
TOUCH-UP ART & LETTERING **Stephen Dutro**
DESIGN **Shawn Carrico**
EDITOR **Annette Roman**

SOUSEI NO ONMYOJI © 2013 by Yoshiaki Sukeno
All rights reserved.
First published in Japan in 2013 by SHUEISHA Inc., Tokyo.
English translation rights arranged by SHUEISHA Inc.

The stories, characters and incidents mentioned in this
publication are entirely fictional.

Printed in Canada

Published by VIZ Media, LLC
P.O. Box 77010
San Francisco, CA 94107

10 9 8 7 6 5 4 3 2 1
First printing, January 2019

shonenjump.com

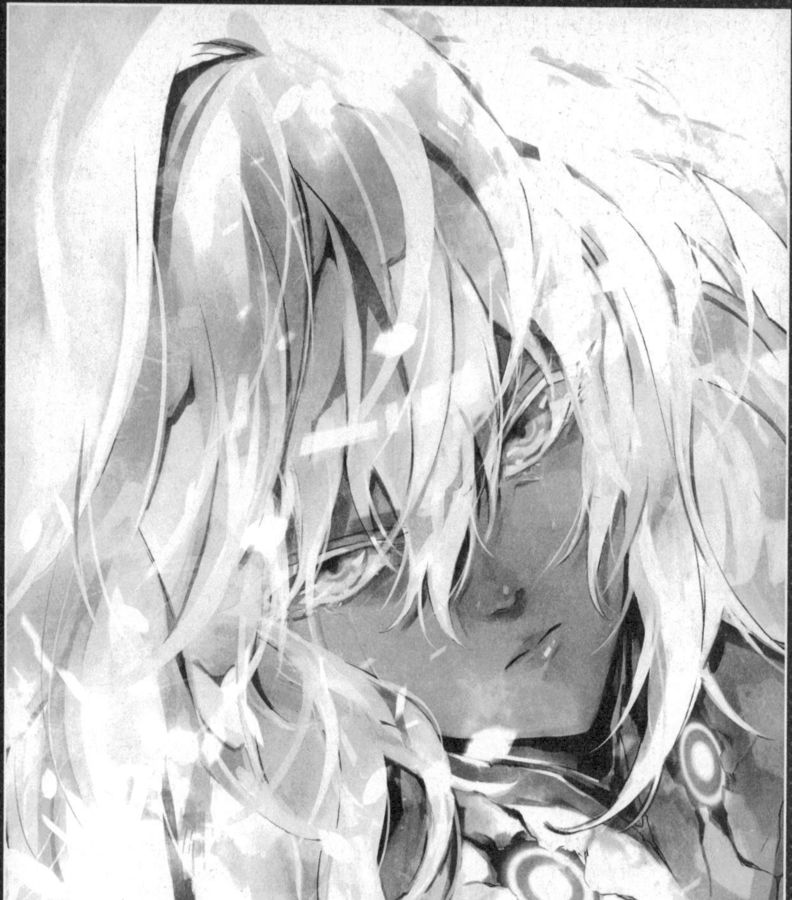
As Benio begins the ritual to claim her true form, she is attacked! An unlikely ally comes to her aid... Meanwhile, Rokuro is eager to embark on the expedition to exorcise Benio's brother Yuto, but a more pressing crisis arises!
VOLUME 15

Twin Star Exorcists
ONMYOJI

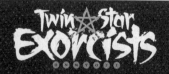

THE PROMISED NEVERLAND

STORY BY **KAIU SHIRAI**

ART BY **POSUKA DEMIZU**

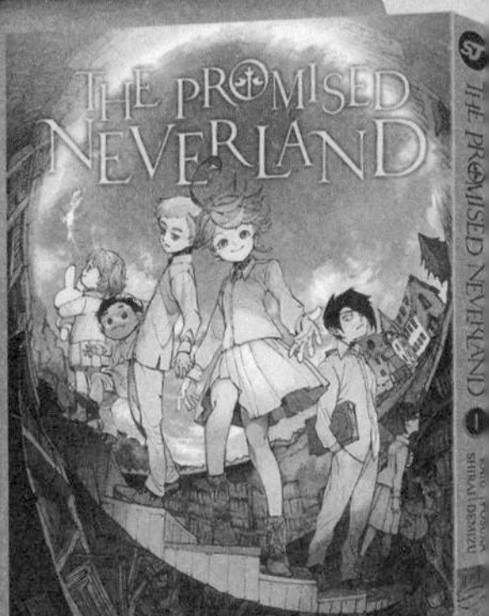

Emma, Norman and Ray are the brightest kids at the Grace Field House orphanage. And under the care of the woman they refer to as "Mom," all the kids have enjoyed a comfortable life. Good food, clean clothes and the perfect environment to learn—what more could an orphan ask for? One day, though, Emma and Norman uncover the dark truth of the outside world they are forbidden from seeing.

DEATH NOTE

ALL-IN-ONE EDITION

Story by Tsugumi Ohba   **Art by Takeshi Obata**

Light Yagami is an ace student with great prospects—
and he's bored out of his mind. But all that changes
when he finds the Death Note, a notebook dropped by
a rogue Shinigami death god. Any human whose name
is written in the notebook dies, and now Light has
vowed to use the power of the Death Note to rid the
world of evil. But when criminals begin dropping dead,
the authorities send the legendary detective L to track
down the killer. With L hot on his heels, will Light lose
sight of his noble goal...or his life?

Includes a
NEW epilogue
chapter!

All 12 volumes in ONE
monstrously large edition!

YOU'RE READING THE **WRONG WAY!**

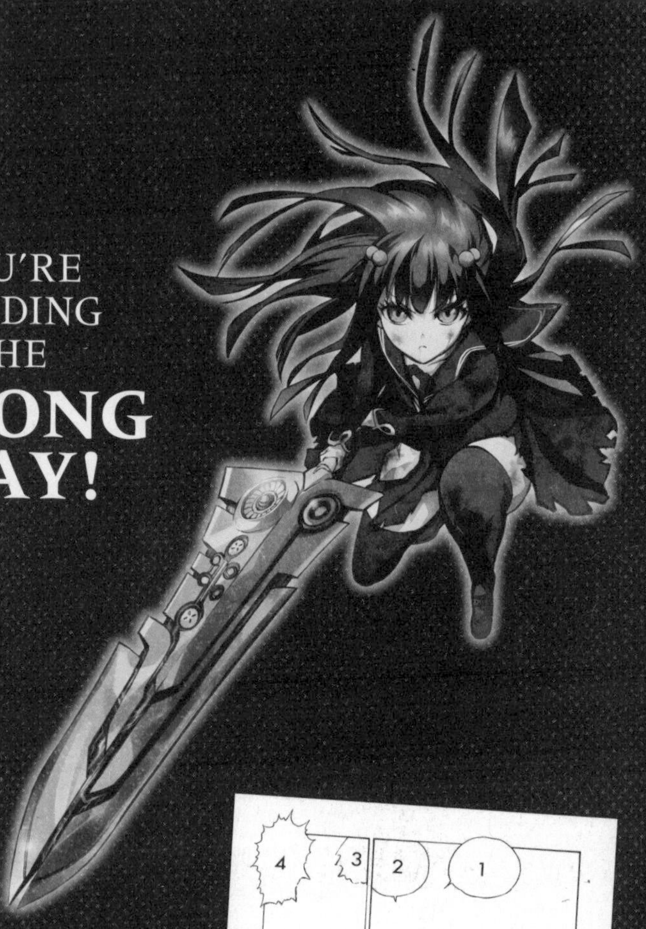

Twin Star Exorcists reads from right to left, starting in the upper-right corner. Japanese is read from right to left, meaning that action, sound effects and word-balloon order are completely reversed from English order.

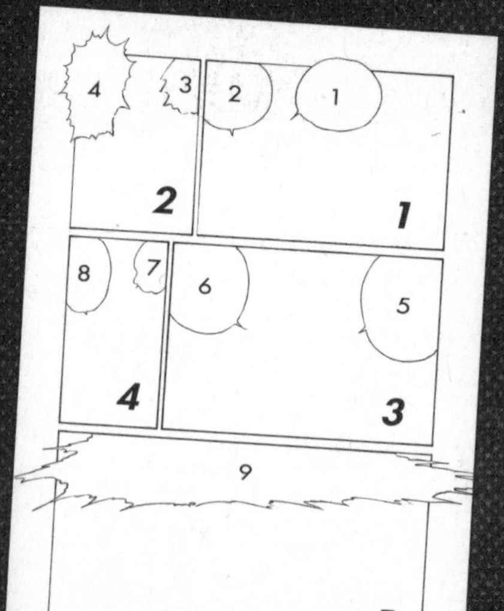
1
2
1
3
4
2
5
6
3
7
8
4
9
5
142